George Lillie Craik

The English of Shakespeare

Illustrated in a Philological Commentary on His Julius Caesar

George Lillie Craik

The English of Shakespeare
Illustrated in a Philological Commentary on His Julius Caesar

ISBN/EAN: 9783337054717

Printed in Europe, USA, Canada, Australia, Japan

Cover: Foto ©Thomas Meinert / pixelio.de

More available books at **www.hansebooks.com**

THE ENGLISH OF SHAKESPEARE

ILLUSTRATED IN

A Philological Commentary

ON HIS

JULIUS CÆSAR.

BY

GEORGE L. CRAIK,

PROFESSOR OF HISTORY AND OF ENGLISH LITERATURE IN
QUEEN'S COLLEGE, BELFAST.

FOURTH EDITION, **REVISED** AND CORRECTED.

LONDON:
CHAPMAN **AND** HALL, 193, PICCADILLY.
1869.

JOHN CHILDS AND SON, PRINTERS.

CONTENTS.

	Page
PROLEGOMENA.	
Shakespeare's Personal History	1
Shakespeare's Works	3
The Sources for the Text of Shakespeare's Plays .	9
The Shakespearian Editors and Commentators .	25
The Modern Shakespearian Texts . . .	27
The Mechanism of English Verse, and the Prosody of the Plays of Shakespeare	30
Shakespeare's *Julius Cæsar*	44
PHILOLOGICAL COMMENTARY, WITH TEXT OF THE PLAY	61

PREFACE.

In this attempt to illustrate the ENGLISH OF SHAKESPEARE, I would be understood to have had a twofold purpose, in conformity with the title of the volume, which would naturally be taken to promise something of exposition in regard both to the language or style of Shakespeare and to the English Language generally.

My first business I have considered to be the correct exhibition and explanation of the noble work of our great dramatist with which the volume professes to be specially occupied. I will begin, therefore, by stating what I have done, or endeavoured to do, for the Play of JULIUS CÆSAR.

I have given what I believe to be a more nearly authentic Text than has yet appeared. *Julius Cæsar* is, probably, of all Shakespeare's Plays, the one of which the text has come down to us in the least unsatisfactory state. From whatever cause it has happened, the passages in this Play as to the true reading of which there can be much reasonable doubt are, comparatively, very few. Even when anything is wrong in the original edition, the manner in which it is to be set to rights is for the most part both pretty obvious and nearly certain. There are perhaps scarcely so many as half-a-dozen lines of any importance which must be given up as hopelessly incurable or even doubtful. It is, I should think, of all the Plays, by much the easiest to edit; both the settlement of the text and its explanation are, I conceive, simpler than would be the case in any other; and it is for that reason partly that I have selected it for the present attempt.

The alterations which I have found it necessary to make upon the commonly received text do not amount to very many; and the considerations by which I have been guided are in every instance fully stated in the Commentary. The only conjectural innovations which I have ventured upon of my own are, the change of "What night is this?" into "What a night is this!" in the speech numbered 117; the insertion of "not" after "Has he," in that numbered 402; and the transposition of the two names *Lucilius* and *Lucius* in that numbered 521. The first and second of these three corrections are of little moment, though both, I think, clearly required; the third I hold to be both of absolute certainty and necessity, and also of considerable importance, affecting as it does the whole course of the Fourth Act of the Play, restoring propriety and consistency to the conduct of the action and the parts sustained by the various personages, and vindicating a reading of the First Folio in a subsequent speech (571) which, curiously enough, had never been previously noticed by anybody, but has been silently ignored and departed from even by those of the modern editors who have professed to adhere the most scrupulously to that original text.

For the rest, the present text differs in nothing material from that which is found in all the modern editions, unless it be that I have restored from the First Folio one or two antiquated forms,—such as *'em* for *them*, and *moe* in several places for *more*,—which have been usually suppressed, although *'em* remains familiar enough in our colloquial speech, or at any rate is still perfectly intelligible and unambiguous, and *moe* is sometimes the only form that will suit the exigencies of the verse.

A merely mechanical innovation in the typographical exhibition of the text will at once catch the eye. The present is, I suppose, the first edition of a Play, in any language, with the speeches numbered. Possibly it may be the first time that any one has thought of counting the speeches in a Play.* In that case, the result arrived at, that there are about eight hundred separate utterances, or divisions of the dialogue, long and short, in the drama here examined, may be received as one of some little curiosity and interest. At any rate, such a method as I have adopted seems to afford the only available means for distinct and expeditious reference. It has a double advantage over the mere pagination; first, inasmuch as a speech is usually much shorter than a page, and, secondly, inasmuch as the division into speeches is the same for all editions. The only other plan that has been, or that, apparently, can be taken, is to make shift with the ordinary division into Acts and Scenes. This is what has been commonly done in the various verbal indexes to Shakespeare. But to be told simply

---

* Since the first publication of the present work, however, Mr J. A. Ellis has obligingly forwarded to me copies of editions of Shakespeare's *Tempest* and *Macbeth*, in what is called the Phonetic spelling, brought out under his care at London in 1849, in which the speeches in each Scene are separately numbered for the purpose of reference in the notes, mostly explanatory, but sometimes critical or conjectural, appended at the foot of the page. But, besides that there is no general summation, the text of Shakespeare is not fully given in these editions, so that even the process of adding up the speeches in the several scenes would not give us the entire number in the Play. The plan of one continuous enumeration throughout would seem to be simpler and more convenient for all purposes.

that a word or phrase which we are in search of occurs in a certain Scene of one of Shakespeare's Plays is in most cases only a degree better than being told that it may be found somewhere within the compass of the Play. We may be often half an hour in finding it. The Scenes in Shakespeare (the notation of which, by the bye, is for the most part the work of his modern editors) continually run out to dimensions which make this kind of reference a mere tantalizing and tormenting mockery. In any liberally printed library edition, such as those of Mr Knight or Mr Collier, with a very small proportion of the space taken up by foot-notes, it is not unusual to find that the Scene to which we have been directed extends over twenty or thirty pages. Even in the present edition of *Julius Cæsar*, compactly printed as it is, several of the Scenes cover seven or eight pages. In the entire Play, filling about sixty pages, there are only eighteen Scenes, so that the average throughout is considerably above three pages for each. Even Jennens's more scientific division gives us only twenty-six Scenes for this Play, making an average of above two of our pages for each; and that of Hanmer, which Warburton follows, and which is the most minute that has been proposed, gives us only thirty-seven, each therefore extending over a space of not much less than two of our pages on an average. This is the utmost amount of definiteness attainable by the system of reference to Scenes. The enumeration of the speeches reduces the average space which a reference includes to about the thirteenth part of a page. As there are about eight hundred speeches in the Play, and only eighteen Scenes (according to the common division), it follows that the one method of reference must be on the whole between forty and fifty times more precise, and consequently more serviceable, than the other.

Mrs Cowden Clarke's *Concordance to Shakspere* is a noble monument of the fair compiler's loving patience and carefulness; its correctness, especially when we take into account the multitude of mere figures and symbols which there was nothing in the sense or the context to protect from perversion, is wonderful; it would be hard to name a printed volume either of more difficult or of more faultless execution; it is rare to find a single figure or letter wrong; it may be questioned if any equally elaborate work, literary or of any other kind, so remarkable for exactness and freedom from error, ever before proceeded from the female head or hand; even as it stands, it is invaluable, and in a manner indispensable, for critical purposes. But it is much to be wished that before it was undertaken there had existed an edition of the Plays with the speeches numbered throughout, as in the present edition of the *Julius Cæsar*, to which it might have been accommodated. We should in that case have found whatever we might seek by its assistance in about a fiftieth part of the average time that it now takes us.*

---

* What is stated in the above paragraph will explain my preference for the plan of enumeration I have adopted over that subsequently employed by Herr Karl Elze in his edition of *Hamlet* (in the original English), with notes in German, published at Leipzig, in 1857. He has simply divided each page of the Play into so many paragraphs of equal, or nearly equal, length (he makes 241 of them in all); and, in a complimentary reference to my book, which had reached him while his own was passing through the press, he observes that I had made an attempt to furnish a similar indispensable requisite for the philological study of Shakespeare:—"einen Versuch hierzu hat allerdings ganz kürzlich Professor Craik in Belfast gemacht." It will be seen that Herr Elze's method would not serve the more general purpose which I had in view. I have not seen Meyer's edition of the *Julius Cæsar* which he notices as having been published at Hamburg in the same year 1857, and the numbering in which he says is quite useless, inasmuch as it does not admit of being transferred to other editions.

As for the present Commentary on the Play of *Julius Cæsar*, it will be perceived that it **does not at all** aspire to what is commonly distinguished **as the** higher criticism. It does not seek to examine or to expound this **Shakespearian drama æsthetically, but only philologically, or with respect to the language.** The only kind of criticism which it professes is what is called verbal criticism. Its whole aim, in so far as it relates to the particular work to which it is attached, is, as far as may be done, first to ascertain **or** determine the text, secondly to explain it; to inquire, **in other** words, **what** Shakespeare really **wrote, and how what he has written is to be** read and construed.

Wherever either the earliest text **or that which is commonly** received has been deviated from to **the extent of a** word or a syllable, the alteration has been distinctly indicated. **In this** way a complete representation is given, **in so far at least** as regards **the** language, both of the **text of** the *editio princeps* **and of** the *textus receptus*. **I have not** sought to register with the same exactness the **various readings of the** other texts, **ancient and** modern; **but I believe,** nevertheless, **that all will be** found **to be noted that are of any interest either in** the Second Folio **or among the** conjectures of **the long array** of editors **and** commentators **extending from** Rowe **to our** own **day.**

Then, **with regard to the** explanation of the **text:—I confess that here my** fear is rather **that I shall be thought to have done too** much **than too little. But I have been desirous to** omit nothing **that any** reader **might require for the** full understanding **of the Play, in so far as I was** able to supply it. **I have even** retained **the** common schoolboy explanations **of the few points of Roman** antiquities **to** which allusions occur, such as the arrangements of the Calendar, the usages of the Lupercalia, etc. The *expression*, however, is what I have chiefly dwelt upon. The labours of scores of expositors, embodied in hundreds of volumes, attest the existence in the writings of Shakespeare of numerous words, phraseologies, and passages the import of which is, to say the least, not obvious to ordinary readers of the present day. This comes partly from certain characteristics of his style, which would probably have made him occasionally a difficult author in any circumstances; but much more from the two facts, of the corrupted or at least doubtful state of the text in many places, and the changes that our national speech has undergone since his age. The English of the sixteenth century is in various respects a different language from that of the nineteenth. The words and constructions are not throughout the same, and when they are they have not always the same meaning. Much of Shakespeare's vocabulary has ceased to fall from either our lips or our pens; much of the meaning which he attached to so much of it as still survives has dropt out of our minds. What is most misleading of all, many words and forms have acquired senses for us which they had not for him. All such cases that the Play presents I have made it my object to notice. Wherever there seemed to be any risk of the true meaning being mistaken, I have, in as few words as possible, stated what I conceived it to be. Where it was not clear to myself, I have frankly confessed my inability to explain it satisfactorily.

In so far as the Commentary relates to the particular Play which it goes over, and professes to elucidate, it is intended to be as complete as I could make it, in the sense of not leaving any passage unremarked upon which seemed to be difficult or obscure. But, of course, it puts forward no pretensions to a similar completeness, or thoroughness, in respect of any further purpose. It is far from embracing the whole subject of the *English of Shakespeare*, or making any attempt to do so. **It is** merely an introduction **to** that subject. In the *Prolegomena*, nevertheless, I have sought to lay a foundation for the full and systematic treatment of an important department of it in the exposition which is given of some principles of our prosody, **and some** peculiarities of Shakespeare's versification, which **his** editors have not in general sufficiently attended to. **Such** investigations are, I conceive, full of promise of new light **in** regard to the history both of the Plays and **of** the mind of their **author.**

Still less can the Commentary pretend to any completeness **in** what it may contain in reference to the history **and** constitution of the language generally, or of particular **classes of** words and constructions. Among the fragments, or specimens, however—for they can be nothing more—which occur in it of this kind of speculation are **a** few which will be found, perhaps, to carry out **the** examination of a principle, or the survey of a group of connected facts, farther than had before been done; **such** as those in the notes on *Merely* (45), on *Its* (54), on *Shrew* and *Shrewd* (186), on *Statue* (246), on *Deliver* **(348), on the prefix** *Be* (390), on *The* in combination **with a** comparative (675), etc.*

* **I may add a** remark **on** the **word** *business*, **noticed** in 496. **Whether our** *busy* be or be not the same with the German *böse*, signifying *wicked* (even **as both** *wicked* and *weak* have been supposed to be identical with *quick*,—*Vid.* 267), and whatever may be the origin of the French *besogne* and ***besoin*,** and the Italian *bisogna* and *bisogno*, **there can,** I conceive, **be no** doubt that our *business*, which never (at **least in** modern English) means the condition or quality of being busy, **is** really nothing more **than the** French *besoins* or *besognes*, formerly

PREFACE.

This new edition has been revised throughout with the greatest care; and it will be found to present a considerable number of alterations, additions, **and improvements** as compared with the former. A difference between the two conspicuous at first sight is that the **Text** of the Play is now much more conveniently placed **for all the** purposes **of such a book by** being incorporated with the Commentary.*

busoignes,—as, for example, in the Stat. of the 25th of Edward I. (*Confirmatio Chartarum*):—"les aides e les mises les queles il **nous** unt fait avaunt ces houres pur nos guerres e autres busoignes;" or in an answer of Edward III. to Archbishop Stratford in 1341:—"Queu chose le Roi ottreia. Mes il dit, q'il voleit que **les busoignes touchantes** l'estat du Roialme et commune profit fussent **primes mys en exploit, et** puis il ferroit exploiter **les autres"** (*Rot. Par.* II. 127). The *ness*, therefore, is here not **the substantival affix, but merely a misrepresenta-**tion of the final letters **of the word in its plural form. "Go about your** business" is go about your (own) **needs, occasions, affairs. We speak** of the *busy* bee, **and of a** *busy* man, or a man who is *busy*, but we do not (now at least) call **the condition or the natural quality the** *busi-ness* of either the man or of the bee. What we understand by a man's *business* is (grammatically or logically) something of the same kind, not with his *goodness*, but **rather with** his *goods*. The irregular or exceptional pronunciation of the word *business* would alone indicate some peculiarity of origin or formation. *Business*, pronounced in two syllables, is evidently not a word of the same kind with *heaviness*, for instance, pronounced in three.

* I have retained, it will be observed, in speech 363 the emendation of Mr Collier's MS. annotator—"A curse shall light upon the loins of men." But since this **part of the volume has** been printed off I confess that I have, although at first very much opposed to it, been more and more impressed, the more I consider it, in favour of a new reading for **which** a strong case has been made out, and urged upon my attention, by a distinguished literary friend,—"A curse shall fall upon *these impious* men." In the first place, on looking at the passage, every reader will, I think, be struck with something incongruous and improbable **in the denunciation here of** a curse upon men generally,—upon the whole human race,—let it be regarded with reference whether to the occasion, and to the circumstances on which Antony founds it, or to the calamities about to fall merely upon Italy

Although very much disinclined to depart from established usage in such a matter as mere expression, I have to which the prophecy immediately narrows itself. It is an exordium followed up by no adequate amplification or specification, but rather the contrary. *These* men—the murderers of his friend Cæsar—and not either the *limbs* or the *loins* of mankind universally—must, one would say, have been uppermost at such a moment in his mind and in his impassioned words. Without something more, however, such general considerations as this would hardly entitle us to touch the passage. There would be no end of conjectural emendation if it were permitted us, in the text of Shakespeare or of any other writer, to disturb an authorized or accepted reading on no other ground than that it might, as we may think, be improved. This is the sort of wild disorganizing work with which so many would be reformers and restorers, male and female, busy themselves, without so much as a suspicion, in many cases, of the nature of a single canon or principle of critical science, or that such a science exists. But here, secondly, we have, almost universally admitted, what is the almost indispensable preliminary to any attempt at emendation,—a manifest flaw in the ordinary reading. "*Limbs* of men" pleases nobody, or hardly anybody. Thirdly and lastly, then—for, if that can be made out, nothing more in the way of mere conjecture is possible,—can it be shown to be at all probable that the supposed words "these impious men," if written by Shakespeare, would or might have been mistaken by the printer of the First Folio for what he has given us—"the limbs of men?" It is not necessary to assume that he has adhered to the exact spelling of what he believed himself to have before him in his copy or manuscript. What he set up as "the limbs of" may have seemed to him to be written "the Limbes of." Only, now, suppose farther that the writing was somewhat close or crowded, or rather that it appeared to him to be so, and it would not be very unlikely that what he took for a "the" followed by a capital L, with its final curve running possibly below the line, was really a "these," written, of course, with a long *ſ;* and then it would not be difficult for him, thus misled, to convert the "impious" into "imbs of," or "imbes of." It may be thought that some confirmation is lent to this conjecture by the fact that Zachary Jackson, the printer, who published in 1818 a work entitled "A Few Concise Examples of Seven Hundred Errors in Shakespeare's Plays, now corrected and elucidated" (reprinted the following year under the title of "Shakespeare's Genius Justified,"), proposes to read "these imps of men."

I am not blind to the bearing which this ingenious emendation, if

in the new editions both of the present and of another elementary philological work felt it indispensable to abandon the ordinary fashion of designating our national speech as *Saxon* or *Anglo-Saxon* before, and as *English* only since, the Norman Conquest. I cannot call to mind another customary form of words which involves so much at once of unfounded or questionable assumption and of positive misstatement as this. The common name for the language among the people themselves always has been, not Saxon, but English. It was so before the Conquest, as it is so still. Modern philologists, who call the earlier form of it Saxon or Anglo-Saxon, do so on the assumption that the portion of the population distinguished as the Saxons had a language of their own, known by their own name, before they left the continent for Britain, and that the common language of England before the Norman Conquest was identical with that. But nothing of all this is either proved or probable. There is much more reason for believing that the language was called English than that it was called Saxon on the continent as well as afterwards in Britain. In fact, there is no reason at all for supposing that it was ever at any time commonly or properly known as Saxon. There is, indeed, a Germanic dialect which philologists have baptised Old Saxon, or Continental Saxon, and of which their system supposes what it calls

---

it were held to be established, might be alleged to have upon the hypothesis that has been proposed in the *Prolegomena* in regard to the authority belonging to the corrections of Mr Collier's manuscript annotator. Can he, it may be argued, have had the author's or any other authentic copy of the Plays before him, if he has passed over so important a restoration as ought to have been made here? Of this particular passage, at least, he could not be supposed to have had any such copy. On the other hand, however, this necessary consequence would obviously tell as much against the proposed reading as that does against the hypothesis.

Anglo-Saxon, or the Saxon of England, to be **a modification**; but the one name is as much a modern invention as the other; we have no remains **of this** so-called Old Saxon of so early a date by several centuries as the first settlement of the Angles and Saxons in Britain; and, **although it and what is called the Saxon of England were no doubt nearly related, we have no evidence whatever either** that the former was the mother and the latter the **daughter, or even that** their relationship was that of **parent and child at all. So far,** however, we have gratuitous assumption **only, or little more. In** what comes next we have downright contradiction **and absurdity.** If **the** language was Saxon before the Norman Conquest, **how** did it or could it **come to** be English after that catastrophe? How is it that it is English **now?** The only effect that the Conquest had, or possibly could have, upon **it was to** make it, not more, but less purely, less exclusively, English than it was before.

G. L. C.

Queen's College Belfast;
   March, 1859.

P.S. Leaving the preceding note on pp. xiii and xiv **as it** stood, **I** take the opportunity of a revised impression **to say here that I** do not now **feel** the incongruity **of the curse in the** passage under consideration being made to extend to the whole human race, nor do I think that Antony's prophecy can **be** fairly affirmed **to** narrow itself in what immediately follows to the calamities about to fall **merely** upon Italy. I revert, therefore, to my original preference for the reading of the Collier Folio :—
"A curse shall light upon the loins of men."

November, 1863.

THE
ENGLISH OF SHAKESPEARE,
ETC.

PROLEGOMENA.

I. SHAKESPEARE'S PERSONAL HISTORY.

WILLIAM SHAKESPEARE was born at Stratford-upon-Avon, in the county of Warwick, in April 1564. His baptism is recorded in the parish register as having taken place on Wednesday the 26th, and the inscription on his tomb makes him to have been in his fifty-third year when he died on the 23rd, of April 1616; his birth-day, therefore, cannot have been later than the 23rd. It was more probably some days earlier. It is commonly assumed, nevertheless, to have been the 23rd, which, besides being also the day of his death, is the day dedicated to St George the Martyr, the patron saint of England.

His father was John Shakespeare; his mother, Mary Arderne, or Arden. The Ardens were among the oldest of the county gentry; many of the Shakespeares also, who were numerous in Warwickshire, were of good condition. The name in provincial speech was probably sounded *Shackspeare* or *Shacksper;* but even in the poet's own day its more refined or literary pronunciation seems to have been the same that now prevails. It was certainly recognised as a combination of the two words

Shake and *Spear*. His own spelling of it, however, in a few instances in which that, our only known fragment of his handwriting, has come down to us, is *Shakspere*.

John Shakespeare appears to have followed the business of a glover, including no doubt the making of gloves as well as the selling of them. He seems to have fallen latterly into decayed circumstances; but in his better days it is evident that he ranked with the first class of the burgesses of his town. He was for many years an alderman, and twice filled the office of High Bailiff, or chief magistrate. He was also, though perhaps never very wealthy, but rather always a struggling man, possessed of some houses in Stratford, as well as of a small freehold estate acquired by his marriage; and his connexion with the Arden family would itself bring him consideration. His marriage probably took place in 1557. He lived till 1602, and his wife till 1608. Of eight children, four sons and four daughters, William was the third, but the eldest son.

Shakespeare's father, like the generality of persons of his station in life of that day, appears to have been unable to write his name; all his signature in the books of the corporation is his cross, or mark; but there can be no doubt that the son had a grammar-school education. He was in all probability sent to the free-school of his native town. After he left school it has been thought that he may have spent some time in an attorney's office. But in 1582, when he was only eighteen, he married; his wife, Anne Hathaway, of Shottery, in the neighbourhood of Stratford, was about eight years older than himself; children soon followed,—first a daughter, then twins, a son and daughter; and this involvement may be conjectured to have been what drove him to London, in the necessity of finding some way of supporting his family which required no apprenticeship. He became first an actor, then a writer for the stage. Already by the year

1589 he had worked his way up to be one of the proprietors of the Blackfriars Theatre. But he seems to have always continued to look upon Stratford as his home; there he left his wife and children; he is said to have made a point of revisiting his native town once a year; and thither, after he had, by the unceasing activity of many years, secured a competency, he returned to spend the evening of his days in quiet. So that we may say he resorted to London, after all, only as the sailor goes to sea, always intending to come back. He appears to have finally retired to Stratford, and settled there on a property which he had purchased, about the year 1612; his wife still lived, and also his two daughters, of whom the elder, Susanna, was married to Dr John Hall, a physician, in 1607; the younger, Judith, to Mr Thomas Quiney, in February 1616. But he had lost his only son, who was named Hamnet, in 1596, when the boy was in his twelfth year. Shakespeare died at Stratford, as already mentioned, on the 23rd of April 1616; and he lies interred in the parish church there.

His wife survived till August 1623. Both his daughters had families;—Susanna, a daughter, who was twice married; Judith, three sons; but no descendant of the great poet now exists. The last was probably Elizabeth, daughter of Dr Hall, who became the wife first of Thomas Nash, Esq., secondly of Sir John Barnard, and died without issue by either husband in February 1670. Nor is it known that there are any descendants even of his father remaining, although one of his brothers and also one of his sisters are ascertained to have been married, and to have had issue.

II. SHAKESPEARE'S WORKS.

The first work of Shakespeare's which was printed with his name was his poem entitled *Venus and Adonis*, in stanzas consisting each of an alternately rhyming quatrain followed by a couplet. It appeared in 1593, with a Dedication to the Earl of Southampton, in which the author styles it the first heir of his invention. This was followed in 1594 by *The Rape of Lucrece*, in stanzas of seven lines, one rhyming to the fourth being here inserted before the closing couplet; it is also dedicated to Lord Southampton, to whom the author expresses the most unlimited obligation:—"What I have done," he says, "is yours; what I have to do is yours; being part in all I have, devoted yours." The *Venus and Adonis* was thrice reprinted in Shakespeare's lifetime; the *Lucrece*, five or six times.

His other works, besides his Plays, are *The Passionate Pilgrim*, a small collection of poems, first printed in 1599; and his *Sonnets*, 154 in number, with the poem entitled *A Lover's Complaint* (in the same stanza as the *Lucrece*), which appeared together in 1609. But the Sonnets, or some of them at least, were well known long before this. "As the soul of Euphorbus was thought to live in Pythagoras," says a writer named Francis Meres in his *Palladis Tamia*, published in 1598, "so the sweet witty soul of Ovid lives in mellifluous and honey-tongued Shakespeare: witness his *Venus and Adonis*, his *Lucrece*, his sugared *Sonnets* among his private friends." It was still a common practice for works to be circulated to a limited extent in manuscript while they were withheld from the press.

The first edition of Shakespeare's collected Dramatic Works appeared in 1623, or not till seven years after his death, in a folio volume. A second edition, with numerous verbal alterations, but no additional Plays, was brought out in the same form in 1632. In 1664 appeared a third edition, also in folio, containing seven additional Plays. And a fourth and last folio reprint followed in 1685.

The Plays that are now commonly received as Shakespeare's are all those that are contained in the First Folio, being thirty-six in number, together with *Pericles, Prince of Tyre*, one of the seven added in the Third Folio. Besides the other six in that edition,—entitled *The Tragedy of Locrine, The First Part of the Life of Sir John Oldcastle, The Chronicle History of Thomas Lord Cromwell, The London Prodigal, The Puritan*, and *A Yorkshire Tragedy*,—there have been ascribed to Shakespeare in more recent times the old Plays of *The Reign of King Edward the Third* and *The Tragedy of Arden of Feversham;* and by certain German critics those of *The Comedy of George-a-Green* (generally held to be the work of Robert Greene), *The Comedy of Mucedorus, The Birth of Merlin*, and *The Merry Devil of Edmonton*. Some of these are among the humblest productions of the human intellect; that the notion of their being Shakespeare's should have been taken up by such men as Schlegel and Tieck is an illustrious instance of how far the blinding and extravagant spirit of system may go. Finally, the Play of *The Two Noble Kinsmen*, commonly included among those of Beaumont and Fletcher, has been attributed in part to Shakespeare; it is described on the title-page of the first edition, published in 1634, as written by Fletcher and Shakespeare, and the opinion that Shakespeare had a share in it has been revived in our own day.

Of the thirty-seven Plays generally held to be genuine, eighteen are known to have been separately printed, some of them oftener than once, in Shakespeare's lifetime:— *Titus Andronicus, Romeo and Juliet, Love's Labour's Lost, Midsummer Night's Dream, Much Ado about Nothing, Merchant of Venice, Lear, Troilus and Cressida, Pericles, Richard the Second, First Part of Henry the Fourth, Second Part of Henry the Fourth, Richard the Third* (all substantially as we now have them); *Hamlet*, in three editions, two of them greatly differing the one from the other; and, in forms more or less unlike our present copies, *The Merry Wives of Windsor, Henry the Fifth,* and the *Second* and *Third Parts of Henry the Sixth*, under the titles of "The First Part of the Contention betwixt the Houses of York and Lancaster," and "The True Tragedy of Richard Duke of York" (often referred to as "The Second Part of the Contention"). Nor is it improbable that there may have been early impressions of some others of the Plays, although no copies are now known. The *Tragedy of Othello* was also printed separately in 1622. All these separately published Plays are in quarto, and are familiarly known as the old or early *Quartos*.

The following eighteen Plays appeared for the first time, as far as is known, in the Folio of 1623:—*The Tempest, The Two Gentlemen of Verona, Measure for Measure, The Comedy of Errors, As You Like It, The Taming of the Shrew, All's Well that Ends Well, Twelfth Night, A Winter's Tale, King John,* The First Part of *Henry the Sixth, Henry the Eighth, Coriolanus, Timon of Athens, Julius Cæsar, Macbeth, Antony and Cleopatra,* and *Cymbeline.*

There is reason to believe that the first edition of *Titus Andronicus* was printed in 1594, although the earliest of which any copy is now known is dated 1600. The earliest existing editions of *Romeo and Juliet, Richard the Second,* and *Richard the Third,* bear the date of 1597. The dates of the other Quartos (except *Othello*) all range between 1598 and 1609. It appears, however, from Francis Meres's book, mentioned above, that by the year 1598, when it was published, Shakespeare had already produced at least the following Plays, several of which, as we have seen, are not known to have been printed till they were included a quarter of a century afterwards in the First Folio:—*The Two Gentlemen of Verona, The Comedy of Errors, Love's Labour's Lost, Midsummer Night's Dream, The Merchant of Venice, Richard the Second, Richard the Third, Henry the Fourth, King John, Titus Andronicus, Romeo and Juliet,* and another called *Love's Labour's Won,* which has been commonly supposed to be that now entitled *All's Well that Ends Well*.* And Meres cannot be

* But the play of *All's Well that Ends Well* seems to have its present title built or wrought into it, and as it were incorporated with it. It is Helena's habitual *word*, and the thought that is never absent from her mind. "All's well that ends well," she exclaims, in the fourth Scene of the Fourth Act;

"Still the fine's the crown :
Whate'er the course, the end is the renown."

And again in the first Scene of the Fifth Act:—

"All's well that ends well yet."

So also the King, in the concluding lines of the Play :—

"All yet seems well; and, if it end so meet
The bitter past, more welcome is the sweet;"

and then to the audience :—

"The king's a beggar, now the play is done;
All is well ended, if this suit be won,
That you express content."

There would be no nature or meaning in the dialogue circling around the phrase in question, or continually returning upon it, in this way, unless it formed the name of the Play. On the other hand, there is not an expression throughout the piece that can be fairly considered as allusive to such a title as *Love's Labour's Won*.

Another notion that has been taken up is that the Play now known as *The Tempest* is that designated *Love's Labour's Won* by Meres. This is the theory of the Reverend Joseph Hunter, first brought forward in a "Disquisition on the Tempest," published in 1841, and reproduced in the Second Part of his "New Illustrations of the Life, Studies, and Writings of Shakespeare," 1844. But, notwithstanding all the learning and ingenuity by which it has been set forth and defended, it has probably not met with much acceptance. One would as soon believe with Ulrici that *The Tempest* is the very latest of all Shakespeare's Plays, as with Mr Hunter that it is one of his earliest,—"nearly the first in time," he calls it, "as the first in place [meaning as it stands in the original collective edition], of the dramas which are wholly his."

May not the true *Love's Labour's Won* be what we now call *The Taming of the Shrew?* That Play is founded upon an older one called *The Taming of A Shrew*; it is therefore in the highest degree improbable that it was originally produced under its present name. The de-

held to profess to do more than to instance some of the works by which Shakespeare had by this time in his opinion proved himself the greatest English writer that had yet arisen both in tragedy and in comedy.

Six years before this, or in 1592, Robert Greene, accounted by himself and others one of the chief lights of that early morning of our drama, but destined to be soon completely outshone and extinguished, had, perhaps with some presentiment of his coming fate, in a pamphlet which he entitled "Greene's Groatsworth of Wit," thus vented his anger against the new luminary; "There is an upstart crow, beautified with our feathers, that, with his tiger's heart wrapped in a player's hide, supposes he

signation by which it is now known, in all likelihood, was only given to it after its predecessor had been driven from the stage, and had come to be generally forgotten. Have we not that which it previously bore indicated in one of the restorations of Mr Collier's MS. annotator, who directs us, in the last line but one of the Second Act, instead of "in this case of *wooing*," to read "in this case of *winning*," thus giving us what may stand, in want of a better, for a rhyme to the "if I fail not of my cunning" of the line following? The lines are pretty evidently intended to rhyme, however rudely. The Play is, besides, full of other repetitions of the same key-note. Thus, in the second Scene of Act I., when Hortensio informs Gremio that he had promised Petrucio, if he would become suitor to Katharine, that they "would be contributors, And bear his charge of wooing, whatsoe'er," Gremio answers, "And so we will, provided that he win her." In the fifth Scene of Act IV., when the resolute Veronese has brought the shrew to a complete submission, Hortensio's congratulation is, "Petrucio, go thy ways; the field is won." So in the concluding scene the lady's father exclaims, "Now fair befall thee, good Petrucio! The wager thou hast won;" to which the latter replies, "Nay, I will win my wager better yet." And his last words in passing from the stage, as if in pointed allusion to our supposed title of the piece, are—

"'Twas I won the wager, though you [*Lucentio*] hit the white;
And, being a winner, God give you good night!"

The title of *Love's Labour's Won*, it may be added, might also comprehend the underplot of Lucentio and Bianca, and even that of Hortensio and the Widow, though in the case of the latter it might rather be supposed to be the lady who should be deemed the winning party.

is as well able to bombast out a blank verse as the best of you; and, being an absolute *Johannes Factotum*, is, in his own conceit, the only *Shake-scene* in a country." This would seem to imply, what is otherwise probable enough, that up to this time Shakespeare had chiefly made himself known as a dramatic writer by remodelling and improving the works of his predecessors. He may, however, have also even already produced some Plays wholly of his own composition. If *Titus Andronicus* and the Three Parts of *Henry the Sixth* are to be accounted his in any sense, they probably belong to this earliest stage of his career.

Of the thirty-seven Plays there are *seven* the authenticity of which has been more or less questioned. The Three Parts of *King Henry the Sixth* (especially the First) and *Titus Andronicus*, if they are by Shakespeare, have very little of his characteristic manner; *Pericles* has come down to us in so corrupted a state that the evidence of manner and style is somewhat unsatisfactory, though it is probably his; *Timon of Athens* is generally admitted to be only partly his; and much of *King Henry the Eighth*, which has only recently come to be suspected, is also evidently by another hand.*

III. THE SOURCES FOR THE TEXT OF SHAKESPEARE'S PLAYS.

From what has been stated it appears that, of the entire number of thirty-seven Plays which are usually regarded as Shakespeare's, there are only *fourteen* (including *Hamlet*) of which, in what may be called their completed state or ultimate form, we possess impressions published in his lifetime; together with *four* others (reckoning the Second and Third Parts of *Henry the Sixth* to be the same with the Two Parts of the *Contention*) of which in

---

* See a paper by Mr Spedding, in the *Gentleman's Magazine* for August 1850, and various subsequent communications by Mr Hickson and others in the *Notes and Queries*.

an immature and imperfect state we have such impressions. Of one other, *Othello*, we have also an edition, printed indeed after the author's death, but apparently from another manuscript than that used for the First Folio. For the remaining *eighteen* Plays our oldest authority is that edition. And the only other sources for which any authority has been claimed are; 1. The Second, Third, and Fourth Folios; 2. A manuscript of the First Part and some portions of the Second Part of *Henry the Fourth*, which is believed to be nearly of Shakespeare's age, and of which an impression has been edited by Mr Halliwell for the *Shakespeare Society*; 3. The manuscript emendations, extending over all the Plays, with the exception only of *Pericles*, made in a handwriting apparently of about the middle of the seventeenth century, in a copy of the Second Folio belonging to Mr Collier.

None of these copies can claim to be regarded as of absolute authority. Even the least carelessly printed of the Quartos which appeared in Shakespeare's lifetime are one and all deformed by too many evident and universally admitted errors to make it possible for us to believe that the proofs underwent either his own revision or that of any attentive editor or reader; it may be doubted if in any case the Play was even set up from the author's manuscript. In many, or in most, cases we may affirm with confidence that it certainly was not. Some of these Quartos are evidently unauthorized publications, hurriedly brought out, and founded probably in the main on portions of the dialogue fraudulently furnished by the actors, with the lacunæ filled up perhaps from notes taken by reporters in the theatre.

The First Folio (1623) is declared on the title-page to be printed "according to the true original copies;" and it is probable that for most of the Plays either the author's autograph, or, at any rate, some copy belonging to the theatre, was made use of. The volume was put forth in the names of two of Shakespeare's friends and fellow-actors, *John Heminge* and *Henrie Condell*, who introduce what they style "these trifles," the "remains" of their deceased associate, by a Dedication to the Earls of Pembroke and Montgomery,—who, they observe, had been pleased to think the said trifles something,—and by a Preface, in which, after confessing that it would have been a thing to be wished "that the author himself had lived to have set forth and overseen his own writings," they desire that they his surviving friends may not be envied the office of their care and pains in collecting and publishing them, and so publishing them as that, whereas formerly, they continue, addressing the Reader, "you were abused with divers stolen and surreptitious copies, maimed and deformed by the frauds and stealths of injurious impostors that exposed them [that is, exposed them for sale, or published them], even those are now offered to your view cured and perfect of their limbs, and all the rest absolute in their numbers,* as he conceived them. Who, as he was a happy imitator of nature, was a most gentle expresser of it: his mind and hand went together; and what he thought he uttered with that easiness, that we have scarce received from him a blot in his papers."

Here we have certainly, along with an emphatic and undiscriminating condemnation of all the preceding impressions, a distinct declaration by the publishers of the present volume that they had the use of the author's manuscripts. It is the only mention to be found anywhere of any of the Plays being in existence in his own

* This Latinism has no special reference, as has sometimes been supposed, to the verse; it means merely perfect in all their parts, or in all respects. So Sir Roger Twysden, in the Preface to his "Historiæ Anglicanæ Scriptores Decem" (1652), speaking of the pains that had been taken to ensure the accuracy of the text, says:—"Nihil unquam apud nos, tanti saltem conaminis, . . . adeo *omnibus numeris absolutum* prodiisse memini."

handwriting. No doubt can reasonably be entertained that such of his papers as were in possession of the Blackfriars Theatre, to which Heminge and Condell, like himself, belonged, were placed at their disposal. And we may assume that from these the edition of 1623 was set up, so far as they went and could be made available.

But it would be a great straining of such premises to conclude that the First Folio is to be accepted throughout as anything like an infallible authority in all cases for what Shakespeare actually wrote. That would, for one thing, be to suppose an accuracy and correctness of printing and editing of which there is no example in the published popular literature of that age, least of all in the drama, which was hardly looked upon as belonging to literature, and in regard to which the Press, when it was resorted to, was always felt to be at best but an imperfect and unnatural substitute for the proper mode of publication by means of the Stage. The writer, it would seem to have been thought, could not well claim as a *work* what called itself only a *play*. Nor do the publishers in the present instance make profession of having bestowed any special care upon the editing of their volume; what they say (or more probably what some regular author of the day, Ben Jonson, as it has been conjectured, or another, had been got to write in their names) is nothing more than the sort of recommendation with which it was customary for enlarged and improved editions to be introduced to the world, and the only positive assertion which it can be held to involve is, that the new impression of the Plays had been set up, at least in part, from the author's own manuscript. They lay claim, and we may therefore be sure could lay claim, to nothing further. They even admit, as we have seen, that it would have been better if the author himself had superintended the publication. Of correction of the press there is not one word. That, we may be pretty certain, was left merely to the printer. It is not likely that the two players, who, with the exception of this Dedication and Preface, to which their names are attached, are quite unknown in connexion with literature, were at all qualified for such a function, which is not one to be satisfactorily discharged even by persons accustomed to writing for the press without some practice.

But this is not all. The materials which Heminge and Condell, or whoever may have taken charge of the printing of the First Folio, had at their command were very possibly insufficient to enable them to produce a perfect text, although both their care and their competency had been greater than they probably were. In the first place, there is nothing in what they say to entitle us to assume that they had the author's own manuscript for more than some of the Plays. But, further, we do not know what may have been the state of such of his papers as were in their hands. We are told, indeed, that they were without a blot, and the fact is an interesting one in reference to Shakespeare's habits of composition; but it has no bearing upon the claims of the text of this First Folio to be accounted a correct representation of what he had written. He had been in his grave for seven years; the latest of the original copies of the Plays were of that antiquity at the least; most of them must have been much older. If, as is probable, they had been ever since they were written in use at the theatres, it can hardly have been that such of them as were not quite worn out should not have suffered more or less of injury, and have become illegible, or legible only with great difficulty, in various passages. Nor may the handwriting, even when not partially obliterated, have been very easy to decipher. The very rapidity with which the poet's "thick-coming fancies" had been committed to the paper may have made the record of them, free from blots as it was, still one not to be read running, or unlikely to trip a reader to whom it was not familiar.

When we take up and examine the volume itself, we find it to present the very characteristics which these considerations would lead us to expect. As a typographical production it is better executed than the common run of the English popular printing of that date. It is rather superior, for instance, in point of appearance, and very decidedly in correctness, to the Second Folio, produced nine years later. Nevertheless it is obviously, to the most cursory inspection, very far from what would now be called even a tolerably well printed book. There is probably not a page in it which is not disfigured by many minute inaccuracies and irregularities, such as never appear in modern printing. The punctuation is throughout rude and negligent, even where it is not palpably blundering. The most elementary proprieties of the metrical arrangement are violated in innumerable passages. In some places the verse is printed as plain prose; elsewhere, prose is ignorantly and ludicrously exhibited in the guise of verse. Indisputable and undisputed errors are of frequent occurrence, so gross that it is impossible they could have been passed over, at any rate in such numbers, if the proof-sheets had undergone any systematic revision by a qualified person, however rapid. They were probably read in the printing-office, with more or less attention, when there was time, and often, when there was any hurry or pressure, sent to press with little or no examination. Everything betokens that editor or editing of the volume, in any proper or distinctive sense, there could have been none. The only editor was manifestly the head workman in the printing-office.

On closer inspection we detect other indications. In one instance at least we have actually the names of the actors by whom the Play was performed prefixed to their portions of the dialogue instead of those of the *dramatis personæ*. Mr Knight, in noticing this circumstance, observes that it shows very clearly the text of the Play in which it occurs (*Much Ado About Nothing*) to have been taken from the play-house copy, or what is called the prompter's book.* But the fact is that the scene in question is given in the same way in the previous Quarto edition of the Play, published in 1600; so that here the printers of the Folio had evidently no manuscript of any kind in their hands, any more than they had any one over them to prevent them from blindly following their printed copy into the most transparent absurdities. The Quarto, to the guidance of which they were left, had evidently been set up from the prompter's book, and the proof-sheets could not have been read either by the author or by any other competent person. In the case of how many more of the Plays the Folio in like manner may have been printed only from the previously published separate editions we cannot be sure. But other errors with which the volume abounds are evidence of something more than this. In addition to a large number of doubtful or disputed passages, there are many readings in it which are either absolutely unintelligible, and therefore certainly corrupt, or, although not purely nonsensical, yet clearly wrong, and at the same time such as are hardly to be sufficiently accounted for as the natural mistakes of the compositor. Sometimes what is evidently the true word or expression has given place to another having possibly more or less resemblance to it in form, but none in signification; in other cases, what is indispensable to the sense, or to the continuity and completeness of the dramatic narrative, is altogether omitted. Such errors and deficiencies can only be explained on the supposition that the compositor had been left to depend upon a manuscript which was imperfect, or which could

* Library Shakspere, II. 366.

not be read. It is remarkable that deformities of this kind are apt to be found accumulated at one place; there are as it were nests or eruptions of them; they run into constellations; showing that the manuscript had there got torn or soiled, and that the printer had been obliged to supply what was wanting in the best way that he could by his own invention or conjectural ingenuity.*

Of the other Folio Editions, the Second, dated 1632, is the only one the new readings introduced in which have ever been regarded as of any authority. But nothing is known of the source from which they may have been derived. The prevailing opinion has been that they are nothing more than the conjectural emendations of the unknown editor. Some of them, nevertheless, have been adopted in every subsequent reprint.

The manuscript of *Henry the Fourth* (belonging to Sir Edward Dering, Bart., of Surrenden in Kent) is curious and interesting, as being certainly either of Shakespeare's own age or close upon it, and as the only known manuscript copy of any of the Plays of nearly that antiquity. But it appears to have been for the greater part merely transcribed from some printed text, with such omissions and modifications as were deemed expedient in reducing the two Plays to one.† The *First Part* of

* I have discussed the question of the reliance to be placed on the First Folio at greater length in an article on *The Text of Shakespeare*, in the 40th No. of the *North British Review* (for February 1854). It is there shown, from an examination of the First Act of Macbeth, that the number of readings in the First Folio (including arrangements of the verse and punctuations affecting the sense) which must be admitted to be either clearly wrong or in the highest degree suspicious probably amounts to not less than twenty on an average per page, or about twenty thousand in the whole volume. Most of them have been given up and abandoned even by those of the modern editors who profess the most absolute deference to the general authority of the text in which they are found.

† I am informed by a friend, upon whose accuracy I can rely, that a collation of a considerable portion of the MS. with the Quarto of

Henry the Fourth had been printed no fewer than five times, and the *Second Part* also once, in the lifetime of the author. The Dering MS., however, exhibits a few peculiar readings. One of them is remarkable.

For the lines, in the speech by the King with which the *First Part* opens, commonly given as—

" No more the thirsty entrance of this soil
Shall daub her lips with her own children's blood "—

we have in the MS.—

" No more ye thirsty bosome of this land
Shall wash her selfe in her owne childrens bloud."

Here are in the compass of two lines no fewer than five variations;—*bosom* for *entrance*, *land* for *soil*, *wash* for *daub*, *self* for *lips*, *in* for *with*,—the last being, moreover, a correction deliberately interlined over an erasure of the other reading.

The substitution of *wash* for *daub* is not without importance, the more especially as *daub* is commonly assumed to be the old reading, whereas it is really, I believe, nothing more than a modern conjectural emendation of the *damb* (or *damp* ?) of the early copies.

But the most important variation is that of *bosom* for *entrance*. Now, in the first place, although *entrance* is the reading of the *First* and *Second*, and, I believe, also of the *Third Folio*, another reading, *entrails*, is not, as has been sometimes supposed, the conjecture of Mr Douce, but is found in the *Fourth Folio*. I confess, however, that I can make nothing of *entrance*, and, if possible, still less of *entrails*. We are told that the " entrance of this soil" means the *mouth* of this soil. If a single instance can be produced from any writer, not confessedly insane, in which the mouth either of a real person, or of something represented as a living person, is

1613 leaves no doubt of that being the printed edition on which it was formed.

c

styled his, her, or its *entrance*, I shall be satisfied. Such a mode of expression, it appears to me, would at once destroy the personification. We speak, indeed, of the *entrance* of a cavern, for the *mouth* of a cavern; but here we are not calling a *mouth* an *entrance*, but an *entrance* a *mouth:* the proper prosaic name of the aperture by which we enter the cave is its *entrance*, which, when we animate the cave, we change into its *mouth;* but the opposite process is, I apprehend, unknown either in prose or in verse, in written eloquence or in the loosest colloquial speech. Any one who should talk of the *entrance* of a man, or of a lion, or of a dog, meaning the mouth, would not be understood. So in Latin we have the entrance to a river very often called its *os*, but nowhere the mouth of any living creature, or of any poetical personification, ever spoken of as its *ostium*.*

Nothing, also, can be more indisputable than that the two *hers*—"her lips" (or herself) and "her own children's blood"—must have the same reference. This is what syntax and common sense alike imperatively demand. Steevens's notion, therefore, that by "her lips" may be meant the lips of *peace*, mentioned four lines before, would be untenable, were there no other objection to it than that it would, apparently, give the *her* of "her lips" one reference and the *her* of "her own children" another.

The lips and the children must plainly be understood to be either those of the soil, or those of that, whatever it may have been, the designation of which has given rise to the various readings, *entrance, entrails, entrants*, as proposed by Steevens, *bosom*, &c. One's first inclination is to suppose some personage animating or presiding over

---

* The only interpretation of *entrance* having the least plausibility appears to me to be that thrown out by Theobald:—"I presume the sense is, 'blood-thirsty invasion of this country shall no more stain it with its own children's gore.' But is this idea conveyed by *thirsty entrance?*" Letter to Warburton, dated 13 January 1730, in Nichols's *Illustrations of the Literary History of the Eighteenth Century*, II. 402.

the soil; and hence such conjectures as that of Monk Mason,—"the thirsty *Erinnys* of this soil,"—which has been adopted in many editions, and which might mean that the Spirit of Discord should no more daub either her own lips with the blood of her own children, or the lips of the soil with the blood of the children of the soil. The circumstance of the word *Erinnys* being a Shakespearian ἅπαξ λεγόμενον, or not elsewhere found, would make it more likely to have been mistaken by the printer. So also might be interpreted "the thirsty *Genius* of this soil," as proposed in the First Edition of the present work.

But to both these readings there is this objection, which I apprehend must be held to be fatal. On the one hand, the epithet *thirsty*, standing where it does, seems clearly to bind us to understand that the lips described as to be no more daubed, or moistened, were those, not of the soil, but of the imaginary personage (the *Erinnys* or the *Genius*) to whom the performance of the act of daubing is attributed; on the other, the people could not be called the children of either the one of these personages or the other. And I do not think it would be possible to find any other mythological personage who could, more than either of these two, be represented as at once the owner of the lips and the parent of the children. It may be added that against "the thirsty *Genius*" this objection is of double force; inasmuch as, *Genius* being always conceived to be a male, the "*her* lips" (as well as "*her* own children") would in that case have of necessity to be understood as signifying the lips (and children) of the soil,—which would leave the epithet "thirsty" without meaning.

I do not think, therefore, that there is any other known reading which can compete with that of the Dering MS. The *bosom* of the soil, or ground, or earth, is one of the commonest and most natural forms of figurative expression, and is particularly natural and appropriate when the soil or ground is represented, as here, under the personification of a mother with her children. So **Friar** Lawrence says, in *Romeo and Juliet*, when setting out from his cell, basket **in** hand, at the dawn of day, to gather his "baleful weeds and precious-juiced flowers"—

> "**The earth,** that's nature's mother, is her tomb;
> What is her burying grave, that is her womb;
> **And** from her womb children of divers kind
> **We,** sucking on her natural bosom, find."

Then for the authority on which this reading rests, the probability surely is that the deviation from the common printed text was not made **on mere** conjecture; great pains appear to have **been taken with** the **MS.**; it is carefully corrected throughout in the handwriting of Sir Edward Dering, who died in 1644; **and he may very** well be supposed to have had access to other **sources of information,** both documentary and oral, in addition **to the** printed books. A strong case might **be** made out **for** such **a MS. as** being entitled to quite as much **deference** as any of the early printed copies, quarto or folio.

The first or outside page of the manuscript from which **this Play had** been originally set up may very probably have been **in** a somewhat dilapidated state when it was put into the **hands of the** printer. In addition to the five variations **in the two** lines that have been quoted, **it is** doubtful **whether in the first** line of the speech we ought to read "*wan* **with care**" or "*worn* with care;" the latter is the correction of Mr Collier's MS. annotator, and certainly it would **seem to** be more natural for the **King to** speak of his anxieties as wearing him down and **wasting** him away than as merely blanching his complexion.

It is only upon this supposition of the old text **of the** Plays having been printed from a partially obliterated or otherwise imperfectly legible manuscript, which, as we see, meets and accounts for other facts and peculiar ap pearances, while it is also so probable in itself, that the remarkable collection of emendations in Mr Collier's copy of the Second Folio can, apparently, be satisfactorily explained. The volume came into Mr Collier's hands in 1849, and was some time afterwards discovered by him to contain a vast number of alterations of the printed text inserted by the pen, in a handwriting certainly of the seventeenth century, and possibly of not much later date than the volume. They extend over all the thirty-six Plays, and are calculated to amount in all to at least 20,000. Here is, then, a most elaborate revision—an expenditure of time and painstaking which surely could only have been prompted and sustained by a strong feeling in the annotator of admiration for his author, and the most anxious and scrupulous regard for the integrity of his text. Such motives would be very inconsistent with the substitution generally for the old words of anything that might merely strike him as being *possibly* a preferable reading. The much more probable presumption is that he followed some guide. Such a labour is only to be naturally accounted for by regarding it as that of the possessor of a valued but very inaccurately printed book who had obtained the means of collating it with and correcting it by a trustworthy manuscript. And, when we come to examine the new readings, we find everything in sufficient correspondence with this hypothesis; some things almost, we may say, demonstrating it. Some of the alterations are of a kind altogether transcending the compass of conjectural emendation, unless it had taken the character of pure invention and fabrication. Such in particular are the entire lines inserted in various passages of which we have not a trace in the printed text. The number, too, of the new readings which cannot but be allowed to be either indisputable, or, at the least, in the highest degree ingenious and plausible, is of itself almost conclusive against our attributing them to nothing better than conjecture. Upon this supposition this unknown annotator would have outdone all that has been accomplished in the way of brilliant and felicitous conjecture by all other labourers upon the Shakespearian text taken together. On the other hand, some of his alterations are in all probability mistaken, some of his **new readings** apparently inadmissible;* and many pas-

---

* **Among such** must be reckoned undoubtedly the alteration, in Lady Macbeth's passionate rejoinder (*Macbeth, i.* 7),—

"What beast was't, then,
    That **made you break** this enterprise **to** me?"—

of *beast* into *boast*. This is to convert the forcible and characteristic not merely into tameness but into **no-meaning; for** there is no possible sense of the word *boast* which will answer here. But in this case the corrector was probably left to mere conjecture in making his selection between the two words; for in the handwriting of the earlier part of the seventeenth century the *e* and *o* are frequently absolutely undistinguishable. In the specimen of the annotator's own handwriting which Mr Collier gives, the two *e*'s of the word *briefely* are as like *o*'s **as** *e*'s, and what Mr Collier reads *bleeding* might be equally **read** *blooding*, if that were a word. Would Mr Collier thus correct Tennyson's

"Were not his words delicious, I a beast
    To take them as I did?"

Edwin Morris.

There cannot, I conceive, **be a** question that a celebrated passage in **another Play has been** seriously injured by the same mistake which the annotator has made in the instance under consideration. Is it not self-evident that the speech of Polixenes **in** the Third Scene of the Fourth Act of the *Winter's Tale* should run as follows?—

"Nature is made better by no mean
But nature makes that mean. So *ever* that art,
Which you say adds to nature, **is** an art
That nature makes. . . . .
The art itself is nature."

The "*o'er* that art" of the modern editions is "*over* that art" in the old copies.—In other cases, again, the *ever* and the *even* have evidently been confounded; as in *The Merry Wives of Windsor, iv.* 6, where Fenton describes Mrs Page as "even strong against" the marriage of her daughter with Slender, "and firm for Doctor Caius." The error here, if it be one, however, has apparently been left uncorrected by **Mr** Collier's MS. annotator.

sages which there can hardly be a doubt are corrupt are passed over by him without correction. All this becomes intelligible upon our hypothesis. Working possibly upon the same manuscripts (whether those of the author or no) from which the printed text had been set up, he would with more deliberation, or by greater attention and skill, succeed in deciphering correctly much of the difficult or faded writing which had baffled or been misread by the printer. In other places, again, he was able to make nothing of it, or it deceived him. In some cases he may have ventured upon a conjecture, and when he does that he may be as often wrong as right. The manuscripts of which he had the use—whether the author's original papers or only transcripts from them—probably belonged to the theatre; and they might now be in a much worse condition in some parts than when they were in the hands of Heminge and Condell in 1623. The annotator would seem to have been connected with the stage. The numerous and minute stage directions which he has inserted look as if it might have been for the use of some theatrical Company, and mainly with a view to the proper representation of the Plays, that his laborious task was undertaken.*

* I do not remember having seen it noticed that the theatres claimed a property in the Plays of Shakespeare, and affected to be in possession of the authentic copies, down to a comparatively recent date. The following *Advertisement* stands prefixed to an edition of Pericles, in 12mo, published in 1734, and professing to be " printed for J. Tonson, and the rest of the Proprietors :"—" Whereas R. Walker, and his accomplices, have printed and published several of Shakespeare's Plays, and, to screen their innumerable errors, advertise that they are printed as they are acted; and industriously report that the said Plays are printed from copies made use of at the Theatres ; I therefore declare, in justice to the Proprietors, whose right is basely invaded, as well as in defence of myself, that no person ever had, directly or indirectly, from me any such copy or copies; neither would I be accessary, on any account, to the imposing on the public such useless, pirated, and maimed editions, as are published by the said R. Walker. W. CHET-

Mr Collier has given an account of his annotated Folio in a volume which he published in 1852, entitled "Notes and Emendations to the text of Shakespeare's Plays, from Early Manuscript Corrections in a Copy of the Folio, 1632." A second edition of this volume appeared in 1853; and meanwhile he had also given to the world the same year an edition, in one volume, of "The Plays of Shakespeare: The Text regulated by the Old Copies, and by the recently discovered Folio of 1632, containing early Manuscript Emendations." But the most distinct statement that he has made upon the subject is that contained in a subsequent volume entitled "Seven Lectures on Shakespeare and Milton, by the late S. T. Coleridge; A List of all the MS. Emendations in Mr Collier's Folio, 1632; and an Introductory Preface;" 8vo, Lon. 1856. Of this volume the account of the annotations, headed "A List of Every Manuscript Note and Emendation in Mr Collier's Copy of Shakespeare's Works, Folio, 1632," is spread over about 120 pages. Instead of 20,000, how-

---

WOOD, *Prompter to His Majesty's Company of Comedians at the Theatre Royal in Drury-Lane*." On the subject of this *Chetwood* see Malone's *Inquiry into the Shakespeare Papers*, pp. 350—352. In Tonson's similar editions of *The History of Sir John Oldcastle* and *The Tragedy of Locrine* (both declared on the title-page to be "By Mr William Shakespear"), he speaks in like manner of himself "and the other Proprietors of the Copies of Shakespear's Plays," and complains that "one Walker has proposed to pirate all Shakespear's Plays, but, through ignorance of what Plays were Shakespear's, did in several Advertisements propose to print *Œdipus King of Thebes* as one of Shakespear's Plays, and has since printed Tate's *King Lear* instead of Shakespear's, and in that and *Hamlet* has omitted almost one half of the genuine editions printed by J. Tonson and the Proprietors." It would appear from Nichols's *Illustrations*, II. 199, that Theobald in the Preface to the Second Edition of his Play of *The Double Falsehood*, which he pretended was written by Shakespeare, spoke of private property perhaps standing so far in his way as to prevent him from putting out a complete edition of Shakespeare's Works. The passage, which does not occur in the first edition (1728), is retained in the third (1767).

ever, as originally stated (see *Notes and Emendations, Introduction*, p. iv.), the alterations here enumerated cannot much exceed 3000. Those omitted are probably (though nothing to that effect is said) only corrections of what are called literal errors, or such misprints as rather disfigure than injure the sense. Among them, however, are such as the alteration of *dambe* into *daub* in the passage quoted above from the beginning of the *First Part of Henry the Fourth*, which is mentioned in the *Notes and Emendations*, though passed over in the *List*. It would be more satisfactory if everything were given.*

IV. THE SHAKESPEARIAN EDITORS AND COMMENTATORS.

The four Folios were the only editions of the Plays of Shakespeare brought out in the seventeenth century; and, except that the First, as we have seen, has a Dedication and Preface signed by Heminge and Condell, two actors belonging to the Blackfriars Theatre, nothing is known, and scarcely anything has been conjectured, as to what superintendence any of them may have had in passing through the press. The eighteenth century produced a long succession of editors:—Rowe, 1709 and 1714; Pope, 1725 and 1728; Theobald, 1733 and 1740; Hanmer, 1744; Warburton, 1747; Johnson, 1765; Steevens, 1766; Capell, 1768; Reed, 1785; Malone, 1790; Rann, 1786—1794. The editions of Hanmer, Johnson, Steevens, Malone, and Reed were also all reprinted once or oftener, for the most

* Nearly the same views in most respects which I had announced in the *North British Review* in 1854, both on the Shakespearian text and on the new readings supplied by Mr Collier's MS. annotator, are ably advocated in an article in the *Edinburgh Review*, No. 210, for April 1856. The writer refers to a paper, which I have not seen, in a number of the *North American Review* for the preceding year, as containing " by far the best and most thoroughly reasoned discussion " of the subject with which he had met.

part with enlargements; and all the notes of the preceding editions were at last incorporated in what is called Reed's Second Edition of Johnson and Steevens, which appeared, in 21 volumes 8vo, in 1803. This was followed in 1821 by what is now the standard *Variorum* edition, also in 21 volumes, which had been mostly prepared by Malone, and was completed and carried through the press by his friend Mr James Boswell. We have since had the various editions of Mr Knight and Mr Collier, from both of whom, in addition to other original research and speculation, both bibliographical and critical, we have received the results of an examination of the old texts more careful and extended than they had previously been subjected to. New critical editions by the late Mr Singer and by Mr Staunton have also appeared within the last few years; and there are in course of publication the Cambridge edition by Mr Clark and Mr Wright, and another since commenced by Mr Dyce, besides the magnificent edition by Mr Halliwell, which is to extend to 20 volumes folio.

The list of commentators, however, includes several other names besides those of the editors of the entire collection of Plays; in particular, *Upton*, in " Critical Observations," 1746; *Dr Zachary Grey*, in " Critical, Historical, and Explanatory Notes," 1755; *Heath*, in " A Revisal of Shakespeare's Text," 1765; *Kenrick*, in a "Review of Johnson's Edition," 1765, and " Defence of Review," 1766; *Tyrwhitt*, in " Observations and Conjectures," 1766; *Dr Richard Farmer*, in " Essay on the Learning of Shakespeare," 1767; *Charles Jennens*, in annotated editions of " King Lear," 1770,—" Othello," 1773, —" Hamlet," 1773,—" Macbeth," 1773,—and " Julius Cæsar," 1774; *John Monck Mason*, in " Comments on the Last Edition of Shakespeare's Plays," 1785, and " Further Observations," 1798; *A. Beckett*, in "A Concordance to Shakespeare, to which are added three hundred Notes and Illustrations," 1787; *Ritson*, in " The Quip

Modest," 1781, and "Cursory Criticisms," 1792; *Whiter*, in "A Specimen of a Commentary," 1794; *George Chalmers*, in "Apology for the Believers in the Shakespearian Papers," 1797, and "Supplemental Apology," 1799; *Douce*, in "Illustrations of Shakespeare and of Ancient Manners," 1807; *Reverend Joseph Hunter*, in "Illustrations of the Life, Studies, and Writings of Shakespeare," 1844; and *Reverend Alexander Dyce*, in "Remarks on Mr Collier's and Mr Knight's Editions," 1844, and "A Few Notes on Shakespeare," 1853. To these names and titles may be added the *Reverend Samuel Ayscough's* "Index to the Remarkable Passages and Words made use of by Shakespeare," 1790; "A Complete Verbal Index to the Plays of Shakespeare," in 2 vols., by *Francis Twiss, Esq.*, 1805; and *Mrs Cowden Clarke's* "Complete Concordance to Shakspere," 1847. Finally, there may be mentioned *Archdeacon Nares's* "Glossary of Words, etc., thought to require Illustration in Shakespeare and his Contemporaries," 1822.*

V. THE MODERN SHAKESPEARIAN TEXTS.

No modern editor has reprinted the Plays of Shakespeare exactly as they stand in any of the old Folios or Quartos. Neither the spelling, nor the punctuation, nor the words of any ancient copy have been retained unaltered, even with the correction of obvious errors of the Press. It has been universally admitted by the course that has been followed that a genuine text is not to be obtained without more or less of conjectural emendation: the only difference has been as to the extent to which it should be carried. The most recent texts, however, beginning with that of Malone, and more especially those of Mr Knight and of Mr Collier (in his eight volume edition), have been formed upon the principle of adhering

* Of this important work a new edition, with large additions, has lately been announced as in preparation.

to the original copies as closely as possible; **and** they have given us back many old readings which had been rejected by preceding editors. There has been **some** difference of opinion among editors of **the modern** school in **regard to** whether the preference should **be given** in certain cases to the First Folio or **to** some previous **Quarto** impression of the **Play** produced in the lifetime of **the author;** and Steevens latterly, in opposition **to** Malone, who had originally **been** his coadjutor, set up **the** doctrine that the Second Folio was a safer guide than the First. This heresy, however, **has** probably now been abandoned by everybody.

But, besides the correction of what are believed to be errors of the **Press in** the old copies, the text of Shakespeare has been subjected to certain modifications **in all** the modern reprints:—

1. The spelling has been reduced to the modern standard. The original spelling is certainly no **part of the composition.** There is no reason to believe **that it is even** Shakespeare's own spelling. In all probability **it is** merely that of the person who set up the types. Spenser may be suspected to have had some peculiar notions upon the subject of orthography; but, apparently, it was not a matter about which Shakespeare troubled himself. In departing from the original editions **here,** therefore, we lose nothing **that is really his.**

2. **The actual form of the word** in certain cases has **been modernized.** This deviation is not so clearly defensible upon principle, **but** the change is so slight, and the convenience and advantage so considerable, that it may fairly be held to be justifiable nevertheless on the ground of expediency. The case of most frequent occurrence is that of the word *than*, which with Shakespeare, as **generally with** his contemporaries and predecessors, **is** always *then*. "Greater *then* a king" would be intolerable to the modern ear. *Then* standing in this position is there-

fore quietly converted by all the modern editors into our modern *than*. Another form which was unquestionably part of the regular phraseology and grammar of his day is what is sometimes described as the conjunction of a plural nominative with a singular verb, but is really only a peculiar mode of inflecting the verb, by which the plural is left undistinguished from the singular. Shakespeare and his contemporaries, although they more usually said, as we do, "words sometimes *give* offence," held themselves entitled to say also, if they chose, "words sometimes *gives* offence." But here again so much offence would be given by the antiquated phraseology to the modern ear, accustomed to such an apparent violation of concord only from the most illiterate lips, that the detrimental *s* has been always suppressed in the modern editions, except only in a few instances in which it happens to occur as an indispensable element of the rhyme—as when *Macbeth*, in his soliloquy before going in to murder the sleeping King (*ii.* 1) says,—

"Whiles I threat he lives:
Words to the heat of deeds too cold breath *gives;*"

or, as when *Romeo* says to Friar Lawrence (*ii.* 3),

" Both our remedies
Within thy help and holy physic *lies.*"

A few contractions also, such as *upon't, on's* head, etc., which have now become too vulgarized for composition of any elevation, are usually neglected in constructing the modern text, and without any appreciable injury to its integrity.

3. In some few cases the editors have gone the length of changing even the word which Shakespeare may very possibly have written, or which may probably have stood in the manuscript put into the hands of the original printers, when it has been held to be palpably or incontrovertibly wrong. In *Julius Cæsar*, for instance (*ii.* 1), they have upon this principle changed "the *first* of

March" into "the *ides* of March" (149), and afterwards "*fifteen* days" into "*fourteen* days" (154). It is evident, however, that alterations of this kind ought to be very cautiously made.

VI. THE MECHANISM OF ENGLISH VERSE, AND THE PROSODY OF THE PLAYS OF SHAKESPEARE.

The mechanism of verse is a thing altogether distinct from the music of verse. The one is matter of rule, the other of taste and feeling. No rules can be given for the production of music, or of the musical, any more than for the production of poetry, or the poetical.

The law of the mechanical construction of verse is common to verse of every degree of musical quality,—to the roughest or harshest (provided it be verse at all), as well as to the smoothest and sweetest. Music is not an absolute necessity of verse. There are cases in which it is not even an excellence or desirable ingredient. Verse is sometimes the more effective for being unmusical. The mechanical law or form is universally indispensable. It is that which constitutes the verse. It may be regarded as the substance; musical character, as the accident or ornament.

In every language the principle of the law of verse undoubtedly lies deep in the nature of the language. In all modern European languages, at least, it is dependent upon the system of accentuation established in the language, and would probably be found to be modified in each case according to the peculiarities of the accentual system. In so far as regards these languages, verse may be defined to consist in a certain arrangement of accented and unaccented syllables.

The Plays of Shakespeare are all, with the exception only of occasional couplets, in unrhymed or what is called *Blank* verse. This form of verse was first exemplified in

English in a translation of the Fourth Book of the Æneid by the unfortunate Lord Surrey, who was executed in 1547 ; it was first employed in dramatic writing by Thomas Sackville (afterwards Lord Buckhurst and Earl of Dorset) in his *Gorboduc* (or *Ferrex and Porrex*), produced in 1561; and, although not much used in poetical compositions of any other kind, either translated or original, till Milton brought it into reputation by his *Paradise Lost* in the latter part of the following century, it had come to be the established or customary verse for both tragedy and comedy before Shakespeare began to write for the stage. Our only legitimate English Blank verse is that commonly called the Heroic, consisting normally in a succession of five feet of two syllables each, with the pressure of the voice, or accent, on the latter of the two, or, in other words, on the second, fourth, sixth, eighth, and tenth syllables of each line. After the tenth syllable, an unaccented syllable, or even two, may be added without any prosodical effect. The rhythm is completed with the tenth syllable, and what follows is only as it were a slight reverberation or echo.

But this general statement is subject to certain important modifications :—

1. In any of the feet an accent on the first syllable may be substituted for one on the second, providing it be not done in two adjoining feet. This transference of the accent is more unusual in certain of the feet than in others—most of all in the fifth, next to that in the second ; —but is not in any foot a violation of the law of the verse, or what is properly to be called a licence.

2. It is a universal law of English verse, that any syllable whatever, falling in the place of the accent either immediately before or immediately after a foot of which one of the syllables is truly accented, will be accounted to be accented for the purposes of the verse. The *-my* of *enemy*, for instance, or the *in-* of *intercept*, is always so

accounted in heroic verse, in virtue of the true accent upon *en-* and upon *-cept;* but in dactylic or anapæstic verse, these syllables, although pronounced precisely in the same manner, are always held to be unaccented, the law of those kinds of verse not requiring another accent within the distance at which the *-my* stands removed from the *en-*, or the *in-* from the *-cept*. This, in so far as regards the heroic line, is equivalent to saying that every alternate foot may be without a really accented syllable in it at all. Or the line might be defined as consisting, not of five feet of two syllables each, with one of them accented, but of two and a half feet, each of four syllables, with at least one of the four accented; the half foot, which need not have an accent, occurring sometimes at the beginning of the line, sometimes in the middle, sometimes at the end. Practically, the effect is, that anywhere in the line we may have a sequence of three syllables (none of them being superfluous) without any accent; and that there is no word in the language (such as Horace was plagued with in Latin) *quod versu dicere non est,—* none, whether proper name or whatever else, which the verse does not readily admit.

3. It is by no means necessary (though it is commonly stated or assumed to be so) that the syllables alternating with the accented ones should be unaccented. Any or all of them *may* be accented also.

4. Further, in any of the places which may be occupied by an unaccented syllable it is scarcely an irregularity to introduce two or even more such unaccented syllables. The effect may be compared to the prolongation or dispersion of a note in music by what is called a shake. Of course, such a construction of verse is to be resorted to sparingly and only upon special grounds or occasions; employed habitually, or very frequently, it crowds and cumbers the rhythm, and gives it a quivering and feeble character. But it can nowhere be said to be illegitimate,

—although, in **ordinary** circumstances, it may **have a less** agreeable effect in some places of the line than in others.

These four modifications of its normal **structure are** what, along with **the artistic distribution of the pauses and** cadences, principally **give** its variety, freedom, **and** life to our Heroic verse. **They are what** the intermixture of dactyls and spondees **is to the** Greek **or** Latin **Hexameter.** They are none of them of the nature of what is properly denominated a poetic **licence, which is not a modification but** a violation **of** the rule, permissible only upon rare occasions, and altogether **anarchical and destructive** when too frequently committed. **The first three of** our four modifications are taken advantage **of habitually** and incessantly by every writer of verse **in the language;** and the fourth, **to a greater or less extent, at least** by nearly all our blank **verse poets.**

So much cannot **be said for another form of verse (if it is to be so called) which has also** been supposed **to be found in** Shakespeare; **that, namely, in which a line,** evidently perfect **both at the beginning and the end,** wants a syllable in **the middle.** Such, for instance, is the well-known line in *Measure for Measure, ii.* 2, as it stands in the First Folio,—

"Than the soft myrtle. But man, proud man."

Here, it will be observed, we **have** not a hemistich **(by which we mean any portion of a verse** perfect **so far as it** extends, **whether** it be the commencing **or** concluding portion), but something which professes to **be a complete verse.** The present is not merely a *truncated* line of nine syllables, or one where the defect consists in **the want of** either the first or the last syllable; the defect here would not be cured **by any** addition **to either the beginning or** the end of the **line;** the syllable that is wanting is **in the** middle.

The existing text **of** the Plays presents us with **a con-**

siderable number of verses of this description. In many of these, in all probability, the text is corrupt; the wanting syllable, not being absolutely indispensable to the sense, has been dropt out in the copying or setting up by some one (a common case) not much alive to the demands of the prosody. The only other solution of the difficulty that has been offered is, that we have a substitute for the omitted syllable in a *pause* by which the reading of the line is to be broken. This notion appears to have received the sanction of Coleridge. But I cannot think that he had fully considered the matter. It is certain that in no verse of Coleridge's own does any mere pause ever perform the function which would thus be assigned to it. Nor is any such principle recognized in any other English verse, modern or ancient, of which we have a text that can be absolutely relied upon. It is needless to observe that both in Shakespeare and in all our other writers of verse we have abundance of lines broken by pauses of all lengths without any such effect being thereby produced as is here assumed. If the pause be really equivalent to a syllable, how happens it that it is not so in every case? But that it should be so in any case is a doctrine to which I should have the greatest difficulty in reconciling myself. How is it possible by any length of pause to bring anything like rhythm out of the above quoted words,—

"Than the soft myrtle. But man, proud man"?

If this be verse, there is nothing that may not be so designated.

I should be inclined to say, that, wherever there seems to be no reason for suspecting the loss of a syllable, we ought in a case of this sort to regard the words as making not one line, but two hemistichs, or truncated lines. Thus, the passage in *Measure for Measure* would stand—

" Merciful heaven!
Thou rather, with thy sharp and sulphurous bolt,

> Splitt'st the unwedgeable and gnarled oak
> Than the soft myrtle.
> But man, proud man,
> Dress'd in a little brief authority:" &c.

This is nothing more than what has been done with the words "Merciful heaven!" which all the modern editors print as a hemistich, but which both in the First Folio and in all the others is made to form a line with the words that immediately precede; thus;—

> "Nothing but thunder: Mercifull héauen."

What mainly gives its character to the English Heroic line is its being poised upon the tenth syllable. It is by this, as well as by the number of feet, that its rhythm or musical flow is distinguished, for instance, from that of what is called the Alexandrine, or line of twelve syllables, the characteristic of which is that the pressure is upon the sixth and the twelfth. Without this twelve syllables will no more make an Alexandrine than they will a common Heroic line. There are in fact many Heroic lines consisting of twelve syllables, but still, nevertheless, resting upon the tenth.

It follows that generally in this kind of verse the tenth syllable will be strongly accented. That is the normal form of the line. When there is rhyme, the consonance is always in the tenth syllable. As, however, in dancing (which is a kind of visible verse,—the poetry of motion, as it has been called), or in architecture (which is another kind, and may be styled the visible poetry of repose), the pressure upon that which really sustains is sometimes sought to be concealed, or converted into the semblance of its opposite, and the limb or the pillar made to appear to be rather drawn towards the ground than resting upon it, so in word-poetry too we have occasionally the exhibition of a similar feat. Instead of a strongly accented syllable, one taking only a very slight accent, or none at all, is made to fill the tenth place. One form, indeed, of this peculiarity of **structure** is extremely common, **and is** resorted to by all our poets as often for mere convenience as for **any** higher purpose, that, namely, **in which the** weak tenth syllable is the termination of a word of which **the syllable** having the accent has already done duty in its proper place in the preceding foot. It is in this **way** that, **both in** our blank and **in** our rhymed verse, the large classes of words ending in *-ing*, *-ness*, *-ment*, *-y*, etc., **and accented on** the antepenultimate, are made available **in** concluding so many lines. The same thing happens when we have at the end of the line a short or unaccented monosyllable which either coalesces like an enclitic with the preceding word or at least belongs to the same clause of the expression; as in Beaumont and Fletcher's

"By my dead father's soul, you stir not, Sir!"
(*Humorous Lieutenant*, ii. 2);

or,

"And yields all thanks to me for that dear care
Which I was bound to have in training you."
(*King and No King*, ii.).

But another **case is more remarkable.**

This is when the weak **or unaccented tenth** syllable is **neither** the final syllable of a word the accented syllable of which has already done service in the preceding foot, nor **in any way a** part of the same clause of the expression to **which that** foot belongs, but a separate monosyllabic word, frequently **one,** such as *and*, *but*, *if*, *or*, *of*, even *the*, or *a*, or *an*, among the slightest and most rapidly uttered in the language, and belonging syntactically and in natural utterance **to** the succeeding line. We may be said to have the strongest or most illustrious exemplifications of this mode of versifying in the

"Labitur ripa, Jove non probante, u—
—**xorius amnis,"**

and other similar exhibitions of "linked sweetness" in

Horace, Pindar, and the Greek dramatists in their choral passages (if we may accept the common arrangement),—to say nothing of sundry modern imitations in the same bold style, even in our own vernacular, which need not be quoted. Such a construction of verse, however, when it does not go the length of actually cutting a word in two, is in perfect accordance with the principles of our English prosodical system; for, besides that the *and*, *or*, *of*, or *if* is not really a slighter syllable than the termination *-ty* or *-ly*, for instance, which is so frequently found in the same position, these and other similar monosyllables are constantly recognized, under the second of the above laws of modification, as virtually accented for the purposes of the verse in other places of the line. Still when a syllable so slight meets us in the place where the normal, natural, and customary rhythm demands the greatest pressure, the effect is always somewhat startling. This unexpectedness of effect, indeed, may be regarded as in many cases the end aimed at, and that which prompts or recommends the construction in question. And it does undoubtedly produce a certain variety and liveliness. It is fittest, therefore, for the lighter kinds of poetry. It is only there that it can without impropriety be made a characteristic of the verse. It partakes too much of the nature of a trick or a deception to be employed except sparingly in poetry of the manliest or most massive order. Yet there too it may be introduced now and then with the happiest effect, more especially in the drama, where variety and vivacity of style are so much more requisite than rhythmical fulness or roundness, and the form of dialogue, always demanding a natural ease and freedom, will justify even irregularities and audacities of expression which might be rejected by the more stately march of epic composition. It has something of the same bounding life which Ulysses describes Diomed as showing in "the manner of his gait":—

> "He rises on the toe: that spirit of his
> In aspiration lifts him from the earth."

Two things are observable with regard to Shakespeare's employment of this peculiar construction of verse:—

1. It will be found upon an examination of his Plays that there are some of them in which it occurs very rarely, or perhaps scarcely at all, and others in which it is abundant. It was certainly a habit of writing which grew upon him after he once gave in to it. Among the Plays in which there is little or none of it are some of those known to be amongst his earliest; and some that were undoubtedly the product of the latest period of his life are among those that have the most of it. It is probable that the different stages in the frequency with which it is indulged in correspond generally to the order of succession in which the Plays were written. A certain progress of style may be traced more or less distinctly in every writer; and there is no point of style which more marks a poetic writer than the character of his versification. It is this, for instance, which furnishes us with the most conclusive or at least the clearest evidence that the play of *King Henry the Eighth* cannot have been written throughout by Shakespeare. It is a point of style which admits of precise appreciation to a degree much beyond most others; and there is no other single indication which can be compared with it as an element in determining the chronology of the Plays. It is therefore extremely difficult to believe that the three Roman plays, *Julius Cæsar*, *Antony and Cleopatra*, and *Coriolanus*, can all belong to the same period (Malone assigns them severally to the years 1607, 1608, and 1610), seeing that the second and third are among the plays in which verses having in the tenth place an unemphatic monosyllable of the kind in question are of most frequent occurrence, while the only instances of anything of the sort in the first are, I believe, the following:—

51. "I had as lief not be as live to be
  In awe of such a thing as I myself."

54.   "And Cassius is
  A wretched creature, and must bend his body."

54. "A man of such a feeble temper should
  So get the start of the majestic world."

55. "I do believe that these applauses are
  For some new honours that are heaped on Cæsar.

155.   "All the interim is
  Like a phantasma."

307. "Desiring thee that Publius Cimber may
  Have an immediate freedom of repeal."

355. "And am moreover suitor, that I may
  Produce his body to the market-place."

358. "And that we are contented Cæsar shall
  Have all true rites and awful ceremonies."

406. "But yesterday the word of Cæsar might
  Have stood against the world."

494.   "Or here, or at
  The Capitol."

Not only does so comparatively rare an indulgence in it show that the habit of this kind of versification was as yet not fully formed, but in one only of these ten instances have we it carried nearly so far as it repeatedly is in some other Plays: *be,* and *is,* and *should,* and *may,* and *shall,* and *might,* and *are,* all verbs, though certainly not emphatic, will yet any of them allow the voice to rest upon it with a considerably stronger pressure than such lightest and slightest of "winged words" as *and, or, but, if, that* (the relative or conjunction), *who, which, than, as, of, to, with, for,* etc. The only decided or true and perfect instance of the peculiarity is the last in the list.

2. In some of the Plays at least the prosody of many of the verses constructed upon the principle under consideration has been misconceived by every editor, including the most recent. Let us take, for example, the play of

Coriolanus, in which, as has just been observed, such verses are very numerous. Here, in the first place, we have a good many instances in which the versification is correctly exhibited in the First Folio, and, of course, as might be expected, in all subsequent editions; such as—

> "Only in strokes, but with thy grim looks and
> The thunder-like percussion of thy sounds."—i. 4.

> "I got them in my country's service, when
> Some certain of your brethren roared and ran."—ii. 3.

> "The thwartings of your dispositions, if
> You had not showed them how you were disposed."—iii. 2.

> "Come, my sweet wife, my dearest mother, and
> My friends of noble touch, when I am forth."—iv. 2.

> "Permitted by our dastard nobles, who
> Have all forsook me."—iv. 5.

> "Mistake me not, to save my life; for if
> I had feared death, of all the men i' the world."—iv. 5.

> "Had we no quarrel else * to Rome, but that
> Thou art thence banished, we would muster all."—iv. 5.

---

* The reading of all the copies is "No other quarrel else;" but it is evident that *other* is merely the author's first word, which he must be supposed to have intended to strike out, if he did not actually do so, when he resolved to substitute *else*. The prosody and the sense agree in admonishing us that both words cannot stand. So in *Antony and Cleopatra*, iv. 10, in the line "To the young Roman boy she hath sold me, and I fall;" *young* is evidently only the word first intended to be used, and never could be meant to be retained after the expression *Roman boy* was adopted. Another case of the same kind is unquestionably that of the word *old* in the line (*As You Like It*, iv. 3),—

> "Under an (old) oak, whose boughs were mossed with age."

Nor can I have any doubt that another text, equally familiar to the modern ear, has suffered a similar corruption,—Bassanio's—

> "In my school-days, when I had lost one shaft,
> I shot his fellow of the self-same flight
> The self-same way with more advised watch,
> To find the other forth; and by adventuring both
> I oft found both."

"You have holp to ravish your own daughters, and
    To melt the city leads upon your pates."—iv. 6.

"Your temples burned in their cement; and
    Your franchises, whereon you stood, confined."—iv. 6.

"Upon the voice of occupation, and
    The breath of garlic-eaters."—iv. 6.

"I do not know what witchcraft's in him; but
    Your soldiers use him as the grace 'fore meat."—iv. 7.

"Mine ears against your suits are stronger than
    Your gates against my force."—v. 3.

"As if Olympus to a molehill should
    In supplication nod."—v. 3.

"Hath an aspect of intercession, which,
    Great Nature cries, Deny not."—v. 3.

"Aufidius, and you Volsces, mark; for we'll
    Hear nought from Rome in private."—v. 3.

"That thou restrain'st from me the duty which
    To a mother's part belongs."—v. 3.

"And hale him up and down; all swearing, if
    The Roman ladies bring not comfort home."—v. 4.

"The city posts by this hath entered, and
    Intends to appear before the people, hoping."—v. 5.

"I seemed his follower, not partner; and
    He waged me with his countenance, as if
    I had been mercenary."—v. 5.

"At a few drops of women's rheum, which are
    As cheap as lies."—v. 5.

"With our own charge; making a treaty where
    There was a yielding."—v. 5.

"That prosperously I have attempted, and
    With bloody passage led your wars, even to
    The gates of Rome."—v. 5.

To find forth may, I apprehend, be safely pronounced to be neither English nor sense. The *forth* has apparently been transferred from the preceding line, which was either originally written "The same way forth," or, more probably, was so corrected after having been originally written "The self-same way."

"Breaking his oath and resolution, like
A twist of rotten silk."—v. 5.

"Though in this city he
Hath widowed and unchilded many a one."—v. 5.

These instances are abundantly sufficient to prove the prevalence in the Play of the peculiarity under consideration, and also its recognition, whether consciously and deliberately or otherwise does not matter, by the editors. But further, we have also some instances in which the editors most attached to the original printed text have ventured to go the length of rearranging the verse upon this principle where it stands otherwise in the First Folio. Such are the following:

"Commit the war of white and damask in
Their nicely gauded cheeks."—ii. 1.

Here the Folio includes *their* in the first line.

"A kinder value of the people than
He hath hereto prized them at."—ii. 2.

The Folio gives this as prose.

"To allay my rages and revenges with
Your colder reasons."—v. 3.

The Folio gives from "My rages" inclusive as a line.

After this it is surely very strange to find in our modern editions such manifest and gross misconceptions of the versification as the following arrangements exhibit:—

"My gentle Marcius, worthy Caius,
And—By deed-achieving honour duly named."—ii. 1.

"I have seen the dumb men throng to see him,
And—The blind to hear him speak."—ii. 1.

"Have made them mutes, silenced their pleaders,
And—Dispropertied their freedoms."—ii. 1.

"Having determined of the Volsces,
And—To send for Titus Lartius."—ii. 2.

"To gratify his noble service, that hath
Thus—Stood for his country."—ii. 2.

"That valour is the chiefest virtue,
And—Most dignifies the haver."—ii. 2.

"Pray you, go fit you to the custom;
And—Take to you, as your predecessors have."—ii. 2.

"I have seen and heard of; for your voices
Have—Done many things, some less, some more; your voice."
—ii. 3.

"Endue you with the people's voice:
Remains—That, in the official marks invested,
You—Anon do meet the senate."—ii. 3.

"Would think upon you for your voices,
And—Translate his malice towards you into love."—ii. 3.

"The apprehension of his present portance,
Which—Most gibingly, ungravely, he did fashion."—ii. 3.

"For the mutable, rank-scented many,
Let them—Regard me as I do not flatter,
And—Therein behold themselves."—iii. 1.

"That would depopulate the city,
And—Be every man himself."—iii. 1.

In all these instances the words which I have separated from those that follow them by a dash belong to the preceding line; and, nearly every time that the first of the two lines is thus put out of joint, the rhythm of both is ruined.

The modern editor who has shown the most disposition to tamper with the old text in the matter of the versification is Steevens. The metrical arrangement of the First Folio is undoubtedly wrong in thousands of instances, and it is very evident that the conception which the persons by whom the printing was superintended had of verse was extremely imperfect and confused. They would be just as likely to go wrong as right whenever any intricacy or indistinctness in the manuscript threw them upon their own resources of knowledge and critical sagacity. But Steevens set about the work of correction on false principles. Nothing less would satisfy him than to reduce the prosody of the natural dramatic blank verse of Shakespeare, the characteristic product of the sixteenth century, **to the** standard **of** the trim rhyming couplets into which **Pope** shaped **his** polished epigrams in the eighteenth. **It is a** mistake, however, **to** speak **of** Steevens as having no ear for verse. His **ear** was a practised and correct enough one, only that **it** had been trained in a narrow school. Malone, **on** the other hand, had **no notion** whatever of verse beyond what he could obtain **by counting the** syllables on his fingers. Everything **else but** the mere number of the syllables went with him **for nothing.** This is demonstrated **by all** that he has written **on** the subject. And, curiously enough, Mr James Boswell, the associate of his labours, appears to have been **endowed with** nearly an equal share of the same singular insensibility.

VII. SHAKESPEARE'S JULIUS CÆSAR.

Shakespeare's *Julius Cæsar* was first printed, **as far as** is known, in the First Folio collection of his **Plays,** published in 1623; it stands there between *Timon of Athens* and *Macbeth*, filling, in the division **of** the volume which begins with *Coriolanus* and extends to the end, being that **occupied** with the *Tragedies*,—which **is** preceded by those containing the *Comedies* and **the** *Histories*,—the double-columned **pages** from **109 to 130** inclusive.* Here, at **the beginning and over each** page, **it is** entitled "The **Tragedie of Julius Cæsar;" but** in the *Catalogue* at the **beginning of the volume it** is entered as "The Life and **Death of** Julius **Cæsar;"** other entries in the list being, among the *Histories*, "The Life and Death **of King** John," **"The** Life and Death of Richard the **Third,"** "The Life of King Henry the Eighth," and, **among the** *Tragedies*, "The Tragedy of Coriolanus," "The Tragedy **of** Macbeth," "The Tragedy of **Hamlet," "King** Lear," "Othello, the Moore of Venice." **In the Second** Folio

* There is a break in the pagination from 101 to 108 inclusive.

(1632), where this series of pages includes *Troilus and Cressida*, " The Tragedy of Julius Cæsar," as it is entered both in the running title and in the Catalogue, extends from page 129 to 150 inclusive. In both editions the Play is divided into Acts, but not into Scenes; although the First Act is headed in both " Actus Primus. Scœna Prima." There is no list in either edition of the *Dramatis Personæ*, as there is with several others of the Plays.

Malone, in his " Attempt to ascertain the Order in which the Plays of Shakespeare were written," assigning *Hamlet* to the year 1600, *Othello* to 1604, *Lear* to 1605, *Macbeth* to 1606, *Antony and Cleopatra* to 1608, and *Coriolanus* to 1610, fixes upon the year 1607 as the date of the composition of *Julius Cæsar*. But nothing can be more inconclusive than the grounds upon which he comes to this conclusion. His reasoning is principally, or, indeed, we may say almost wholly, founded upon the fact of a rhyming play on the same subject by William Alexander, afterwards Earl of Sterline, or Stirling, having been first printed at London in that year (it had been originally printed in Scotland three years before), which he thinks may be presumed to have preceded Shakespeare's. "Shakespeare, we know," he observes, in his disquisition on the Chronological Order (*Variorum* edition, II. 445-451), "formed at least twelve plays on fables that had been unsuccessfully managed by other poets; but no contemporary writer was daring enough to enter the lists with him in his lifetime, or to model into a drama a subject which had already employed his pen; and it is not likely that Lord Sterline, who was then a very young man, and had scarcely unlearned the Scotch idiom, should have been more hardy than any other poet of that age." Elsewhere (XII. 2) he says: " In the two Plays many parallel passages are found, which might perhaps have proceeded only from the two authors drawing from the same source. However, there are some reasons for thinking the coincidence more than accidental." The only additional reason he gives is that "a passage in *The Tempest* ("The cloud-capped towers, etc.") seems to have been copied from one in *Darius*, another Play of Lord Sterline's, printed at Edinburgh in 1603." Upon the subject of these alleged imitations by Shakespeare of one of the most uninspired of his contemporaries, see Mr Knight's article on this *William Alexander* in the "Biographical Dictionary of the Society for the Diffusion of Useful Knowledge," Vol. II. pp. 4-7. They may safely be pronounced to be one and all purely imaginary. The passage in *Darius* (which Play is also in rhyme), it may be noted, was removed by Lord Stirling from his Play when he reprinted it in a revised form in 1637. This would have been a singularly self-denying course for the noble versifier to have taken if the notion that it had been either plagiarized or imitated by the great English dramatist had ever crossed his mind. The resemblance, in fact, is no greater than would be almost sure to occur in the case of any two writers in verse, however widely remote in point of genius, taking up the same thought, which, like the one we have here, is in itself almost one of the commonplaces of poetical or rhetorical declamation, however pre-eminently it has been arrayed by Shakespeare in all the "pride, pomp, and circumstance of glorious *words*."

A Latin Play upon the subject of the death of Cæsar —"Epilogus Cæsaris Interfecti"—the production of a Dr Richard Eedes, whom Meres, in his *Wit's Commonwealth*, published in 1598, mentions as one of the best tragic writers of the time, appears to have been brought out at Christ's Church, Oxford, in 1582. And there is also an anonymous English Play of Shakespeare's age, entitled "The Tragedy of Cæsar and Pompey, or Cæsar's Revenge," of which two editions have come down to us, one bearing the date of 1607 (the same year in which

Alexander's *Julius Cæsar* was printed at London), the other without date, but apparently earlier. This Play is often confounded with another of the same title by George Chapman, which, however, was not printed till 1631. The anonymous Play appears to have been first produced in 1594. See *Henslowe's Diary, by Collier*, p. 44. Malone observes that " in the running title it is called *The Tragedy of Julius Cæsar;* perhaps the better to impose it on the public for the performance of Shakespeare." It is not pretended, however, that it and Shakespeare's Play have anything in common.*

Shakespeare's *Julius Cæsar* is alluded to as one of the most popular of his Plays by Leonard Digges (a younger brother of Sir Dudley, the popular parliament man in the time of Charles I., and afterwards Master of the Rolls), in a copy of verses prefixed to the First Folio :—

" Nor shall I e'er believe or think thee dead, . . .
. . . till I hear a scene more nobly take
Than when thy half-sword parlying Romans spake."

In the Prologue, also, to Beaumont and Fletcher's tragedy entitled *The False One*,† the subject of which is the loves of Cæsar and Cleopatra in Egypt, the authors vindicate themselves from the charge of having taken up the same ground with Shakespeare in the present Play:—

* From a comedy called *Every Woman in her Humour*, printed in 1609, Malone quotes a passage from which he infers that there was an ancient droll or puppet-shew on the subject of Julius Cæsar :—" I have seen the City of Nineveh and Julius Cæsar acted by mammets." " I formerly supposed," Malone adds, " that this droll was formed on the play before us; but have lately observed that it is mentioned with other *motions* (Jonas, Ninevie, and the Destruction of Jerusalem) in Marston's *Dutch Courtesan*, printed in 1605, and was probably of a much older date." (*Chronological Order*, 449.) But it is not so clear that the mention of the *motion*, or puppet-shew, in 1605 would make it impossible that it should have been posterior to Shakespeare's Play.

† It has been disputed whether by *The False One* we are to understand Cæsar or another character in the Play, the villain Septimius. A friend suggests that it may be Cleopatra that is intended to be so designated.

"Sure to tell
Of Cæsar's amorous heats, and how he fell
I' the Capitol, can never be the same
To the judicious."

But in what year *The False One* was brought out is not known. It certainly was not before 1608 or 1609.

Finally, it has been remarked that the quarrel scene between Brutus and Cassius in Shakespeare's Play has evidently formed the model for a similar one between the two friends Melantius and Amintor in the Third Act of Beaumont and Fletcher's *Maid's Tragedy*. All that is known, however, of the date of that Play is, that it was probably brought out before 1611, in which year another Play entitled *The Second Maiden's Tragedy* was licensed. But even this is doubtful; for there is no resemblance, or connexion of any kind, except that of the names, between the two Plays.*

On the whole, it may be inferred from these slight evidences that the present Play can hardly be assigned to a later date than the year 1607; but there is nothing to prove that it may not be of considerably earlier date.

It is evident that the character and history of Julius Cæsar had taken a strong hold of Shakespeare's imagina-

* "This tragedy," says Malone, "(as I learn from a MS. of Mr Oldys) was formerly in the possession of John Warburton, Esq., Somerset Herald, and since in the library of the Marquis of Lansdown." (*Chronological Order*, 450.) It is one of the three Plays which escaped destruction by Mr Warburton's cook. It has now been printed "from the original MS., 1611, in the Lansdown Collection" (British *Museum*), in the First No. of *The Old English Drama*, Lon. 1824, -25, the eight Nos. of which, making two vols., are commonly regarded as making a supplement to the last, or 12 volume, edition of *Dodsley*. The title of *The Second Maiden's Tragedy* appears to have been given to the present Play by Sir George Buc, the master of the Revels. The MS., he states, had no name inscribed on it. On the back of the MS. the Play is attributed to **William** *Goughe*. Afterwards *William* has been altered to **Thomas**. Then this name has been obliterated, and *George Chapman* substituted. Finally, this too has been scored through, and the authorship assigned to *William Shakspear*.

tion. There is perhaps no other historical character who is so repeatedly alluded to throughout his Plays.

"There was never anything so sudden," says the disguised Rosalind in *As You Like It* (*v.* 2) to Orlando, speaking of the manner in which his brother Oliver and her cousin (or sister, as she calls her) Celia had fallen in love with one another, "but the fight of two rams, and Cæsar's thrasonical brag of I came, saw, and overcame: for your brother and my sister no sooner met, but they looked; no sooner looked, but they loved; no sooner loved, but they sighed;" etc.

"O! such a day," exclaims Lord Bardolph in the *Second Part of King Henry the Fourth* (*i.* 1) to old Northumberland in his misannouncement of the issue of the field of Shrewsbury,

"So fought, so hononred, and so fairly won,
Came not till now to dignify the times
Since Cæsar's fortunes."

And afterwards (in *iv.* 3) we have Falstaff's magnificent gasconade:—"I have speeded hither with the very extremest inch [?] of possibility: I have foundered ninescore and odd posts; and here, travel-tainted as I am, have, in my pure and immaculate valour, taken Sir John Coleville of the Dale, a most furious [famous?] knight, and valorous enemy. But what of that? He saw me, and yielded; that I may justly say, with the hook-nosed fellow of Rome, I came, saw, and overcame."

"But now behold," says the Chorus in the Fifth Act of *King Henry the Fifth*, describing the triumphant return of the English monarch from the conquest of France,

"In the quick forge and working-house of thought,
How London doth pour out her citizens.
The mayor, and all his brethren, in best sort,
Like to the senators of the antique Rome,
With the plebeians swarming at their heels,
Go forth, and fetch their conquering Cæsar in."

In the three Parts of *King Henry the Sixth*, which are

so thickly sprinkled with classical allusions of all kinds, there are several to the great Roman Dictator. "Henry the Fifth! thy ghost I invocate;" the **Duke of** Bedford apostrophizes his deceased brother in the *First Part* (*i*. 1);

> "Prosper this realm, keep it from civil broils!
> Combat with adverse planets in the heavens!
> **A far** more glorious star thy soul will make
> Than Julius Cæsar, or bright Cassiope."*

In the next Scene the Maid, setting out to raise the siege of Orleans, and deliver her king **and** country, compares herself to

> 'That proud insulting ship
> **Which** Cæsar and his fortunes bare at once."

In the *Second* **Part** (*iv.* 1) we have Suffolk, when hurried away to execution by the seamen who had captured **him,** consoling himself with—

> "Great men oft die by vile bezonians:
> A Roman sworder and banditto slave
> Murdered sweet Tully; Brutus' bastard **hand**
> Stabbed Julius Cæsar; savage islanders
> Pompey the great; and Suffolk dies by **pirates.**"

---

* The *Cassiope* is supplied **by** Mr Collier's MS. annotator. But Theobald had proposed *Cassiopeia,* and **not without** supporting his conjecture **by some** ingenious and plausible **reasoning.** See his letter to Warburton, dated 29th **January 1730,** in Nichols's *Illustrations*, II. 451—453. This, then, is one **of those remarkable** instances in which the recently discovered MS. **is found to** concur with a previously published conjectural emendation,—like **two** independent witnesses testifying separately to the same fact, and so at once adding confirmation to the fact and corroborating each other's testimony, sagacity, or judgment. It is proper to add, however, that Theobald was afterwards induced to **give up this reading.** Writing again to Warburton on the **12th of February,** he says:—" I have received the pleasure of **yours** dated February 3, **with a** kind and judicious refutation **of** *Cassiopeia;* and, **with a just deference** to your **most convincing reasons, I shall** with great **cheerfulness banish** it as a bad and unsupported conjecture." (*Illustrations,* II. 478).

And afterwards (*iv.* 7) we have Lord Say, in somewhat similar circumstances, thus appealing to Cade and his mob of men of Kent :—

> "Hear me but speak, and bear me where you will.
> Kent, in the Commentaries Cæsar writ,
> Is termed the civilest place of all this isle;
> Sweet is the country, because full of riches;
> The people liberal, valiant, active, worthy;
> Which makes me hope you are not void of pity."

"O traitors! murderers!" Queen Margaret in the *Third Part* (*v.* 5) shrieks out in her agony and rage when the Prince her son is butchered before her eyes;—

> "They that stabbed Cæsar shed no blood at all,
> Did not offend, nor were not worthy blame,
> If this foul deed were by to sequel it:
> He was a man; this, in respect, a child;
> And men ne'er spend their fury on a child."

In *King Richard the Third* (*iii.* 1) is a passage of great pregnancy. "Did Julius Cæsar build that place, my lord?" the young Prince asks Buckingham when it is proposed that he shall retire for a day or two to the Tower before his coronation. And, when informed in reply that the mighty Roman at least began the building, "Is it," he further inquires,

> "upon record, or else reported
> Successively from age to age, he built it?"

"It is upon record, my gracious lord," answers Buckingham. On which the wise royal boy rejoins,—

> "But say, my lord, it were not registered,
> Methinks the truth should live from age to age,
> As 'twere retailed to all posterity,
> Even to the general all-ending day."

And then, after a "What say you, uncle?", he explains the great thought that was working in his mind in these striking words:—

> "That Julius Cæsar was a famous man:
> With what his valour did enrich his wit
> His wit set down to make his valour live.
> Death makes no conquest of this conqueror,*
> For now **he** lives in fame, though not in life."

Far away from anything Roman as the fable and **locality** of *Hamlet* are, various passages testify how much **Cæsar** was in the mind of Shakespeare while writing that **Play.** First, we have the famous **passage** (*i.* 1) so closely resembling one in the Second **Scene** of the Second Act of *Julius Cæsar:*—

> "In the most high and palmy state of Rome,
> A little ere the mightiest Julius fell,
> The graves stood tenantless, and the sheeted **dead**
> Did squeak and gibber in the Roman streets;
> As † stars with trains of fire, and dews of blood,
> Disasters in the sun; and the moist star,
> Upon whose influence Neptune's empire stands,
> Was sick almost to doomsday with eclipse." ‡

Then there is (*iii.* 2) the conversation between Hamlet and Polonius, touching the histrionic exploits of the latter in his university days:—"I did enact **Julius Cæsar: I was killed i'** the Capitol; Brutus killed me." "It was a *brute* part of him to kill so *capital* a calf there" (surely, by the bye, to be spoken *aside*, though not so marked).— Lastly, there is the **Prince's** rhyming moralization (*v.* 1):—

> "Imperial Cæsar, dead and turned to clay,
> Might stop a hole to keep the wind away.
> O, that that earth which kept the world in awe
> Should patch a **wall** to expel the winter's flaw!"

---

* "*His* conqueror" is the reading of all the Folios. "*This*" was restored by Theobald from the Quarto of 1597, and has been adopted by Malone and most modern editors.

† Something is evidently wrong here; but even Mr **Collier's** annotator gives us no help.

‡ This passage, however, is found only in the Quartos, and is omitted in all the Folios. Nor, although retained by Mr Collier in his "regulated" **text, is it stated** to be restored by his MS. annotator.

Many notices of Cæsar occur, as might be expected, in *Cymbeline*. Such are the boast of Posthumus to his friend Philario (*ii.* 4) of the valour of the Britons:—

> "Our countrymen
> Are men more ordered than when Julius Cæsar
> Smiled at their lack of skill, but found their courage
> Worthy his frowning at;"

Various passages in the First Scene of the Third Act:—

> "When Julius Cæsar (whose remembrance yet
> Lives in men's eyes, and will to ears and tongues
> Be theme and hearing ever) was in this Britain,
> And conquered it, Cassibelan, thine **uncle**
> (Famous in Cæsar's praises no whit less
> Than in his feats deserving it)," etc. ;

> "There be many Cæsars,
> Ere such another Julius;"

> "A kind of conquest
> Cæsar made here ; but made not here his brag
> Of *came*, and *saw*, and *overcame :* with shame
> (The first that ever touched him) he was carried
> From off our coast twice beaten ; and his shipping
> (Poor ignorant baubles !) on our terrible seas,
> Like egg-shells moved upon their surges, cracked
> As easily 'gainst our rocks. For joy whereof
> The famed Cassibelan, who was once at point
> (O giglot Fortune !) to master Cæsar's sword,
> Made Lud's town with rejoicing fires bright,
> And Britons strut with courage ;"

"Our kingdom is stronger than it was at that time; and, as I said, there is no more such Cæsars ; other of them may have crooked noses ; but to owe such straight arms, none ;"

> "Cæsar's ambition
> (Which swelled so much that it did **almost stretch**
> The sides o' the world) against all **colour, here,**
> Did put the yoke upon us ; which to shake **off**
> Becomes **a** warlike people, whom we reckon
> Ourselves **to** be."

Lastly, we have a few **references** in *Antony and Cleopatra;* such as :—

"Broad-fronted Cæsar,
When thou wast here above the ground, I was
A morsel for a monarch" (*i.* 4);

"Julius Cæsar,
Who at Philippi the good Brutus ghosted" (***ii.* 6**);

"What was it
That **moved pale Cassius to** conspire? And what
Made the all-honoured, honest, Roman Brutus,
With the armed rest, courtiers of beauteous freedom,
To drench the Capitol, but that **they** would
Have one man but a man?" (*ii.* 6);

"Your fine Egyptian cookery
Shall have the fame. I have heard that Julius Cæsar
Grew fat with feasting there" (*ii.* 6);

"When Antony found Julius Cæsar dead,
He cried almost to roaring; and he wept
When at Philippi he found Brutus slain" (*iii.* 2);

Thyreus.—"Give me grace to lay
My duty on your hand.
Cleopatra.—"Your Cæsar's father oft,
When he hath mused of taking kingdoms in,
Bestowed his lips on that unworthy place
As it rained kisses" (***iii.* 11).**

These passages taken all together, and some of them **more** particularly, will probably be thought to afford a considerably **more** comprehensive representation of "the **mighty Julius**" than the Play which bears his name. **We cannot be sure** that that Play was so entitled by **Shakespeare.** "The Tragedy of Julius Cæsar," or "The **Life and** Death of Julius Cæsar," would describe no more **than the** half of it. Cæsar's part in it terminates **with** the opening of the Third Act; after that, on to the **end, we** have nothing more of him but his dead body, his ghost, **and** his memory. The Play **might more** fitly be called after Brutus than after Cæsar. And still more remark-**able is the partial delineation** that we have of the man.

We have a distinct exhibition of little else beyond his vanity and arrogance, relieved and set off by his good-nature or affability. He is brought before us only as "the spoilt child of victory." All the grandeur and predominance of his character is kept in the background or in the shade—to be inferred, at most, from what is said by the other *dramatis personæ*—by Cassius on the one hand and by Antony on the other in the expression of their own diametrically opposite natures and aims, and in a very few words by the calmer, milder, and juster Brutus—nowhere manifested by himself. It might almost be suspected that the complete and full-length Cæsar had been carefully reserved for another drama. Even Antony is only half delineated here, to be brought forward again on another scene: Cæsar needed such reproduction much more, and was as well entitled to a stage which he should tread without an equal. He is only a subordinate character in the present Play; his death is but an incident in the progress of the plot. The first figures, standing conspicuously out from all the rest, are Brutus and Cassius.

Some of the passages that have been collected are further curious and interesting as being other renderings of conceptions that are also found in the present Play, and as consequently furnishing data both for the problem of the chronological arrangement of the Plays and for the general history of the mind and artistic genius of the writer. After all the commentatorship and criticism of which the works of Shakespeare have been the subject, they still remain to be studied in their totality with a special reference to himself. The man Shakespeare as read in his works—Shakespeare as there revealed, not only in his genius and intellectual powers, but in his character, disposition, temper, opinions, tastes, prejudices,—is a book yet to be written.

It is remarkable that not only in the present Play, but also in *Hamlet* and in *Antony and Cleopatra*, the assassination of Cæsar should be represented as having taken place in the Capitol. From the Prologue, quoted above, to Beaumont and Fletcher's tragedy of *The False One*, too, it would appear as if this had become the established popular belief; but the notion may very probably be older than Shakespeare.

Another deviation from the literalities of history which we find in the Play, is the making the Triumvirs in the opening scene of the Fourth Act hold their meeting in Rome. But this may have been done deliberately, and neither from ignorance nor forgetfulness.

I have had no hesitation in discarding, with all the modern editors, such absurd perversions as *Antonio, Flavio, Lucio*, which never can have proceeded from Shakespeare, wherever they occur in the old copies; and in adopting Theobald's rectification of *Murellus* (for *Marullus*), which also cannot be supposed to be anything else than a mistake made in the printing or transcription. But it seems hardly worth while to change our familiar *Portia* into *Porcia* (although Johnson, without being followed, has adopted that perhaps more correct spelling in his edition).

The peculiarity of the form given to the name of Cæsar's wife in this Play does not seem to have been noticed. The only form of the name known to antiquity is *Calpurnia*. And that is also the name even in North's English translation of *Plutarch*, Shakespeare's great authority.* The *Calphurnia* of all the old copies of the Play, adopted by all the modern editors, may be nothing better than an invention of the printers. I have not, how-

* Mr Senior, in his late reprint of Bacon's *Essays*, at p. 99, gives the name *Calfurnia*; but that form is not to be found, I apprehend, in any of the old copies.

ever, ventured to rectify it, in the possibility that, although a corrupt form, it *may* be one which Shakespeare found established in the language and in possession of the public ear. In that case, it will be to be classed with *Anthony*, *Protheus*, and *Bosphorus*, the common modern corruption of the classic *Bosporus*, which even Gibbon does not hesitate to use.

The name of the person called *Decius* Brutus throughout the play was *Decimus* Brutus. *Decius* is not, like *Decimus*, a prænomen, but a gentilitial name. The error, however, is as old as the edition of Plutarch's Greek text produced by Henry Stephens in 1572;* and it occurs likewise in the accompanying Latin translation, and both in Amyot's and Dacier's French, as well as in North's English. It is also found in Philemon Holland's translation of *Suetonius*, published in 1606. Lord Stirling in his *Julius Cæsar*, probably misled in like manner by North, has fallen into the same mistake with Shakespeare. That *Decius* is no error of the press is shown by its occurrence sometimes in the verse in places where *Decimus* could not stand.

Finally, it may be noticed that it was really this Decimus Brutus who had been the special friend and favourite of Cæsar, not Marcus Junius Brutus the conspirator, as represented in the Play. In his misconception upon this point our English dramatist has been followed by Voltaire in his tragedy of *La Mort de César*, which is written avowedly in imitation of the *Julius Cæsar* of Shakespeare.

The wholly new readings in the Play of *Julius Cæsar* which Mr Collier appears to have obtained from his manuscript annotator are the following, twenty-three in number:—

* Ἐν δὲ τούτῳ Δέκιος Βροῦτος ἐπίκλησιν Ἀλβῖνος. *Vit. Cæs.* p. 1354.

ACT I.
102. He was quick *mettled* when he went to school.

But this, although given in the *Regulated Text* of the Plays, is not noticed either in the *Notes and Emendations* or in the *List*.

109. These are their *seasons*,—they are natural.

ACT II.
187. And after seem to chide 'em. This shall *mark*.
202. Enjoy the *heavy honey-dew* of slumber.

ACT III.
285. *That* touches *us? Ourself* shall be last served.
303. *Casca.* Are we all ready?—*Cæs.* What is now amiss, &c

But this is not noticed in the *List*.

305. These *crouchings*, and these lowly courtesies.
— *Low-crouched* courtesies, and base spaniel fawning.
346. Our arms in strength of *welcome*, and our hearts.
363. A curse shall light upon the *loins* of men.
461. And things *unlikely* charge my fantasy.

ACT IV.
496. And graze *on* commons.
541. I shall be glad to learn of **abler** men.
542. I said, an *older* soldier, **not a better.**

But this is only given in the *Regulated Text*.

559. A flatterer's would not, though they *did* appear.
620. Come on refreshed, *new-hearted*, and encouraged.

ACT V.
687. The posture of your blows *is* yet unknown.
690. *While* damned Casca, like a cur, behind.

But this is only given in the *Regulated Text*.

692. Have added slaughter to the *word* of *traitor*.
704. Coming from Sardis, on our *forward* ensign.
709. To stay the providence of *those* high powers.
711. Must end that work the ides of March *began*.

But this is only given in the *Regulated Text*.

794. He only, in a *generous* honest thought
    Of common good to all, made one of them.

And the emendations in the MS. also include the following eleven readings which had been conjecturally proposed before its discovery:—

ACT I.

56. That her wide *walls* encompassed but one man.
57. Under *such* hard conditions as this time.
130. *In* favour's like the work we have in hand.

ACT II.

238. *We are* two lions, littered in one day.
246. *Of* evils imminent; and on her knee.

ACT III.

305. Into the *law* of children. Be not fond.
349. Signed in thy spoil, and crimsoned in thy *death*.
358. Have all *due* rites, and lawful ceremonies.
459. I heard *them* say, Brutus and Cassius.

ACT IV.

530. Brutus, *bay* not me.

ACT V.

709. The *term* of life; arming myself with patience.

Finally, the reading of the First Folio, which had been altered in the Second, is restored by the MS. annotator in the following ten instances:—

ACT I.

50. That I profess *myself* in banqueting.
54. But *for* my single self.
89. But there's *no* heed to be taken of them

ACT II.

160. Buried in their *cloaks*.
199. Caius Ligarius doth bear Cæsar *hard*.
233. The noise of battle *hurtled* in the air.

ACT IV.

529. I had rather be a dog, and *bay* the moon.
634. Poor knave, I blame thee *not*.

ACT V.

758. And bring us *word* unto Octavius' tent.
779. My heart doth joy, that yet, *in* all my life.

Of these forty four corrections, thirty two are adopted in the present text; and, of the remaining twelve, only **one or two can** be regarded, **I** think, as clearly wrong.

I have not thought it necessary to distinguish the **cases** in which the verbal affix -*ed* is to be united in **the pronunciation** with the preceding syllable by the usual **substitution** of the apostrophe **in** place of the silent **vowel.** **Why** should the word *loved,* **for** example, so sounded **be** represented differently in verse from what it always **is in** prose? It is **true that** the cases in **which the -*ed*** makes a separate syllable are more numerous **in Shakespeare** than **in** the poetry of the present day; but the reader who **cannot** detect such **a** case on the instant is disqualified by some natural deficiency for the reading of verse. If **any** distinction **were necessary,** the better plan would **be** to **represent the** one form by "loved," the other by "lov-ed."

I **have not thought it** necessary in the present revision to make the numerous typographical rectifications which would have been required **in** the margin of every page, and also in **many** of the references, to remove the traces of an unimportant error **of *one* in** the numbering of the speeches from 249 (on p. 180), which ought to be 248, onwards to the end of the play.—1863.

PHILOLOGICAL COMMENTARY

ON

SHAKESPEARE'S JULIUS CÆSAR.

PERSONS REPRESENTED.

JULIUS CÆSAR.
OCTAVIUS CÆSAR, \
MARCUS ANTONIUS, } *Triumvirs, after the death of Julius Cæsar.*
M. ÆMIL. LEPIDUS, /
CICERO, PUBLIUS, POPILIUS LENA; *Senators.*
MARCUS BRUTUS, \
CASSIUS, |
CASCA, |
TREBONIUS, } *Conspirators against Julius Cæsar.*
LIGARIUS, |
DECIUS BRUTUS, |
METELLUS CIMBER, |
CINNA, /
FLAVIUS and MARULLUS, *Tribunes.*
ARTEMIDORUS, *a Sophist of Cnidos.*

A SOOTHSAYER.
CINNA, *a Poet.*—Another POET.
LUCILIUS, TITINIUS, MESSALA, Young CATO, and VOLUMNIUS; *Friends to Brutus and Cassius.*
VARRO, CLITUS, CLAUDIUS, STRATO, LUCIUS, DARDANIUS; *Servants to Brutus.*
PINDARUS, *Servant to Cassius.*

CALPHURNIA, *Wife to Cæsar.*
PORTIA, *Wife to Brutus.*

SENATORS, CITIZENS, GUARDS, ATTENDANTS, ETC.

SCENE, *during a great part of the Play, at Rome; afterwards at Sardis; and near Philippi.*

ACT I.

SCENE I.—*Rome. A Street.*

Enter FLAVIUS, MARULLUS, *and a Rabble of* CITIZENS.

1. *Flav.* Hence; home, you idle creatures, get you home;
Is this a holiday? What! know you not,
Being mechanical, you ought not walk,
Upon a labouring day, without the sign
Of your profession?—Speak, what trade art thou?

1 *Cit.* Why, Sir, a carpenter.

Mar. Where is thy leather apron, and thy rule?
What dost thou with thy best apparel on?—
You, Sir; what trade are you?

2 *Cit.* Truly, Sir, in respect of **a** fine workman, I am but, as you **would** say, a cobbler.

Mar. But what trade art thou? Answer me directly.

6. 2 *Cit.* A trade, Sir, that, I hope, I may use with a safe **con**science; which is, indeed, Sir, a mender of bad soles.
7. *Mar.* What trade, thou knave? thou naughty knave, what trade?
8. 2 *Cit.* Nay, I beseech you, **Sir, be not** out with me: yet if you **be** out, Sir, I can mend you.
9. *Mar.* What mean'st thou by **that?** Mend me, thou saucy fellow?

2 *Cit.* Why, Sir, cobble you.

Flav. Thou art a cobbler, art thou?

12. 2 *Cit.* **Truly,** Sir, all that **I live by** is, with the awl: **I** meddle **with no** tradesman's matters, nor women's matters, but with awl. I am, indeed, Sir, a surgeon to old shoes; when they are in great danger, I recover them. As proper men as ever trod upon neat's leather have gone upon my handiwork.

Flav. But wherefore art not in thy shop to-day?
Why dost thou lead these men about the streets?

2 *Cit.* Truly, Sir, to wear out their shoes, to get myself into **more** work. But, indeed, Sir, we make holiday to see Cæsar, **and to** rejoice in his triumph.

15. *Mar.* Wherefore rejoice? What conquest **brings** he home?
What tributaries follow him to Rome,
To grace in captive bonds his chariot wheels?
You blocks, you stones, **you worse** than senseless things!
O, **you** hard hearts, you **cruel men** of Rome,
Knew you not Pompey? **Many a** time and oft
Have you climbed up to walls and battlements,
To towers and windows, yea, to chimney-tops,
Your infants in your arms, and there have sat
The live-long **day, with** patient expectation,
To see great Pompey pass the streets of Rome:
And, when you saw his chariot but appear,
Have you not made an universal shout,
That Tiber trembled underneath her banks,
To hear the replication of your sounds
Made in her concave shores?
And do you now put on your best attire?
And do **you now cull out a holiday?**

And do you now strew flowers in his way,
That comes in triumph over Pompey's blood?
Be gone!
Run to your houses, fall upon your knees,
Pray to the gods to intermit the plague
That needs must light on this ingratitude.

16. *Flav.* Go, go, good countrymen, and, for this fault,
Assemble all the poor men of your sort;
Draw them to Tiber banks, and weep your tears
Into the channel, till the lowest stream
Do kiss the most exalted shores of all. [*Exeunt* CITIZENS.
See, whe'r their basest metal be not moved!
They vanish tongue-tied in their guiltiness.
Go you down that way towards the Capitol;
This way will I: Disrobe the images,
If you do find them deckt with ceremonies.

17. *Mar.* May we do so?
You know, it is the feast of Lupercal.

18. *Flav.* It is no matter; let no images
Be hung with Cæsar's trophies. I'll about,
And drive away the vulgar from the streets;
So do you too, where you perceive them thick.
These growing feathers pluckt from Cæsar's wing,
Will make him fly an ordinary pitch;
Who else would soar above the view of men,
And keep us all in servile fearfulness. [*Exeunt*

Act I. Scene I., etc.—The heading here in the original text is:—"*Actus Primus. Scoena Prima. Enter Flavius, Murellus, and certaine Commoners over the Stage.*" *Murellus* stands throughout not only in all the Folios, but also in the editions of both Rowe and Pope. The right name was first inserted by Theobald.

This opening scene may be compared with the first part of that of *Coriolanus*, to which it bears a strong general resemblance.

1. *You ought not walk.*—The history and explanation of this now disused construction may be best collected from a valuable paper by Dr Guest "On English Verbs, Substantive and Auxiliary," read before the Philological Society, 13th March, 1846, and printed in their *Proceed-*

ings, II. 223. "Originally," says Dr Guest, "the *to* was prefixed to the gerund, but never to the present infinitive; as, however, the custom gradually prevailed of using the latter in place of the former, the *to* was more and more frequently prefixed to the infinitive, till it came to be considered as an almost necessary appendage of it. Many idioms, however, had sunk too deeply into the language to admit of alteration; and other phrases, to which the popular ear had been familiarized, long resisted the intrusive particle." The ancient syntax is still retained in all cases with the auxiliary verbs, as they are called, *shall, will, can, may, do*, and also with *must* and *let*, and oftener than not with *bid, dare, hear, make, see*, and perhaps some others. *Vid.* 634. *Cause* is frequently so used; and so is *help*, sometimes,—as in Milton's Sonnet to his friend Lawrence:—

"Where shall we sometimes meet, and by the fire
Help waste a sullen day?"

But, even since the language may be said to have entered upon the stage of its existence in which it still is, several of the verbs just enumerated as not admitting the *to* are occasionally found following the common example and taking it; and others, again, which at the present day have completely conformed to the ordinary construction, formerly used now and then to dispense with it. One of Dr Guest's quotations exemplifies both these archaisms; it is from the portion of *The Mirror for Magistrates* contributed by John Higgins in 1574 (*King Albanact*, 16):—

"And, though we owe the fall of Troy requite,
Yet let revenge thereof from gods to light."

That is, "Though we ought to requite, . . . yet let revenge light," as we should now say. Here we have *let* with the *to*, and *owe* (of which *ought* or *owed* is the preterite), as in Shakespeare's expression before us, without it. Others of Dr Guest's citations from the same writer exhibit the auxiliaries *may, will, can* with the *to*. And he also produces from Spenser (*F. Q.*, iv. 7. 32),—

"Whom when on ground she grovelling *saw to* roll;"

and from Shakespeare (*Othello, iv.* 2)—

"I *durst*, my Lord, *to* wager she is honest."

Other verbs that are found in Shakespeare sometimes construed in the same manner are *endure, forbid, intend, vouchsafe;* as,

"The treason that my haste forbids me show."
Rich. II., v. 3.

"How long within this wood intend you stay?"
Mid. N. Dr., ii. 1.

"Your betters have endured me say my mind."
Tam. of Shrew, iv. 3.

"Most mighty Duke, vouchsafe me speak a word."
Com. of Er. v. 1.

The verb to *owe*, it may further be observed, is etymologically the same with *own*. Shakespeare repeatedly has *owe* where *own* would be now employed; as in Iago's diabolical self-gratulation (in *Othello, iii.* 3):—

"Not poppy, nor mandragora,
Nor all the drowsy syrops of the world,
Shall ever medicine thee to that sweet sleep
Which thou *owed'st* yesterday."

The original English word is *ágan*,—the *ag*, or radical part, of which is evidently the same with the εχ of the Greek ἔχειν, signifying to hold, to possess, to have for one's property, or what we call one's *own*. If we suppose the *a* to have been pronounced broad, as in our modern *all*, and the *g* to have come to be softened as *g* final usually is in modern German, *ag* and *owe*, unlike as they are to the eye, will be only different ways of spelling, or representing by letters, almost the same vocal utterance. The sound which the vowel originally had is more nearly preserved in the Scotch form of the word, *awe*. The *n* which we have in the form *own* is either merely the common annexation which the vowel sound is apt to seek as a support or rest for itself, or, probably, in this case it may be the *en* of the ancient past participle (*ágen*) or the *an* of the infinitive (*ágan*). So we have both to *awake* and to *awaken*, to *ope* and to *open*. In so short a word as the one under consideration, and one in such active service, these affixes would be the more liable to get confounded with the root. It may sound odd to speak of a man as *owning* what he *owes;* yet, if we will think of it, there are few things that can rightly be said to be more a man's own than his debts; they are emphatically *proper* to him, or his *property*, clinging to him, as they do, like a part of himself. Again, that which a man owns in this sense, or *owes*, is that which it is *proper* for him, or which he *has*, to perform or to discharge (as the case may be); hence the secondary meaning of *ought* as applied to that which is one's duty, or which is fitting. For another explanation of these forms, however, the reader is referred to the Second Edition of Dr Latham's *Handbook of the English Language* (1855), pp. 304 and 309. Dr Latham distinguishes the *own* in such expressions as " He owned his fault" by the name of the *Own concedentis* (of concession or acknowledgment). But may not this sense be explained as equivalent to I make my own, I take as my own ?

1. *Upon a labouring day.*—*Labouring* is here a substantive, not a participle. It is as when we say that we love labouring, or that labouring is conducive to health of mind as well as of body. It is not meant that the day labours; as when we speak of a labouring man, or a labouring ship, or a labouring line—

("When Ajax strives some rock's vast weight to throw,
The line too labours, and the words move slow ").

A labouring day is an expression of the same kind with *a walking stick*, or *a riding coat;* in which it is not asserted that the stick walks, or that the coat rides; but, two substantives being conjoined, the one characterizes or qualifies the other,—performs, in fact, the part of an adjective,—just as happens in the expressions *a gold ring, a silver tankard, a leather apron, a morning draught, the evening bells.*

An expression used by Cowper (in his verses composed in the name of Alexander Selkirk), "the sound of the church-going bell," has been passionately reprobated by Wordsworth. "The epithet *church-going* applied to a bell," observes the critic (in an Appendix upon the subject of Poetic Diction, first attached, I believe, in 1820 to the Preface originally published with the Second Edition of the *Lyrical Ballads,* 1800), "and that by so chaste a writer as Cowper, is an instance of the strange abuses which poets have introduced into their language, till they and their readers take them as matters of course, if they do not single them out expressly as matters of admiration." A *church-going bell* is merely a bell for church-going; and the expression is constructed on the same principle with a thousand others that are and always have been in familiar use;—such as a marauding or a sight-seeing expedition, a banking or a house-building speculation, a fox-hunting country, a lending library, a writing desk, a looking glass, a dining room, a dancing school, a dwelling house, a lying-in hospital, etc., etc. What would Wordsworth have said to such a daring and extreme employment of the same form as we have in Shakespeare, where he makes Cleopatra (in *Antony and Cleopatra, iii.* 11) say, speaking of the victorious Cæsar,—

"From his *all-obeying* breath I hear
The doom of Egypt?"

But these audacities of language are of the very soul of poetry.

The peculiar class of substantives under consideration cannot, properly speaking, be regarded as even present participles in disguise. Their true history has been given for the first time by **Mr** Richard Taylor in his Additional Notes to Tooke's *Diversions of Purley*, 1829 and 1840; *vid*. edition of 1840, pp. xxxix.-liv. The old termination of the present participle in English was **and** or **end;** and **when** that **part of** the verb **was used** substantively it denoted **the** *agent*, or performer of the verbal **act**. Thus, *Haelend* signified the **Healer**, or Saviour; *Scyppend*, the **Shaper**, or Creator. *Ing* or *ung*, on the other hand, was **the** regular termination **of that** description of verbal substantive which denoted the *act*. Thus *Brennung* was what **in** Latin would **be** called *Combustio*, and what in our **modern** English **is** still **called** the *Burning*. In other tongues of the same Gothic stock to which our own in part belongs both forms are still preserved. In German, for instance, we have, as anciently in English, *end* for the termination universally of the present participle, and *ung* for that of a numerous class of verbal substantives all signifying the act or thing done. It never could **have** been supposed that in that language these **verbal substantives** in *ung* were present participles.

But in English the fact is, as Mr Taylor **has** observed, **that it is** not the verbal substantive **denoting** the act which has assumed the form **of the present** participle, but the latter which has thrown **away its** own proper termi**nation and** adopted that **of the former.** This change appears **to** have commenced as early as the twelfth century, **and to have been completely** established by **the fourteenth. Even after** the middle of the sixteenth century, however, we have the old distinction between **the** two terminations (the *end* or *and* for the present participle, or the agent, and the *ing* for the verbal act) still adhered to by the Scottish **writers.**

The consequence of the two forms having **thus** become confounded is, as **Dr Latham has remarked** (*English Language*, 3rd edit. **pp.** 349, 350), that we now construct our verbal **substantives in** *ing* upon a false analogy. It has long been understood, or assumed, at least, that the present participle of any English verb may be used substantively to express the verbal act or state.

1. *What trade art thou?*—The rationale of this mode of expression may be seen from the answer to the question:—" Why, Sir, a carpenter." The trade and the person practising it are used indifferently the one for the other: " What trade art thou?" is equivalent to " What tradesman art thou?" So in 6 we have—" A trade . . . which is, indeed, a mender of bad soles." The *thou*, as here and in 5, 7, 9, 11, 13, was still common in the English of Shakespeare's age; it was the ordinary form in addressing an inferior; only when he was treated, or affected to be treated, as a gentleman, the mechanic received the more honourable compellation of *you ;*—as in 3, " You, Sir, what trade are you?" *Thou, Sir,* would have been incongruous in the circumstances.

6. *Soles.*— Quasi *souls ;* — an immemorial quibble, doubtless. It is found also (as Malone notes) in Fletcher's *Woman Pleased*. Yet we might seem to have a distinction of pronunciation between *soul* and *sole* indicated in *The Merchant of Venice*, iv. 1, " Not on thy sole, but on thy soul, harsh Jew."

7. This speech in the old copies is given to *Flavius;* and it is restored to him by Mr Knight, who observes that the modern editors "assume that only one [of the tribunes] should take the lead; whereas it is clear that the dialogue is more natural, certainly more dramatic, according to the original arrangement, where Flavius and Marullus alternately rate the people, like two smiths smiting on the same anvil." But this will not explain or account for the " mend *me*" of Marullus in 9. That proves beyond controversy that the preceding speech (8) was addressed to Marullus ; and it is equally clear that the *you* of speech 8 is the person to whom speech 7 belongs. The rating, besides, is as much alternate, or in-

termingled, in the one way as in the other: Mr Knight gives six speeches to Flavius and five to Marullus; the common arrangement gives five to Flavius and six to Marullus. Mr Collier, however, also gives the present speech to Flavius.

The other changes which Mr Knight charges the modern editors with proposing unnecessarily in the allotment of the speeches in this scene were all proposed, I believe, before the substitution of *Marullus* for *Flavius* in 7, which was made by Capell.

8. *Be not out with me; yet, if you be out.*—The two senses of being *out* are obvious: "They are out with one another," or, simply, "They are out;" and "He is out at the elbows," or in any other part of his dress. For another play upon the various senses of the word *out* see the dialogue between Rosalind and Orlando in *As You Like It, iv.* 1.

9. *Mend me.*—The answer shows that *mend*, not *me*, is the emphatic word.

12. *But with awl.*—Mr Knight and Mr Collier print "with all." This, apparently, would accord with Farmer's notion, who maintains that the true reading is "I meddle with no trade, man's matters," etc., understanding *with awl*, or *with all*, I suppose, to involve, as one of its meanings, that of "with all trades." The original reading is, "but withal I am indeed, Sir, a surgeon," etc. And the Second Folio has "*woman's* matters."

12. *As proper men.*—A *proper* man is a man such as he should be. In *The Tempest, ii.* 2, we have the same expression that we have here distributed into two successive speeches of the drunken Stephano:—"As proper a man as ever went on four legs;" and "Any emperor that ever trod on neat's leather." But, in the prevailing tone of its inspiration at least, it is not with the present Play that one would compare *The Tempest*, but rather with *The Winter's Tale*.

15. *Wherefore rejoice? etc.*—This was in the beginning of B. C. 44 (A. U. C. 709), when Cæsar, having returned from Spain in the preceding October, after defeating the sons of Pompey at the Battle of Munda (fought 17th March, B. C. 45), had been appointed Consul for the next ten years and Dictator for life. The festival of the Lupercalia, at which he was offered and declined the crown, was celebrated 13th February, B. C. 44; and he was assassinated 15th March following, being then in his fifty-sixth year.

15. *Many a time and oft.*—This old phrase, which is still familiar, may be held to be equivalent to many and many a time, that is, many times and yet again many more times. The old pointing of this line is, "Knew you not Pompey many a time and oft?" It is like what all the Folios give us in *Macbeth*, i. 5:—

"Your face, my thane, is as a book where men
May read strange matters, to beguile the time."

What follows,—"Have you climbed up," etc.,—is, of course, made a second question.

15. *To see great Pompey pass the streets of Rome.*— In modern English to *pass* a street, or a bridge, is to abstain from walking along it. It would be satisfactory with respect to this line, if other instances could be produced of the usage of the language being different in Shakespeare's day.

15. *That Tiber trembled underneath her banks.*—The proper antecedent of *that* (*so*, or *in such wise*) is left unexpressed, as sufficiently obvious.—Some of the modern editors have taken the unwarrantable liberty of changing *her* into *his* in this line and the next but one, because *Tiber* is one of those names of rivers which are always masculine in Latin. This is to give us both language and a conception different from Shakespeare's.

15. *Made in her concave shores.*—An imperfect line (or

hemistich, as it is commonly called), but prosodically regular so far as it goes, which is all we have a right to look for. The occasional use of such shortened lines would seem to be, at least in dramatic poetry, one of the proper and natural prerogatives of blank verse, according well, as it does, with the variety of pause and cadence which makes the distinctive charm of verse of that form. But, apparently, it need not be assumed, as is always done, that the fragment must necessarily be in all cases the beginning of a line. Why should not the poet be supposed sometimes, when he begins a new sentence or paragraph in this manner, to intend that it should be connected, in the prosody as well as in the meaning, with what follows, not with what precedes? A few lines lower down, for instance, the words "Be gone" might be either the first foot of the verse or the last.

16. *Weep your tears.*—We should scarcely now speak of weeping tears absolutely, though we might say "to weep tears of blood, or of agony, or of bitterness," or "to weep an ocean of tears, or our fill of tears." This sense of the verb *weep* is quite distinct from the sense it commonly has when used transitively, which is to weep for, or to lament; as when in *Cymbeline* (*i.* 5) Iachimo speaks of "those that weep this lamentable divorce." It more resembles what we have in the phrases *To sin the sin, To die the death, To sing a song;*—expressive forms, to which the genius of our tongue has never been very prone, and to which it is now decidedly averse. They owe their effect, in part, indeed, to a certain naturalness, or disregard of strict propriety, which a full-grown and educated language is apt to feel ashamed of as something rustic or childish. Perhaps, however, a distinction should be drawn between such an expression as *To weep tears* and such as *To sin the sin, To sing a song,* in which the verb is merely a synonyme for to act, to perform, to execute.

16. *Till the lowest stream,* etc.—The hot-tempered tri-

bune talks fast. It is evident that no augmentation of the water will ever make the *lowest* stream touch the highest shores. In the *do kiss* we have a common archaism, the retention of the auxiliary, now come to be regarded, when it is not emphatic, as a pleonasm enfeebling the expression, and consequently denied alike to the writer of prose and to the writer of verse. It is thus in even a worse predicament than the separate pronunciation of the final *ed* in the preterite indicative or past participle passive. It was only the first fervour of an acquaintance with and admiration of our old literature that could have led Keats to mar the fine poetry of many of his pieces by a recurrence to these extinct forms. But in the age of Shakespeare they were both, though beginning to be abandoned, still part and parcel of the living language, and there is therefore no affectation in his frequent use of them. Instances both of the unemphatic *do* and of the distinct syllabication of the final *ed* are numerous in the present Play. The modern forms probably were as yet completely established only in the spoken language, which commonly goes before that which is written and read in such economical innovations.—For the modern stage direction *Exeunt Citizens*, the original text has here *Exeunt all the Commoners*.

16. *See whe'r their basest metal.*—*Whe'r* is *whether*. The contraction is common both in Shakespeare and in other writers of his age. Thus we have in his 59th Sonnet:—

"*Whether* we are mended, or *whe'r* better they,
Or *whether* revolution be the same."

The *er* may be supposed to have been pronounced as the *er* is in *her*. In the old copies the word, when thus contracted, is usually printed exactly as the adverb of place always is, *where*. But if it were to be here spelled *whether* at full length, and pronounced as a dissyllable, we should have no more of prosodical irregularity than we have in many other lines. And it is occasionally in similar circumstances so presented in the old copies.

16. *Deckt with ceremonies.*—To *deck* (the same with the Latin *teg-ere* and the German *deck-en*) signifies properly no more than to cover. Hence the *deck* of a ship. *Thatch* (the German *Dach*) is another formation from the same root. To *deck*, therefore, has no connexion with to *decorate*, which is of the same stock with *decent* (from the Latin *decus*, or *decor*, and *decet*). The supposition that there was a connexion, however, has probably helped to acquire for *deck* its common acceptation, which now always involves the notion of decoration or adornment. And that was also its established sense when Shakespeare wrote. By *ceremonies* must here be meant what are afterwards in 18 called "Cæsar's trophies," and are described in 95 as "scarfs" which were hung on Cæsar's images. No other instance of this use of the word, however, is produced by the commentators; nor is such a sense of it given either by Johnson (though himself an editor of Shakespeare) or by Webster. The Latin *ceremonia* is of unknown or disputed origin, but its only meaning is a religious rite. In our common English the meaning of *ceremony* has been extended so as to include also forms of civility and outward forms of state. We have it in that sense in 27. And we shall find lower down that Shakespeare uses it in still another sense, which is peculiar to himself, or which has now at least gone out. *Vid.* 194.

17. *The feast of Lupercal.*—The Roman festival of the *Lupercalia* (*-ium* or *-iorum*), whatever may be the etymology of the name, was in honour of the god Pan. It was celebrated annually on the Ides (or 13th) of February, in a place called the *Lupercal*, at the foot of Mount Aventine. A third company of *Luperci*, or priests of Pan, with Antony for its chief, was instituted in honour of Julius Cæsar.

18. *It is no matter*, etc.—The Second Folio goes, or stumbles, on—

> "let on Images
> Be hung with the *Cæsars* Trophees."

Mr Collier does not state that this is corrected by his MS. annotator.

18. *Will make him fly.*—A modern sentence constructed in this fashion would constitute the *him* the antecedent to the *who*, and give it the meaning of the person generally who (in this instance) else would soar, etc., or whoever would. But it will be more accordant with the style of Shakespeare's day to leave the *him* unemphatic, and to regard *Cæsar* as being the antecedent to *who*. It was not then so unusual, or accounted so inelegant, as it would now be, in our more precise and straitened syntax, thus to separate the relative from its true antecedent by the interposition of another false or apparent one, or to tack on the relative clause to the completed statement as if it had been an afterthought. Thus, again in the present Play, we have, in 704,—

> "Coming from Sardis, on our former ensign
> Two mighty eagles fell, and there they perched,
> Gorging and feeding from our soldiers' hands;
> Who to Philippi here consorted us;

and in 716,—

> "O Cassius, Brutus gave the word too early;
> Who, having some advantage on Octavius,
> Took it too eagerly."

SCENE II.—*The same. A Public Place.*

Enter, in Procession with Music, CÆSAR; ANTONY, *for the course;* CALPHURNIA, PORTIA, DECIUS, CICERO, BRUTUS, CASSIUS, *and* CASCA, *a great crowd following, among them a* SOOTHSAYER.

Cæs. Calphurnia,—
Casca. Peace, ho! Cæsar speaks. [*Music ceases.*
Cæs. Calphurnia,—
Cal. Here, my lord.

23. *Cæs.* Stand you directly in Antonius' way,
    When he doth **run** his course.—Antonius.
    Ant. Cæsar, my lord.
25. *Cæs.* Forget not, in your speed, Antonius,
    To **touch** Calphurnia; for our elders say,
    The barren, touched in this holy chase,
    Shake off their sterile curse.
    Ant. I shall remember:
When Cæsar says, *Do this,* **it is** performed.
    Cæs. Set on; and leave **no** ceremony out.   [*Music.*
    Sooth. Cæsar.
    Cæs. Ha! who calls?
    Casca. Bid every noise be still:—Peace yet again. [*Music ceases.*
    Cæs. Who is it in the press that calls on me?
I hear a tongue, shriller than all the music,
Cry, Cæsar. Speak; Cæsar is turned to hear.
32. *Sooth.* Beware the ides of March.
    Cæs. What man is that?
34. *Bru.* A soothsayer, bids you beware the ides of **March.**
    Cæs. Set him before me; let me see his face.
    Cas. Fellow, come from the throng: Look upon Cæsar.
    Cæs. What say'st thou to me now? Speak once again.
    Sooth. Beware the ides of March.
39. *Cæs.* He is **a** dreamer: let us leave him;—pass.
            [*Sennet. Exeunt all but* BRUTUS *and* CASSIUS.
    Cas. Will you go see the order of the course?
    Bru. Not I.
    Cas. I pray you do.
    Bru. **I am not gamesome: I do lack some part**
Of that quick spirit that is in Antony.
Let me not hinder, Cassius, your desires;
I'll leave you.
44. *Cas.* Brutus, I do observe you now **of late:**
I have not from your eyes that gentleness,
And show of love, as I was wont to have:
You bear too stubborn and too strange a hand
Over your friend that loves you.
45. *Bru.* Cassius,
Be not deceived: if I have veiled my look,
I turn the trouble of my countenance
Merely upon myself. Vexed I am,
Of late, with passions of some difference,
Conceptions only proper to myself,

    Which give some soil, perhaps, to my behaviours:
    But let not therefore my good friends be grieved
    (Among which number, Cassius, be you one);
    Nor construe any further my neglect,
    Than that poor Brutus, with himself at war,
    Forgets the shews of love to other men.
46. *Cas.* Then, Brutus, I have much mistook your passion;
    By means whereof, this breast of mine hath buried
    Thoughts of great value, worthy cogitations.
    Tell me, good Brutus, can you see your face?
47. *Bru.* No, Cassius: for the eye sees not itself,
    But by reflection, by some other things.
48. *Cas.* 'Tis just:
    And it is very much lamented, Brutus,
    That you have no such mirrors as will turn
    Your hidden worthiness into your eye,
    That you might see your shadow. I have heard,
    Where many of the best respect in Rome
    (Except immortal Cæsar), speaking of Brutus,
    And groaning underneath this age's yoke,
    Have wished that noble Brutus had his eyes.
    Bru. Into what dangers would you lead me, Cassius,
    That you would have me seek into myself
    For that which is not in me!
50. *Cas.* Therefore, good Brutus, be prepared to hear:
    And, since you know you cannot see yourself
    So well as by reflection, I, your glass,
    Will modestly discover to yourself
    That of yourself which you yet know not of.
    And be not jealous on me, gentle Brutus:
    Were I a common laugher, or did use
    To stale with ordinary oaths my love
    To every new protester; if you know
    That I do fawn on men, and hug them hard,
    And after scandal them; or if you know
    That I profess myself in banqueting
    To all the rout, then hold me dangerous. [*Flourish and shout.*
51. *Bru.* What means this shouting? I do fear, the people
    Choose Cæsar for their king.
    Cas. Ay, do you fear it?
    Then must I think you would not have it so.
53. *Bru.* I would not, Cassius; yet I love him well.—
    But wherefore do you hold me here so long?

What is it that you would impart to me?
If it be aught toward the general good,
Set Honour in one eye, and Death i' the **other**,
And I will look on both indifferently:
For, let the gods so speed me, as I love
The name of Honour more than I **fear Death**.

54. *Cas.* I know that virtue to be in you, **Brutus**,
As well as I do know your outward favour.
Well, Honour is the subject of my **story.**—
I cannot tell what **you** and other men
Think of this life; but, for my single self,
I had as lief not be as live to be
In awe of such a thing as I myself.
I was born free as Cæsar; so were you:
We both have fed as well; and we can both
Endure the winter's cold as well as he.
For once, upon a raw and gusty day,
The troubled Tiber chafing with her shores,
Cæsar said to me, *Dar'st thou, Cassius, now
Leap in with me into this angry flood,
And swim to yonder point?* Upon the word,
Accoutred as I was, I plunged in,
And bade him follow: so, indeed, he did.
The torrent roared; and we did buffet it
With lusty sinews; throwing it aside,
And stemming it with hearts of controversy.
But ere we could arrive **the** point proposed,
Cæsar cried, *Help me, Cassius, or I sink.*
I, as Æneas, our great ancestor,
Did from the flames of Troy **upon his shoulder**
The old Anchises bear, so, from **the waves** of Tiber
Did I the tired Cæsar: And this **man**
Is now become a god; and Cassius is
A wretched creature, and must bend his body
If Cæsar carelessly **but nod** on him.
He had a fever when he was **in** Spain,
And, when the fit was on him, I did mark
How he did shake: 'tis true, this god did shake:
His coward lips did from their colour fly;
And that same eye, whose bend **doth** awe **the world**,
Did lose his lustre: I did **hear him groan**:
Ay, and that tongue of **his, that bade the** Romans
Mark him, and write his **speeches in** their books,

    Alas! it cried, *Give me some drink, Titinius,*
    As a sick girl. Ye gods, it doth amaze me,
    A man of such a feeble temper should
    So get the start of the majestic world,
    And bear the palm **alone.**   [*Shout. Flourish.*
55. *Bru.* Another **general shout!**
    I do believe, that these applauses are
    For some new honours that are heaped on Cæsar.
56. *Cas.* Why, man, he doth bestride **the narrow world.**
    Like a Colossus; and we petty men
    Walk under his huge legs, and peep about
    To find ourselves dishonourable graves.
    Men at some time are masters of their fates:
    The fault, dear Brutus, is not in our stars,
    But in ourselves, **that we are underlings.**
    Brutus and Cæsar: What should be in that Cæsar?
    Why should that name be sounded **more than yours?**
    Write them together, yours is as fair **a name;**
    Sound them, it doth become the mouth **as well;**
    Weigh them, it is **as heavy;** conjure with 'em,
    Brutus will start **a spirit as** soon as Cæsar.   [*Shout.*
    Now, in the names of all the gods at once,
    Upon what meat doth this our Cæsar feed,
    That he is grown so great? Age, thou art shamed:
    Rome, thou hast lost the breed of noble bloods!
    When went there by an **age, since** the great flood,
    But it was famed with more than with **one** man?
    When could they say, till **now,** that talked of Rome,
    That her wide walls encompassed but one man?
    Now is it Rome indeed, and room **enough,**
    When there is in it but one only man.
    O! **you and** I have heard our fathers say,
    There was a Brutus once, **that** would have brooked
    The eternal devil **to** keep his state in Rome
    As easily **as a** king.
57. *Bru.* That you do **love me,** I am nothing jealous·
    What you would **work me to,** I have **some** aim;
    How I have **thought of this,** and of these times,
    I shall recount hereafter; **for this present,**
    I would not, so with love **I might entreat you,**
    Be any further moved. **What you have said,**
    I will consider; what you have **to say,**
    I will with patience hear: **and find a time**

Both meet to hear, and answer, such high things.
Till then, my noble friend, chew upon this:
Brutus had rather be a villager,
Than to repute himself a son of Rome
Under these hard conditions as this time
Is like to lay upon us.

58. *Cas.* I am glad, that my weak words
Have struck but this much shew of fire from Brutus.

Re-enter CÆSAR, *and his Train.*

Bru. The games are done and Cæsar is returning.

60. *Cas.* As they pass by, pluck Casca by the sleeve;
And he will, after his sour fashion, tell you
What hath proceeded, worthy note, to-day.

61. *Bru.* I will do so:—But, look you, Cassius,
The angry spot doth glow on Cæsar's brow,
And all the rest look like a chidden train:
Calphurnia's cheek is pale; and Cicero
Looks with such ferret and such fiery eyes,
As we have seen him in the Capitol,
Being crossed in conference by some senators.

62. *Cas.* Casca will tell us what the matter is.
Cæs. Antonius.
Ant. Cæsar.

35. *Cæs.* Let me have men about me that are fat;
Sleek-headed men, and such as sleep o' nights:
Yond Cassius has a lean and hungry look;
He thinks too much: such men are dangerous.

66. *Ant.* Fear him not, Cæsar; he's not dangerous.
He is noble Roman, and well given.

67. *Cæs.* Would he were fatter.—But I fear him not.
Yet, if my name were liable to fear,
I do not know the man I should avoid
So soon as that spare Cassius. He reads much;
He is a great observer, and he looks
Quite through the deeds of men: he loves no plays,
As thou dost, Antony; he hears no music:
Seldom he smiles; and smiles in such a sort,
As if he mocked himself, and scorned his spirit
That could be moved to smile at any thing.
Such men as he be never at heart's ease,
Whiles they behold a greater than themselves;
And therefore are they very dangerous.
I rather tell thee what is to be feared

Than what I fear; for always I am Cæsar.
Come on my right hand, for this ear is deaf,
And tell me truly what thou think'st of him.
[*Sennet. Exeunt* CÆSAR *and his Train.* CASCA *stays behind.*
Casca. You pulled me by the cloak; Would you speak with me?
69. *Bru.* Ay, Casca; tell us what hath chanced to-day,
That Cæsar looks so sad.
Casca. Why, you were with him, were you not?
Bru. I should not then ask Casca what had chanced.
Casca. Why, there was a crown offered him: and, being offered him, he put it by with the back of his hand, thus; and then the people fell a-shouting.
Bru. What was the second noise for?
Casca. Why, for that too.
Cas. They shouted thrice; What was the last cry for?
Casca. Why, for that too.
Bru. Was the crown offered him thrice?
78. *Casca.* Ay, marry, was't, and he put it by thrice, every time gentler than other; and, at every putting by, mine honest neighbours shouted.
Cas. Who offered him the crown?
Casca. Why, Antony.
Bru. Tell us the manner of it, gentle Casca.
82. *Casca.* I can as well be hanged, as tell the manner of it: it was mere foolery. I did not mark it. I saw Mark Antony offer him a crown;—yet 'twas not a crown neither, 'twas one of these coronets;—and, as I told you, he put it by once; but, for all that, to my thinking, he would fain have had it. Then he offered it to him again; then he put it by again; but, to my thinking, he was very loath to lay his fingers off it. And then he offered it the third time; he put it the third time by: and, still as he refused it, the rabblement shouted, and clapped their chopped hands, and threw up their sweaty night-caps, and uttered such a deal of stinking breath because Cæsar refused the crown, that it had almost choked Cæsar; for he swooned, and fell down at it. And, for my own part, I durst not laugh, for fear of opening my lips, and receiving the bad air.
83. *Cas.* But, soft, I pray you: What? did Cæsar swoon?
Casca. He fell down in the market-place, and foamed at mouth, and was speechless.
85. *Bru.* 'Tis very like: he hath the falling sickness.
86. *Cas.* No, Cæsar hath it not; but you and I,
And honest Casca, we have the falling sickness.
87. *Casca.* I know not what you mean by that; but I am sure Cæsar

fell down. If the tag-rag people did not clap him, and hiss him, according as he pleased and displeased them, as they use to do the players in the theatre, I am no true man.

Bru. What **said he, when he came** unto himself?

89. *Casca.* **Marry, before he fell** down, when he perceived the common **herd was glad he refused** the crown, he plucked me ope his doublet, and offered them his throat to cut.—An I had been a man of any occupation, **if I** would not have taken him at **a** word, I would I might go to hell among the rogues. And so he fell. When he came to himself **again, he said,** If he had done, or said, anything amiss, he desired their worships to think it was his infirmity. Three or four wenches, where I stood, cried *Alas, good soul!*—and forgave him with all their hearts: But **there's no** heed to be taken of them; if Cæsar had stabbed their mothers, they would have done no less.

Bru. And after that, he came, thus **sad, away?**

Casca. Ay.

Cas. Did **Cicero say** anything?

Casca. Ay, he spoke Greek.

Cas. To what effect?

95. *Casca.* **Nay, an** I tell you that, I'll ne'er look you **i' the face** again: But **those** that understood him smiled at one another, **and** shook their heads; but, for my own part, it was Greek to **me.** I could tell you more news too: Marullus and **Flavius, for pulling** scarfs off Cæsar's images, are put to silence. Fare you **well. There** was more foolery yet, if I could remember it.

Cas. Will you sup with me to-night, Casca?

97. *Casca.* No, I am promised forth.

Cas. **Will** you dine with **me to-morrow?**

Casca. Ay, if I be alive, **and your mind** hold, and your dinner worth the eating.

Cas. Good: I **will expect you.**

Casca. Do so: **Farewell, both.** [*Exit* CASCA.

102. *Bru.* **What a blunt** fellow is this grown to be! He was quick mettle when he went to school.

103. *Cas.* So is he **now, in** execution
Of any bold or noble enterprise,
However he puts on this tardy form.
This rudeness is a sauce to his good wit,
Which gives men stomach to digest his words
With better appetite.

104. *Bru.* And so it is. For **this time I will leave you:**
To-morrow if you please to speak with me,
I will come home to you; or, if you will,

Come home to me, and I will wait for you.
105. *Cas.* I will do so:—till then, think of the world.
[*Exit* BRUTUS.

Well, Brutus, thou art noble; yet, I see,
Thy honourable metal may be wrought
From that it is disposed: Therefore it is meet
That noble minds keep ever with their likes:
For who so firm, that cannot be seduced?
Cæsar doth bear me hard; but he loves Brutus:
If I were Brutus now, and he were Cassius,
He should not humour me. I will this night,
In several hands, in at his windows throw,
As if they came from several citizens,
Writings all tending to the great opinion
That Rome holds of his name; wherein obscurely
Cæsar's ambition shall be glanced at:
And, after this, let Cæsar seat him sure;
For we will shake him, or worse days endure. [*Exit.*

Scene II.—The original heading here is:—"*Enter Cæsar, Antony for the Course, Calphurnia, Portia, Decius, Cicero, Brutus, Cassius, Caska, a Soothsayer: after them Murellus and Flavius.*" The three stage directions about the Music are all modern.

23. *Stand you directly*, etc.—The sacerdotal runners wore only a cincture of goat-skins, the same material of which their thongs were made. The passage in Plutarch's Life of Julius Cæsar as translated by Sir Thomas North is as follows:—

"At that time the feast Lupercalia was celebrated, the which in old time, men say, was the feast of Shepherds or Herdsmen, and is much like unto the feast of Lyceians [Λυκεῖα] in Arcadia. But, howsoever it is, that day there are divers noblemen's sons, young men (and some of them magistrates themselves that govern them), which run naked through the city, striking in sport them they meet in their way with leather thongs. And many noble women and gentlewomen also go of purpose to stand in their way, and do put forth their hands to be stricken, persuading themselves that, being with child, they shall have good delivery, and also, being barren, that it will make them conceive with child. Cæsar sat to behold that sport upon the pulpit for orations, in a chair of gold, apparelled in triumphant manner. Antonius, who was Consul at that time, was one of them that ronne this holy course"

Here, and in 25, as generally throughout the Play, *Antonius* is *Antonio* in the original text, and in all the editions down to that of Pope.

25. *Their sterile curse.*—Our English formations from Latin words terminating in *-ilis* are in an unsatisfactory state in respect both of spelling and pronunciation. Of the Latin words some have the *il* long, others short; and the former ought naturally to give in English *-ile* (sounded as in *mile*), the latter *-il*. But, instead of this, the common usage is to spell them all indiscriminately with the *e*, and to pronounce them as if they were without it. Thus we have not only *puerile, servile, subtile, juvenile, hostile* (from *puerīlis, servīlis, juvenīlis, hostīlis*), but also *docile, sterile, versatile, agile, fragile* (from *docĭlis, sterĭlis, versatĭlis, agĭlis, fragĭlis*). And, as for the pronunciation, while Walker, holding the general rule to be that the *i* is short, makes *Exile, Senile, Edile,* and *Infantile* (together with *Reconcile, Chamomile,* and *Estipile,*—which last, however, is not in his Dictionary, or in any other that I have consulted), to be the only exceptions, Smart (1849) gives no rule upon the subject (that I can find), leaves *Senile* unmarked, and (omitting both *Estipile* and *Chamomile*) seems to add *Mercantile*, and distinctly adds *Gentile*, to *Exile* and *Edile*, as having the *i* long, and in *Infantile* seems to give it short in the Dictionary, but distinctly marks it as long in the section of his "Principles" to which a reference is made from the word. Further, as if the confusion were not bad enough without such mechanical carelessness and blundering, in the stereotyped 8vo edition of Walker, 1819 (called the 21st edition), in a list given at page 36 (the same page in which the strange word *Estipile* occurs) the *i* is printed with the long instead of the short mark in *Gentile, Virile, Sub-*

tile, Coctile, Quintile, Hostile, Servile, and *Sextile*, in direct contradiction both to the Dictionary and to the very statement with which the list is headed and introduced. The present tendency of our pronunciation seems to be to extend the dominion of the long *i* both in these forms and even in the termination *ite*. In reading, at least, the—*ile* is now perhaps more usually pronounced long than short in *Hostile, Servile*, and some other similar instances; and we sometimes hear even *infinite* pronounced with the *ite* long (as in *finite*), though such a pronunciation is still only that of the uneducated populace in *Opposite* or *Favourite*.

32. *The Ides of March.*—In the Roman Kalendar the Ides (*Idus*) fell on the 15th of March, May, July, and October, and on the 13th of the eight remaining months.

34. *A soothsayer, bids.*—That is, It is a soothsayer, who bids. It would not otherwise be an answer to Cæsar's question. The omission of the relative in such a construction is still common.

39. The old stage direction here is;—"*Sennet. Exeunt. Manet Brut. et Cass.*" The word *Sennet* is also variously written *Sennit, Senet, Synnet, Cynet, Signet*, and *Signate*. Nares explains it as "a word chiefly occurring in the stage directions of the old plays, and seeming to indicate a particular set of notes on the trumpet, or cornet, different from a flourish." In Shakespeare it occurs again in the present Play at 67, in the heading to *Antony and Cleopatra, ii.* 7, in *King Henry VIII, ii.* 4, and in *Coriolanus, i.* 1 and 2, where in the first scene we have "A Sennet. Trumpets sound." In the heading of the second scene of the fifth act of Beaumont and Fletcher's *Knight of Malta* we have "*Synnet*, i. e. *Flourish of Trumpets.*" But in Dekker's *Satiromastix* (1602) we have " Trumpets sound a flourish, and then a sennet." Steevens says;— "I have been informed that *sennet* is derived from *senneste*, an antiquated French tune formerly used in the

army; but the Dictionaries which I have consulted exhibit no such word."

44. *That gentleness . . . as I was, etc.*—We should now say "that gentleness *that* I was wont to have." But *that* and *as* are by origin words of the same signification; *that*, or *thaet*, being the neuter form of the Original English article or demonstrative, and *as* being in all probability (as remarked by Horne Tooke, *Diversions of Purley*, p. 147) identical with the German *es* (still in continual use in that language for our *that* or *it*). "The word *as*," observes Dr Latham (*English Language*, p. 423), "properly a conjunction, is occasionally used as a relative—*the man* as *rides to market*. This expression is not to be imitated." Clearly not. Such syntax is no longer, if it ever was, a part of the language. But in many other expressions which everybody uses, and the propriety of which nobody has ever questioned, *as* is manifestly not a conjunction, but a relative pronoun. For example, in Pope's "All such reading as was never read," *as* is the nominative to the verb. It acts in the same capacity in the common phrases, "as is said," "as regards," "as appears," and others similarly constructed. It is not very long since the conjunction *as* was used at least in one case in which we now always employ *that*. "*So—as*," says Bishop Lowth (*Introd. to Eng. Gram.*), "was used by the writers of the last [17th] century to express a consequence, instead of *so—that*. Swift [who died 1745], I believe, is the last of our good writers who has frequently used this manner of expression. It seems improper, and is deservedly grown obsolete." That it is obsolete cannot be disputed, and it would therefore be an impropriety in modern writing; but Horne Tooke is right in objecting to Lowth that there is nothing naturally or essentially wrong in it; it is wrong, if at all, only conventionally. Exactly corresponding to this formerly common use of the conjunctions *so* and *as* is Shakespeare's

use in the present passage, and many others, of the pronouns *that* and *as*. In "as I was wont to have," *as* is the accusative of the relative pronoun governed by *have*, "*that* gentleness, and show of love," being the antecedent. The practice, common in most or all languages, of employing the same word as demonstrative and relative, is familiarized to us in English by our habitual use of *that* in both capacities.

44. *Over your friend that loves you.*—It is *friends* in the Second Folio.

45. *Merely upon myself.*—*Merely* (from the Latin *merus* and *mere*) means purely, only. It separates that which it designates or qualifies from everything else. But in so doing the chief or most emphatic reference may be made either to that which is included, or to that which is excluded. In modern English it is always to the latter; by "merely upon myself" we should now mean upon nothing else except myself; the *nothing else* is that which the *merely* makes prominent. In Shakespeare's day the other reference was the more common, that namely to what was included; and "merely upon myself" meant upon myself altogether, or without regard to anything else. *Myself* was that which the *merely* made prominent. So when Hamlet, speaking of the world, says (*i.* 2) "Things rank and gross in nature possess it *merely*," he by the *merely* brings the *possession* before the mind, and characterizes it as complete and absolute ; but by the same term now the prominence would be given to something else from which the possession might be conceived to be separable; "possess it merely" would mean have nothing beyond simply the possession of it (have, it might be, no right to it, or no enjoyment of it). It is not necessary that that which is included, though thus emphasized, should therefore be more *definitely* conceived than that with which it is contrasted. So, again, when in *Henry VIII., iii.* 2 (whoever may have written that Play, or this passage),

the Earl of Surrey charges Wolsey with having sent large supplies of substance to Rome "to the mere undoing of all the kingdom," he means to the complete undoing of all the kingdom, to nothing less than such undoing; but in our modern English the words would sound as if the speaker's meaning were, to nothing more than the undoing of the kingdom. The *mere* would lead us to think of something else, some possible aggravation of the undoing (such, for instance, as the disgrace or infamy), from which that was to be conceived as separated.

The use of *merely* here is in exact accordance with that of *mere* in *Othello*, ii. 2, where the Herald proclaims the tidings of what he calls "the mere perdition of the Turkish fleet" (that is, the entire perdition or destruction). In Helena's " Ay, surely, mere the truth," in *All's Well that Ends Well*, iii. 5, *mere* would seem to have the sense of *merely* (that is, simply, exactly), if there be no misprint.

Attention to such changes of import or effect, slight as they may seem, which many words have undergone, is indispensable for the correct understanding of our old writers. Their ignorance of the old sense of this same word *merely* has obscured a passage in Bacon to his modern editors. In his 58th *Essay*, entitled " Of Vicissitudes of Things," he says; "As for conflagrations and great droughts, they do not *merely* dispeople and destroy" —meaning, as the train of the reasoning clearly requires, that they do not *altogether* do so. Most of the editors (Mr Montague included) have changed "*and* destroy" into "*but* destroy;" others leave out the " not " before *merely;* either change being subversive of the meaning of the passage and inconsistent with the context. The reading of the old copies is confirmed by the Latin translation, done under Bacon's own superintendence :—" Illæ populum *penitus* non absorbent aut destruunt."

So in the 3rd *Essay*, " Of Unity in Religion," when we are told that extremes would be avoided " if the points fundamental and of substance in religion were truly discerned and distinguished from points not merely of faith, but of opinion, order, or good intention," the meaning is, from points not *altogether* of faith,—not, were distinguished *not only* from points of faith, as a modern reader would be apt to understand it.

45. *Passions of some difference.*—The meaning seems to be, of some discordance, somewhat conflicting passions. So we have a few lines after, " poor Brutus, with himself at war."

45. *Conceptions* **only** *proper to myself.*—Thoughts and feelings relating exclusively to myself.

45. *To my behaviours.*—We have lost this plural. But we still say, though with some difference of meaning, both " **My manner**" and " **My** manners."

45. *Be you one.*—There are various kinds of *being*, or of existing. What is here meant is, Be in your belief and assurance; equivalent to Rest assured that you are.

45. *Nor construe any further my neglect.*—*Further* is the word in the old copies; but Mr Collier, I observe, in his one volume edition prints *farther*. Is this one of the corrections of his MS. annotator? It is sometimes supposed that, as *farther* answers to *far*, so *further* answers to *forth*. But *far* and *forth*, or *fore*, are really only different forms of the same word, different corruptions or modernizations of the old Original English *feor* or *forth*.

46. *I have much mistook your passion.*—That is, the feeling under which you are suffering. *Patience* and *passion* (both from the Latin *patior*) equally mean suffering; the notions of quiet and of agitation which they have severally acquired, and which have made the common signification of the one almost the opposite of that of the other, are merely accidental adjuncts. It may be seen, however, from the use of the word *passion* here and in the preceding speech, that its proper meaning was not so completely obscured and lost sight of in Shakespeare's

day as it has come to be in ours, when it retains the notion of *suffering* only in two or three antique expressions; such as the iliac *passion*, and the *passion* of our Saviour (with *Passion* Week).—Though it is no longer accounted correct to say I have *mistook*, or I have *wrote*, such forms were in common use even till far on in the last century. Nor has the analogy of the reformed manner of expression been yet completely carried out. In some cases we have even lost the more correct form after having once had it: we no longer, for instance, say I have *stricken*, as they did in Shakespeare's day, but only I have *struck*.

47. *But by reflection*, etc.—The "other things," must, apparently, if we interpret the words with reference to their connexion, be the reflectors or mirrors spoken of by Cassius. Taken by itself, however, the expression might rather seem to mean that the eye discovers its own existence by its power of seeing other things. The verse in the present speech is thus ingeniously broken up in the original edition:—

"No, Cassius:
For the eye sees not itself but by reflection,
By some other things."

It may still be suspected that all is not quite right, and possibly some words have dropped out. "By reflection, by some other things" is hardly Shakespeare's style. It is not customary with him to employ a word which he finds it necessary thus to attempt immediately to amend, or supplement or explain, by another.—It is remarkable that in the first line of this speech the three last Folios turn the *itself* into *himself*. Mr Collier, nevertheless, prints *itself*. Is this a restoration of his MS. annotator?

There is a remarkable coincidence, both of thought and of expression, between what we have here and the following passage in *Troilus and Cressida, iii.* 3;—

"Nor doth the eye itself,
That most pure spirit of sense, behold itself."

And it may be worth noting that these lines appear only in the two original Quarto editions of the Play (1609), and are not in any of the Folios.

48. *Many of the best respect.*—A lost phrase, no longer permissible even in poetry, although our only modern equivalent is the utterly unpoetical " many persons of the highest respectability." So, again, in the present Play, we have in 780, " Thou art a fellow of a good respect."

50. *Therefore, good Brutus,* etc.—The eager, impatient temper of Cassius, absorbed in his own one idea, is vividly expressed by his thus continuing his argument as if without appearing to have even heard Brutus's interrupting question; for such is the only interpretation which his *therefore* would seem to admit of.

50. *And be not jealous on me.*—This is the reading of all the Folios; and it has been restored to the text by Mr Knight, who does not, however, produce any other example of the same syntax. The other modern editors generally, with the exception of Mr Collier, have changed the *on* into *of*. And everywhere else, I believe, Shakespeare writes *jealous of*. But there seems to be no natural reason, independently of usage, why the adjective might not take the one preposition as well as the other. They used to say *enamoured on* formerly. In the same manner, although the common form is *to eat of*, yet in *Macbeth*, *i.* 3, we have, as the words stand in the first three Folios, " Have we eaten *on* the insane root." So, although we commonly say " seized *of*," we have in *Hamlet*, *i.* 1, " All those his lands Which he stood seized *on*." And there is the familiar use of *on* for *of* in the popular speech, of which we have also an example in *Hamlet* in the Clown's " You lie out on't, Sir " (*v.* 1).

50. *Were I a common laugher.*—Pope made this correction, in which he has been followed by all subsequent editors. In all the editions before his the reading is *laughter;* and the necessity or propriety of the change is

perhaps not so unquestionable as it has been generally thought. Neither word seems to be perfectly satisfactory. "Were **I a common** laughter" might seem **to** derive some support from the expression **of** the same speaker in 562: "Hath **Cassius** lived to be **but** mirth and laughter to his Brutus?"

50. *To stale with ordinary oaths my love.*—Johnson, the only commentator **who notices** this expression, interprets it as meaning, "to invite every new protester to my affection by the stale, or allurement, of customary oaths." But surely the more common sense of the word *stale*, both **the** verb and the noun, involving the notion of insipid **or of** little **worth or estimation**, is far more natural here. Who forgets **Enobarbus's phrase** in his enthusiastic description of Cleopatra (*Antony and Cleopatra, ii. 2*); "Age cannot wither her, nor **custom** *stale* Her infinite variety"? So in 498, "*Staled* by other **men**."

50. *And after scandal them.*—We have lost the **verb** *scandal* altogether, and we scarcely use the other form to *scandalize*, except in **the** sense of the **Hellenistic** σκανδαλίζω, to shock, to give offence. Both **had formerly also the sense of to** defame **or traduce**.

51. *What means this shouting?* etc.—Here is the manner in which this passage **is given in** the original edition:—

> "*Bru.* What means this Showting?
> **I do** feare, **the** People choose *Cæsar*
> **For their** King.
> *Cassi.* I, do you feare it?"

53. *If it be aught toward.*—All that the prosody demands here is that the word *toward* be **pronounced in two syllables; the** accent may **be** either **on the first or the second**. *Toward* when an adjective **has, I believe**, always the **accent on** the first syllable **in** Shakespeare; but its customary pronunciation may have been otherwise **in** his day when it was a preposition, as it is here. Milton,

however, in the few cases in which he does not run the two syllables into one, always accents the first. And he uses both *toward* and *towards*.

53. *Set Honour in one eye*, etc.—This passage has occasioned some discussion. Johnson's explanation is:— " When Brutus first names Honour and Death, he calmly declares them indifferent; but, as the image kindles in his mind, he sets Honour above life." It does not seem to be necessary to suppose any such change or growth either of the image or the sentiment. What Brutus means by saying that he will look upon Honour and Death indifferently, if they present themselves together, is merely that, for the sake of the honour, he will not mind the death, or the risk of death, by which it may be accompanied; he will look as fearlessly and steadily upon the one as upon the other. He will think the honour to be cheaply purchased even by the loss of life; that price will never make him falter or hesitate in clutching at such a prize. He must be understood to set honour above life from the first; that he should ever have felt otherwise for a moment would have been the height of the unheroic.—The convenient elisions *i' the* and *o' the* have been almost lost to our modern English verse, at least in composition of the ordinary regularity and dignity. Byron, however, has in a well-known passage ventured upon " Hived in our bosoms like the bag o' the bee."

54. *Your outward favour.*—A man's *favour* is his aspect or appearance. "In beauty," says Bacon, in his 43rd *Essay*, " that of favour is more than that of colour; and that of decent and gracious motion more than that of favour." The word is now lost to us in that sense; but we still use *favoured* with *well*, *ill*, and perhaps other qualifying terms, for featured or looking; as in *Gen. xli.* 4 :— " The ill-favoured and lean-fleshed kine did eat up the seven well-favoured and fat kine." *Favour* seems to be used for *face* from the same confusion or natural trans-

ference of meaning between the expressions for the feeling in the mind and the outward indication of it in the look that has led to the word *countenance*, which commonly denotes the latter, being sometimes employed, by a process the reverse of what we have in the case of *favour*, in the sense of at least one modification of the former; as when we speak of any one giving something his *countenance*, or *countenancing* it. In this case, however, it ought to be observed that *countenance* has the meaning, not simply of favourable feeling or approbation, but of its expression or avowal. The French terms from which we have borrowed our *favour* and *countenance* do not appear to have either of them undergone the transference of meaning which has befallen the English forms. But *contenance*, which is still also used by the French in the sense of material capacity, has drifted far away from its original import in coming to signify one's aspect or physiognomy. It is really also the same word with the French and English *continence* and the Latin *continentia*.

54. *For my single self.*—Here is a case in which we are still obliged to adhere to the old way of writing and printing *my self. Vid.* 56.

54. *I had as lief.*—*Lief* (sometimes written *leef*, or *leve*), in the comparative *liefer* or *lever*, in the superlative *liefest*, is the Original English *leof*, of the same meaning with our modern *dear*. "No modern author, I believe," says Horne Tooke (*D. of P.* 261), "would now venture any of these words in a serious passage; and they seem to be cautiously shunned or ridiculed in common conversation, as a vulgarity. But they are good English words, and more frequently used by our old English writers than any other word of a corresponding signification." The common modern substitute for *lief* is *soon*, and for *liefer, sooner* or *rather*, which last is properly the comparative of *rath*, or *rathe*, signifying *early*, not found in Shakespeare, but used in one expression—"the rathe

primrose" (*Lycidas,* 142)—by Milton, who altogether ignores *lief. Lief, liefer,* and *liefest,* are all common in Spenser. Shakespeare has *lief* pretty frequently, but never *liefer;* and *liefest* occurs only in the *Second Part of King Henry VI.,* where, in *iii.* 1, we have " My *liefest* liege." In the same Play, too (*i.* 1), we have " Mine *alderliefest* sovereign," meaning dearest of all. " This beautiful word," says Mr Knight, "is a Saxon compound. *Alder,* of all, is thus frequently joined with an adjective of the superlative degree,—as *alderfirst, alderlast.*" But it cannot be meant that such combinations are frequent in the English of Shakespeare's day. They do occur, indeed, in a preceding stage of the language. *Alder* is a corrupted or at least modified form of the Original English genitive plural *aller,* or *allre;* it is that strengthened by the interposition of a supporting *d* (a common expedient). *Aller,* with the same signification, is still familiar in German compounds.—The effect and construction of *lief* in Middle English may be seen in the following examples from Chaucer:—" For him was lever han at his beddes head" (*C. T. Pro.* 295), that is, To him it was dearer to have (*lever* a monosyllable, *beddes* a dissyllable); " Ne, though I say it, I n' am not lefe to gabbe" (*C. T.* 3510), that is, I am not given to prate; " I hadde lever dien," that is, I should hold it preferable to die. And Chaucer has also " Al be him loth or lefe" (*C. T.* 1839), that is, Whether it be to him agreeable or disagreeable; and " For lefe ne loth" (*C. T.* 13062), that is, For love nor loathing.—We may remark the evidently intended connexion in sound between the *lief* and the *live,* or rather the attraction by which the one word has naturally produced or evoked the other.

54. *Cæsar said to me,* etc.—In the Second Folio it is " Cæsar saies to me." And three lines lower down it is there " Accounted as I was." Other errors of that copy

in the same speech are "chasing with her shores," and
"He had a Feaher when he was in Spaine."

54. *Arrive the point proposed.*—*Arrive* without the now
indispensable *at* or *in* is found also in the *Third Part of
King Henry VI.* (*v.* 3) :—

> "Those powers that the queen
> Hath raised in Gallia have arrived our coast."

And Milton has the same construction (*P. L. ii.* 409) :—

> "Ere he arrive
> The happy isle."

54. *I, as Æneas*, etc.—This commencement of the sentence, although necessitating the not strictly grammatical repetition of the first personal pronoun, is in fine rhetorical accordance with the character of the speaker, and vividly expresses his eagerness to give prominence to his own part in the adventure. Even the repetition (of which, by the by, we have another instance in this same speech) assists the effect. At the same time, it may just be noted that the *I* here is not printed differently in the original edition from the adverb of affirmation in "*Ay*, and that tongue of his," a few lines lower down. Nor are the two words anywhere distinguished. It may be doubted whether Macbeth's great exclamation (*ii.* 2) should not be printed (as it is by Steevens) "Wake Duncan with thy knocking: Ay, would thou could'st!" (instead of "I would," as commonly given).

54. *The old Anchises*, etc.—This is a line of six feet; but it is quite different in its musical character from what is called an Alexandrine, such as rounds off the Spenserian stanza, and also frequently makes the second line in a rhymed couplet or the third in a triplet. It might perhaps be going too far to say that a proper Alexandrine is inadmissible in blank verse. There would seem to be nothing in the principle of blank verse opposed to the occasional employment of the Alexandrine; but the

custom of our modern poetry excludes such a variation even from dramatic blank verse; and unquestionably by far the greater number of the lines in Shakespeare which have been assumed by some of his editors to be Alexandrines are only instances of the ordinary heroic line with the very common peculiarity of certain superfluous short syllables. That is all that we have here,—the ordinary heroic line overflowing its bounds,—which, besides that great excitement will excuse such irregularities, or even demand them, admirably pictures the emotion of Cassius, as it were acting his feat over again as he relates it,—with the shore the two were making for seeming, in their increasing efforts, to retire before them,—and panting with his remembered toil.

54. *His coward lips did from their colour fly.*—There can, I think, be no question that Warburton is right in holding that we have here a pointed allusion to a soldier flying from his colours. The lips would never otherwise be made to fly from their colour, instead of their colour from them. The figure is quite in Shakespeare's manner and spirit. But we may demur to calling it, with Warburton, merely "a poor quibble." It is a forcible expression of scorn and contempt. Such passions are, by their nature, not always lofty and decorous, but rather creative and reckless, and more given to the pungent than the elegant.

54. *Did lose his lustre.*—There is no personification here. *His* was formerly neuter as well as masculine, or the genitive of *It* as well as of *He;* and *his* lustre, meaning the lustre of the eye, is the same form of expression that we have in the texts:—" The fruit-tree yielding fruit after *his* kind, whose seed is in *itself*" (*Gen.* i. 11); " *It* shall bruise thy head, and thou shalt bruise *his* heel" (*Gen. iii.* 15); "If the salt have lost *his* savour" (*Matt. v.* 13, and *Luke xiv.* 34); "If the salt have lost *his* saltness" (*Mark ix.* 50); "When they were past the first

and the second ward, they came unto the iron gate that leadeth unto the city, which opened to them of *his* own accord" (*Acts xii.* 10); "His throne was like the fiery flame, and *his* wheels as burning fire" (*Dan. vii.* 9); and others. The word *Its* does not occur in the authorized translation of the Bible; its place is always supplied either by *His* or by *Thereof*. So again, in the present Play, in 523, we have "That every nice offence should bear *his* comment;" and in *Antony and Cleopatra, v.* 1, "The heart where mine *his* thoughts did kindle." One of the most curious and decisive examples of the neuter *his* occurs in *Coriolanus, i.* 1:—

> "*it* [the belly] tauntingly replied
> To the discontented members, the mutinous parts
> That envied *his* receipt."

Its, however, is found in Shakespeare. There is one instance in *Measure for Measure, i.* 2, where Lucio's remark about coming to a composition with the King of Hungary draws the reply, "Heaven grant us *its* peace, but not the King of Hungary's." The *its* here, it may be observed, has the emphasis. It is printed without the apostrophe both in the First and in the Second Folio. But the most remarkable of the Plays in regard to this particular is probably *The Winter's Tale*. Here, in i. 2, we have so many as three instances in a single speech of Leontes:—

> "How sometimes Nature will betray it's folly?
> It's tendernesse? and make it selfe a Pastime
> To harder bosomes? Looking on the Lynes
> Of my Boyes face, me thoughts I did requoyle
> Twentie-three yeeres, and saw my selfe vnbreech'd,
> In my greene Velvet Coat; my Dagger muzzel'd,
> Least it should bite it's Master, and so prove
> (As Ornaments oft do's) too dangerous."

So stands the passage in the First Folio. Nor does the new pronoun here appear to be a peculiarity of expression characteristic of the excited Sicilian king; a little while after in the same scene we have the same form from the mouth of Camillo:—

> "Be plainer with me, let me know my Trespas
> By it's owne visage."

And again, in iii. 3, we have Antigonus, when about to lay down the child in Bohemia, observing that he believes it to be the wish of Apollo that

> "it should heere be laide
> (Either for life, or death) vpon the earth
> Of it's right Father."

Nor is this all. There are two other passages of the same Play in which the modern editors also give us *its;* but in these the original text has *it*. The first is in ii. 3, where Leontes, in directing Antigonus to carry away the "female bastard" to some foreign land, enjoins him that he there leave it

> "(Without more mercy) to it owne protection."

The other is in iii. 2, where Hermione's words stand in both the First and Second Folio,

> "The innocent milke in it most innocent mouth."

It is a mistake to assume, as the modern editors do, that *it* in these instances is a misprint for *its:* Dr Guest (*Phil. Pro.* i. 280) has observed that in the dialects of the North-Western Counties formerly *it* was sometimes used for *its;* and that, accordingly, we have not only in Shakespeare's *King John, ii.* 1, "Goe to yt grandame, child . . . . and it grandame will give yt a plumb," but in Ben Jonson's *Silent Woman, ii.* 3, "It knighthood and it friends." So in *Lear, i.* 4, we have in a speech of the Fool, "For you know, Nunckle, the Hedge-Sparrow fed the Cuckoo so long, that it's had it head bit off by it young" (that is, that it has had its head,—not that it had its head, as the modern editors give the passage, after the Second **Folio, in** which it stands, "that **it had its** head bit off by it young"). This use of *it* is still familiar in the popular speech of the West Riding of Yorkshire, and **even in the** English of some parts of Ireland. So, long before *its* was generally received, **we have** *it self* commonly **printed in** two words, evidently **under** the impression that *it* **was** a possessive, of the same syntactical force with the **pronouns** in *my self, your self, her self.* And even now we do not write *itsself.* Formerly, too, according to Dr **Guest, they often** said even "The King wife," etc., for "**The King's** wife." So he holds that in **such** modern **phrases as** "The idea of a thing being **abstracted,**" or "of it being abstracted," *thing* and *it* are genitives, for *thing's* and *its.*

We have also either *it* or *its* in another passage of *Lear,* where Albany, **in iv. 2,** speaks of "that **nature** which condemns its origin." The passage is not **in the Folios;** but, if we may trust to Jennens, the First Quarto **has** *ith,* the Second *it,* for the *its* of the modern text. Both those Quartos are of 1608; and there is also **a third of the** same year, **but** the reading in that is **not noted** by the commentators.

I am indebted to Dr Trench, **the Dean of** Westminster, **for calling my** attention **to one passage in** our English **Bible,** *Levit. xxv.* 5, **in** which, although the modern reprints give us "that which groweth of its own accord," the reading **in the original** edition is "of it own accord." In Luther's German version the phrase here is the same **that is** employed in *Acts xii.* 10, quoted above, where **we have** "of his own accord:"—*von ihm selber* in **the one case,** *von ihr selbst* in the other.

Dr Guest asserts that *its* was used **generally by the dramatists of** the age to which **the authorized** version of **the Bible belongs, and also** by many of their contemporaries. Dr Trench, **in his** *English, Past and Present,* doubts whether Milton has once admitted it into *Paradise*

Lost, "although, when that was composed, others frequently allowed it." The common authorities give us no help in such matters as this; no notice is taken of the word *Its* either in Todd's *Verbal Index* to Milton, or in Mrs Clarke's elaborate *Concordance* to Shakespeare. But Milton does use *Its* occasionally; as, *e. g.* (*P. L. i.* 254), "The mind is *its* own place, and in itself;" and (*P. L. iv.* 813), "No falsehood can endure Touch of celestial temper, but returns Of force to *its* own likeness." Generally, however, he avoids the word, and easily manages to do so by personifying most of his substantives; it is only when this cannot be done, as in the above examples, that he reluctantly accepts the services of the little *parvenu* monosyllable.

Mr Singer, in a note to his edition of the *Essays* and *Wisdom of the Ancients*, p. 200, seems to intimate that *its* is nowhere used by Bacon. Like Shakespeare and other writers of the time, he has frequently *his* in the neuter.

Dr Trench notices the fact of the occurrence of *its* in *Rowley's Poems* as decisive against their genuineness. He observes, also, that "Dryden, when, in one of his fault-finding moods with the great men of the preceding generation, he is taking Ben Jonson to task for general inaccuracy in his English diction, among other counts of his indictment, quotes this line of *Catiline*, 'Though heaven should speak with all his wrath at once;' and proceeds, '*Heaven* is ill syntax with *his*.'" This is a curious evidence of how completely the former humble condition and recent rise of the now fully established vocable had come to be generally forgotten in a single generation.

The need of it, indeed, must have been much felt. If it was convenient to have the two forms *He* and *It* in the nominative, and *Him* and *It* in the other cases, a similar distinction between the Masculine and the Neuter of the genitive must have been equally required for perspicuous expression. Even the personifying power of *his* was impaired by its being applied to both genders. Milton, consequently, it may be noticed, prefers wherever it is possible the feminine to the masculine personification, as if he felt that the latter was always obscure from the risk of the *his* being taken for the neuter pronoun. Thus we have (*P. L. i.* 723) "The ascending pile Stood fixed **her** stately height;" (*ii.* 4) "The gorgeous East with richest hand Showers on *her* kings;" (*ii.* 175) "What if all *Her* stores were opened, and this firmament Of hell should spout *her* cataracts of fire;" (*ii.* 271) "This desert soil Wants not *her* hidden lustre;" (ii. 584) "Lethe, the river of oblivion, rolls *Her* watery labyrinth;" (*ix.* 1103) "The fig-tree . . . spreads *her* arms;" (*Com.* 396) "Beauty . . . had need . . . To save *her* blossoms and defend *her* fruit;" (*Com.* 468) "The soul grows clotted . . . till *she* quite lose The divine property of *her* first being;" and so on, continually and habitually, or upon system. His masculine personifications are comparatively rare, and are only ventured upon either where **he does not** require to use the pronoun, or where **its gender cannot** be mistaken.

Milton himself, however, nowhere, I believe, uses *his* in a neuter sense.* He felt too keenly the annoyance of such a sense of it always coming in the way to spoil or prevent any other use he might have made of it. The modern practice is the last of three distinct stages through which the language passed as to this matter in the course of less than a century. First, we have *his* serving for

---

* Unless the following were to be considered as an instance:—

"It was a mountain, at whose verdant feet
A spacious plain, outstretched in circuit wide,
Lay pleasant; from *his* side two rivers flowed."

Par. Reg. iii. 255.

But the *feet*, instead of *foot*, would seem to intimate that we are to regard the mountain as personified here.

both masculine and neuter; secondly, we have *his* restricted to the masculine, and the neuter left without or with hardly any recognized form; thirdly, we have the defect of the second stage remedied by the frank adoption of the heretofore rejected *its*. And the most curious thing of all in the history of the word *its* is the extent to which, before its recognition as a word admissible in serious composition, even the occasion for its employment was avoided or eluded. This is very remarkable in Shakespeare. The very conception which we express by *its* probably does not occur once in his works for ten times that it is to be found in any modern writer. So that we may say the invention, or adoption, of this form has changed not only our English style, but even our manner of thinking.

The Original English personal pronoun was, in the Nominative singular, *He* for the Masculine, *Heó* for the Feminine, and *Hit* for the Neuter. *He* we still retain; for *Heó* we have substituted *She*, apparently a modification of *Seó*, the Feminine of the Demonstrative (*Se*, *Seó*, *Thaet*); *Hit* we have converted into *It* (though the aspirate is still often heard in the Scottish dialect). The Genitive was *Hire* for the Feminine (whence our modern *Her*), and *His* both for the Masculine and the Neuter. So also the modern German has *ihr* for the Feminine, and only one form, *sein*, for both the Masculine and the Neuter. But in the inflection of this single form the two genders in our ancient English were distinguished both in the Nominative and in the Accusative, whereas in German they are distinguished in the Accusative only. They are the same in the Genitive and Dative in both languages.

It is to be understood, of course, that the *its*, however convenient, is quite an irregular formation: the *t* of *it* (originally *hit*) is merely the sign of the neuter gender, which does not enter into the inflection, leaving the natural genitive **of that** gender (*hi, hi-s*) substantially identical with that of the masculine (*he, he-s, hi-s*).

54, 55.—*And bear the palm alone.—Another general shout!*—Two hemistichs or broken lines thus following one another are not necessarily to be regarded **as prosodically connected,** any more than if they **were several** sentences asunder. The notion that two such consecutive fragments were always intended **by** Shakespeare to make **a** complete verse has led the modern editors, more especially Steevens, **into a great** deal of uncalled-for chopping **and** tinkering of the old text.

56. *But in ourselves.*—In the original edition divided "our selves," exactly as "our stars" in the preceding line. And so always with *our self, your self, her self, my self, thy self,* **and also** *it self,* but never with *himself,* or *themselves. Vid.* **54.**

56. *What should be in that Cæsar?*—A form of **speech** now gone out. It was a less blunt and direct way **of** saying What **is** there? or What may there **be?** These more subtle and delicate modes of expression, **by the use** of the subjunctive for the indicative and of **the past** for the present, which characterize not only **the** Greek and Latin languages but even the German, have for the greater **part** perished in **our modern** English. The deep insight **and creative** force—the "**great** creating nature"—which **gave birth to** our tongue **has dried** up under the benumbing tòuch **of the** logic **by which it** has been trained and cultivated.

56. *More than yours.*—Here and everywhere else, it **may be noticed** once **for** all, our modern *than* is *then* in the old **text.** *Vid.* Prolegomena, *Sect. v.*

56. *Become the mouth as well.*—Always **aswell,** as one word, in the First Folio.

56. *The breed of noble bloods.*—**We scarcely** now use this plural. Shakespeare **has it several times**; as afterwards in 645, "I know young bloods look for a time of

rest;" in *Much Ado About Nothing, iii.* 3, where Boracio remarks how giddily fashion "turns about all the hot bloods between fourteen and five and thirty;" in *The Winter's Tale, i.* 1, where Leontes says, "To mingle friendship far is mingling bloods;" in *King John, ii.* 1, where Philip of France, to the boast of John before the walls of Angiers that he brings as witnesses to his right and title "twice fifteen thousand hearts of English breed," replies (*aside*) that

> "As many and as well-born bloods as those
> Stand in his face to contradict his claim."

56. *That her wide walls encompassed but one man.*—The old reading is "wide *walks.*" Despite the critical canon which warns us against easy or obvious amendments, it is impossible not to believe that we have a misprint here. What Rome's wide *walks* may mean is not obvious; still less, how she could be encompassed by her *walks*, however wide. The correction to *walls* has the authority of Mr Collier's MS. annotator, but had been conjecturally adopted down to the time of Malone by most of the modern editors, from Rowe inclusive.

56. *Now is it Rome indeed, and room enough.*—Shakespeare's pronunciation of *Rome* seems to have been *Room*. Besides the passage before us we have afterwards in the present Play (368) "No Rome of safety for Octavius yet;" and in *King John*, iii. 1, "That I have *room* with Rome to curse a while." In the *First Part of King Henry the Sixth*, it is true, we have the other pronunciation; there (*iii.* 2), the Bishop of Winchester having exclaimed "Rome shall remedy this," Warwick replies "*Roam* thither, then." This little fact is not without its significance in reference to the claim of that Play to be laid at Shakespeare's door.

56. *But one only man.*—In the original text "but one *onely* man," probably indicating that the pronunciation

of the numeral and of the first syllable of the adverb was the same.

56. *There was a Brutus once, that would have brooked.*—To *brook* (originally *brucan*), for to endure, to submit to, is one of those old words which every one still understands but no one uses, unless it may be some studious imitator of the antique.

57. *That you do love me, I am nothing jealous.*—I am nowhat jealous, doubtful, suspicious, in regard to its being the fact that you love me. This seems to be the grammatical resolution of a construction which, like many similar ones familiar to the freer spirit of the language two centuries ago, would now scarcely be ventured upon.

57. *I have some aim.*—*Aim*, in old French *eyme*, *esme*, and *estme*, is the same word with *esteem* (from the Latin *æstimatio* and *æstimare*), and should therefore signify properly a judgment or conjecture of the mind, which is very nearly its meaning here. We might now say, in the same sense, I have some notion. In modern English the word has acquired the additional meaning of an intention to hit, or catch, or in some other way attain, that to which the view is directed. It does not seem impossible that the French name for the loadstone, *aimant*, may be from the same root, although it has usually been considered to be a corruption of *adamant*. A ship's reckonings are called in French *estimes*, which is undoubtedly the same word with our *aims*. In the French of the early part of the sixteenth century we find *esme* and *esmé* (or *esmez*, as it was commonly written) confounded with the totally different *aimer*, to love. Rabelais, for instance, writes *bien aymez* for *bien esmez*, well disposed. See Duchat's Note on liv. I., ch. 5.

57. *For this present.*—So, in the *Absolution*, "that those things may please him which we do at this present." This expression, formerly in universal use and good repute,

now remains only a musty law phrase, never admitted into ordinary composition except for ludicrous effect.

57. *So with love I might entreat you.*—This form of expression is still preserved both in our own language and in German. Thus (*John i.* 25):—" Warum taufest du denn, so du nicht Christus bist?" or, "So Gott will" (If God please). The conjunction thus used is commonly said to be equivalent to *if*. But *so*, according to Horne Tooke (*D. of P.*, 147), is merely the Mœso-Gothic demonstrative pronoun, and signifies properly *this* or *that*. In German, though commonly, as with ourselves, only an adverb or conjunction, it may still be also used pronominally; as *Das Buch, so ihr mir gegeben habt* (the book which you gave me). Something of the same kind, as we have already seen (44), takes place even in English with *as*, which is perhaps only another form of *so* or *sa*. Upon this theory, all that *so* will perform in such a passage as the present will be to mark and separate the clause which it heads by an emphatic introductory compendium: —*That* (or *this*), namely, that with love I might, etc.; and the fact of the statement in the clause being a supposition, or assumption, will be left to be inferred. That fact, however, would be *expressed* by the *so* according to the doctrine of Dr Webster, who conceives the word to be derived from some Hebrew or other root signifying *to compose, to set, to still.* "This sense," he affirms, "is retained in the use of the word by milkmaids, who say to cows *so, so*, that is, stand still, remain as you are." Such an application of the term, I apprehend, is not peculiar to the milkmaid tongue,—a familiarity with which, however, is certainly carrying linguistic knowledge a great way.—The First Folio points, blunderingly, "I would not so (with love I might intreat you)."

57. *Be any further moved.*—Here again, as in 45, Mr Collier prints *farther*, though *further* is the reading of both the First and the Second Folio.

57. *Chew upon this.*—We have lost the native word in this application; but we retain the metaphor, only translating *chew* into the Latin equivalent, *ruminate.*

57. *Brutus had rather be . . . than to repute.*—The sense of the verb *Have* in the phrase *Had rather* is peculiar. Johnson calls it barbarous. Webster asks, "Is not this phrase a corruption of *would rather?*" It has the same sense, as we have seen (54), in *Had as lief*, and in the older *Had liefer*, or *lever*. This verb (one very variously applied in some other languages,—witness the *il y a* of the French, the *vi ha* or *havvi* of the Italian, the *ha* or *hay* of the Spanish, as well as certain constructions of the Greek ἔχειν) may have been employed by us formerly with more latitude of signification than now. We still say *Have at him*, and, with a somewhat different sense, *Have at you.* Even Shakespeare has, in *Rich. II., iii.* **3**,

"Me rather had my heart might feel your love
Than my unpleased eye see your courtesy."

There is also the phrase, *Had like*, not yet quite gone out, of which all that Dr Webster has to say is, that it seems to be a corruption,—unless, he adds, *like* be here a noun, and used for resemblance or probability (which it may be safely affirmed that it is not). The *to* before *repute* is, apparently, to be defended, if at all, upon the ground that *had rather* is equivalent in import to *would prefer*, and that, although it is only an auxiliary before *be a villager*, it is to be taken as a common verb before *to repute*. It is true that, as we have seen (1), the *to* was in a certain stage of the language sometimes inserted, sometimes omitted, both after auxiliaries and after other verbs; but that was hardly the style of Shakespeare's age. We certainly could not now say "I had rather *to* repute;" and I do not suppose that any one would have *directly* so written or spoken then. The irregularity is softened or disguised in the passage before us by the intervening words.

57. *Under these hard conditions as.*—This is the reading in all the old copies; *these—as* where we should now say *such—as*, or *those—that*. If *such, so,* **as, that** (or *this*) be all etymologically of the same or nearly the same signification, they would naturally, till custom regulated their use, and assigned a distinct function to each, be interchangeable one with another. Thus in 129 we have " To *such* a man *That* is no fleering tell-tale." Although *those—as*, or *that—as*, is common, however, *these—as* is certainly at any rate unusual. Mr Collier prints, upon the authority of his MS. corrector, " under *such* hard conditions." I should suspect the true reading to be " under *those* hard conditions." *Vid.* 44.

57. *Is like.*—This form of expression is not quite, but nearly, gone out. We now commonly say *is likely*.

58. *I am glad* **that my** *weak words.*—In this first line of the speech of Cassius and the last of the preceding speech of Brutus we have two hemistichs, having no prosodical connexion. It was never intended that they should form one line, and no torturing can make them do so.

Re-enter Cæsar.—In the original text it is *Enter*.

60. *What hath proceeded.*—That is, simply, happened, —a sense which the verb has now lost.

61. *I will do so,* etc.—Throughout the Play, the *ius* of *Cassius* (as also of *Lucilius*) makes sometimes only one syllable, sometimes two, as here.

62. *Being crossed in conference,* etc.—If the *being* and *conference* be fully enunciated, as they will be in any but the most slovenly reading, we have two supernumerary syllables in this line, but both so short that neither the mechanism nor the melody of the verse is at all impaired by them.

65. *Let me have men about me,* etc.—Some of the expressions in this speech are evidently suggested by those of North in his translation of Plutarch's Life of Cæsar:

—" When Cæsar's friends complained unto him of Antonius and Dolabella, that they pretended [i. e. *intended*] some mischief towards him, he answered; As for those fat men and smooth-combed heads (quoth he), I never reckon of them; but these pale-visaged and carrion-lean people, I fear them most; meaning Brutus and Cassius."

65. *Such as sleep o' nights.*—That is, on nights; as *o'clock* is on clock, and also as *aboard* is on board, *aside* on side, *aloft* on loft, *alive* in life, etc. In the older stages of the language the meanings that we now discriminate by *on* and *in* are confused, and are both expressed by *an, on, un, in*, or in composition by the contractions *a* or *o*. The form here in the original text is *a-nights*.

65. *Yond Cassius.*—Though *yond* is no longer in use, we still have both **yon** and *yonder*. The *d* is probably no proper part of the word, but has been added to strengthen the sound, as in the word *sound* itself (from the French *son*), and in many other cases. See, upon the origin of *Yonder*, Dr Latham's *Eng. Lang.* 375.

66. *Well given.*—Although we no longer say absolutely *well* or *ill given* (for well or ill disposed), we still say given to study, given to drinking, etc.

67. *Yet, if my name.*—A poetic idiom for "Yet, if I, bearing the name I do." In the case of Cæsar the name was even more than the representative and most precise expression of the person; it was that in which his power chiefly resided, his renown. Every reader of Milton will remember the magnificent passage (*P. L. ii.* 964):—

> "Behold the throne
> Of Chaos, and his dark pavilion spread
> Wide on the wasteful deep; with him enthroned
> Sat sable-vested Night, eldest of things,
> The consort of his reign; and by them stood
> Orcus and Ades, and *the dreaded name*
> Of Demogorgon."

67. *Liable to fear.*—The word *liable* has been somewhat restricted in its application since Shakespeare's time.

We should scarcely now speak of a person as liable to fear. And see 249 for another application of it still farther away from our present usage.

67. *Such men as he*, etc.—In this and the following line we have no fewer than three archaisms, words or forms which would not and could not be used by a writer of the present day:—*be* (for are), *at heart's ease* (for in ease of mind), *whiles* (for while). It would be difficult to show that the language has not in each of these instances lost something which it would have been the better for retaining. But it seems to be a law of every language which has become thoroughly subdued under the dominion of grammar, that perfectly synonymous terms cannot live in it. If varied forms are not saved by having distinct senses or functions assigned to each, they are thrown off as superfluities and encumbrances. One is selected for use, and the others are reprobated, or left to perish from mere neglect. The logic of this no doubt is, that verbal expression will only be a correct representation of thought if there should never be any the slightest variation of the one without a corresponding variation of the other. But the principle is not necessarily inconsistent with the existence of various forms which should be recognized as differing in no other respect whatever except only in vocal character; and the language would be at least musically richer with more of this kind of variety. It is what it regards as the irregularity or lawlessness, however, of such logically unnecessary variation that the grammatical spirit hates. It would be argued that with two or more words of precisely the same signification we should have really something like a confusion of two or more languages.

67. For the present stage direction at the end of this speech, we have in the original text " *Sennit. Exeunt Cæsar and his Traine.*"

69. *What hath chanced to-day.*—So in 71; where, also,

most of the modern editions have "**what** *hath* chanced," **Mr** Collier's one-volume edition included, although *had* is the **word in all** the Folios. Instead of *to chance* in this sense we now usually say **to** *happen*. *Chance* is a French word (from the *cas-* of the Latin *casus* strengthened by the common expedient of inserting an *n*); *happen*, *hap*, and also *happy*, appear to be derivatives **from a** Welsh **word,** *hap* or *hab*, luck, fortune. The Original **English verb was** *befeallan*, **from which** also we have still **to** *befall*.

78. *Ay, marry, was't*.—This term of asseveration, *marry*, which Johnson seems to speak **of** as still in common use **in** his day, is found in Chaucer in the form *Mary*, and appears to be merely a mode of swearing **by** the Holy Virgin.

78. *Every time gentler than other.*—I do not know that this use of *other* will be admitted to be of the same **nature** with that which we have in *Macbeth, i.* 7, where the reading of the First Folio is "Vaulting ambition, **which o'er-leaps** itself, And falls on the other." The *other* **in both passages** ought perhaps to be considered **as a substantive, as** it still is in other cases, **though it is no longer** used exactly in this way. So in *Meas. for Meas. iv.* 4;—"Every letter he hath **writ** hath **disvouched other."**

82. *The rabblement shouted.*—The **first** three Folios have **howted, the Fourth** *houted*. The common reading is *hooted*. But this is entirely inconsistent with the context. The people applauded when Cæsar refused **the** crown, and only hissed or hooted when they thought **he** was about to accept it. *Shouted* was substituted **on conjecture by** Hanmer, and almost indicates itself; **but** it has **also the support of Mr** Collier's MS. annotator.

82. *Their chopped hands.*—**In** the **old** copies *chopt*. Mr Collier, however, **has** *chapped*.

82. *For he swooned.*—*Swoonded* is the word in all the Folios.

83. *Did Cæsar swoon?*—Here *swound* is the word in all the Folios.

85. *'Tis very like: he hath the falling sickness.*—*Like* is likely, or probable, as in 57. I am surprised to find Mr Collier adhering to the blundering punctuation of the early copies, "'Tis very like he hath," etc. Cæsar's infirmity was notorious; it is mentioned both by Plutarch and Suetonius.

86. *And honest Casca*, etc.—The slight interruption to the flow of this line occasioned by the supernumerary syllable in *Casca* adds greatly to the effect of the emphatic *we* that follows. It is like the swell of the wave before it breaks.

87. *If the tag-rag people.*—In *Coriolanus, iii.* 1, we have "Will you hence, before the *tag* return." "This," says Nares, "is, perhaps, the only instance of *tag* without his companions *rag* and *bobtail*, or at least one of them."

87. *No true man.*—No honest man, as we should now say. Jurymen, as Malone remarks, are still styled "good men and true."

89. *He plucked me ope his doublet.*—Though we still use *to ope* in poetry, *ope* as an adjective is now obsolete. As for the *me* in such a phrase as the present, it may be considered as being in the same predicament with the *my* in *My Lord*, or the *mon* in the French *Monsieur*. That is to say, it has no proper pronominal significancy, but merely serves (in so far as it has any effect) to enliven or otherwise grace the expression. How completely the pronoun is forgotten,—or we may say, quiescent—in such a case as that of *Monsieur* is shown by the common phrase "*Mon* cher monsieur." *Vid.* 205 and 471.

The best commentary on the use of the pronoun that we have here is the dialogue between Petrucio and his servant Grumio, in *Tam. of Shrew, i.* 2:—"*Pet.* Villain, I say, knock me here soundly. *Gru.* Knock you here, sir? Why, sir, what am I, sir, that I should knock you here, sir? *Pet.* Villain, I say, knock me at this gate, and rap me well, **or** I'll knock your knave's pate. ***Gru.*** My master is grown quarrelsome: **I** should knock **you** first, And then **I know** after who comes by the worst. . . . ***Hortensio.*** How now, what's the **matter?** . . . ***Gru.*** Look you, sir,—he bid me knock him, and rap him soundly, **sir:** Well, was it fit for a servant to use his master so? . . . ***Pet.*** **A senseless** villain!—Good Hortensio, I bade **the rascal** knock upon your gate, And could not get him for my heart to **do it.** *Gru.* Knock at the gate?—O heavens! **Spake you not these** words plain,—'Sirrah, knock me here, Rap me here, knock me well, **and** knock me soundly?' And come you now with—knocking at the gate?"

89. *A man of any occupation.*—This is explained **by** Johnson as meaning "a mechanic, one of the plebeians **to whom he** offered his throat." But it looks as if it had **more in it than** that. In the Folios it is "*and* **I** had been a man;" and again in 95 "*and* I tell you." So also Bacon **writes** (Essay 23rd):—"Certainly **it is the** nature of extreme self-lovers, as they will **set an house on** fire, and **it were but to** roast their eggs;" and (Essay 40th):—"For time is to be honoured and respected, and it were but for her daughters, Confidence and Reputation."

95. *Marullus and Flavius.*—In **this** instance the *Marullus* **is** *Murrellus* in **the First Folio** (instead of *Murellus*, as elsewhere).

97. *I am promised forth.*—An old phrase for I have an engagement.

102. ***He was*** *quick mettle.*—This is the reading **of all** the old copies. Mr Collier, however, in his regulated text, has *mettled*, but not, it would appear, on the authority of his MS. corrector. I have allowed **the** distinction made by the modern editors between *metal* and *mettle* to stand throughout the Play, although there can be little doubt **that** the **latter form is** merely a corruption of the **former, and that the supposed** two words are the same.

In the First Folio it is always *mettle ;* in 16 and 105, as well as here and in 177 and 506. Dr Webster, however, thinks that *mettle* may be the Welsh *mezwl* or *methwl*, mind.

103. *However he puts on.*—We should hardly now use *however*, in this sense, with the indicative mood. We should have to say, "However he may put on."—*This tardy form :* this shape, semblance, of tardiness or dulness.

104. *I will come home to you . . . Come home to me.*—To *come home to* one, for to come to one's house, is another once common phrase which is now gone out of use.

105. *Think of the world.*—The only meaning that this can have seems to be, Think of the state in which the world is.

105. *From that it is disposed.*—Here we have the omission, not only of the relative, which can easily be dispensed with, but also of the preposition governing it, which is an essential part of the verb; but, illegitimate as such syntax may be, it is common with our writers down to a date long subsequent to Shakespeare's age. *Vid.* 224.

105. *Therefore it is meet.*—*It is* (instead of *'tis*) is the reading of the First Folio, which has been restored by Mr Knight. The excess here is of a syllable (the *fore* of *therefore*) not quite so manageable as usual, and it makes the verse move ponderously, if we must not say halt ; but perhaps such a prosody may be thought to be in accordance with the grave and severe spirit of the passage.

105. *With their likes.*—We scarcely use this substantive now.

105. *Cæsar doth bear me hard.*—Evidently an old phrase for does not like me, bears me a grudge. It occurs again in 199, and a third time in 345. In 199, and there only, the editor of the Second Folio has changed *hard* into *hatred*, in which he has been followed by the Third and Fourth Folios, and also by Rowe, Pope, Hanmer, and

even Capel. **Mr** Collier's MS. annotator restores the *hard*. It is remarkable that the expression, **meeting us** so often in **this** one Play, should **be found** nowhere else in Shakespeare. Nor have the **commentators been able to refer** to an instance of its **occurrence** in any other writer.

105. *He should not humour me.*—The meaning **seems** to be, **If I** were in his position (a favourite with Cæsar), **and** he in mine (disliked by **Cæsar**), he should not cajole, or turn **and** wind, me, as **I** now do him. *He* and *me* are to be contrasted **by** the emphasis, **in** the same manner as *I* **and** *he* in the preceding line. This **is** Warburton's explanation; whose remark, however, that the words convey a reflection on **Brutus's** ingratitude, seems unfounded. It is rather Brutus's simplicity that Cassius has in his mind. It would be satisfactory, however, if other examples could be produced of the use of the verb *to humour* in the sense assumed. Johnson appears to have quite mistaken the meaning of the passage: he takes the *he* to be not Brutus, but Cæsar; and his interpretation **is**, "his (that is, Cæsar's) love should not take hold of **my** affection, **so as to** make **me** forget **my principles.**"

105. *In several hands.*—Writings in several hands.

105. *Let Cæsar seat him sure.*—Seat himself firmly (as on horseback).

SCENE III.—*The same.* *A Street.*

Thunder and Lightning. Enter, from opposite sides, Casca, *with his sword drawn, and* Cicero.

106. *Cic.* **Good** even, Casca; Brought you Cæsar home?
Why are you breathless? and why stare you so?

107. *Casca.* Are not you moved, when all the **sway of earth**
Shakes, like a thing unfirm? O Cicero,
I have seen tempests, **when the scolding winds**
Have rived the knotty oaks; and I have seen
The ambitious ocean swell, and rage, and foam,
To be exalted with the threatening clouds:

sc. 3.] JULIUS CÆSAR. 117

But never till to-night, never till now,
Did I go through a tempest dropping fire.
Either there is a civil strife in heaven,
Or else the world, too saucy with the gods,
Incenses them to send destruction.
108. *Cic.* Why, saw you anything more wonderful?
109. *Casca.* A common slave (you know him well by sight)
Held up his left hand, which did flame and burn
Like twenty torches joined; and yet his hand,
Not sensible of fire, remained unscorched.
Besides (I have not since put up my sword),
Against the Capitol I met a lion,
Who glared upon me, and went surly by,
Without annoying me: And there were drawn
Upon a heap a hundred ghastly women,
Transformed with their fear; who swore they saw
Men, all in fire, walk up and down the streets.
And yesterday the bird of night did sit,
Even at noon-day, upon the market-place,
Hooting, and shrieking. When these prodigies
Do so conjointly meet, let not men say,
These are their reasons,—they are natural;
For, I believe, they are portentous things
Unto the climate that they point upon.
110. *Cic.* Indeed, it is a strange-disposed time:
But men may construe things after their fashion,
Clean from the purpose of the things themselves.
Comes Cæsar to the Capitol to-morrow?
  Casca. He doth; for he did bid Antonius
Send word to you, he would be there to-morrow.
112. *Cic.* Good night, then, Casca: this disturbed sky
Is not to walk in.
  Casca. Farewell, Cicero.   [*Exit* CICERO.
              Enter CASSIUS.
  Cas. Who's there?
  Casca. A Roman.
  Cas. Casca, by your voice.
117. *Casca.* Your ear is good. Cassius, what a night is this!
  Cas. A very pleasing night to honest men.
  Casca. Who ever knew the heavens menace so?
120. *Cas.* Those that have known the earth so full of faults.
For my part, I have walked about the streets,
Submitting me unto the perilous night;

And, thus unbraced, Casca, as you see,
Have bared my bosom to the thunder-stone:
And, when the cross blue lightning seemed to open
The breast of heaven, I did present myself
Even in the aim and very flash of it.
  Casca. But wherefore did you so much tempt the heavens?
It is the part of men to fear and tremble,
When the most mighty gods, by tokens, send
Such dreadful heralds to astonish us.

122. *Cas.* You are dull, Casca; and those sparks of life
That should be in a Roman you do want,
Or else you use not: You look pale, and gaze,
And put on fear, and cast yourself in wonder,
To see the strange impatience of the heavens:
But if you would consider the true cause,
Why all these fires, why all these gliding ghosts,
Why birds, and beasts, from quality and kind;
Why old men, fools, and children calculate;
Why all these things change from their ordinance,
Their natures, and pre-formed faculties,
To monstrous quality; why, you shall find,
That heaven hath infused them with these spirits,
To make them instruments of fear and warning
Unto some monstrous state. Now could I, Casca,
Name to thee a man most like this dreadful night;
That thunders, lightens, opens graves, and roars,
As doth the lion, in the Capitol:
A man no mightier than thyself, or me,
In personal action; yet prodigious grown,
And fearful, as these strange eruptions are.
  Casca. 'Tis Cæsar that you mean: Is it not, Cassius?

124. *Cas.* Let it be who it is: for Romans now
Have thews and limbs like to their ancestors,
But, woe the while! our fathers' minds are dead,
And we are governed with our mothers' spirits;
Our yoke and sufferance show us womanish.
  Casca. Indeed, they say, the senators to-morrow
Mean to establish Cæsar as a king:
And he shall wear his crown by sea and land,
In every place, save here in Italy.

126. *Cas.* I know where I will wear this dagger, then;
Cassius from bondage will deliver Cassius:
Therein, ye gods, you make the weak most strong;

Therein, ye gods, you tyrants do defeat:
Nor stony tower, nor walls of beaten brass,
Nor airless dungeon, nor strong links of iron,
Can be retentive to the strength of spirit;
But life, being weary of these worldly bars,
Never lacks power to dismiss itself.
If I know this, know all the world besides,
That part of tyranny that I do bear
I can shake off at pleasure.   [*Thunder still.*

127. *Casca.* So can I:
So every bondman in his own hand bears
The power to cancel his captivity.

128. *Cas.* And why should Cæsar be a tyrant, then?
Poor man! I know, he would not be a wolf,
But that he sees the Romans are but sheep:
He were no lion, were not Romans hinds.
Those that with haste will make a mighty fire
Begin it with weak straws: What trash is Rome,
What rubbish, and what offal, when it serves
For the base matter to illuminate
So vile a thing as Cæsar? But, O, grief!
Where hast thou led me? I, perhaps, speak this
Before a willing bondman: Then I know
My answer must be made. But I am armed,
And dangers are to me indifferent.

129. *Casca.* You speak to Casca; and to such a man,
That is no fleering tell-tale. Hold, my hand:
Be factious for redress of all these griefs;
And I will set this foot of mine as far
As who goes farthest.

130. *Cas.* There's a bargain made.
Now know you, Casca, I have moved already
Some certain of the noblest-minded Romans
To undergo, with me, an enterprise
Of honourable-dangerous consequence;
And I do know by this they stay for me
In Pompey's porch: for now, this fearful night
There is no stir or walking in the streets;
And the complexion of the element
In favour's like the work we have in hand,
Most bloody, fiery, and most terrible.

                Enter CINNA.

Casca. Stand close awhile, for here comes one in haste.
Cas. 'Tis Cinna, I do know him by his gait;

He is a friend.—Cinna, where haste you so?
Cin. To find out you: Who's that? Metellus Cimber?

134. **Cas.** No, it is Casca; one incorporate
To our attempts. Am I not staid for, Cinna?

135. *Cin.* I am glad on't. What a fearful night is this!
There's two or three of us have seen strange sights.

136. *Cas.* Am I not staid for? Tell me.

137. *Cin.* Yes, you are.—
O Cassius, if you could
But win the noble Brutus **to our party!**

138. **Cas.** Be you content. Good Cinna, take this paper,
And look **you lay it in the** prætor's chair,
Where Brutus may but find it; and throw this
In at his window: set this up with **wax**
Upon **old** Brutus' statue: all this done,
Repair to Pompey's porch, where you shall find **us**.
Is Decius Brutus, and Trebonius, there?

139. *Cin.* All but Metellus Cimber; and he's gone
To seek you at your house. Well, I will hie,
And so bestow these papers as you bade me.

140. *Cas.* That done, repair to Pompey's theatre.   [*Exit* CINNA.
Come, **Casca,** you and I will, yet, ere day,
See Brutus at his house: three parts of him
Is ours already; and the man entire,
Upon the next encounter, yields him ours.

Casca. O, he sits high in all the **people's hearts;**
And that, which would **appear offence in us,**
His countenance, like richest **alchymy,**
Will change to virtue, and to worthiness.

142. *Cas.* **Him, and his worth, and our great** need of him,
You have right well conceited. Let us go,
For it is after midnight; **and, ere** day,
We will awake him, and be sure of him.   [*Exeunt.*

The heading of *Scene III.* in the old copies is only "Thunder and Lightning. Enter Casca, and Cicero."

106. *Brought you Cæsar home?—Bring,* which **is now ordinarily** restricted **to the sense of carrying** *hither* (so that **we cannot** say Bring *there*), **was formerly** used in that **of carrying or** conveying generally. To bring one on his way, for **instance, was** to accompany him even if he had been leaving the **speaker.** So "Brought you Cæsar home?" is Did you go home with Cæsar? The word re-

tains its old sense in the expression *To bring forth* (fruit, or young), if not also in To *bring down* (a bird with a gun). To *fetch*, again, seems always to have meant more than to *bring* or to *carry*. "A horse cannot fetch, but only carry," says Launce in *The Two Gent. of Ver. iii.* 1.

107. *All the sway of earth.*—*Sway, swing, swagger*, are probably all of the same stock with *weigh*, and also with *wave*. The *sway of earth* may be explained as the balanced swing of earth.

107. *Like a thing unfirm.*—We have now lost the adjective *unfirm*, and we have appropriated *infirm* almost exclusively to the human body and mind, and their states and movements. For *infirm* generally we can only say *not firm*.

107. *Have rived.*—We have nearly lost this form, which is the one Shakespeare uses in the only two passages in which (if we may trust to Mrs Clarke) the past participle passive of the verb *to rive* is found in his works. The other is also in this Play:—"Brutus hath *rived* my heart," in 554. Milton, again, has our modern *riven* in the only passage of his poetry in which any part of the verb *to rive* occurs:—(*P. L. vi.* 449), "His *riven* arms to havoc hewn."

107. *To be exalted with.*—That is, in order, or in the effort, to be raised to the same height with.

107. *A tempest dropping fire.*—In the original text these three words are joined together by hyphens.

107. *A civil strife in heaven.*—A strife in which one part of heaven wars with another.

108. *Any thing more wonderful.*—That is, anything more that was wonderful. So in *Coriolanus, iv.* 6:—

> "The slave's report is seconded, and more,
> More fearful, is delivered."

So also in *King John, iv.* 2:—

> "Some reasons of this double coronation
> I have possessed you with, and think them strong;
> And more, more strong, ...
> I shall endue you with."

109. *You know him well by sight.*—Is it to be supposed that Casca really means to say that the common slave whom he chanced to meet was a particular individual well known to Cicero? Of what importance could that circumstance be? Or for what purpose should Casca notice it, even supposing him to have been acquainted with the fact that Cicero knew the man well, and yet knew him only by sight? It is impossible not to suspect some interpolation or corruption. Perhaps the true reading may be, "you *knew* him well by sight," meaning that any one would have known him at once to be but a common slave (notwithstanding the preternatural appearance, as if almost of something godlike, which his uplifted hand exhibited, burning but unhurt).

109. *Besides (I have not since*, etc.—In the Folios "I ha' not since."

109. *Against the Capitol.*—Over against, opposite to.

109. *Who glared upon me.*—In all the Folios the word is *glazed*. Pope first changed it to *glared*. Malone afterwards substituted *gazed*, partly on the strength of a passage in Stowe's Chronicle,—which gave Steevens an opportunity of maliciously rejoining, after quoting other instances of Shakespeare's use of *glare;*—"I therefore continue to repair the poet with his own animated phraseology, rather than with the cold expression suggested by the narrative of Stowe; who, having been a tailor, was undoubtedly equal to the task of mending Shakespeare's hose, but, on *poetical* emergencies, must not be allowed to patch his dialogue." *Glared* is also the correction of Mr Collier's MS. annotator. The only other instance known of the use of *glazed*, in apparently the sense which it would have here, is one produced by Boswell, from King James's translation of the *Urania* of Du Bartas: "I gave a lusty glaise." Boswell adds that "Du Bartas's original affords us no assistance."

109. *Drawn upon a heap.*—Gathered together in a heap,

or crowd. "Among this princely heap," says Gloster in *King Richard III.*, *ii.* 1. *Heap* was in common use in this sense throughout the seventeenth century.

109. *The bird of night.*—The owl; as the "bird of dawning" (the cock) in *Hamlet, i.* 1.

109. *Hooting and shrieking.*—*Howting* is the word in the first three Folios, *houting* in the Fourth.

109. *Even at noonday*, etc.—There may be a question as to the prosody of this line; whether we are to count *even* a monosyllable and throw the accent upon *day*, or, making *even* a dissyllable and accenting *noon*, to reckon *day* supernumerary.

109. *These are their reasons*, etc.—That such and such are their reasons. It is the same form of expression that we have afterwards in 147 :—" Would run to these and these extremities." But the present line has no claim to either a distinctive type or inverted commas. It is not as if it were "These are *our* reasons." Is it possible that Mr Collier can hold the new reading which he gives us in his one volume edition, on the authority of his MS. annotator, " These are their *seasons*," to be what Shakespeare really wrote? *This is their season* might have been conceivable; but who ever heard it remarked of any description of phenomena that *these are their seasons?*

109. *Unto the climate.*—The region of the earth, according to the old geographical division of the globe into so many *Climates*, which had no reference, or only an accidental one, to differences of temperature.

110. *A strange-disposed time.*—We should now have to use the adverb in this kind of combination. If we still say *strange-shaped*, it is because there we seem to have a substantive for the adjective to qualify; just as we have in *high-mind-ed, strong-mind-ed, able-bodi-ed,* and other similar forms. In other cases, again, it is the adjective, and not the adverb, that enters into the composition of the verb; thus we say *strange-looking, mad-look-*

ing, *heavy-looking*, etc., because the verb is *to look strange*, etc., not *to look strangely* (which has quite another meaning). *Foreign-built* may be regarded as an irregular formation, occasioned probably by our having no such adverb as *foreignly*. Even in *home-built, home-baked, home-brewed, home-grown, home-made,* etc., the adverb *home* has a meaning (*at home*) which it never has when standing alone.

110. *Clean from the purpose.*—A use of *clean* (for *completely*) **now** come to be accounted inelegant, though common **in the** translation of the Bible. "*From* the purpose" is away from the purpose.

112. The metre of this speech stands, or rather stumbles, thus in the original edition:—

"Good-night then, Caska:
This disturbed Skie is not to walke in."

117. ***Your ear is good***, etc.—The old copies **have** "What night is this?" But, notwithstanding the supernumerary short syllable, the only possible reading seems to be the one which I have given; "Cassius, what a night is this!" The *a* is plainly indispensable; for surely Casca **cannot** be supposed to ask what day of **the month it is.** What he says can only be **understood as an** exclamation, similar to that of **Cinna, in** 135: "**What a** fearful night is this!" **As for the slight irregularity in** the prosody, **it is of** perpetual **occurrence. Thus,** only thirty lines lower down (in **122) we have an** instance of it produced exactly as here:—"**Name to** thee a man most like this **dreadful** night." **And** so again in 155:—"Are then in council; and the state of a man."

120. *So full of faults.*—The word *fault*, formerly, though often signifying **no** more than it now does, carried sometimes (as here) **a** much greater **weight of** meaning than we now attach to it. *Conf.* 143.

120. **The** *thunder-stone.*—**The** thunder-stone is the imaginary product **of the** thunder, **which** the ancients called *Brontia*, mentioned **by** Pliny (*N. H. xxxvii.* 10) as

a species of gem, and **as that** which, falling with the lightning, does the mischief. It is the fossil commonly called the Belemnite, or Finger-stone, and now known to be a shell. We still talk of the *thunder-bolt*, which, however, is commonly confounded with the lightning. The *thunder-stone* was **held** to be quite distinct from the lightning, **as may be seen from** the song of Guiderius and Arviragus in *Cymbeline, iv. 2.*

" *Guid.* Fear no more the lightning-flash.
Arv. Nor the all-dreaded thunder-stone."

It is also alluded to in *Othello, v. 2:*—

" Are there no stones in **heaven,**
But what serve for the thunder ? "

122. *You are dull,* etc.—The commencement of this speech is a brilliant specimen of the blank verse of the original edition:—

" You are dull, Caska :
And those sparkes of Life, that should be in a Roman,
You doe want, or else you use not.
You looke pale, and gaze, and put on feare,
And cast your selfe in wonder,
To see," etc.

122. *Cast yourself in wonder.*—Does this mean *throw yourself into* a paroxysm of wonder? Or may *cast yourself* mean **cast** *your self*, or your mind, *about*, as in idle conjecture? The Commentators are mute. Shakespeare sometimes **has** *in* **where** we should now **use** *into*. In an earlier **stage** of the language, **the** distinction **now** established between *in* **and** *into* **was** constantly disregarded; and in some idiomatic expressions, **the** radical fibres of **a** national speech, **we still** have *in* used **to express** what is commonly and regularly **expressed by** *into*. *To fall in love* is a familiar **example. Perhaps** we continue to say *in love* as marking **more forcibly the** opposition to what **Julia in** the concluding line of *The Two Gentlemen of*

Verona calls *out of love*. The expression *cast yourself in wonder* seems to be most closely paralleled by another in *King Richard III.*, i. 3 :—" Clarence, whom I, indeed, have cast in darkness," as it stands in the First Folio, although the preceding Quartos (of which there were five, 1597, 1598, 1602, 1612 or 1613, 1622) have all "laid in darkness." We have another instance of Shakespeare's use of *in* where we should now say *into* in the familiar lines in *The Merchant of Venice*, v. 1 ;—

> "How sweet the moonlight sleeps upon this bank !
> Here we will sit, and let the sounds of music
> Creep in our ears."

122. *Why old men*, etc.—Blackstone's novel pointing of this passage is ingenious :—" Why old men fools" (*i. e.* why we have all these fires, etc., why we have old men fools). But the amendment is hardly required ; or, at any rate, it would not go far to give us a perfectly satisfactory text. Nor does there seem to be any necessity for assigning to *calculate* the singular sense of *prophesy* (which the expression adduced by Johnson, *to calculate a nativity*, is altogether insufficient to authorize). There is probably some corruption ; but the present line may be very well understood as meaning merely, why not only old men, but even fools and children, speculate upon the future ; or, still more simply, why all persons, old and young, and the foolish as well as the wise, take part in such speculating and prognosticating. Shakespeare may have been so far from thinking, with Blackstone, that it was something unnatural and prodigious for old men ever to be fools, that he has even designed to classify them with foolish persons generally, and with children, as specially disqualified for looking with any very deep insight into the future. And so doubtless they are apt to be, when very old.

122. *Unto some monstrous state.*—That is, I suppose,

some monstrous or unnatural state of things (not some overgrown commonwealth).

122. *And roars*, etc.—That is, roars in the Capitol as doth the lion. Many readers, I believe, go away with the notion that Cæsar is here compared by Cassius to some live lion that was kept in the Capitol. Or perhaps it may be sometimes imagined that he alludes to the same lion which Casca (though not in his hearing) has just been telling Cicero that he had met "against the Capitol." —The Second and two following Folios have *tears* for roars. Mr Collier, however, prints *roars*, although it is not stated that that word is restored by his MS. annotator.

122. *No mightier than thyself, or me.*—Of course, in strict grammar it should be *than I*. But the personal pronouns must be held to be, in some measure, emancipated from the dominion or tyranny of syntax. Who would rectify even Shelley's bold

> "lest there be
> No solace left for *thou* and me?"

The grammatical law has so slight a hold that a mere point of euphony is deemed sufficient to justify the neglect of it.

As we have *me* for *I* in the present passage, we have *I* for *me* in Antonio's "All debts are cleared between you and I" (*Merchant of Venice, iii.* 2). Other examples of the same irregularity are the following:—

> "Which none but Heaven, and you and I, shall hear."
> *King John, i.* 1.

> "Which none may hear but she and thou."
> *Coleridge, Day Dream.*

In both these passages *but* can only be the preposition. So where Corin, in his conversation with Touchstone, in *As You Like It, iii.* 2, says, "You told me you salute not at the court but you kiss your hands," he does not mean that there is no saluting at court, only kissing of hands, but that people never salute without kissing hands. There ought to be no comma after *court*. The form of phrase is the same that we have afterwards in *iii.* 5 :—

> "The common **executioner** . . .
> Falls not the axe upon the humbled **neck**
> But first begs pardon;"—

that is, without first asking pardon.

·124. ***Let it*** *be who it is*.—Not who it *may be;* Cassius, in his **present** mood, is above that subterfuge. While he abstains from pronouncing **the name,** he will not allow it to be supposed that there is **any doubt** about the actual existence of the man **he has** been describing.

124. *Thews and limbs*.—The common signification of the word *thews* in our old writers is manners, or qualities of mind and disposition. This is the sense in which it is always used both by Chaucer and by Spenser. It is also the only sense of the Original English *theaw*. And even at a comparatively late date any other **sense seems to** have been felt to be strange. The editors **of the Third** and Fourth Folios (1664 **and** 1685) substitute *sinews* in the present passage. Pope, on the other **hand,** retaining, or restoring, *thews*, explains **it as meaning** here *manners or* **capacities.** But, even **if the true** meaning of the word **were** disputable in this passage **considered** by itself, the **other instances** of **its use by** Shakespeare would clearly **show what sense he attached** to it. They are only two. "Care I," says Falstaff, **in the** *Second Part of King Henry IV., iii.* 2, "for the limb, the *thews,* the **stature,** bulk, and big assemblance **of a** man? Give me the spirit, **Master Shallow."** And exactly in the same **way** it is used by Laertes in *Hamlet, i.* 3 :—

> "For nature, crescent, does not grow alone
> In *thews* and bulk; but, as this temple waxes,
> The inward service of the mind and soul
> Grows wide withal."

In all the three passages by *thews* Shakespeare means unquestionably brawn, nerves, muscular vigour. And to this sense, and this only, the word has now settled down; the other sense, which was formerly so familiar in our literature, is quite gone out and forgotten. Shakespeare's use of it had probably been always common in the popular language. There appear in fact to have been two Original English words, *theaw* and *theow*, the latter the original of our modern *thigh* and also of Shakespeare's *thew*. It is preserved, too, in the Scottish *thowless*, meaning feeble or sinewless. Only one or two instances, however, have been discovered of the word being used by any other English writer before Shakespeare in his sense of it. One is given by Nares from George Turbervile, who, in his translation of *Ovid's Epistles*, first printed in 1567, has "the *thews* of Helen's passing [that is, surpassing] form." In the earlier version of *Layamon's Brut*, also, which belongs to the end of the twelfth century, we have in one place (*verse* 6361), " Monnene strengest of maine and of *theawe* of alle thissere theode" (of men strongest of main, or strength, and of sinew, of all this land). But Sir Frederic Madden remarks (III. 471) :—"This is the only instance in the poem of the word being applied to bodily qualities, nor has any other passage of an earlier date than the sixteenth century been found in which it is so used." It may be conjectured that it had only been a provincial word in this sense, till Shakespeare adopted it.

124. *But, woe the while!*—This, I believe, is commonly understood to mean, alas for the present time; but may not the meaning, here at least, rather be, alas for what hath come to pass in the mean while, or in the interval that has elapsed since the better days of our heroic ancestors?

124. *And we are governed with.*—We now commonly employ *by* to denote agency, and *with* where there is only instrumentality; but that distinction was not formerly so

fully established, and *with* was used more frequently than it is with us. Shakespeare even has (*Rich. II.*, *iii.* 3) "I live *with* bread like you, feel want, taste **grief.**"

125. *I know where I will wear this dagger, then.*—The true meaning of this line is ruined by its being printed, as it is in the old, and also in most of the modern editions, without the comma. Cassius does not intend to be understood as intimating that he is prepared to plunge his dagger into his heart at that *time*, but in that *case*.

126. *Can be retentive to.*—Can retain or confine the spirit.

126. *If I know this*, etc.—The logical connexion of "If I know this" is with "That part of tyranny," etc.; but there is also a rhetorical connexion with "Know all the world besides." As if he had said, "Knowing this, I can shake off, etc.; and, I knowing this, let all others too know and be aware that I can," etc.

127. *The power to cancel*, etc.—Here, it will be observed, we have *power* reduced to a monosyllable, although it had been employed as a dissyllable only five lines before, "Never lacks power," etc.

128. *He were no lion*, etc.—His imagination is still filled with the image by which he has already pictured the tyranny of the Dictator;—"roars, as doth the lion, in the Capitol."—*Hind*, a she stag, is correctly formed from the Original English *hinde*, of the same meaning; our other *hind*, a peasant, was originally *hine* and *hina*, and has taken the *d* only for the sake of a fuller or firmer enunciation. It may be noted, however, that, although there is a natural tendency in certain syllables to seek this addition of breadth or strength, it is most apt to operate when it is aided, as here, by the existence of some other word or form to which the *d* properly belongs. Thus, *soun* (from *sonner* and *sono*) has probably been the more easily converted into *sound* from having become confounded in the popular ear and understanding with

the adjective *sound* and the verb *to sound*, meaning to search; and such obsolete or dialectic forms as *drownd* and *swound* (for *drown* and *swoon*) may be supposed to have been the more readily produced through the misleading influence of the parts of the verb which actually and properly end in *d* or *ed*. As we have confounded the old *hinde* and *hine*, so we have also the Original English *herd*, or *heord*, meaning a flock or crowd (the modern German *heerde*), with *hyrd*, meaning a keeper or tender (the modern German *hirt*); our one form for both being now *herd*.

128. *My answer must be made.*—I must answer for what I have said.

129. *To such a man, That is,* etc.—*Vid.* 57.—To *fleer* (or *flear*, as is the old spelling) is to mock, or laugh at. The word appears to have come to us from the Norse or Scandinavian branch of the Gothic,—one of the roots of our English tongue which recent philology has almost abjured, although, besides all else, we owe to it even forms of such perpetual occurrence as the *are* of the substantive verb and the ordinary sign of our modern genitive (for such a use of the preposition *of*, common to us with the Swedish, is unknown to the classical English of the times before the Norman Conquest, although we have it in full activity, probably adopted from the popular speech of the northern counties, in the written language of the twelfth century).

129. *Hold, my hand.*—That is, Have, receive, take hold (of it); there is my hand. The comma is distinctly marked in the early editions.

129. *Be factious for redress of all these griefs.*—Here *factious* seems to mean nothing more than active or urgent, although everywhere else, I believe, in Shakespeare the word is used in the same disreputable sense which it has at present. *Griefs* (the form still used in the French language, and retained in our own with another meaning)

is his by far more common word for what we now call *grievances*, although he has that form too occasionally (which Milton nowhere employs). *Vid.* **436**.

130. *To undergo, with me, an enterprise.*—We should now rather say to *undertake* where there is anything to **be done**.

130. *Of honourable-dangerous.*—These two words were probably intended to make a compound adjective, although the hyphen with which they are connected by most of the modern editors is not in the oldest printed text. The language does **not now, at least** in serious composition, indulge in compounds of this description. Shakespeare, **however, has** apparently several such. Thus:—

"More active-valiant, or more valiant-young."
1 Hen. IV., v. 1.

"But pardon me, I am too sudden-bold."
Love's Lab. Lost, ii. 1.

"More fertile-fresh than all the field to see."
Mer. W. of Wind., v. 5.

"So full of shapes is fancy,
That it alone is high-fantastical."—
Twelfth Night, i. 1.

130. *By this they stay for me.*—That is, by this time. And it is a mode of expression which, like so many others which the language once possessed, we have now lost. Yet we still say, in the same sense, ere *this*, before *this*, after *this*, the preposition **in** these phrases being felt to be suggestive of the notion of time in a way that *by* is not.

130. *There is no . . . walking.*—In another connexion **this might** mean, that there was no possibility of walking; but here the meaning apparently is that there was no walking going on.

130. *The complexion of the element.*—That is, of the **heaven**, of the sky. North, in **his** *Plutarch*, speaks of "the fires **in** the element." The word in this sense was much in favour with the fine writers or talkers of Shake-

speare's day. He has a hit at the affectation in his *Twelfth Night*, iii. 1, where the Clown, conversing with Viola, says, "Who you are, and what you would, are out of my welkin: I might say, element: but the word is overworn." Of course, *welkin* is, and is intended to be, far more absurd. Yet we have *element* for the sky or the air in other passages besides the present. Thus:—

"The element itself, ...
Shall not behold her face at ample view."
Twelfth Night, i. 1.

" I, in the clear sky of fame, o'ershine you as much as the full moon doth the cinders of the element, which show like pins' heads to her" (*Falstaff*, in 2 *Hen. IV*., iv. 3).

It is curious to find writers of the present day who are scrupulous about the more delicate proprieties of expression still echoing Shakespeare's dissatisfaction: "The territorial *element*, to use that favourite word," says Hallam, *Mid. Ages*, I. 297 (*edit.* of 1855), probably without any thought of the remark of the all-observing dramatist two centuries and a half before.

130. *In favour's like the work.*—The reading in all the Folios is "Is favors" (or "favours" for the Third and Fourth). The present reading, which is that generally adopted, was first proposed by Johnson; and it has the support, it seems, of Mr Collier's *MS*. annotator. *Favour*, as we have seen (*vid.* 54), means aspect, appearance, features. Another emendation that has been proposed (by Steevens) is "Is favoured." But to say that the complexion of a thing is either featured like, or in feature like, to something else is very like a tautology. I should be strongly inclined to adopt Reed's ingenious conjecture, "Is feverous," which he supports by quoting from *Macbeth*, ii. 3, "Some say the earth Was feverous and did shake." So also in *Coriolanus*, i. 4 ;—" Thou mad'st thine enemies shake, as if the world Were feverous and did tremble." *Feverous* is exactly the sort of word that, if

not very distinctly written, would be apt to puzzle and be mistaken by a compositor. It may perhaps count, too, for something, though not very much, against both "favour's like" and "favoured like" that a very decided comma separates the two words in the original edition.

134. *One incorporate To our attempts.*—One of our body, one united with us in our enterprise. The expression has probably no more emphatic import.

135. *There's two or three.*—The contraction *there's* is still used indifferently with a singular or a plural; though *there is* scarcely would be.

136. *Am I not staid for?*—This is the original reading, which has been restored by Mr Knight. The common modern reading is, "Am I not staid for, Cinna?" the last word being inserted (and that without notice, which is unpardonable) only to satisfy the supposed demands of the prosody.

137. This speech stands thus in the First Folio:—

"Yes, you are. O Cassius,
If you could but winne the Noble Brutus
To our party—."

The common metrical arrangement is:—

"Yes,
You are. O Cassius, if you could but win
The noble Brutus to our party."

No person either having or believing himself to have a true feeling of the Shakespearian rhythm can believe this to be right. Nor am I better satisfied with Mr Knight's distribution of the lines, although it is adopted by Mr Collier:—

" Yes, you are.
O, Cassius, if you could but win the noble Brutus,
To our party;"

which gives us an extended line equally unmusical and undignified whether read rapidly or slowly, followed (to make matters worse which were bad enough already) by what could scarcely make the commencement of any kind of line. I cannot doubt that, whatever we are to do with "Yes, you are,"—whether we make these comparatively unimportant words the completion of the line of which Cassius's question forms the beginning, or take them along with what follows, which would give us a line wanting only the first syllable (and deriving, perhaps, from that mutilation an abruptness suitable to the occasion)— the close of the rhythmic flow must be as I have given it:—

"O Cassius, if you could
But win the noble Brutus to our party."

138. *Where Brutus may but find it.*—If *but* be the true word (and be not a misprint for *best*), the meaning must be, Be sure you lay it in the prætor's chair, *only* taking care to place it so that Brutus may be sure to find it.

138. *Upon old Brutus' statue.*—Lucius Brutus, who expelled the Tarquins, the reputed ancestor of Marcus Lucius Brutus; also alluded to in 56, "There was a Brutus once," etc.

139. *I will hie.*—To *hie* (meaning to hasten) is used reflectively, as well as intransitively, but not otherwise as an active verb. Its root appears to be the Original English *hyge*, meaning mind, study, earnest application; whence the various verbal forms *hyggan*, *hygian*, *hiegan*, *higgan*, *higian*, *hogian*, *hugian*, and perhaps others. *Hug* is probably another modern derivative from the same root.

139. *And so bestow these papers.*—This use of *bestow* (for to place, or dispose of) is now gone out; though something of it still remains in *stow*.

140. *Pompey's theatre.*—The same famous structure of Pompey's, opened with shows and games of unparalleled cost and magnificence some ten or twelve years before the present date, which has been alluded to in 130 and 138.

142. *You have right well conceited.*—To *conceit* is an-

other form of our still familiar to *conceive*. And the noun *conceit*, which survives with a limited meaning (the conception of a man by himself, which is so apt to be one of over-estimation), is also frequent in Shakespeare with the **sense**, nearly, of what we now call *conception*, in general. So in 349. Sometimes **it is** used in a sense which might almost be said to be the opposite of what it now means; **as** when Juliet (in *Romeo and Juliet, ii. 5*) employs **it as** the term to denote her all-absorbing affection for Romeo:—

> " Conceit, more rich **in matter than in** words,
> Brags of his substance, not of **ornament**:
> They are but beggars that can count their worth;
> But my true love is grown to such excess,
> I cannot sum the sum of half my wealth."

Or as when Gratiano, in *The Merchant of Venice, i.* 1, speaks of a sort of men who

> "do a wilful stillness entertain,
> With purpose to be dressed in an opinion
> Of wisdom, gravity, profound conceit"—

that is, deep **thought**.

So, again, when **Rosaline, in** *Love's Labour's Lost, ii.* 1, speaking of Biron, describes **his " fair tongue "** as " **conceit's** expositor," all that she **means is** that speech is the expounder of thought. **The** scriptural expression, still in familiar use, " wise **in his** own conceit " means merely wise **in his** own thought, **or in his** own eyes, as we are told **in** the margin the Hebrew literally signifies. In the New Testament, where we have " in their own conceits," **the** Greek is simply παρ' ἑαυτοῖς (in or with themselves).

ACT II.

SCENE I.—*The same.* BRUTUS'S *Orchard.*
Enter BRUTUS.

143. *Bru.* What, Lucius! ho!
I cannot, by the progress of the stars,

Give guess how near to day.—Lucius, I say!—
I would it were my fault to sleep so soundly.—
When, Lucius? when? Awake, I say: What, Lucius!

Enter LUCIUS.

  Luc. Called you, my Lord?
  Bru. Get me a taper in my study, Lucius:
When it is lighted, come and call me here.
  Luc. I will, my lord.   [*Exit.*

147. *Bru.* It must be by his death: and, for my part,
I know no personal cause to spurn at him,
But for the general. He would be crowned:—
How that might change his nature, there's the question.
It is the bright day that brings forth the adder;
And that craves wary walking. Crown him?—That;—
And then, I grant, we put a sting in him,
That at his will he may do danger with.
The abuse of greatness is, when it disjoins
Remorse from power; and, to speak truth of Cæsar,
I have not known when his affections swayed
More than his reason. But 'tis a common proof,
That lowliness is young ambition's ladder,
Whereto the climber upward turns his face:
But when he once attains the upmost round,
He then unto the ladder turns his back,
Looks in the clouds, scorning the base degrees
By which he did ascend. So Cæsar may.
Then, lest he may, prevent. And, since the quarrel
Will bear no colour for the thing he is,
Fashion it thus; that what he is, augmented,
Would run to these and these extremities:
And therefore think him as a serpent's egg,
Which, hatched, would, as his kind, grow mischievous;
And kill him in the shell.

Re-enter LUCIUS.

148. *Luc.* The taper burneth in your closet, Sir.
Searching the window for a flint, I found
This paper, thus sealed up; and, I am sure,
It did not lie there when I went to bed. [*Gives him the letter.*
149. *Bru.* Get you to bed again; it is not day.
Is not to-morrow, boy, the ides of March?
  Luc. I know not, Sir.
  Bru. Look in the calendar, and bring me word.

Luc. I will, Sir. [*Exit.*

153. *Bru.* The exhalations, whizzing in the air,
Give so much light, that I may read by them.
[*Opens the letter, and reads.*
" Brutus, *thou sleep'st ; awake, and see thyself.*
Shall Rome, &c. *Speak, strike,* redress *!"* —
Brutus, thou sleep'st ; awake.
Such instigations have been often dropped
Where I have took them up.
Shall Rome, &c. Thus must I piece it out :—
Shall Rome stand under one man's awe ? What ! Rome ?
My ancestors did from the streets of Rome
The Tarquin drive, when he was called a king.
Speak, strike, redress !
Am I entreated
To speak, and strike? O Rome! I make thee promise,
If the redress will follow, thou receivest
Thy full petition at the hand of Brutus.

Re-enter LUCIUS.

154. *Luc.* Sir, March is wasted fourteen days. [*Knock within.*
155. *Bru.* 'Tis good. Go to the gate ; somebody knocks.
[*Exit* LUCIUS.
Since Cassius first did whet me against Cæsar,
I have not slept.
Between the acting of a dreadful thing
And the first motion, all the interim is
Like a phantasma, or a hideous dream :
The genius, and the mortal instruments,
Are then in council ; and the state of a man,
Like to a little kingdom, suffers then
The nature of an insurrection.

Re-enter LUCIUS.

156. *Luc.* Sir, 'tis your brother Cassius at the door,
Who doth desire to see you.
Bru. Is he alone ?
158. *Luc.* No, Sir, there are moe with him.
Bru. Do you know them ?
160. *Luc.* No, Sir ; their hats are pluckt about their ears,
And half their faces buried in their cloaks,
That by no means I may discover them
By any mark of favour.
161. *Bru.* Let 'em enter. [*Exit* LUCIUS

They are the faction. O Conspiracy!
Sham'st thou to show thy dangerous brow by night,
When evils are most free! O, then, by day,
Where wilt thou find a cavern dark enough
To mask thy monstrous visage? Seek none, Conspiracy;
Hide it in smiles, and affability :
For, if thou path, thy native semblance on,
Not Erebus itself were dim enough
To hide thee from prevention.

Enter CASSIUS, CASCA, DECIUS, CINNA, METELLUS CIMBER, *and* TREBONIUS.

162. *Cas.* I think we are too bold upon your rest :
Good morrow, Brutus; Do we trouble you?
  Bru. I have been up this hour; awake, all night.
Know I these men that come along with you?
  Cas. Yes, every man of them; and no man here
But honours you; and every one doth wish
You had but that opinion of yourself
Which every noble Roman bears of you.
This is Trebonius.
  Bru. He is welcome hither.
  Cas. This, Decius Brutus.
  Bru. He is welcome too.
168. *Cas.* This, Casca; this, Cinna; and this, Metellus Cimber.
  Bru. They are all welcome.
What watchful cares do interpose themselves
Betwixt your eyes and night?
  Cas. Shall I entreat a word?   [*They whisper.*
  Dec. Here lies the east : Doth not the day break here?
  Casca. No.
173. *Cin.* O, pardon, Sir, it doth; and yon grey lines,
That fret the clouds, are messengers of day.
174. *Casca.* You shall confess, that you are both deceived.
Here, as I point my sword, the sun arises;
Which is a great way growing on the **south**,
Weighing the youthful season of the year.
Some two months hence, **up** higher toward **the north**
He first presents his fire; **and the high east**
Stands, as the Capitol, directly **here**.
175. *Bru.* Give me your hands all over, **one by one.**
  Cas. And let us swear our resolution.
177. *Bru.* No, not an oath : If not the face of men,

The sufferance of our souls, the time's abuse,—
If these be motives weak, break off betimes,
And every man hence to his idle bed;
So let high-sighted tyranny range **on**,
Till each man drop by lottery. But if these,
As I am sure they do, bear fire enough
To kindle cowards, and to steel with valour
The melting spirits of women; then, countrymen,
What need we any spur, **but our own cause,**
To prick us to redress? **what other** bond,
Than secret Romans, that have spoke the word,
And will not palter? And what other oath,
Than honesty to honesty engaged
That this shall be, or we will fall for it?
Swear priests, and cowards, and men cautelous,
Old feeble carrions, and such suffering souls
That welcome wrongs; unto bad causes swear
Such creatures as men doubt: but do not stain
The even virtue of our enterprise,
Nor the insuppressive mettle of our spirits,
To think that or our cause or our performance
Did need an oath; when every drop of blood,
That every Roman bears, and nobly bears,
Is guilty of a several bastardy,
If he do break the smallest particle
Of any promise that hath passed from him.

178. *Cas.* But what **of Cicero**? Shall we sound him?
I think, **he will stand very** strong with us.
  Casca. Let us not leave him out.
  Cin. No, by no means.

181. *Met.* O let us have him; **for his silver hairs**
Will purchase us a good opinion,
And **buy men's** voices to commend our deeds:
It shall be said, his judgment ruled our hands;
Our youths, and wildness, shall no whit appear,
But **all be** buried in his gravity.

182. *Bru.* O, **name** him not; let us not break with him;
For **he will never** follow anything
That other men begin.
  Cas. Then leave him out.
  Casca. Indeed, he **is not fit.**
  Dec. **Shall** no man **else be** touched but only Cæsar?

186. *Cas.* **Decius,** well urged:—I think it is not meet,

Mark Antony, so well beloved of Cæsar,
Should outlive Cæsar: We shall find of him
A shrewd contriver; and, you know, his means,
If he improve them, may well stretch so far
As to annoy us all: which to prevent,
Let Antony and Cæsar fall together.

187. *Bru.* Our course will seem too bloody, Caius Cassius,
To cut the head off, and then hack the limbs,
Like wrath in death, and envy afterwards:
For Antony is but a limb of Cæsar.
Let us be sacrificers, but not butchers, Caius.
We all stand up against the spirit of Cæsar;
And in the spirit of men there is no blood:
O, that we then could come by Cæsar's spirit,
And not dismember Cæsar! But, alas,
Cæsar must bleed for it! And, gentle friends,
Let's kill him boldly, but not wrathfully;
Let's carve him as a dish fit for the gods,
Not hew him as a carcass fit for hounds:
And let our hearts, as subtle masters do,
Stir up their servants to an act of rage,
And after seem to chide 'em. This shall mark
Our purpose necessary, and not envious:
Which so appearing to the common eyes,
We shall be called purgers, not murderers.
And for Mark Antony, think not of him;
For he can do no more than Cæsar's arm
When Cæsar's head is off.

188. *Cas.* Yet I do fear him.
For in the ingrafted love he bears to Cæsar,——

189. *Bru.* Alas, good Cassius, do not think of him:
If he love Cæsar, all that he can do
Is to himself, take thought, and die for Cæsar:
And that were much he should; for he is given
To sports, to wildness, and much company.

190. *Treb.* There is no fear in him; let him not die;
For he will live, and laugh at this hereafter.   [*Clock strikes.*
   Bru. Peace, count the clock.

192. *Cas.* The clock hath stricken three.
   Treb. 'Tis time to part.

194. *Cas.* But it is doubtful yet
Whether Cæsar will come forth to-day or no:
For he is superstitious grown of late;

Quite from the main opinion he held once
Of fantasy, of dreams, and **ceremonies**;
It may be, these apparent prodigies,
The unaccustomed **terror** of this night,
And **the persuasion** of his augurers,
May **hold him from** the Capitol to-day.

195. *Dec.* Never fear that: If he **be so resolved,**
I can o'ersway **him**: for he loves to hear
That unicorns may be betrayed with trees,
And bears with glasses, elephants with holes,
Lions with toils, and men with flatterers;
But, when I tell him he hates flatterers,
He says he does; **being then most flattered.**
Let me work:
For I can give his humour the **true bent;**
And I will bring him to **the Capitol.**
  Cas. **Nay,** we will all **of us be** there to fetch him.

197. *Bru.* **By the** eighth hour: **Is** that the uttermost?
  Cin. **Be that** the uttermost, and fail not then.

199. *Met.* Caius Ligarius doth bear Cæsar hard,
Who rated him for speaking well of Pompey;
I wonder none of you have thought of him.

200. *Bru.* Now, good Metellus, go along by him:
He loves me well, and I have given him reasons;
Send him but hither, and I'll fashion him.

201. *Cas.* The morning comes upon us: **We'll leave you, Brutus:—**
And, friends, disperse yourselves: **but all remember**
What you have said, **and show yourselves true Romans.**

202. *Bru.* **Good gentlemen, look fresh and merrily;**
Let not our looks put on our purposes:
But bear it as our Roman actors do,
With untired spirits, **and** formal constancy:
And so, good morrow to you every one. [*Exeunt all but* BRUTUS.
Boy! Lucius!—Fast asleep? It is no matter;
Enjoy the heavy honey-dew of slumber:
Thou **hast** no figures, nor no fantasies,
Which busy care draws in the brains of men;
Therefore thou sleep'st **so sound.**

  Enter PORTIA.

  Por. Brutus, my lord!
  Bru. Portia, what mean you? Wherefore rise you now?
It is not for your health, thus to commit

Your weak condition to the raw-cold morning.
205. *Por.* Nor for yours neither. You've ungently, Brutus,
Stole from my bed: And yesternight, at supper,
You suddenly arose, and walked about,
Musing, and sighing, with your arms across:
And, when I asked you what the matter was,
You stared upon me with ungentle looks:
I urged you further; then you scratched your head,
And too impatiently stamped with your foot:
Yet I insisted, yet you answered not;
But, with an angry wafture of your hand,
Gave sign for me to leave you: So I did;
Fearing to strengthen that impatience,
Which seemed too much enkindled; and, withal,
Hoping it was but an effect of humour,
Which sometime hath his hour with every man.
It will not let you eat, nor talk, nor sleep;
And, could it work so much upon your shape,
As it hath much prevailed on your condition,
I should not know you, Brutus. Dear my lord,
Make me acquainted with your cause of grief.
    Bru. I am not well in health, and that is all.
    Por. Brutus is wise, and, were he not in health,
He would embrace the means to come by it.
    Bru. Why, so I do.—Good Portia, go to bed.
209. *Por.* Is Brutus sick? and is it physical
To walk unbraced, and suck up the humours
Of the dank morning? What, is Brutus sick;
And will he steal out of his wholesome bed,
To dare the vile contagion of the night?
And tempt the rheumy and unpurged air
To add unto his sickness? No, my Brutus;
You have some sick offence within your mind,
Which, by the right and virtue of my place,
I ought to know of: And, upon my knees,
I charm you, by my once commended beauty,
By all your vows of love, and that great vow,
Which did incorporate and make us one,
That you unfold to me, yourself, your half,
Why you are heavy; and what men to-night
Have had resort to you: for here have been
Some six or seven, who did hide their faces
Even from darkness.

  Bru. Kneel not, gentle Portia.
211. *Por.* I should not need, if you were gentle Brutus.
Within the bond of marriage, tell me, Brutus,
Is it excepted, **I should** know no secrets
That appertain to you? Am I yourself
But, **as** it **were, in** sort, or limitation;
To keep with you at meals, comfort your bed,
And talk to you sometimes? Dwell I but in the suburbs
Of your good pleasure? If it be no more,
Portia is Brutus' harlot, not his wife.
  Bru. You are my true and honourable wife;
As dear to me as are the ruddy drops
That visit my sad heart.
213. *Por.* If this were true, then should I know this secret.
I grant, I am a woman; but, withal,
A woman that lord Brutus took to wife:
I grant, I am a woman; but, withal,
A woman well reputed; Cato's daughter.
Think you, I am no stronger than my sex,
Being so fathered, and so husbanded?
Tell me your counsels, I will not disclose 'em:
I have made strong proof of my constancy,
Giving myself a voluntary wound
Here, in the thigh: Can I bear that with patience,
And not my husband's secrets?
214. *Bru.* O ye gods,
Render me **worthy of this** noble **wife!**   [*Knocking within.*
Hark, **hark!** one knocks: Portia, go **in a while**;
And by and by thy **bosom shall partake**
The secrets of my heart.
All my engagements I will construe to thee,
All the charactery of my sad brows:—
Leave me with haste.   [*Exit* PORTIA.

    Enter LUCIUS *and* LIGARIUS.

Lucius, who's that, knocks?
  Luc. Here is a sick man, that would speak with you.
  Bru. Caius Ligarius, that Metellus spake of.—
Boy, stand aside.—Caius Ligarius! how?
217. *Lig.* Vouchsafe good-morrow from a feeble tongue.
218. *Bru.* O, what a **time have you chose out,** brave Caius,
To wear **a kerchief?** Would you were not sick!
  Lig. I am not sick, if Brutus have in hand

Any exploit worthy the name of honour.
  Bru. Such an exploit have I in hand, Ligarius,
Had you a healthful ear to hear of it.
221. *Lig.* By all the gods that Romans bow before
I here discard my sickness. Soul of Rome!
Brave son, derived from honourable loins!
Thou, like an exorcist, hast conjured up
My mortified spirit. Now bid me run,
And I will strive with things impossible,
Yea, get the better of them. What's to do?
  Bru. A piece of work that will make sick men whole.
  Lig. But are not some whole, that we must make sick?
224. *Bru.* That must we also. What it is, my Caius,
I shall unfold to thee, as we are going
To whom it must be done.
225. *Lig.* Set on your foot;
And, with a heart new-fired, I follow you,
To do I know not what: but it sufficeth,
That Brutus leads me on.
  Bru. Follow me then.   [*Exeunt.*

Scene I.—The heading here in the Folios (in which there is no division into Scenes), is merely "*Enter Brutus in his Orchard.*" Assuming that Brutus was probably not possessed of what we now call distinctively an orchard (which may have been the case), the modern editors of the earlier part of the last century took upon them to change *Orchard* into *Garden.* But this is to carry the work of rectification (even if we should admit it to be such) beyond what is warrantable. To deprive Brutus in this way of his orchard was to mutilate or alter Shakespeare's conception. It is probable that the words *Orchard* and *Garden* were commonly understood in the early part of the seventeenth century in the senses which they now bear; but there is nothing in their etymology to support the manner in which they have come to be distinguished. In *Much Ado About Nothing,* ii. 3, although the scene is headed "*Leonato's Garden,*" Benedick, sending the Boy for a book from his chamber-window, says, "Bring it hither to me in the orchard." A *Garden* (or *yard*, as it is still called in Scotland) means merely a piece of ground girded in or enclosed; and an *Orchard* (properly *Ortyard*) is, literally, such an enclosure for *worts*, or herbs. At one time *Orchard* used to be written *Hortyard*, under the mistaken notion that it was derived from *hortus* (which may, however, be of the same stock).

143. *How near to day.*—How near it may be to the day.

143. *I would it were my fault.*—Compare the use of *fault* here with its sense in 120.

143. *When, Lucius? when?*—This exclamation had not formerly the high tragic or heroic sound which it would now have. It was merely a customary way of calling impatiently to one who had not obeyed a previous **summons**. So in *Richard the Second* (i. 2) John of Gaunt calls to his son—"When, Harry? when? Obedience bids, I should not bid again."

147. *But for the general.*—The *general* was formerly a common expression for what we now call the community or the people. Thus Angelo in *Measure for Measure*, ii. 4:—

> "The general, subject to a well-wished king,
> Quit their own part, and in obsequious fondness
> Crowd to his presence."

147. *And that craves.*—It might be questioned whether *that* here be the demonstrative (as it is commonly considered) or the relative (to the antecedent "the bright day").

147. *Crown him? That.*—Here the emphatic *that* appears to be used exactly as *so* (etymologically of the same import) often is. *Vid.* 57. Either, or any equivalent term, thus used, might obviously serve very well for the sign of affirmation; in the present passage we might substitute *yes* for *that* with the same effect. It used to be held that the French *oui*, anciently *oyl*, was merely the

ill of the classic *ill-e*, *ill-a*, *ill-ud*, and that the old Provençal *oc* was *hoc*. It appears however, that *oui* or *oyl* is really *voul* (or *je voul*), the old present of *vouloir*. The common word for *yes* in Italian, again, *si* (not unknown in the same sense to the French tongue), may be another form of *so*. The three languages used to be distinguished as the *Langue d'Oyl* (or *Lingua Oytana*), the *Langue d'Oc* (or *Lingua Occitana*), and the *Lingua di Si*.—The pointing in the First Folio here is "Crowne him that, And then," etc.

147. *Do danger.*—*Danger*, which we have borrowed from the French, is a corruption of the middle age Latin *domigerium*, formed from *damno*. It is, in fact, radically the same with *damage*. A detail of the variations of meaning which the word has undergone in both languages would make a long history. In French also it anciently bore the same sense (that of mischief) which it has here. Sometimes, again, in both languages, it signified power to do mischief or to injure; as when Portia, in *The Merchant of Venice* (iv. 1), speaking to Antonio of Shylock, says, "You stand within his danger, do you not?"

147. *The abuse of greatness is*, etc.—The meaning apparently is, "The abuse to which greatness is most subject is when it deadens in its possessor the natural sense of humanity, or of that which binds us to our kind; and this I do not say that it has yet done in the case of Cæsar; I have never known that in him selfish affection, or mere passion, has carried it over reason." *Remorse* is generally used by Shakespeare in a wider sense than that to which it is now restricted.

147. *But 'tis a common proof.*—A thing commonly proved or experienced (what commonly, as we should say, proves to be the case).

A frequent word with Shakespeare for *to prove* is *to approve*. Thus, in the *Two Gentlemen of Verona*, v. 4, we have—

> "O, 'tis the curse in love, and still approved,
> When women cannot love where they're beloved."

So, in *Much Ado About Nothing*, we have, in *iv.* 1, "an approved wanton," and afterwards "Is he not approved in the height a villain?" When Don Pedro in the same Play, *ii.* 1, describes Benedick as "of approved valour," the words cannot be understood as conveying any notion of what we now call approval, or approbation; the meaning is merely, that he had *proved* his valour by his conduct. This is, no doubt, also, the meaning of the word in the last verse of Sir Thomas Wyat's passionately earnest lines entitled "To his Mistress" (supposed to be Anne Boleyn):—

> "Forget not, then, thine own approved,
> The which so long hath thee so loved,
> Whose steadfast faith yet never moved;
> **Forget not** this!"

So in *Hamlet, i.* 1, Marcellus says, speaking of Horatio and the Ghost,—

> "——I have entreated him along
> With us to watch the minutes of this **night**,
> That, if again this apparition come,
> He may approve our eyes, and speak **to it**;"

that is, prove our eyes true. And in *Meas. for Meas., i.* 3, Claudio says,—

> "**This day my sister** should the cloister enter,
> And there receive her approbation"—

for what we now call *probation*. This sense of the word (which **we still** retain in the law-term an *approver*, in Latin *probator*) occurs repeatedly both in the Bible and in Milton, and in fact is the most common sense which it **has in** our earlier English. It is strange that it should not be noticed at all by Nares, and that the only reference for it in *Boucher* is in the following insertion by Stephenson:—"To bring proof of.—'Matabrun in likewise en-

devored her on the other syde to *approve* the said iniury
. . . bi hir commised and purpensed.'—*Heylas*, p. 27."

147. *Whereto the climber upward*, etc.—There is no hyphen in the original text connecting *climber* and *upward*, as there is in some modern editions; but any doubt as to whether the adverb should be taken along with *climber* or with *turns* might be held to be determined by the expression in *Macbeth*, *iv.* 2:—"Things at the worst will cease, or else climb upwards To what they were before."

147. *The upmost round.*—The step of a ladder has come to be called a *round*, I suppose, from its being usually cylindrically shaped. Mr Knight (whose collation of the old copies is in general so remarkably careful) has here (probably by a typographical error) *utmost*.

147. *The base degrees.*—The lower steps of the ladder —*les bas degrés* (from the Latin *gradus*) of the French. The epithet *base*, however, must be understood to express something of contempt, as well as to designate the position of the steps.

147. *By which he did ascend.*—It is not the syntax of our modern English to use the auxiliary verb in such a case as this. *Vid.* 16.

147. *Then, lest he may, prevent.*—We should not now say *to prevent lest*. But the word *prevent* continued to convey its original import of *to come before* more distinctly in Shakespeare's day than it does now. *Vid.* 161 and 709.

147. *Will bear no colour for the thing he is.*—Will take no shew, no plausibility, no appearance of being a just quarrel, if professed to be founded upon what Cæsar at present actually is. The use of *colour*, and *colourable*, in this sense is still familiar.

147. *What he is, augmented.*—What he now is, if augmented or heightened (as it is the nature of things that it should be).

147. *Would run to these*, etc.—To such and such ex-

tremities (which we must suppose to be stated and explained). *Vid.* 109.

147. *Think him as.*—The verb *to think* has now lost this sense, though we might still say "Think him a serpent's egg," "Think him good, or wicked," and also "To think a good or evil thought."

147. *As his kind.*—Like his species.

147. *And kill him in the shell.*—It is impossible not to feel the expressive effect of the hemistich here. The line itself is, as it were, killed in the shell.

148. This speech is headed in the Folios "*Enter Lucius.*" The old stage direction, "*Gives him the Letter,*" is omitted by most of the modern editors.

149. *The ides of March.*—The reading of all the ancient copies is "the *first* of March;" it was Theobald who first made the correction, which has been adopted by all succeeding editors (on the ground that the day was actually that of the ides). At the same time, it does not seem to be impossible that the poet may have intended to present a strong image of the absorption of Brutus by making him forget the true time of the month. The reply of Lucius after consulting the Calendar—" Sir, March is wasted fourteen days "—sounds very much as if he were correcting rather than confirming his master's notion. Against this view we have the considerations stated by Warburton:—" We can never suppose the speaker to have lost fourteen days in his account. He is here plainly ruminating on what the Soothsayer told Cæsar [*i.* 2] in his presence [*Beware the ides of March*]." Mr Collier also prints "the *ides;*" but the correction does not appear to be made by his MS. annotator. Mr Knight, I apprehend, must be mistaken in saying that Shakespeare found "the *first* of March" in North's *Plutarch:* the present incident is not, I believe, anywhere related by Plutarch.

153. *Brutus, thou sleep'st; awake.*—I have endeavour-

ed to indicate by the printing that the second enunciation of these words is a repetition by Brutus to himself, and not, as it is always made to appear, a further portion of the letter. The letter unquestionably concluded with the emphatic adjuration, "Speak, strike, redress!" It never, after this, would have proceeded to go over the ground again in the same words that had been already used. They would have only impaired the effect, and would have been quite inappropriate in their new place. We see how the speaker afterwards repeats in the like manner each of the other clauses before commenting upon it.

153. *Where I have took.*—*Vid.* 46.

153. *Speak, strike, redress!*—*Am I entreated,* etc.—The expression is certainly not strengthened by the *then* which was added to these words by Hanmer, in the notion that it was required by the prosody, and has been retained by Steevens and other modern editors. At the same time Mr Knight's doctrine, that "a pause, such as must be made after *redress,* stands in the place of a syllable," will, at any rate, not do here; for we should want two syllables after *redress.* The best way is to regard the supposed line as being in reality two hemistichs; or to treat the words repeated from the letter as no part of the verse. How otherwise are we to manage the preceding quotation, "Shall Rome, etc."?

153. *I make thee promise.*—I make promise to thee. In another connexion, the words might mean I make thee to promise. The Second Folio has "*the* promise." The heading that follows this speech, and also 155, in the First Folio is *Enter Lucius.*

153. *Thou receivest.*—Mr Collier prints *receiv'st,*—it is not apparent why.

154. *March is wasted fourteen days.*—In all the old editions it is *fifteen.* The correction was made by Theobald. *Vid.* 149. Mr Collier has also *fourteen;* but he does not here appear to have the authority of his MS. annotator.

—The heading which precedes is "*Enter Lucius*" in the original text.

155. *The genius and the mortal instruments.*—The commentators have written and disputed lavishly upon these celebrated words. Apparently, by the *genius* we are to understand the contriving and immortal mind, and most probably the *mortal instruments* are the earthly passions. The best light for the interpretation of the present passage is reflected from 186, where Brutus, advising with his fellow conspirators on the manner in which they should dispatch their mighty victim, not as blood-thirsty butchers, but as performing a sacrifice of which they lamented the necessity, says:—

"Let our hearts, as subtle masters do,
Stir up their servants to an act of rage,
And after seem to chide 'em."

The *servants* here may be taken to be the same with the *instruments* in the passage before us. It has been proposed to understand by the *mortal instruments* the bodily powers or organs; but it is not obvious how these could be said to hold consultation with the genius or mind. Neither could they in the other passage be so fitly said to be stirred up by the heart.

The bodily organs, however, seem to be distinctly designated the *instruments* and *agents*, in *Coriolanus*, *i.* 1, where, first, Menenius Agrippa says, in his apologue of the rebellion of the other members of the body against the belly,—

"The other instruments
Did see and hear, devise, instruct, walk, feel,
And, mutually participate, did minister
Unto the appetite and affection common
Of the whole body"—

and, shortly after, the Second Citizen asks,—

"The former agents, if they did complain,
What could the belly answer?"

So again, in *Macbeth*, *i.* 7:—

"I am settled, and bent up
Each corporal agent to this terrible feat."

We have, apparently, the word *Genius* used for the spirit or mind in what the Duke says, in *The Comedy of Errors*, *v.* 1, of the two Antipholuses and the two Dromios:—

"One of these men is genius to the other;
And so of these: which is the natural man,
And which the spirit?"

155. *And the state of a man.*—This is the original reading, in which the prosodical irregularity is nothing more than what frequently occurs. The common reading omits the article. There is certainly nothing gained in vividness of expression by so turning the concrete into the abstract. We have elsewhere, indeed, in *Macbeth*, *i.* 3, "My single state of man;" and Falstaff, in the *Second Part of Henry IV.*, *iv.* 4, speaks of "This little kingdom, man;" but in neither of these cases is the reference in the word *man* to an individual, as here.—The *Exit Lucius* attached to the first line of this speech is modern.

156. *Your brother Cassius.*—Cassius had married Junia, the sister of Brutus.

158. *No, Sir, there are moe with him.*—*Moe*, not *more*, is the word here and in other passages, not only in the First, but in all the Four Folios. It was probably the common form in the popular speech throughout the seventeenth century, as it still is in Scotland in the dialectic *meh'* (pronounced exactly as the English *may*). No confusion or ambiguity is produced in this case by the retention of the old word, of continual occurrence both in Chaucer and Spenser, such as makes it advisable to convert the *then*, which the original text of the Plays gives us after the comparative, into our modern *than*. In some cases, besides, the *moe* is absolutely required by the verse; as in Balthazar's Song in *Much Ado About Nothing* (*ii.* 3):— '

"Sing no more ditties, sing no moe,
    Or dumps so dull and heavy;
The frauds of men were ever so,
    Since summer first was leavy."

160. *Pluckt about their ears.* — Pulled down about their ears.

160. *By any mark of favour.*—That is, of feature or countenance. *Vid.* 54.

161. *When evils are most free!*—When evil things have most freedom.

161. *To mask thy monstrous visage?*—The only prosodical irregularity in this line is the common one of the one supernumerary short syllable (the *age* of *visage*). The two unaccented syllables which follow the fifth accented one have no effect.

161. *Hide it in smiles.*—This is the old reading, which Mr Knight has restored. He states that all the modern editions have *in it*.

161. *For, if thou path, thy native semblance on.*— Coleridge has declared himself convinced that we should here read "if thou *put* thy native semblance on;" and Mr Knight is inclined to agree with him, seeing that *putte* might be easily mistaken for *pathe*. If *path* be the word, the meaning must be, If thou go forth. *Path* is employed as a verb by Drayton, but not exactly in this sense: he speaks of pathing a passage, and pathing a way, that is, making or smoothing a passage or way. There is no comma or other point after *path* in the old copies.

161. *To hide thee from prevention.*—To prevent (præ-venire) is to come before, and so is equivalent in effect with to *hinder*, which is literally to make behind. I make that behind me which I get before.—The heading that follows is in the old copies;—" *Enter the Conspirators, Cassius, Casca, Decius, Cinna, Metellus, and Trebonius.*"

162. *We are too bold upon your rest.*—We intrude too boldly or unceremoniously upon your rest.

168. *This, Casca; this, Cinna;* etc.—I print this speech continuously, as it stands in the original edition, and as Mr Knight has also given it. It might perhaps be possible, by certain violent processes, to reduce it to the rude semblance of a line of verse, or to break it up, as has also been attempted, into something like a pair of hemistichs; but it is far better to regard it as never having been intended for verse at all, like many other brief utterances of the same level kind interspersed in this and all the other Plays.

173. *And yon grey lines.*—This is the reading of all the Folios. Why does Mr Collier print *yond'* ?

174. *Which is a great way*, etc.—The commentators, who flood us with their explanations of many easier passages, have not a word to say upon this. Casca means that the point of sunrise is as yet far to the south (of east), weighing (that is, taking into account, or on account of) the unadvanced period of the year. But is there not some allusion, which the look and tone of the speaker might express more clearly than his words, to the great act about to be performed in the Capitol, and the change, as of a new day, that was expected to follow it? Otherwise, it is difficult to understand the elaborate emphasis of the whole speech,—more especially the closing words—

"and the high east
Stands, as the Capitol, directly here."

175. *Give me your hands all over.*—That is, all included. The idiom is still common.

177. *If not the face of men.*—The commentators are all alive here, one proposing to read *fate* of men, another *faith* of men, another *faiths* (as nearer in sound to *face*). It is difficult to see much difficulty in the old reading, understood as meaning the looks of men. It is prefer-

able, at any rate, to anything which it has been proposed to substitute.

177. *The time's abuse.*—This, apparently, must be taken to mean the prevalence of abuse generally, all the abuses of the time.

177. *Hence to his idle bed.*—That is, bed of idleness, or in which he may lie doing nothing (not vacant or unoccupied bed, as some would understand it).

177. *So let high-sighted tyranny.*—High-looking, proud.—Some modern editions have *rage* instead of *range*, probably by an accidental misprint.

177. *Till each man drop by lottery.*—That is, probably, as if by chance, without any visible cause why he in particular should be struck down or taken off. It has been suggested, however, that there may be an allusion to the process of decimation.

177. *Than secret Romans.*—Romans bound to secrecy.

177. *And will not palter?*—To *palter* (perhaps etymologically connected with *falter*) means to shuffle, to equivocate, to act or speak unsteadily or dubiously with the intention to deceive. It is best explained by the well-known passage in *Macbeth* (*v.* 7):—

> "And be these juggling fiends no more believed,
> That palter with us in a double sense;
> That keep the word of promise to our ear,
> And break it to our hope."

177. *Or we will fall for it?*—Will die for it.

177. *Men cautelous.*—*Cautelous* is given to *cautels*, full of *cautels*. A *cautel*, from the Roman law-term *cautela* (a caution, or security), is mostly used in a discreditable sense by our old English writers. The caution has passed into cunning in their acceptation of the word;—it was natural that caution should be popularly so estimated;—and by *cautels* they commonly mean craftinesses, deceits. Thus we have in *Hamlet* (*i.* 3);—

"And now no soil nor cautel doth besmirch
The virtue of his will."

And in the passage before us *cautelous* is cautious and wary at least to the point of cowardice, if not to that of insidiousness and trickery.

177. *Old feeble carrions.*—*Carrions*, properly masses of dead and putrefying flesh, is a favourite term of contempt with Shakespeare.

177. *Such suffering souls*, etc.—See the note on *that gentleness as* in 44. In the present speech we have both the old and the new phraseology;—*such . . . that* in one line, and *such . . . as* in the next.—*Suffering souls* are patient, all-enduring souls.

177. *The even virtue of our enterprise.*—The *even virtue* is the firm and steady virtue. The *our* is emphatic.

177. *Nor the insuppressive mettle.*—The keenness and ardour incapable of being suppressed (however illegitimate such a form with that sense may be thought to be). So we have in *As You Like It* (*iii.* 2) "The fair, the chaste, and *unexpressive* she." And even Milton has (*Lycidas*, 176) "And hears the *unexpressive* nuptial song." —For *mettle* see 102.

177. *To think that.*—The easiest supplement, or filling up of the ellipsis, is, so as to think.

177. *Is guilty of a several bastardy.*—The etymology of the word *bastard* is uncertain. Shakespeare probably took his notion of what it radically expressed from the convertible phrase *base-born*. Thus, in *Lear*, *i.* 2, Edmund soliloquizes,—"Why bastard? Wherefore base?" By *a several bastardy* here is meant a special or distinct act of baseness, or of treason against ancestry and honourable birth. For *several* see 444.

178. *But what of Cicero?* etc.—Both the prosody and the sense direct us to lay the emphasis on *him*.

178. *He will stand very strong.*—He will take part with us decidedly and warmly.

181. *It shall be said, his judgment*, etc.—Dr **Guest**, in the paper " On English Verbs," in the Second Volume of the *Proceedings of the Philslogical Society*, which has been already referred to, adduces **some examples to show that the** primary sense of *shall* **is to owe. Hence the use of *should*** which is still **common in** the sense of ought. " **The use** of *shall* to denote future time," Dr Guest continues, " may be traced to a remote antiquity in our language; that of *will* is of much later origin, and prevailed chiefly in our northern dialects.—Writers, however, who paid much attention to their style **generally used** these terms with greater precision. The assertion of will or of duty seems **to** have been considered by them as implying **to** a certain extent the power to will or to impose a duty. As a **man has** power to will for himself only, it was only in the first person that the verb *will* could be used with this signification; and in the other persons it was left free to take that latitude of meaning which popular usage had given **to** it. Again, the power which overrides the will to impose a duty must proceed from **some** external agency; **and** consequently *shall* could **not be employed to** denote **such** power **in the first person. In the first person,** therefore, it **was left free to follow** the popular meaning, but in **the other two was tied to its** original and **more precise** signification. **These** distinctions still continue a shibboleth for the **natives of** the two sister kingdoms. Walter Scott, **as is well** known to his readers, **could never** thoroughly master the difficulty."

In the Third Edition of Dr Latham's *English Language*, pp. 470—474, **may** be found two other explanations; the first by the late Archdeacon Julius Charles **Hare** (from the *Cambridge Philological Museum*, II. 203), the second by Professor De Morgan (from the *Proceedings of the Philological Society*, IV. 185; No. 90, read 25th Jan. 1850).

The manner of using *shall* and *will* **which** is now so completely established in England, and which throughout the greater part of the country is so perfectly uniform among all classes, was as yet only growing up in the early part of the seventeenth century. This was very clearly shewn some years ago by a writer in *Blackwood's Magazine*, by comparing many passages of the authorized version of the Scriptures, published in 1611, with the same passages in the preceding translation, called *the Bishops' Bible*, which had appeared in 1568. The old use of *shall*, instead of *will*, to indicate simple futurity, with the 2nd and 3rd persons, as well as with the 1st, is still common with Shakespeare. Here, in this and the next line, are two instances:—" It shall be said;" "Shall no whit appear." So afterwards we have, in 187, "This shall mark our purpose necessary;" in 238, "Cæsar should be a beast without a heart;" in 351, "The enemies of Cæsar shall say this;" in 620, "The enemy, marching along by them, By them shall make a fuller number up." We have occasionally the same use of *shall* even in Clarendon:—" Whilst there are Courts in the world, emulation and ambition *will* be inseparable from them; and kings who have nothing to give *shall* be pressed to promise" (*Hist.*, Book xiii). In some rare instances the received text of Shakespeare gives us *will* where we should now use *shall;* as when Portia says, in *The Merchant of Venice, iii. 4*,

" I'll hold thee any wager,
When we are both accoutred like young men,
I'll prove the prettier fellow of the two."

But here we should probably read " *I* prove."

181. *Shall no whit appear.*—*Whit* is the Original English *wiht*, any thing that exists, a creature. It is the same word with *wight*, which we now use only for a man, in the same manner as we have come in the language of the present day to understand *creature* almost exclusively in the sense of a living creature, although it was formerly used freely for every thing created,—as when Bacon says (*Essay, Of Truth*), "The first creature of God, in the

works of the days, was the light of the sense; the last was the light of reason; and his Sabbath work ever **since** is the illumination of his spirit;" or (*Advance. of Learning*, B. *i.*), "The wit and mind of man, if it work upon matter, which is the contemplation of the creatures of **God, work**eth according to the stuff, and is limited thereby;" **or as it is** written **in** our authorized version of the Scriptures (1 ***Tim.*** *iv.* 4), "Every creature of God (πᾶν κτίσμα Θεοῦ) is good, and nothing to be refused, **if it** be received with thanksgiving." We have *creature* used in this extensive sense even by so late a writer as the Scotch metaphysician Dr Reid (who died **in** 1796), in his *Inquiry into the Human Mind, ch.* 1, first published in 1764:—"Conjec**tures** and theories are the creatures of men, and will **always be** found very unlike the creatures of God."—*No whit* is not anything, nowhat, not at all. And our modern *not* (anciently *nought*) is undoubtedly *no whit*:—how otherwise is the *t* to be accounted for? So that our English "I do *not* speak,"=I do *no whit* speak, is an exactly literal translation of the French *Je ne parle pas* (or *point*), which many people believe to contain **a double negative.**

182. *Let **us not break** with him.*—That is, Let us not break the matter to him. This is **the sense** in which the idiom *to break with* is most frequently **found** in Shakespeare. Thus, in *Much Ado About Nothing* (*i.* 1), the Prince, Don Pedro, **says to his** favourite Don Claudio, "**If thou** dost love fair Hero, cherish it; and I will break with her;" that is, I will open the matter to her. And again, in the same scene; "Then after to her father **will** I break." So in *The Two Gentlemen of Verona* (*iii.* **1**), "I am to break with thee of some affairs." **But when in** *The Merry Wives of Windsor* (*iii.* 2), Slender says **to** Ford, in answer to his invitation **to** dinner, "We have appointed to dine with Mistress **Anne, and I** would not break with her for more money than I'll speak of," he means he would not break his engagement with her. The

phrase is nowhere, I believe, used by Shakespeare in the only sense which it now bears, namely, to quarrel with.

186. *A shrewd contriver.* — The adjective *shrewd* is generally admitted to be connected with the substantive *shrew;* and according to Horne Tooke (*Div. of Purley,* 457-9), both are formations from the Original English verb *syrwan, syrewan,* or *syrewian,* meaning to vex, to molest, to cause mischief to, from which he also deduces *sorrow, sorry, sore,* and *sour.* Bosworth (who gives the additional forms *syrwian, syrwyan, searwian, searwan, searian, serian*), interprets the old verb as meaning to prepare, endeavour, strive, arm, to lay snares, entrap, take, bruise. A *shrew,* according to this notion, might be inferred to be one who vexes or molests; and *shrewd* will mean endowed with the qualities or disposition of a shrew. *Shrew,* as Tooke remarks, was formerly applied to a male as well as to a female. So, on the other hand, *paramour* and *lover,* now only used of males, were formerly also applied to females; and in some of the provincial dialects *villain* is still a common term of reproach for both sexes alike.

Both *to shrew* and *to beshrew* are used by our old writers in the sense of to curse, which latter verb, again (originally *cursan* or *cursian*), also primarily and properly signifies to vex or torment. Now, it is a strong confirmation of the derivation of *shrewd* from the verb *to shrew* that we find *shrewd* and *curst* applied to the disposition and temper by our old writers in almost, or rather in precisely, the same sense. Shakespeare himself affords us several instances. Thus, in *Much Ado About Nothing* (*ii.* 1), Leonato having remarked to Beatrice, " By my troth, niece, thou wilt never get a husband if thou be so *shrewd* of thy tongue," his brother Antonio adds, assentingly, " In faith, she's too *curst.*" So, in *A Midsummer Night's Dream* (*iii.* 2), Helena, declining to reply to a torrent of abuse from Hermia, says, " I was never *curst;* I have no gift at all in *shrewishness.*" And in *The Taming of the Shrew* (i. 2), first we **have** Hortensio describing Katharine to his friend Petrucio as "intolerable *curst,* and *shrewd,* and **froward," and** then we have Katharine, the shrew, repeatedly designated "Katharine the *curst.*" At the end of **the Play** she is called "a curst shrew," that is, as **we** might otherwise express it, an ill-tempered shrew.

Shrew, by the way, whether the substantive or the verb, always, I believe, and also *shrewd* very frequently, appear throughout the First Folio with *ow* **as** the diphthong, instead of *ew;* and in *The Taming of the Shrew* the word *shrew* is in various places made to rhyme with the sound **of** *o;* so that there can be little doubt that its common pronunciation in Shakespeare's day was *shrow,* and also that the same vowel sound was given to *shrewd* or *shrowd* in at least some of its applications. It is the reverse of what appears to have happened in the case of the word which probably was formerly pronounced *shew* (as it **is** still often spelled), but now always *show.* Thus Milton, in his 7th Sonnet :—

> "How soon hath Time, the subtle thief of **youth,**
> Stolen on his wing my three and twentieth **year!**
> My hasting days fly on with full career,
> But my late **spring no bud or blossom** *shew'th.*"

So likewise in *Il Penseroso* (171, 172) :—

> "Of every star **that** heaven doth shew,
> And every **herb that** sips the dew."

In **the** case, again, of *strew,* or *strow,* neither **mode** either of spelling or of pronunciation can perhaps **be said** to **have** quite gone out, although the dictionaries, I believe, enjoin us to write **the** word with an *e,* **but** to give it the sound of an *o.* **In the** passage before **us** the First Folio **has** "a shrew'd contriver."

As it **is in words that** ill-temper finds the readiest and most frequent vent, the terms *curst* and *shrew,* and *shrewd*, and *shrewish* are often used with a special reference to the tongue. But sharpness of tongue, again, always implies some sharpness of understanding as well as of temper. The terms *shrewd* and *shrewdly*, accordingly, have come to convey usually something of both of these qualities,—at one time, perhaps, most of the one, at another of the other. The sort of ability that we call *shrewdness* never suggests the notion of anything very high: the word has always a touch in it of the sarcastic or disparaging. But, on the other hand, the disparagement which it expresses is never without an admission of something also that is creditable or flattering. Hence it has come to pass that a person does not hesitate to use the terms in question even of himself and his own judgments or conjectures. We say, "I shrewdly suspect or guess," or "I have a shrewd guess, or suspicion," taking the liberty of thus asserting or assuming our own intellectual acumen under cover of the modest confession at the same time of some little ill-nature in the exercise of it.

Even when *shrewd* is used without any personal reference, the sharpness which it implies is generally, if not always, a more or less unpleasant sharpness. "This last day was a shrewd one to us," says one of the Soldiers of Octavius to his comrade, in *Antony and Cleopatra, iv.* 9, after the encounter in which they had been driven back by Antony near Alexandria. *Shrewdness* is even used by Chaucer in the sense of evil generally; as in *The House of Fame, iii.* 537 :—

> "Speke of hem harm and shreuednesse,
> Instead of gode and worthinesse."

And so too Bacon:—"An ant is a wise creature for it self; but it is a shrewd thing in an orchard or garden." *Essay* 23rd; "Of Wisdom for a Man's Self."

186. *If he improve them.*—That is, if he apply them, if he turn them to account. It is remarkable that no

notice is taken of this sense of the word either by Johnson or Todd. Many examples of it are given by Webster under both *Improve* and *Improvement*. They are taken from the writings, among others, of Tillotson, Addison, Chatham, Blackstone, Gibbon. We all remember

> "How doth the little busy bee
> Improve each shining hour."

Even Johnson himself, in *The Rambler*, talks of a man "capable of enjoying and *improving* life,"—by which he can only mean turning it to account. The *im* of improve must be, or must have been taken to be, the preposition or the intensive particle, not the *in* negative, although it is the latter which we have both in the Latin *improbus* and *improbo*, and also in the French *improuver*, the only signification of which is to disapprove, and although in the latinized English of some of our writers of the sixteenth century to *improve* occurs in the senses both of to reprove and to disprove. In *Much Ado About Nothing*, ii. 3, when Benedick, speaking to himself of Beatrice, says, "They say the lady is fair; ... and virtuous; 'tis so, I cannot *reprove* it," he seems to mean that he cannot disprove it. The manner in which the word *improve* was used in the middle of the seventeenth century may be seen from the following sentences of Clarendon's:—"This gave opportunity and excuse to many persons of quality ... to lessen their zeal to the King's cause; ... and those contestations had been lately improved with some sharpness by the Lord Herbert's carriage towards the Lord Marquis of Hertford" (*Hist., Book vi.*). "Though there seemed reasons enough to dissuade her [the Queen] from that inclination [of retiring from Oxford, when it was threatened with a siege, for Exeter], and his majesty heartily wished that she could be diverted, yet the perplexity of her mind was so great, and her fears so vehement, both improved by her indisposition of health, that all civility and reason obliged everybody to submit" (*Id.*, *Book viii.*).

187. *And envy afterwards.*—*Envy* has here the sense often borne by the Latin *invidia*, or nearly the same with *hatred* or *malice*. And this, as Malone remarks, is the sense in which it is almost always used by Shakespeare.

187. *Let us be sacrificers.*—I cannot think that the *Let's be* of the First Folio indicates more, at most, than that it was the notion of the original printer or editor that *sacrificers* should be pronounced with the emphasis on the second syllable. If we keep to the ordinary pronunciation, the line will merely have two supernumerary short, or unaccented, syllables; that is to say, "sacrificers, but not" will count for only two feet, or four syllables. This is nothing more than what we have in many other lines.

187. *We all stand up*, etc.—*Spirit* is the emphatic word in this line.

187. *And let our hearts*, etc.—*Vid.* 155.

187. *This shall mark.*—For the *shall* see 181.—The old reading is "This shall *make*," which is sense, if at all, only on the assumption that *make* is here equivalent to make to seem. I have no hesitation in accepting the correction, which we owe to Mr Collier's MS. annotator. We have now a clear meaning perfectly expressed;—this will show to all that our act has been a measure of stern and sad necessity, not the product of envy (or private hatred).

187. *Our purpose necessary*, etc.—There is nothing irregular in the prosody of this line, nor any elision to be made. The measure is completed by the *en* of *envious;* the two additional unaccented syllables have no prosodical effect.

188. *Yet I do fear him.*—The old reading is, "Yet I fear him;" the *do* was inserted by Steevens. It improves, if it is not absolutely required by, the sense or

expression as well as the prosody. Mr Knight, by whom it is rejected, says, "The **pause** which naturally occurs before Cassius offers an answer to the impassioned **argument of** Brutus would be most decidedly **marked by a** proper reader or actor." This **pause** Mr Knight would have **to be** equivalent **to a** single **short** syllable, **or half a time.** Surely **one somewhat longer would** have **been necessary for such** an effect **as is** supposed.—The manner **in which** the next line is given **in the** original text shows that the printer or so-called editor **had no** notion of what **the** words meant, **or** whether they **had** any **meaning:** in his exhibition of them, with a full-point after *Cæsar*, they **have none.**

189. *Is to himself*, etc.—*To think*, or **to take thought, seems to have** been formerly used in the sense **of to give way to sorrow** and despondency. Thus, **in** *Antony and Cleopatra, iii.* 11, to Cleopatra's question, after the battle of Actium, "What shall we do, Enobarbus?" the answer of that worthy is, "Think and die."

189. *And that were much he should.*—That **would be** much for him to do.

190. *There is no fear in him.*—That is, cause of fear. It is still common to use *terror* in this active sense,—as when in 551 Brutus says, "There is no terror, Cassius, in your threats."

192. *The clock hath stricken.*—*Vid.* 46.

194. *Whether Cæsar will come forth to day or no.*— *Whether* is thus given uncontracted here in all the **old** copies. And it might have so stood, inoffensively enough, in all the other passages in which the slight irregularity of the superfluous short syllable has been **got** rid **of by its** conversion **into** *where* or *whe'r*.

194. *Quite from the main opinion.*—"**Quite** from" is quite away from. So in *Twelfth Night, v.* 1, Malvolio, charging the Countess with having written the letter, says:—

> "You must not now deny it is your hand;
> Write from it, if you can, in hand or phrase."

Malone remarks that the words "main opinion" occur also in *Troilus and Cressida*, where, as he thinks, they signify, as here, general estimation. The passage is in *i.* 3:—

> "Why then we should our *main opinion* crush
> In taint of our best man."

Johnson's interpretation is perhaps better;—"leading, fixed, predominant opinion." Mason has ingeniously proposed to read "*mean* opinion" in the present passage.

194. *Of fantasy*, etc.—*Fantasy* is fancy, or imagination, with its unaccountable anticipations and apprehensions, as opposed to the calculations of reason. By *ceremonies*, as Malone notes, we are to understand here omens or signs deduced from sacrifices or other ceremonial rites. The word is used again in the same sense in 233. For another sense of it see 16.

194. *These apparent prodigies.*—*Apparent* is here plain, evident, about which there can be no doubt; as in Falstaff's (to Prince Henry) "Were it not here *apparent* that thou art heir *apparent*" (*First part of King Henry the Fourth, i.* 2),—where the *here* is also certainly intended to coincide with the *heir*, giving rise to a suspicion that the latter word may have, sometimes at least, admitted of a different pronunciation in Shakespeare's day from that which it always has now. So when Milton says of our first parents after their fall (*Par. Lost, x.* 112) that

> "Love was not in their looks, either to God
> Or to each other, but apparent guilt,"

he means by "*apparent* guilt" manifest and undoubted guilt. In other cases by *apparent* we mean, not emphatically apparent, or indisputable, but simply apparent, apparent and nothing more, or what we otherwise call probable or seeming. "The sense is apparent" would mean that the sense is plain; "the apparent sense is," that the sense seems to be.

194. *The unaccustomed terror.*—*Unaccustomed* is unusual; we now commonly employ it for unused to. *Terror* has here the active sense, as *fear* has in 190.

194. *And the persuasion of his augurers.*—*Augurer*, formed from the verb, is Shakespeare's usual word, instead of the Latin *augur*, which is commonly employed, and which he too, however, sometimes has. So again in 236.

195. *That unicorns*, etc.—"Unicorns," says Steevens, "are said to have been taken by one who, running behind a tree, eluded the violent push the animal was making at him, so that his horn spent its force on the trunk, and stuck fast, detaining the beast till he was dispatched by the hunter." He quotes in illustration Spenser's description (*F. Q. ii.* 5):—

> "Like as a lion whose imperial power
> A proud rebellious unicorn defies,
> To avoid the rash assault and wrathful stour
> Of his fierce foe him to a tree applies;
> And, when him running in full course he spies,
> He slips aside; the whiles the furious beast
> His precious horn, sought of his enemies,
> Strikes in the stock, ne thence can be releast,
> But to the mighty victor yields a bounteous feast."

"Bears," adds Steevens, "are reported to have been surprised by means of a mirror, which they would gaze on, affording their pursuers an opportunity of taking a surer aim. This circumstance, I think, is mentioned by Claudian. Elephants were seduced into pitfalls, lightly covered with hurdles and turf, on which a proper bait to tempt them was exposed. See Pliny's *Natural History, Book viii.*" Reference might also be made to a speech of Timon to Apemantus in *Timon of Athens, iv.* 3, "If thou wert the lion," etc., which is too long to be quoted. The import of the *For*, with which Decius introduces his statement, is not seen till we come to his "But when I tell him," etc., which, therefore, ought not, as is commonly done, to be separated from what precedes by so strong a point as the colon,—the substitute of the modern editors for the full stop of the original edition.

195. *He says, he does; being then most flattered.*—The *ing* of *being* counts for nothing in the prosody. For the *ed* of *flattered*, see the note on 246.

197. *By the eighth hour.*—It is the *eight* hour in the first three Folios. The author, however, probably wrote *eighth*.

199. *Doth bear Cæsar hard.*—*Vid.* 105. In the Second Folio the *hard* in this passage is changed into *hatred*. But the meaning is manifestly different from what that would give, even if *to bear one hatred* were English at all.

200. *Go along by him.*—Pope, who is followed by the other editors before Malone, changed *by* into *to*. But to go *along by* a person was in Shakespeare's age to take one's way where he was. So afterwards in 620, "The enemy, marching along by them" (that is, through the country of the people between this and Philippi).

200. *I'll fashion him.*—I will shape his mind to our purposes.

201. *The morning comes upon us.*—It may just be noted that all the old copies have "upon's." And probably such an elision would not have been thought inelegant at any time in the seventeenth century.

202. *Let not our looks put on our purposes.*—Put on such expression as would betray our purposes. Compare the exhortation of the strong-minded wife of Macbeth to her husband (*Macbeth*, i. 5):—

> "To beguile the time,
> Look like the time: bear welcome in your eye,
> Your hand, your tongue; look like the innocent flower,
> But be the serpent under it."

But the sentiment takes its boldest form **from the** lips of Macbeth **himself** in the first fervour of his weakness exalted into determined wickedness (*i*. 7):—

> "Away, and mock the time with fairest show:
> False face must hide what the false heart doth know."

202. *Formal constancy.*—Constancy in outward **form, or aspect**; the appearance, at any rate, of perfect freedom from anxiety and the weight of our great design. The original stage direction is; "*Exeunt. Manet Brutus.*'

202. *The heavy honey-dew of slumber.*—This **is** the correction by **Mr** Collier's **MS.** annotator of the old reading "the honey-heavy dew." **I** cannot doubt that it gives **us what** Shakespeare wrote. "The compound," as Mr Collier remarks, "unquestionably is not *honey-heavy*, but *honey-dew*, a well-known glutinous deposit upon the leaves of trees, **etc.; the** compositor was guilty of a transposition." We have a trace, it might be added, of some confusion or indistinctness in the manuscript, perhaps occasioned by an interlineation, and of the perplexity of the compositor, in the strange manner **in which in the First** Folio the *dew* also, as well as the *heavy*, **is** attached **by a** hyphen; thus, "the honey-heavy-Dew."

202. *Thou hast no figures*, etc.—Pictures created by imagination or apprehension. So, in *The Merry Wives of Windsor*, *iv.* 2, Mrs Page, to Mrs Ford's "**Shall we tell our husbands how we have served** him (Falstaff)?" replies, "**Yes, by all** means; if it be but to scrape the figures **out** of your husband's brains."

205. *You've ungently.*—All the Folios have *Y' have;* which, however, was perhaps not pronounced differently from the modern elision adopted in the present text. As **that elision is still common,** it seems unnecessary to substitute **the full *You have*, as most of the** recent editors have done.

205. *Stole from* **my** *bed.*—*Vid.* 46.

205. *I urged you further.*—This is the reading of the old copies. Mr Collier, as elsewhere, has *farther*.

205. *Which sometime hath his hour.*—That is, *its* hour. Vid. 54.

205. *Wafture of your hand.*—*Wafter* is the form of the word in all the Folios.

205. *Fearing to strengthen that impatience.*—For the prosody of such lines see the note on 246.

205. *An effect of humour.* — *Humour* is the peculiar mood, or caprice, of the moment; a state of mind opposed or exceptional to the general disposition and character.

205. *As it hath much prevailed on your condition.*—*Condition* is the general temper or state of mind. We still say *ill-conditioned*, for ill-tempered. Thus, in *The Merchant of Venice, i.* 2, Portia makes the supposition that her suitor the black Prince of Morocco, although his complexion be that of a devil, may have "the condition of a saint." Note how vividly the strong feeling from which Portia speaks is expressed by her repetition of the *much*—" could it work so much As it hath much prevailed."

205.—*Dear my lord.*—So, in *Romeo and Juliet, iii.* 5, Juliet implores her mother, " O, sweet my mother, cast me not away !" For the principle upon which this form of expression is to be explained, see the note on 89. Though now disused in English, it corresponds exactly to the French *Cher Monsieur*. The personal pronoun in such phrases has become absorbed in the noun to which it is prefixed, and its proper or separate import is not thought of. A remarkable instance, in another form of construction, of how completely the pronoun in such established modes of speech was formerly apt to be overlooked, or treated as non-significant, occurs in our common version of the Bible, where in 1 *Kings, xviii.* 7, we have, "And, as Obadiah was in the way, behold, Elijah met him : and he knew him, and fell on his face, and said, Art thou *that my lord* Elijah ? " Still more extraordinary is what we have in *Troilus and Cressida*, v. 2, where (Ulysses having also addressed Troilus, "Nay, good my lord, go off") Cressida exclaims to herself,—

> "Ah! poor our sex! this fault in us I find,
> The error of our eye directs our mind."

209. *Is it physical?*—Medicinal.

209. *Of the dank morning.*—The Second Folio changes *dank* into *dark*. Mr Collier retains *dank*; but it is not stated that the restoration is made by his manuscript annotator.

209. *To add unto his sickness.*—*His* is misprinted *hit* in the First Folio. So in *Macbeth*, i. 5, we have, in the same original text, "the effect and *hit*," apparently for "the effect and *it*" (the purpose),—although the misprint, if it be one, is repeated in the Second Folio, and is, as far as we can gather from Mr Collier, left uncorrected by his MS. annotator. It is even defended as probably the true reading by Tieck. It cannot, at any rate, be received as merely a different way of spelling *it*, deliberately adopted in this instance and nowhere else throughout the volume: such a view of the matter is the very Quixotism of the belief in the immaculate purity of the old text.

209. *You have some sick offence.*—Some pain, or grief, that makes you sick.

209. *By the right and virtue of my place.*—By the right that belongs to, and (as we now say) in virtue of (that is by the power or natural prerogative of) my place (as your wife). The radical meaning of the term *virtue*, connected with *vis*, and perhaps also with *vireo*, and with *vir*, is *force* (which word itself, indeed, with its Latin progenitor *fortis*, may possibly be from the same root). The old spelling of the English word, and that which it has here in the First Folio, is *vertue*, as we still have it in the French *vertu*.

209. *I charm you.*—*Charm* (or *charme*) is the reading of all the old printed copies, and Mr Collier tells us of no correction by his MS. annotator. Pope substituted *charge*, which was adopted also by Hanmer. It must be confessed that the only instance which has been referred to in support of *charm* is not satisfactory. It is adduced by Steevens from *Cymbeline, i.* 7, where Iachimo says to Imogen,—

> "'Tis your graces
> That from my mutest conscience to my tongue
> *Charms* this report out."

This is merely the common application of the verb *to charm* in the sense of to produce any kind of effect as it were by incantation. *Charm* is no doubt a derivative from *carmen*, as *incantation* or *enchantment* is from *cano*. In the passage before us, *I charm you* (if such be the reading) must mean I adjure or conjure you. Spenser uses *charm* with a meaning which it does not now retain; as when he says in his *Shepherd's Kalendar* (*October*, 118), "Here we our slender pipes may safely *charm*," and, in the beginning of his *Colin Clout's Come Home Again*, speaks of "*charming* his oaten pipe unto his peers," that is, playing or modulating (not uttering musical sounds, as explained by Nares, but making to utter them). Still more peculiar is the application of the word by Marvel in a short poem entitled "The Picture of T. C. in a Prospect of Flowers;"—

> "Meanwhile, whilst every verdant thing
> Itself does at thy beauty *charm*;"—

that is, apparently, delights itself in contemplating thy beauty. We do not now use this verb thus reflectively at all. There seems, however, to have been formerly a latitude in the application of it which may possibly have extended to such a sense as that which must be assigned to it if it was really the word here employed by Portia.— Two stage directions are added here by Mr Collier's MS.

annotator:—"*Kneeling*," where Portia says "Upon my knees I charm you;" and "*Raising her*" at 210.

211. *But, as it were, in sort, or limitation.*—Only in a manner, in a degree, in some qualified or limited sense. We still say *in a sort*.

211. *To keep with you,* etc.—To keep company with you. To *keep* in the sense of to live or dwell is of constant occurrence in our old writers; and Nares observes that they still say in the University of Cambridge, Where do you *keep?* I *keep* in such a set of chambers. We sometimes hear it asserted that the word *comfort*, as well as the thing, is exclusively English. But it is also an old French word, though bearing rather the sense of our law term *to comfort*, which is to relieve, assist, or encourage. And it exists, also, both in the Italian and in the Spanish. Its origin is an ecclesiastical Latin verb *conforto* (from *con* and *fortis*), meaning to strengthen.

211. *And talk to you sometimes,* etc.—The true prosodical view of this line is to regard the two combinations "to you" and "in the" as counting each for only a single syllable. It is no more an Alexandrine than it is an hexameter.

213. *Being so fathered, and so husbanded.*—We have here two exemplifications of the remarkable power which our language possesses (though a consequence of its poverty of inflection, or of the loss of their distinctive terminations by the infinitive and present indicative of the verb) of turning almost any noun, upon occasion, into a verb. It may be called its most kingly prerogative, and may be compared to the right of ennobling exercised by the crown in our political constitution,—the more, inasmuch as words too, as well as men, were originally, it is probable, all of equal rank, and the same word served universally as noun at one time and as verb at another. Most of our verbs that are of purely English or Gothic descent are still in their simplest form undistinguishable

from nouns. The noun and the verb might be exhibited together in one system of inflection; *father*, for instance, might be at once declined and conjugated, through *fathered*, and *fathering*, and *have fathered*, and *will father*, and all the other moods and tenses, as well as through *fathers* and *father's*, and *of a father*, and *to a father*, and the other so called *nominal* changes. It is to this their identity of form with the noun that our English verbs owe in a great measure their peculiar force and liveliness of expression, consisting as that does in their power of setting before us, not merely the fact that something has been done or is doing, but the act or process itself as a concrete thing or picture. Shakespeare in particular freely employs any noun whatever as a verb.

It is interesting to note the germ of what we have here in *The Merchant of Venice* (*i.* 2):—

"Her name is Portia; nothing undervalued
To Cato's daughter, Brutus' Portia."

The Merchant of Venice had certainly been written by 1598.

213. *I have made strong proof.*—The prosody concurs here with the sense in demanding a strong emphasis upon the word *strong*.

214. *All the charactery.*—All that is charactered or expressed by my saddened aspect. The word, which occurs also in the *Merry Wives of Windsor*, *v.* 5, is accented on the second syllable there as well as here. And no doubt this was also the original, as it is still the vulgar, accentuation of *character*. Shakespeare, however, always accents that word on the *char-*, as we do, whether he uses it as a noun or as a verb; though a doubt may be entertained as to the pronunciation of the participial form both in the line, "Are visibly charactered and engraved," in *The Two Gentlemen of Verona*, *ii.* 7, and in the "Show me one scar charactered on the skin" of the *Second Part of King*

Henry the Sixth, iii. 1, as well as with regard to that of the compound which occurs in *Troilus and Cressida*, iii. 2,—

> "And mighty states characterless are grated
> To dusty nothing."

—The stage direction near the beginning of this speech is merely *Knock* in the original edition.

214. *Lucius, who's that knocks?*—Who is that who knocks? The omission of the relative is a familiar ellipsis. Vid. 34. *Who's*, and not *who is*, is the reading of all the Folios. It is unnecessary to suppose that the two broken lines were intended to make a whole between them. They are best regarded as distinct hemistichs. Mr Collier, however, prints "Who is't that knocks?" Does he follow his MS. annotator in this?

217. The *Lig.* (for *Ligarius*) is *Cai.* throughout in the original text. The authority for the prænomen *Caius*, by which Ligarius is distinguished throughout the Play, is Plutarch, in his Life of *Brutus*, towards the beginning.

218. *To wear a kerchief.*—*Kerchief* is *cover-chief*, the *chief* being the French *chef*, head (from the Latin *Cap*-ut, which is also the same word with the English *Head* and the German *Haupt*). But, the proper import of *chief* being forgotten or neglected, the name *kerchief* came to be given to any cloth used as a piece of dress. In this sense the word is still familiar in *handkerchief*, though both *kerchief* itself and its other compound *neckerchief* are nearly gone out. In *King John*, iv. 1, and also in *As You Like It*, iv. 3 and v. 2, the word in the early editions is *handkercher*; and this is likewise the form in the Quarto edition of *Othello*.

218. *Would you were not sick!*—I do not understand upon what principle, or in what notion, it is that the Shakespearian editors print *would* in such a construction as this with an apostrophe ('*Would*). Even if it is to be taken to mean *I would*, the *I* will not be a part of the

word which has been cut off, like the *i* of *it* in the contraction *'tis*.

221. *Thou, like an exorcist.*—"Here," says Mason, "and in all other places where the word occurs in Shakespeare, to *exorcise* means to raise spirits, not to lay them; and I believe he is singular in his acceptation of it." The only other instances of its occurrence, according to Mrs Clarke, are;—in the Song in *Cymbeline, iv.* 2:—

> "No exorciser harm thee!
> Nor no witchcraft charm thee!
> Ghost unlaid forbear thee!
> Nothing ill come near thee!"

in *All's Well that Ends Well, v.* 3, where, on the appearance of Helena, thought to be dead, the King exclaims,

> "Is there no exorcist
> Beguiles the truer office of mine eyes?"

and in the *Second Part of King Henry the Sixth, i.* 4, where Bolingbroke asks, "Will her ladyship [the Duchess of Gloster] behold and hear our exorcisms?" meaning the incantations and other operations by which they were to raise certain spirits.—In Mr Collier's regulated text, in this speech, at the words "Soul of Rome," we have the stage direction, "*Throwing away his bandage.*"

221. *My mortified spirit.*—*Mor-ti-fi-ed* here makes four syllables, *spirit* counting for only one. And *mortified* has its literal meaning of *deadened*.

224. *As we are going To whom it must be done.*—While we are on our way to those whom it must be done to. The ellipsis is the same as we have in 105, "From that it is disposed." I do not understand how the words are to be interpreted if we are to separate *going* from what follows by a comma, as is done in most editions.

225. *Set on your foot.*—This was probably a somewhat energetic or emphatic mode of expression. In Scotland they say, "Put down your foot" in exhorting one to walk

on briskly.—At the end of this speech **the old** copies have *Thunder* **as a stage** direction.

SCENE II.—*The same. A Room in* CÆSAR'S *Palace.*

Thunder and Lightning. Enter CÆSAR *in his night-gown.*

227. *Cæs.* Nor heaven, nor earth, have been at peace to-night:
Thrice hath Calphurnia in her sleep cried out,
Help, ho! *they murder Cæsar!*—Who's within?

Enter a SERVANT.

Serv. **My lord?**
229. *Cæs.* Go bid the priests do present sacrifice,
And bring me their opinions of success.
Serv. I will, **my** lord. [*Exit.*

Enter CALPHURNIA.

Cal. **What mean you,** Cæsar? Think you to walk **forth?**
You shall not stir out of your house to-day.
Cæs. Cæsar shall **forth:** The things that threatened me
Ne'er looked but on my back; when they shall see
The face of Cæsar, they are vanished.
233. *Cal.* Cæsar, I never stood on ceremonies,
Yet now they fright me. There is one within,
Besides the things that we have heard and seen,
Recounts most horrid sights seen by **the watch.**
A lioness hath whelped in **the streets;**
And graves have yawned, **and yielded up their dead:**
Fierce fiery warriors fight upon the clouds,
In ranks and squadrons, and right form of war,
Which drizzled blood upon the Capitol:
The noise of battle hurtled in the air,
Horses did neigh, and dying men did groan;
And ghosts did shriek and squeal about the streets.
O Cæsar! these things are beyond all use,
And I **do fear** them.
234. *Cæs.* What can **be avoided,**
Whose end **is** purposed by the mighty gods?
Yet Cæsar shall go forth; for these **predictions**
Are to the world in general, as to Cæsar.
Cal. **When beggars die, there are** no comets seen;
The heavens themselves blaze forth the death of princes
236. *Cæs.* **Cowards die many times** before their deaths;

The valiant never taste of death but once.
Of all the wonders that I yet have heard,
It seems to me most strange that men should fear;
Seeing that death, a necessary end,
Will come, when it will come.

Re-enter a SERVANT.

What say the augurers?
 Serv. They would not have you to stir forth to-day.
Plucking the entrails of an offering forth,
They could not find a heart within the beast.
238. *Cæs.* The gods do this in shame of cowardice:
Cæsar should be a beast without a heart,
If he should stay at home to-day for fear.
No, Cæsar shall not; Danger knows full well
That Cæsar is more dangerous than he.
We are two lions littered in one day,
And I the elder and more terrible;
And Cæsar shall go forth.
239. *Cal.* Alas, my lord,
Your wisdom is consumed in confidence.
Do not go forth to-day: Call it my fear,
That keeps you in the house, and not your own.
We'll send Mark Antony to the senate-house;
And he shall say, you are not well to-day:
Let me, upon my knee, prevail in this.
240. *Cæs.* Mark Antony shall say, I am not well;
And, for thy humour, I will stay at home.

Enter DECIUS.

Here's Decius Brutus, he shall tell them so.
241. *Dec.* Cæsar, all hail! Good morrow, worthy Cæsar:
I come to fetch you to the senate-house.
242. *Cæs.* And you are come in very happy time
To bear my greeting to the senators,
And tell them, that I will not come to-day:
Cannot, is false; and that I dare not, falser:
I will not come to-day: Tell them so, Decius.
 Cal. Say, he is sick.
244. *Cæs.* Shall Cæsar send a lie?
Have I in conquest stretched mine arm so far
To be afeared to tell grey-beards the truth?
Decius, go tell them, Cæsar will not come.
 Dec. Most mighty Cæsar, let me know some cause,

Lest I be laughed at when I tell them so.
245. *Cæs.* The cause is in my will, I will not come;
That is enough to satisfy the senate.
But, for your private satisfaction,
Because I love you, I will let you know.
Calphurnia here, my wife, stays me at home:
She dreamt to-night she saw my statue,
Which like a fountain, with an hundred spouts,
Did run pure blood; and many lusty Romans
Came smiling, and did bathe their hands in it.
And these does she apply for warnings and portents
Of evils imminent; and on **her** knee
Hath begged, that I will stay at home to-day.
246. *Dec.* This dream is all amiss interpreted:
It was a vision fair and fortunate·
Your statue spouting blood in many pipes,
In which so many smiling Romans bathed,
Signifies that from you great Rome shall suck
Reviving blood; and that great men shall press
For tinctures, stains, relics, and cognizance.
This by Calphurnia's dream is signified.
Cæs. And this way have you well expounded it.
249. *Dec.* **I have,** when you have heard what I can say:
And know it now; The senate have concluded
To give this day a crown to mighty Cæsar.
If you shall **send them word you** will not come,
Their minds may change. **Besides,** it were a **mock**
Apt to be rendered, for some one **to say,**
Break **up the senate till** another time,
When Cæsar's wife **shall meet** with better dreams.
If Cæsar hide himself, **shall they not whisper,**
Lo, Cæsar is afraid?
Pardon me, Cæsar; for my dear, dear love
To your proceeding **bids** me tell you this;
And reason to my love is liable.
250. *Cæs.* How foolish do your fears seem now, Calphurnia!
I am ashamed I did yield to them.—
Give me my robe, for I will go:—

Enter PUBLIUS, BRUTUS, LIGARIUS, METELLUS, CASCA, TREBONIUS,
and CINNA.

And look where Publius is come to fetch me.
Pub. Good morrow, Cæsar.

252. *Cæs.* Welcome, Publius.—
What, Brutus, are you stirred so early too?—
Good morrow, Casca.—Caius Ligarius,
Cæsar was ne'er so much your enemy,
As that same ague which hath made you lean.—
What is't o'clock?
253. *Bru.* Cæsar, 'tis strucken eight.
254. *Cæs.* I thank you for your pains and courtesy.

Enter ANTONY

See! Antony, that revels long o'nights,
Is, notwithstanding, up:—
Good morrow, Antony.
  Ant. So to most noble Cæsar.
256. *Cæs.* Bid them prepare within:—
I am to blame to be thus waited for.—
Now, Cinna:—Now, Metellus:—What, Trebonius!
I have an hour's talk in store for you.
Remember that you call on me to-day:
Be near me, that I may remember you.
  Treb. Cæsar, I will:—and so near will I be,
That your best friends shall wish I had been farther.   [*Aside.*
  Cæs. Good friends, go in, and taste some wine with me;
And we, like friends, will straightway go together.
259. *Bru.* That every like is not the same, O Cæsar,
The heart of Brutus yearns to think upon!   [*Aside. Exeunt.*

Scene II. The same. A Room in Cæsar's Palace.—This is not in the old editions; but the stage direction that follows is, only with *Julius Cæsar* (for *Cæsar*).

227. *Nor heaven nor earth*, etc.—This use of *nor* ... *nor* for the usual *neither* ... *nor* of prose (as well as of *or* ... *or* for *either* ... *or*) is still common in our poetry. On the other hand, *either* was sometimes used formerly in cases where we now always have *or;* as in *Luke vi.* 42:—"Why beholdest thou the mote that is in thy brother's eye, but perceivest not the beam that is in thine own eye? Either how canst thou say to thy brother, Brother, let me pull out the mote that is in thine eye, when thou thyself beholdest not the beam that is in thine own eye?"—The strict grammatical principle would of

course require "*has* been at peace;" but where, as here, the two singular substantives are looked at together by the mind, it is more natural to regard them as making a plurality, and to use the plural verb, notwithstanding the disjunctive conjunction (as it is sometimes oddly designated).

229. *Do present sacrifice.*—In this and a good many other cases we are now obliged to employ a verb of a more specific character instead of the general *do*. This is a different kind of archaism from what we have in the "do danger" of 147, where it is not the *do*, but the *danger*, that has a meaning which it has now lost, and for which the modern language uses another word.

229. *Their opinions of success.*—That is, merely, of the issue, or of what is prognosticated by the sacrifice as likely to happen. Johnson remarks (note on *Othello*, *iii.* 3) that *successo* is also so used in Italian. So likewise is *succès* in French. In addition to earlier examples of such a sense of the English word, Boswell adduces from Sidney's *Arcadia*:—"He never answered me, but, pale and quaking, went straight away; and straight my heart misgave me some *evil success*;" and from Dr Barrow, in the latter part of the seventeenth century:—"Yea, to a person so disposed, that *success* which seemeth most *adverse* justly may be reputed the best and most happy." Shakespeare's ordinary employment of the word, however, is accordant with our present usage. But see 735, 736. Sometimes it is used in the sense of our modern *succession;* as in *A Winter's Tale*, *i.* 2:—"Our parents' noble names, In whose success we are gentle." In the same manner the verb *to succeed*, though meaning etymologically no more than to follow, has come to be commonly understood, when used without qualification, only in a good sense. We still say that George II. *succeeded* George I., and could even, perhaps, say that a person or thing had *succeeded* very ill: but when we say simply, that any thing has *succeeded*, we mean that it has had a prosperous issue.

Shakespeare's use of the word *success* may be further illustrated by the following examples:—

" Is your blood
So madly hot, that no discourse of reason,
Nor fear of bad success in a bad cause,
Can qualify the same ? "—*Troil. and Cress.*, ii. 2 ;

"Commend me to my brother: soon at night
I'll send him certain word of my success."
Meas. for Meas., i. 5 ;

" Let this be so, and doubt not but success
Will fashion the event in better shape
Than I can lay it down in likelihood."
Much Ado About Noth., iv. 1;

" And so success of mischief shall be born,
And heir from heir shall hold this quarrel up."
Second Part of Henry IV., iv. 2 ;

" Should you do so, my lord,
My speech should fall into such vile success
Which my thoughts aimed not."—*Othello*, iii. 3.

233. *I never stood on ceremonies.*—*Vid.* 194.

233. *Recounts most horrid sights.*—Who recounts. As in 34 and 214.

233. *Which drizzled blood.*—To *drizzle* is to shed (or to fall) in small drops. The Dictionaries bring it from the German *rieseln* (of the same signification); but the English word probably derives a main part of its peculiar effect from the same initial *dr* which we have in *drip*, *drop*, *drivel*, etc.

233. *The noise of battle hurtled in the air.*—The three last Folios substitute *hurried* for *hurtled*. *Hurtle* is probably the same word with *hurl* (of which, again, *whirl* may be another variation). Chaucer uses it as an active verb in the sense of to push forcibly and with violence; as in *C. T.* 2618 :—

" And he him hurtleth with his hors adoun ; "

and again in *C. T.* 4717 :—

> "O firste moving cruel firmament!
> With thy diurnal swegh that croudest ay,
> And hurtlest all from est til occident,
> That naturally wold hold another way."

Its very sound makes it an expressive word for any kind of rude and crushing, or "insupportably advancing," movement. *Hustle* and *justle* (or *jostle*) may be considered, if not as other forms, or somewhat softened modifications, of the same vocal utterance of thought, as at least fashioned upon the same principle.

233. *Horses did neigh, and dying men did groan.*—This is the reading of the Second and subsequent Folios. The First has "Horses *do* neigh, and dying men *did* grone." We may confidently affirm that no degree of mental agitation ever expressed itself in any human being in such a jumble and confusion of tenses as this,—not even insanity or drunkenness. The "Fierce fiery warriors *fight* upon the clouds," which we have a few lines before, is not a case in point. It is perfectly natural in animated narrative or description to rise occasionally from the past tense to the present; but who ever heard of two facts or circumstances equally past, strung together, as here, with an *and*, and enunciated in the same breath, being presented the one as now going on, the other as only having taken place? Mr Collier's MS. annotator, it is to be presumed, approves or accepts the "*did* neigh" of the Second Folio.

233. *And ghosts did shriek and squeal about the streets.*—It is rare to find Shakespeare coming so near upon the same words in two places as he does here and in dealing with the same subject in *Hamlet*, i. 1:—

> "In the most high and palmy state of Rome,
> A little ere the mightiest Julius fell,
> The graves stood tenantless, and the sheeted dead
> Did squeak and gibber in the Roman streets."

This passage, however, is found only in the Quarto editions of *Hamlet*, and is omitted in all the Folios.

233. *Beyond all use.*—We might still say "beyond all use and wont."

234. *Whose end is purposed*, etc.—The end, or completion, of which is designed by the gods.

236. *What say the augurers?*—*Vid.* 194.—The preceding stage direction is in the original edition, "*Enter a Servant.*"

238. *In shame of cowardice.*—For the shame of cowardice, to put cowardice to shame.

238. *Cæsar should be a beast.*—We should now say Cæsar *would* be a beast. It is the same use of *shall* where we now use *will* that has been noticed at 181. So in *Merchant of Venice*, i. 2, Nerissa, conversing with her mistress Portia about her German suitor, the nephew of the Duke of Saxony, says, "If he should offer to choose, and choose the right casket, you *should* refuse to perform your father's will if you should refuse to accept him." Yet the fashion of saying It *should* appear, or It *should* seem (instead of It *would*), which has come up with the revived study of our old literature, is equally at variance with the principle by which our modern employment of *shall* and *will* is regulated.

238. *We are two lions.*—The old reading, in all the Folios, is *We heare* (or *hear* in the Third and Fourth). Nobody, as far as I am aware, has defended it, or affected to be able to make any sense of it. Theobald proposed *We were*, which has been generally adopted. But *We are*, as recommended by Upton, is at once nearer to the original and much more spirited. It is a singularly happy restoration, and one in regard to which, I conceive, there can scarcely be the shadow of a doubt. It is, however, confirmed, if it needed any confirmation, by its being found among the corrections of Mr Collier's MS. annotator.

239. *Is consumed in confidence.*—As anything is consumed in fire.

240. *For thy humour.*—For the gratification of thy whim or caprice. *Vid.* 205. Mr Collier's MS. annotator directs that Cæsar should here raise Calphurnia, as he had that she should deliver the last line of her preceding speech kneeling.

241. *Cæsar, all hail!*—Hail in this sense is the Original English *hael* or *hál*, meaning hale, whole, or healthy (the modern German *heil*). It ought rather to be spelled *hale*. Hail, frozen rain, is from *haegl, haegel*, otherwise *hagol, hagul*, or *haegol* (in modern German *hagel*).

242. *To bear my greeting.*—To *greet* in this sense is the Original English *gretan*, to go to meet, to welcome, to salute (the *grüssen* of the modern German). The *greet* of the Scotch and other northern dialects, which is found in Spenser, represents quite another verb of the old language, *greotan*, or *graetan*, to lament, apparently the same root which we have in the French *regret* and the Italian *regretto*, as well as in our own *regret* (obtained immediately from the French).

244. *To be afeard.*—The common Scotch form for *afraid* is still *feared*, or *feard*, from the verb *to fear*, taken in the sense of to make afraid; in which sense it is sometimes found in Shakespeare; as in *Measure for Measure, ii.* 1:—

"We must not make a scarecrow of the law,
Setting it up to fear the beasts of prey;"

And in *Antony and Cleopatra, ii.* 6:—

"Thou canst not fear us, Pompey, with thy sails."

In *The Taming of the Shrew, i.* 2, we have in a single line (or two hemistichs) both senses of the verb *to fear*: —"Tush! tush! fear boys with bugs," says Petrucio in scorn; to which his servant Grumio rejoins, *aside*, "For he fears none."

246. *That is enough to satisfy the senate.*—Not (as the

words might in other circumstances mean) enough to ensure their being satisfied, but enough for me to do towards that end.

246. *She dreamt to-night she saw my statue.*—It may be mentioned that both Rowe and Pope substitute *last night*, which would, indeed, seem to be the most natural expression; but it is unsupported by any of the old copies.— The word *statue* is of frequent occurrence in Shakespeare; and in general it is undoubtedly only a dissyllable. In the present Play, for instance, in the very next speech we have

" Your statue spouting blood in many pipes."

And so likewise in 138, and again in 378. Only in one line, which occurs in *Richard the Third, iii. 7,*

" But like dumb statües or breathing stones,"

is it absolutely necessary that it should be regarded as of three syllables, if the received reading be correct. In that passage also, however, as in every other, the word in the First Folio is printed simply *statues*, exactly as it always is in the English which we now write and speak.

On the other hand, it is certain that *statue* was frequently written *statua* in Shakespeare's age; Bacon, for example, always, I believe, so writes it; and it is not impossible that its full pronunciation may have been always trisyllabic, and that it became a dissyllable only by the two short vowels, as in other cases, being run together so as to count prosodically only for one.

" From authors of the times," says Reed, in a note on *The Two Gentlemen of Verona, iv.* 4, " it would not be difficult to fill whole pages with instances to prove that *statue* was at that period a trisyllable." But unfortunately he does not favour us with one such instance. Nor, with the exception of the single line in *Richard the Third*, the received reading of which has been suspected for another reason (*breathing stones* being not improbably, it has been thought, a misprint for *unbreathing stones*), has any decisive instance been produced either by **Steevens**, who refers at that passage to what he designates as Reed's "**very** decisive note," or by any of the other commentators anywhere, or by Nares, who also commences his account of the word in his *Glossary* by telling us that it "was long used in English as a trisyllable."

The only other lines in Shakespeare in which it has been conceived to be other than a word of two syllables are the **one now** under examination, and another which also occurs in the present Play, in 426:—

" Even at the base of Pompey's statue."

These **two lines, it** will **be** observed, are similarly constructed in so far as this word is concerned; in both the supposed trisyllable concludes the verse.

Now, **we have** many verses terminated in exactly the same manner **by** other words, and yet it is very far from being certain that such verses were intended **to** be accounted verses of ten syllables, or were ever **so** pronounced.

First, there is the whole class of **those** ending **with** words in *tion* or *sion*. This termination, **it is** true, usually makes two syllables **in** Chaucer, **and it may do** so sometimes, though it does not **generally, in Spenser**; it is frequently dissyllabic, in **indisputable** instances, even with some of the dramatists of the early part of the seventeenth century, **and** particularly with Beaumont and Fletcher; **but it is only on the** rarest occasions that it is other than monosyllabic in **the** middle of the line with Shakespeare. Is it, then, to be supposed that he employed **it** habitually as a dissyllable at the end of a line? It **is of** continual occurrence in both positions. **For example, in** the following line of the present **speech,**—

" But for your private satisfaction,"—

can we think that the concluding word was intended to

have any different pronunciation from that which it has in the line of *Romeo and Juliet* (*ii.* 2),—

"What satisfaction canst thou have to-night?"

or in this other from Othello (*iii.* 3),—

"But for a satisfaction of my thought?"

Is it probable that it was customary then, any more than it is now, to divide *tion* into two syllables in the one case more than in the other?

Secondly, there are numerous verses terminating with the verbal affix *ed*, the sign of the preterite indicative active or of the past participle passive. This termination is not circumstanced exactly as *tion* is: the utterance of it as a separate syllable is the rare exception in our modern pronunciation; but it evidently was not so in Shakespeare's day; the distinct syllabication of the *ed* would rather seem to have been almost as common then as its absorption in the preceding syllable. For instance, when Juliet, in *Romeo and Juliet*, *iii.* 2, repeating the Nurse's words, exclaims,

"Tybalt is dead, and Romeo banished:
That *banished*—that one word *banished*—
Hath slain ten thousand Tybalts,"

the *ed* in *That banished* clearly makes a distinct syllable; and, that being the case, it must be held to be equally such in the two other repetitions of the word. But in other cases its coalescence with the preceding syllable will only produce the same effect to which we are accustomed when we disregard the antiquated pronunciation of the *tion* at the end of a line, and read it as one syllable. In the present Play, for example, it might be so read in 305,—

"Thy brother by decree is banished;"—

as it was probably intended (in another prosodical position) to be read afterwards in 310,—

"That I was constant Cimber should be banished,"

and as it must be read in 306,—

"For the repealing of my banished brother."

Yet, although most readers in the present day would elide the *e* in all the three instances, it ought to be observed that in the original edition the word is printed in full in the first and with the apostrophe in the two others. And this distinction in the printing is employed to indicate the pronunciation throughout the volume. How such a line as

"Thy brother by decree is banished,"—

being a very common prosodical form in Shakespeare,— was intended by him to be read, or was commonly read in his day, must therefore remain somewhat doubtful. If, however, the *e* was elided in the pronunciation, such verses would be prosodically exactly of the same form or structure with those, also of very frequent occurrence, in which all that we have for a fifth foot is the affix or termination *tion*, on the assumption that that was pronounced only as one syllable.

One way of disposing of such lines would be to regard them as a species of hemistich or truncated line. Verses which, although not completed, are correctly constructed as far as they go, occur in every Play in great numbers and of all dimensions; and those in question would be such verses wanting the last syllable, as others do the two or three or four or five last. This explanation would take in the case of the lines, "She dreamt to-night she saw my statue," and "Even at the base of Pompey's statue," and of others similarly constructed, supposing *statue* to be only a dissyllable, as well as all those having in the last foot only *tion* or *ed*. But most probably this particular kind of truncated line, consisting of nine syllables, would not occur so frequently as it does but for the influence exerted by the memory of the old pronunciation of the two terminations just mentioned even after it had come to be universally or generally disused. For instance, although the word *satisfaction* had already come in the age of Shakespeare to be generally pronounced exactly as it is at the present day, the line " But for your private satisfaction" was the more readily accepted as a sufficient verse by reason of the old syllabication of the word, which, even by those who had abandoned it (as Shakespeare himself evidently had done), was not forgotten. Other lines having nothing more for their tenth syllable than the verbal affix *ed*, in which also an elision had become usual, would be acted upon in the same manner; the *ed* would still retain something of the effect of a separate syllable even when it had ceased to be generally so pronounced. But after the public ear had thus become reconciled and accustomed to such a form of verse, it might be expected to be sometimes indulged in by poetic writers when it had to be produced in another way than through the instrumentality of the half separable *ed* and the half dissyllabic *tion*. The line "But for your private satisfaction," pronounced as we have assumed it to have been, would make such a line as "She dreamt to-night she saw my statue" seem to have an equal right to be accounted legitimate, seeing that its effect upon the ear was precisely the same. Still the conservative principle in language would keep the later and more decided deviation from the normal form comparatively infrequent. Sometimes a singular effect of suddenness and abruptness is produced by such a form of verse; as in the sharp appeal of Menenius, in the opening scene of *Coriolanus*, to the loud and grandiloquent leader of the mutinous citizens,—

" What do *you* think.
You, the great toe of this assembly ? "

Unless, indeed, we are to assume the verse here to be

complete and regular, and that *assembly* is to be read as a word of four syllables, *as-sem-bl-y*. In the present Play, however, at 295, we have an instance to which that objection does not apply. The line there—"Look, how he makes to Cæsar: mark him"—is of precisely the same rhythm with "She dreamt to-night she saw my statue," and also with the one by which it is immediately preceded, —"I fear our purpose is discovered" (in 294), as well as with "He says he does; being then most flattered" (in 195), and many others, read (as it is probable they were intended to be) without the distinct syllabication of the *ed*.

After all, Shakespeare's word may really have been *statua*, as Reed and Steevens suppose. This is decidedly the opinion of Mr Dyce, who, in his *Remarks on Mr Collier's and Mr Knight's editions* (p. 186), calls attention to the following line from a copy of verses by John Harris, prefixed to the 1647 Folio of the Plays of Beaumont and Fletcher;—

"Defaced statua and martyr'd book."

"I therefore have not," he adds, "the slightest doubt that wherever *statue* occurs, while the metre requires three syllables, it is a typographical error for *statua*." Perhaps the best way would be to print *statua* in all cases, and to assume that that was the form which Shakespeare always wrote. *Statua* would have the prosodical value either of a dissyllable or of a trisyllable according to circumstances, just as *Mantua*, for instance, has throughout *Romeo and Juliet*, where we have in one place such a line as

"For then thou canst not pass to Mantu-a" (*iii.* 3),

or

"But I will write again to Mantu-a" (*v.* 2),

and in another such as

"Sojourn in Mantua; I'll find out your man" (*iii.* 3),

or

"So that my speed to Mantua there was stayed" (*v.* 2).

We have a rare example of the termination *-tion* forming a dissyllable with Shakespeare in the middle of a line in Jaques's description of the Fool Touchstone (*As You Like It*, ii. 2) :—

> "He hath strange places crammed
> With observation, the which he vents
> In mangled forms."

This may be compared with the similar prolongation of the *-trance* in the sublime chant of Lady Macbeth (*Macbeth*, i. 5) :—

> "The raven himself is hoarse
> That croaks the fatal *entrance* of Duncan
> Under my battlements;"—

or with what we have in the following line in *The Two Gentlemen of Verona*, ii. 4,

> "And that hath *dazzled* my reason's light;"

or with this in *A Midsummer Night's Dream*, iii. 2,—

> "O me! you *juggler!* you canker-blossom."

The name *Henry*, in like manner, occasionally occurs as a trisyllable both in the three Parts of *Henry VI.*, and also in *Richard III.*

The following are examples of what is much more common, the extension or division of similar combinations at the end of a line :—

> "The parts and graces of the wrestler."
> *As You Like It*, ii. 2;

> "And lasting, in her sad remembrance."
> *Twelfth Night*, i. 1;

> "The like of him. Know'st thou this country?"
> *Ibid.*, i. 3;

> "Which is as bad as die with tickling."
> *Much Ado About Noth.*, iii. 1·

> "O, how this spring of love resembleth."
> *Two Gent. of Ver.*, i. 3;

o

> " And these two Dromios, one in semblance."
> *Com. of Err. i.* 1 ;
> " These are the parents to these children."—*Ibid.*
> " Fair sir, and you my merry mistress."
> *Tam. of Shrew, iv.* 5.

In other cases, however, the line must apparently be held to be a regular hemistich (or truncated verse) of nine syllables; as in

> "Of our dear souls. Meantime sweet sister."
> *Twelfth Night, v.* 1 ;
> " I'll follow you and tell what answer."
> *Third Part of Henry VI., iv.* 3.
> " Be valued 'gainst your wife's commandment."
> *Mer. of Ven., iv.* 1.

Unless, indeed, in this last instance we ought not to read *commandement* (in four syllables), as Spenser occasionally has it; although I am not aware of the occurrence of such a form of the word elsewhere in Shakespeare.

246. *Which, like a fountain with an hundred spouts.*— This is the reading of both the First and Second Folio. Mr Collier, however, has "*a* hundred."

246. *And these does she apply for warnings and portents.* —This is the reading of all the Folios. It is not quite satisfactory; and the suspected corruption has been attempted to be cured in various ways. Shakespeare's habitual accentuation of *portent* seems to have been on the last syllable. If the passage were in any one of certain others of the Plays, I should be inclined to arrange the lines as follows :—

> " And these does **she** apply for warnings and
> Portents of evils imminent; **and on her knee**
> Hath begged that I will **stay at home to-day**."

The crowding of short syllables which this would occasion in the second line is much less harsh and awkward than what the received arrangement produces in the first. But so slight a monosyllable as *and* in the tenth place would give us a structure of verse of which, although common in several of the other Plays, we have no example in this. See *Prolegomena, sect. vi.*

246. *Of evils imminent.*—This conjectural emendation, which appears to be Warburton's, had long been generally accepted; but it has now the authority of Mr Collier's manuscript annotator. The reading in all the old copies is "*And* evils."

247. *For tinctures,* etc.—*Tinctures* and *stains* are understood both by Malone and Steevens as carrying an allusion to the practice of persons dipping their handkerchiefs in the blood of those whom they regarded as martyrs. And it must be confessed that the general strain of the passage, and more especially the expression "shall *press* for tinctures," etc., will not easily allow us to reject this interpretation. Yet does it not make the speaker assign to Cæsar by implication the very kind of death Calphurnia's apprehension of which he professes to regard as visionary? The pressing for tinctures and stains, it is true, would be a confutation of so much of Calphurnia's dream as seemed to imply that the Roman people would be delighted with his death,—

"Many lusty Romans
Came smiling, and did bathe their hands in it."

Do we refine too much in supposing that this inconsistency between the purpose and the language of Decius is intended by the poet, and that in this brief dialogue between him and Cæsar, in which the latter suffers himself to be so easily won over,—persuaded and relieved by the very words that ought naturally to have confirmed his fears,—we are to feel the presence of an unseen power driving on both the unconscious prophet and the blinded victim? *Compare* 408.

Johnson takes both *tinctures* and *cognizance* in the heraldic sense as meaning distinctive marks of honour

o 2

and armorial bearings (in part denoted by colours). But the *stains* and *relics* are not so easily to be accounted for on this supposition; neither would it be very natural to say that men should press to secure such distinctions. The speech altogether Johnson characterizes as "intentionally pompous" and "somewhat confused."

249. *The senate have concluded.*—To **conclude**, for to resolve, is one of numerous expressions, which, although no longer used, are nevertheless almost as universally intelligible as ever. They are the veterans, or *emeriti*, of the language, whose regular active service is over, but who still exist as a reserve force, or retired list, which may always be called out on special occasions.

249. *Apt to be rendered.*—Easy and likely to be thrown out in return or retaliation for your refusing to come.

249. **Shall** *they not whisper?*—We should now say "*Will* they not?" *Vid.* 238.

249. *To your proceeding.*—To your advancement. So in Gloster's protestation, in *Rich. III. iv.* 4,—

"Be opposite all planets of good luck
 To my proceeding! if with dear heart's **love**,
 Immaculate devotion, holy thoughts,
 I tender not thy **beauteous princely daughter;**"

that is, to my prospering, as we should now say.

249. *And reason to my love is liable.*—As if he had said, And, if I have acted wrong in telling you, my excuse is, that my reason where you are concerned is subject to and is overborne by my affection. *Vid.* 67.

250. In the original stage direction the name of *Publius* stands last, instead of first.

252. *Are you stirred.*—We have lost this application of *stirred* (for out of bed). The word now commonly used, *astir*, does not occur in Shakespeare; and, what is remarkable, it has hitherto, although we have long been in the habit of applying it freely in various other ways as

well as in this sense, escaped all or most of our standard lexicographers. I do not find it either in Todd's Johnson, or in Webster, or in Richardson, or in Walker, or in Smart. Of course, the emphasis is on *you.*

253. *'Tis strucken eight.*—Shakespeare uses all the three forms, *struck, strucken,* and *stricken,* of which the existing language has preserved only the first. *Vid.* 192. Mr Collier has here *stricken.* Strictly speaking, of course, the mention of the *striking* of an hour by an old Roman involves an anachronism. Nor is the mode of expression that of the time when here, and in 253 and 272, what we now call eight and nine o'clock in the morning are spoken of as the eighth and ninth hours.

254. *That revels long o' nights.*—Vid. 65. Here again it is *a-nights* in the original text.

256. *Bid them prepare.*—The use of *prepare* thus absolutely (for to make preparation) is hardly now the current language, although it might not seem unnatural in verse, to which some assumption or imitation of the phraseology of the past is not forbidden.

256. *I have an hour's talk*, etc.—*Hour* is here a dissyllable, as such words often are.

259. *That every like is not the same.*—That to be like a thing is not always to be that thing,—said in reference to Cæsar's " We, *like* friends." So the old Scottish proverb, "Like's an ill mark;" and the common French saying, as it has been sometimes converted, "Le vraisemblable n'est pas toujours le vrai." The remark is surely to be supposed to be made aside, as well as that of Trebonius in 257, although neither is so noted in the old copies, and the modern editors, while they retain the direction to that effect inserted by Rowe at 257, have generally struck out the similar one inserted by Pope here. Mr Collier, I see, gives both; but whether on the authority of his MS. annotator does not appear.—In the same manner as here, in *Measure for Measure, v.* 2, to the Duke's

remark, "This is most *likely*," Isabella replies, " O, that it were as *like* as it is true."

259. *The heart of Brutus yearns to think upon.*— *Yearns* is *earnes* in the original text. It has been generally assumed that *yearn* and *earn* are radically the same; the progress of the meaning probably being, it has been supposed, to feel strongly—to desire or long for—to endeavour after—to attain or acquire. But Mr Wedgwood has lately, in a paper published in the *Proceedings* of the *Philological Society*, V. 33 (No. 105, read 21 Feb., 1851), stated strong reasons for doubting whether there be really any connexion between *earn* and either *yearn* or *earnest*. The fundamental notion involved in *earn*, according to the view taken by Mr Wedgwood, is that of harvest or reaping. The primary and essential meaning of *yearn* and *earnest*, again (which are unquestionably of the same stock), may be gathered from the modern German *gern*, willingly, readily, eagerly, which in our Original English was *georn*, and was used as an adjective, signifying desirous, eager, intent. We now commonly employ the verb *to yearn* only in construction with *for* or *after*, and in the sense of to long for or desire strongly. Perhaps the radical meaning may not be more special than to be strongly affected. In the present passage it evidently means to be stung or wrung with sorrow and regret. Shakespeare's construction of the word *yearn*, in so far as it differs from that now in use, may be illustrated by the following examples :—

"It yearns me not if men my garments wear."
Hen. V., iv. 3;

"O, how it yearned my heart, when I beheld."
Rich. II., v. 5.

This is the exclamation of the groom. So Mrs Quickly, in *The Merry Wives of Windsor*, iii. 5 (speaking also, perhaps, in the style of an uneducated person), "Well, she laments, sir, for it, that it would yearn your heart to see it."

"To think upon that every like is" would not have been said in Shakespeare's day, any more than it would be in ours, except under cover of the inversion.

> SCENE III.—*The same. A street near the Capitol.*
>
> *Enter* ARTEMIDORUS, *reading a Paper.*
>
> 260. *Art. Cæsar, beware of* Brutus; *take heed of* Cassius; *come not near* Casca; *have an eye to* Cinna; *trust not* Trebonius; *mark well* Metellus Cimber; Decius Brutus *loves thee not; thou hast wronged* Caius Ligarius. *There is but one mind in all these men, and it is bent against* Cæsar. *If thou be'st not immortal, look about you: Security gives way to conspiracy. The mighty gods defend thee! Thy lover,* Artemidorus.
> Here will I stand, till Cæsar pass along,
> And as a suitor will I give him this.
> My heart laments, that virtue cannot live
> Out of the teeth of emulation.
> If thou read this, O Cæsar, thou mayest live;
> If not, the fates with traitors do contrive. [*Exit.*

260. *Security gives way to.*—In this sense (of leaving a passage open) we should now rather say to make way for. To *give way* has come to mean to yield and break under pressure. The heading of this scene in the original text is merely, *Enter Artemidorus.*

Artemidorus, who was a lecturer on the Greek rhetoric at Rome, had, according to Plutarch, obtained his knowledge of the conspiracy from some of his hearers, who were friends of Brutus, that is, probably, through expressions unintentionally dropt by them.

260. *Thy lover.*—As we might still say " One who loves thee." It is nearly equivalent to friend, and was formerly in common use in that sense. Thus in *Psalm xxxviii.* 11, we have in the old version " My lovers and my neighbours did stand looking upon my trouble," and also in the common version, " My lovers and my friends stand aloof from my sore."—So afterwards in 375 Brutus begins his address to the people, " Romans, countrymen, and

lovers." See other instances from private letters in Chalmers's *Apology*, 165. Another change which has been undergone by this and some other words is that they are now usually applied only to men, whereas formerly they were common to both sexes. This has happened, for instance, to *paramour* and *villain*, as well as to *lover*. But *villain*, as already noticed (186), is still a term of reproach for a woman as well as for a man in some of the provincial dialects. And, although we no longer call a woman a lover, we still say of a man and woman that they are lovers, or a pair of lovers. I find the term *lover* distinctly applied to a woman in so late a work as Smollett's *Count Fathom*, published in 1754:—"These were alarming symptoms to a lover of her delicacy and pride." *Vol. I. ch*. 10.

260. *Out of the teeth of emulation*.— As *envy* (*Vid.* 187) is commonly used by Shakespeare in the sense of hatred or malice, so *emulation*, as here, is with him often envy or malicious rivalry. There are instances, however, of his employing the word, and also the cognate terms *emulator, emulate,* and *emulous*, not in an unfavourable sense.

260. *With traitors do contrive*.—The word **contrive** in the common acceptation is a very irregular derivative from the French *controuver*, an obsolete compound of *trouver* (to find). The English word appears to have been anciently written both *controve* and *contreve* (*Vid.* Chaucer's *Rom. of the Rose*, 4249 and 7547). Spenser, however, has a learned *contrive* of his own (though somewhat irregularly formed too), meaning to spend, consume, wear out, from the Latin *contero, contrivi* (from which we have also *contrite*). And Shakespeare also at least in one place uses the word in this sense:—

"Please you we may contrive this afternoon."
Tam. of Shrew, i. 2.

SCENE IV.—*The same. Another part of the same street, before the house of Brutus.*

Enter PORTIA *and* LUCIUS.

261. *Por.* I pr'ythee, boy, run to the senate-house;
Stay not to answer me, but get thee gone:
Why dost thou stay?
Luc. To know my errand, madam.
263. *Por.* I would have had thee there, and here again,
Ere I can tell thee what thou should'st do there.—
O constancy, be strong upon my side!
Set a huge mountain 'tween my heart and tongue!
I have a man's mind, but a woman's might.
How hard it is for women to keep counsel!—
Art thou here yet?
Luc. Madam, what should I do?
Run to the Capitol, and nothing else?
And so return to you, and nothing else?
Por. Yes, bring me word, boy, if thy lord look well,
For he went sickly forth: And take good note,
What Cæsar doth, what suitors press to him.
Hark, boy! what noise is that?
Luc. I hear none, madam.
267. *Por.* Pr'ythee, listen well;
I heard a bustling rumour, like a fray,
And the wind brings it from the Capitol.
268. *Luc.* Sooth, madam, I hear nothing.

Enter THE SOOTHSAYER.

269. *Por.* Come hither, fellow; Which way hast thou been?
Sooth. At mine own house, good lady.
271. *Por.* What is't o'clock?
Sooth. About the ninth hour, lady.
Por. Is Cæsar yet gone to the Capitol?
Sooth. Madam, not yet; I go to take my stand,
To see him pass on to the Capitol.
Por. Thou hast some suit to Cæsar, hast thou not?
Sooth. That I have, lady: if it will please Cæsar
To be so good to Cæsar as to hear me,
I shall beseech him to befriend himself.
277. *Por.* Why, knowest thou any harm's intended towards him?
278. *Sooth.* None that I know will be, much that I fear may chance.
Good morrow to you.

> Here the street is narrow:
> The throng that follows Cæsar at the heels,
> Of senators, of prætors, common suitors,
> Will crowd a feeble man almost to death;
> I'll get me to a place more void, and there
> Speak to great Cæsar as he comes along. [*Exit.*
> 279. *Por.* I must go in.—Ay me! how weak a thing
> The heart of woman is!
> O Brutus!
> The heavens speed thee in thine enterprise!—
> Sure, the boy heard me:—Brutus hath a suit,
> That Cæsar will not grant.—O, I grow faint:—
> Run, Lucius, and commend me to my lord;
> Say, I am merry, come to me again,
> And bring me word what he doth say to thee. [*Exeunt.*

Scene IV.—The heading of this scene in the original text is only "*Enter Portia and Lucius.*"

261. *Get thee gone.*—An idiom; that is to say, a peculiar form of expression the principle of which cannot be carried out beyond the particular instance. Thus we cannot say either *Make thee gone,* or *He got him* (or *himself*) *gone.* Phraseologies, on the contrary, which are not idiomatic are paradigmatic, or may serve as models or moulds for others to any extent. All expression is divided into these two kinds. And a corresponding division may be made of the inflected parts of speech in any language. Thus, for instance, in Greek or Latin, while certain parts of speech are indeclinable, those that are declined are either paradigmatic (that is, exemplary), such as the noun and the verb, or non-exemplary, such as the articles and the pronouns. They might be distinguished as reproductive and non-reproductive. And such an arrangement of them might be found convenient for some purposes.

263. *O constancy.*—Not exactly our present *constancy*; rather what we should now call firmness or resolution. In the same sense afterwards, in 297, Brutus says, "Cassius, be constant." The French have another use of *constant,—Il est constant* (It is certain),—borrowed from the

Latin impersonal *constat,* and not unknown to *consto.* Vid. 310.

263. *I have a man's mind, but a woman's might.*—That is, but only a woman's might.

263. *How hard it is for women to keep counsel.*— *Counsel* in this phrase is what has been imparted in consultation. In the phrases *To take counsel* and *To hold counsel* it means simply consultation. The two words *Counsel* and *Council* have in some of their applications got a little intermingled and confused, although the Latin *Consilium* and *Concilium*, from which they are severally derived, have no connexion. A rather perplexing instance occurs in a passage towards the conclusion of Bacon's Third Essay, entitled *Of Unity in Religion*, which is commonly thus given in the modern editions:—" Surely in counsels concerning religion, that counsel of the apostle would be prefixed; *Ira hominis non implet justitiam Dei.*" But as published by Bacon himself, if we may trust Mr Singer's late elegant reprint, the words are,—" in Councils concerning Religion, that Counsel of the Apostle—." What are we to say, however, to the Latin version, executed under Bacon's own superintendence?—" Certe optandum esset, ut in omnibus circa Religionem consiliis, ante oculos hominum præfigeretur monitum illud Apostoli." I quote from the Elzevir edition of 1662; p. 20. Does this support *Councils* or *Counsels* concerning Religion? Other somewhat doubtful instances occur in the 20th *Essay*, entitled " Of Counsel," and in the 29th, " Of the True Greatness of Kingdoms and Estates."

267. *I heard a bustling rumour, like a fray.*—Mr Knight has by mistake " I hear."—*Rumour* is here (though not generally in Shakespeare) only a noise; a *fray* is a fight, from the French; *bustle* is apparently connected with *busy,* which is an Original English word, and may perhaps be the same with the German *böse,* wicked. This, if it be so, might lead us to suspect that

quick is also *wicked*. And is *weak* (in Chaucer *wikke* or *wicke*) another variation of the same etymon?

268. Sooth, *madam.*—*Sooth,* when used at all, may still **mean either truth or true.** We see that in Shakespeare's time it also meant truly. The Original English *sóth* is in like manner used in all these different ways. It may be doubted whether this word has any connexion either with our modern verb *to soothe,* or with *sweet* (anciently *sot*), the *süss* of the modern German.

269. *Come hither, fellow; which way hast thou been?*—The line, which stands thus in the original edition, and makes a perfect verse, is commonly cut up into two **hemistichs.** But "*Which* **way hast thou** been" is **not a** possible commencement of **a** verse, unless we were to lay **an** emphasis on *thou,* which would be absurd. **Our** *been,* it may be noted, is here, and commonly elsewhere, *bin* in the old text, as the word is still pronounced. Tyrwhitt would substitute Artemidorus for the Soothsayer in this scene; but the change is not necessary. It is to be observed that we have both Artemidorus and the Soothsayer in the next scene (the First of the Third Act). Nevertheless, there is some apparent want **of artifice** in what may be almost described as the distribution **of** one part **between** two *dramatis* **personæ; and there** may possibly **be** something wrong.

271. *What is't o'clock?*—In the original text *a clocke*. *Vid.* 65.

277. *Why, knowest thou any harm's intended towards him?*—Any harm that is intended. As in 34 and 214.

278. None *that I know,* etc.—Hanmer and **Steevens** object **to** the *may chance* here, as at once unnecessary to the **sense** and injurious to the **prosody. We** should not have **much** missed the **two words, certainly;** but they may be borne **with. The line is bisected in** the original edition; **but, if it is to be accepted, it is** better, perhaps, to consider **it as a prolonged** verse. **In** this somewhat doubtful instance the rhythm will be certainly that of an Alexandrine. Let the three words *know will be*, and also the three *fear may chance*, at any rate, be each and all emphatically enunciated.

278. *I'll get me.*—Compare this with *get thee gone* in 261, and also with *get you home* in 1.

279. *Ay me! how weak a thing.*—This (written *Aye me*) is the reading of all the old copies. That of the modern editions, Mr Collier's one-volume included, is "*Ah me!*" The readers of Milton will remember his "Ay me! I fondly dream, Had we been there," and, again, "Ay me! whilst thee the shores and sounding seas Wash far away," &c. (*Lycidas* 56 and 154). So also in *Comus* 511, and *Samson Agonistes* 330. Even in *Paradise Lost* we have "Ay me! they little know How dearly I abide that boast so vain" (*iv.* 86), and "Ay me! that fear Comes thundering back with dreadful revolution,"—although in the latter passage *ah* has been substituted in many of the modern editions. *Ah me* is a form which he nowhere uses.

279. *The heart of woman is!* etc.—The broken lines here seem to require to be arranged as I have given them. We do not get a complete verse (if that were an object) by the incongruous annexation of the "O Brutus" to the previous exclamation.

279. *Brutus hath a suit,* etc.—This she addresses in explanation to the boy, whose presence she had for a moment forgotten.

279. *Commend me to my lord.*—In this idiomatic or formal phrase the word *commend* has acquired a somewhat peculiar signification. The resolution would seem to be, Give my commendation to him, or Say that I commend myself to him, meaning that I commit and recommend myself to his affectionate remembrance. So we have in Latin "Me totum tuo amori fideique commendo" (*Cicero,* *Epist. ad Att. iii.* 20); and "Tibi me totum

commendo atque trado" (*Id., Epist. Fam.* ii. 6). At the same time, in considering the question of the origin and proper meaning of the English phrase the custom of what was called *Commendation* in the Feudal System is not to be overlooked: the vassal was said to *commend* himself to the person whom he selected for his lord. *Commend* is etymologically the same word with *command*; and both forms, with their derivatives, have been applied, in Latin and the modern tongues more exclusively based upon it, as well as in English, in a considerable variety of ways.

ACT III.

SCENE I.—*The same. The Capitol; the Senate sitting.*

A Crowd of People in the Street leading to the Capitol; among them ARTEMIDORUS *and the* SOOTHSAYER. *Flourish. Enter* CÆSAR, BRUTUS, CASSIUS, CASCA, DECIUS, METELLUS, TREBONIUS, CINNA, ANTONY, LEPIDUS, POPILIUS, PUBLIUS, *and others.*

Cæs. The ides of March are come.
Sooth. Ay, Cæsar; but not gone.
Art. Hail, Cæsar, read this schedule.
283. *Dec.* Trebonius doth desire you to o'er-read,
At your best leisure, this his humble suit.
Art. O, Cæsar, read mine first; for mine's a suit
That touches Cæsar nearer: Read it, great Cæsar.
285. *Cæs.* That touches us? Ourself shall be last served.
Art. Delay not, Cæsar; read it instantly.
Cæs. What, is the fellow mad?
Pub. Sirrah, give place.
289. *Cas.* What, urge you your petitions in the street?
Come to the Capitol.

CÆSAR *enters the Capitol, the rest following. All the* SENATORS *rise.*

Pop. I wish your enterprise to-day may thrive.
Cas. What enterprise, Popilius?
292. *Pop.* Fare you well. [*Advances to* CÆSAR.
Bru. What said Popilius Lena?

Cas. He wished to-day our enterprise might thrive.
I fear our purpose is discovered.
295. *Bru.* Look, how he makes to Cæsar: Mark him.
296. *Cas.* Casca, be sudden, for we fear prevention.—
Brutus, what shall be done? If this be known,
Cassius on Cæsar never shall turn back,
For I will slay myself.
297. *Bru.* Cassius, be constant:
Popilius Lena speaks not of our purposes;
For, look, he smiles, and Cæsar doth not change.
298. *Cas.* Trebonius knows his time; for, look you, Brutus,
He draws Mark Antony out of the way.
             [*Exeunt* ANTONY *and* TREBONIUS. CÆSAR *and the*
              SENATORS *take their seats.*
Dec. Where is Metellus Cimber? Let him go,
And presently prefer his suit to Cæsar.
300. *Bru.* He is addressed: press near and second him.
301. *Cin.* Casca, you are the first that rears your hand.
302. *Casca.* Are we all ready?
Cæs. What is now amiss,
That Cæsar, and his senate, must redress?
304. *Met.* Most high, most mighty, and most puissant Cæsar,
Metellus Cimber throws before thy seat
An humble heart:—   [*Kneeling.*
305. *Cæs.* I must prevent thee, Cimber.
These crouchings, and these lowly courtesies,
Might fire the blood of ordinary men;
And turn pre-ordinance, and first decree,
Into the law of children. Be not fond,
To think that Cæsar bears such rebel blood,
That will be thawed from the true quality
With that which melteth fools; I mean sweet words,
Low-crouched curt'sies, and base spaniel fawning.
Thy brother by decree is banished;
If thou dost bend, and pray, and fawn for him,
I spurn thee like a cur out of my way.
Know, Cæsar doth not wrong; nor without cause
Will he be satisfied.
306. *Met.* Is there no voice more worthy than my own,
To sound more sweetly in great Cæsar's ear
For the repealing of my banished brother?
307. *Bru.* I kiss thy hand, but not in flattery, Cæsar;
Desiring thee that Publius Cimber may

Have an immediate freedom of repeal.
 Cæs. What, Brutus!
309. *Cas.* Pardon, Cæsar; Cæsar, pardon:
As low as to thy foot doth Cassius fall,
To beg enfranchisement for Publius Cimber.
310. *Cæs.* I could be well moved, if I were **as you;**
If I could pray to move, prayers **would move me:**
But I am constant as the northern **star,**
Of whose true fixt and resting quality
There is no fellow in the firmament.
The skies are painted with unnumbered sparks;
They are all fire, and every one doth shine;
But there's but one in all doth hold his place:
So, in the world; 'tis furnished well with men,
And men are flesh and blood, and apprehensive;
Yet, in the number, I do know but one
That unassailable holds on his rank,
Unshaked of motion: and, that I am he,
Let me a little show it, even in this;
That I was constant Cimber should be banished,
And constant do remain to keep him so.
 Cin. O Cæsar,——
312. *Cæs.* Hence! wilt thou lift up Olympus?
 Dec. Great Cæsar,——
314. *Cæs.* Doth not Brutus bootless kneel?
315. *Casca.* Speak, hands, for me.
 [CASCA *stabs* CÆSAR *in the neck.* CÆSAR *catches hold of his arm. He is then stabbed by* **several** *other Conspirators, and at last by* MARCUS BRUTUS.
316. *Cæs. Et tu,* Brute.—Then, **fall,** Cæsar.
 [*Dies. The Senators and People retire in confusion.*
 Cin. Liberty! Freedom! Tyranny is dead!—
Run hence, proclaim, cry it about the streets.
 Cas. **Some** to the common pulpits, and cry out,
Liberty, freedom, and enfranchisement!
319. *Bru.* People, and senators! be not affrighted;
Fly not; stand still:—ambition's debt is paid.
 Casca. Go to the pulpit, Brutus.
 Dec. And Cassius too.
 Bru. Where's Publius?
 Cin. **Here,** quite confounded with this mutiny.
 Met. **Stand** fast together, lest some friend of Cæsar's
Should chance——

325. *Bru.* Talk not of standing: Publius, good cheer;
There is no harm intended to your person,
Nor to no Roman else: so tell them, Publius.
　　Cas. And leave us, Publius; lest that the people,
Rushing on us, should do your age some mischief.
327. *Bru.* Do so;—and let no man abide this deed,
But we the doers.

Re-enter TREBONIUS.

328. *Cas.* Where's Antony?
329. *Tre.* Fled to his house amazed:
Men, wives, and children stare, cry out, and run,
As it were doomsday.
　　Bru. Fates! we will know your pleasures:
That we shall die, we know; 'tis but the time,
And drawing days out, that men stand upon.
331. *Casca.* Why, he that cuts off twenty years of life
Cuts off so many years of fearing death.
　　Bru. Grant that, and then is death a benefit:
So are we Cæsar's friends, that have abridged
His time of fearing death.—Stoop, Romans, stoop,
And let us bathe our hands in Cæsar's blood
Up to the elbows, and besmear our swords:
Then walk we forth, even to the market-place;
And, waving our red weapons o'er our heads,
Let's all cry, Peace! Freedom! and Liberty!
333. *Cas.* Stoop, then, and wash. How many ages hence,
Shall this our lofty scene be acted over
In states unborn, and accents yet unknown!
334. *Bru.* How many times shall Cæsar bleed in sport,
That now on Pompey's basis lies along,
No worthier than the dust!
335. *Cas.* So oft as that shall be,
So often shall the knot of us be called
The men that gave their country liberty.
　　Dec. What, shall we forth?
337. *Cas.* Ay, every man away:
Brutus shall lead; and we will grace his heels
With the most boldest and best hearts of Rome.

Enter a SERVANT.

　　Bru. Soft, who comes here? A friend of Antony's.
339. *Serv.* Thus, Brutus, did my master bid me kneel;
Thus did Mark Antony bid me fall down:

And, being prostrate, thus he bade me say.
Brutus is noble, wise, valiant, and honest;
Cæsar was mighty, bold, royal, and loving:
Say, I love Brutus, and I honour him;
Say, I feared Cæsar, honoured him, and loved him.
If Brutus will vouchsafe, that Antony
May safely come to him, **and be resolved**
How Cæsar hath deserved to lie in death,
Mark Antony shall not love Cæsar dead
So well as Brutus living; but will follow
The fortunes and affairs of noble Brutus,
Thorough the hazards of this untrod state,
With all true faith. So says my master Antony.

340. *Bru.* Thy master is a wise and valiant Roman;
I never thought him worse.
Tell him, so please him come **unto** this place,
He shall be satisfied; and, by my honour,
Depart untouched.
   Serv. I'll fetch him presently.   [*Exit* SERV.

342. *Bru.* I know that we shall have him well to friend.

343. *Cas.* I wish we may: but yet have I a mind
That fears him much; and my misgiving still
Falls shrewdly to the purpose.

   Re-enter ANTONY.

344. *Bru.* But here comes **Antony.—Welcome,** Mark Antony.

345. *Ant.* O mighty Cæsar! Dost thou **lie so low?**
Are all thy conquests, **glories, triumphs, spoils,**
Shrunk to this little measure?—Fare thee **well.**
I know not, gentlemen, what you intend,
Who else must be let blood, who else is rank:
If I myself, there is no hour so fit
As Cæsar's death's hour; nor no instrument
Of half that worth as those your swords, made rich
With the most noble blood of all this world.
I do beseech ye, if you bear me hard,
Now, **whilst your** purpled hands do reek and smoke
Fulfil your pleasure. Live a thousand years,
I shall not find myself so apt to die:
No place will please me so, no mean **of death**
As here, by **Cæsar** and by you, **cut off,**
The choice and master spirits of this age.

346. *Bru.* O Antony! **beg not your** death **of us**

Though now we must appear bloody and cruel,
As, by our hands, and this our present act,
You see we do, yet see you but our hands,
And this the bleeding business they have done:
Our hearts you see not, they are pitiful;
And pity to the general wrong of Rome
(As fire drives out fire, so pity, pity),
Hath done this deed on Cæsar. For your part,
To you our swords have leaden points, Mark Antony:
Our arms, in strength of welcome, and our hearts,
Of brothers' temper, do receive you in
With all kind love, good thoughts, and reverence.
   Cas. Your voice shall be as strong as any man's
In the disposing of new dignities.

348. *Bru.* Only be patient, till we have appeased
The multitude, beside themselves with fear,
And then we will deliver you the cause
Why I, that did love Cæsar when I struck him,
Have thus proceeded.

349. *Ant.* I doubt not of your wisdom.
Let each man render me his bloody hand:
First, Marcus Brutus, will I shake with you:—
Next, Caius Cassius, do I take your hand;—
Now, Decius Brutus, yours;—now yours, Metellus;
Yours, Cinna;—and, my valiant Casca, yours;—
Though last, not least in love, yours, good Trebonius.
Gentlemen all,—alas! what shall I say?
My credit now stands on such slippery ground,
That one of two bad ways you must conceit me,
Either a coward or a flatterer.—
That I did love thee, Cæsar, O, 'tis true:
If then thy spirit look upon us now,
Shall it not grieve thee, dearer than thy death,
To see thy Antony making his peace,
Shaking the bloody fingers of thy foes,
Most noble! in the presence of thy corse?
Had I as many eyes as thou hast wounds,
Weeping as fast as they stream forth thy blood,
It would become me better, than to close
In terms of friendship with thine enemies.
Pardon me, Julius!—Here wast thou bayed, brave hart;
Here didst thou fall; and here thy hunters stand,
Signed in thy spoil, and crimsoned in thy death.

O world! thou wast the forest to this hart;
And this, indeed, O world, the heart of thee.—
How like a deer, strucken by many princes,
Dost thou here lie!
    Cas. Mark Antony,——

351. *Ant.* Pardon me, Caius Cassius:
The enemies of Cæsar shall say this;
Then, in a friend, it is cold modesty.

352. *Cas.* I blame you not for praising Cæsar so;
But what compact mean you to have with us?
Will you be pricked in number of our friends;
Or shall we on, and not depend on you?

353. *Ant.* Therefore I took your hands; but was, indeed,
Swayed from the point, by looking down on Cæsar.
Friends am I with you all, and love you all;
Upon this hope, that you shall give me reasons
Why, and wherein, Cæsar was dangerous.

354. *Bru.* Or else were this a savage spectacle.
Our reasons are so full of good regard,
That, were you, Antony, the son of Cæsar,
You should be satisfied.

355. *Ant.* That's all I seek:
And am moreover suitor, that I may
Produce his body to the market-place;
And in the pulpit, as becomes a friend,
Speak in the order of his funeral.
    Bru. You shall, Mark Antony.

357. *Cas.* Brutus, a word with you.—
You know not what you do; Do not consent
That Antony speak in his funeral:
Know you how much the people may be moved
By that which he will utter?   [*Aside.*

358. *Bru.* By your pardon;—
I will myself into the pulpit first,
And show the reason of our Cæsar's death:
What Antony shall speak, I will protest
He speaks by leave and by permission;
And that we are contented, Cæsar shall
Have all true rites, and lawful ceremonies.
It shall advantage more than do us wrong.

359. *Cas.* I know not what may fall; I like it not.

360. *Bru.* Mark Antony, here, take you Cæsar's body
You shall not in your funeral speech blame us,

But speak all good you can devise of Cæsar,
And say, you do't by our permission;
Else shall you not have any hand at all
About his funeral. And you shall speak
In the same pulpit whereto I am going,
After my speech is ended.
    Ant. Be it so;
I do desire no more.
362. *Bru.* Prepare the body, then, and follow us.
                                [*Exeunt all but* ANTONY.
363. *Ant.* O, pardon me, thou bleeding piece of earth,
That I am meek and gentle with these butchers!
Thou art the ruins of the noblest man
That ever lived in the tide of times.
Woe to the hand that shed this costly blood!
Over thy wounds now do I prophesy,—
Which, like dumb mouths, do ope their ruby lips
To beg the voice and utterance of my tongue:—
A curse shall light upon the loins of men;
Domestic fury, and fierce civil strife,
Shall cumber all the parts of Italy:
Blood and destruction shall be so in use,
And dreadful objects so familiar,
That mothers shall but smile when they behold
Their infants quartered with the hands of war;
All pity choked with custom of fell deeds:
And Cæsar's spirit ranging for revenge,
With Ate by his side, come hot from hell,
Shall in these confines, with a monarch's voice,
Cry *Havoc!* and let slip the dogs of war;
That this foul deed shall smell above the earth
With carrion men, groaning for burial.

                   Enter a SERVANT.

You serve Octavius Cæsar, do you not?
    Serv. I do, Mark Antony.
    Ant. Cæsar did write for him to come to Rome.
366. *Serv.* He did receive his letters, and is coming:
And bid me say to you by word of mouth,—
O Cæsar!——   [*Seeing the Body.*
367. *Ant.* Thy heart is big; get thee apart and weep.
Passion, I see, is catching; for mine eyes,
Seeing those beads of sorrow stand in thine,

Began to water. **Is** thy master coming?
Serv. He lies to-night within seven leagues of Rome.
369. *Ant.* Post back with speed, and tell him what hath chanced:
Here is a mourning Rome, a dangerous **Rome,**
No Rome of safety for Octavius **yet;**
Hie hence, and tell him so. Yet, stay a while;
Thou shalt not back, till I have borne **this corpse**
Into the market-place: there shall I try,
In my oration, **how** the people take
The cruel issue of these bloody men;
According to the which thou shalt discourse
To young Octavius of the state of things.
Lend me your **hand.** [*Exeunt with* CÆSAR'S *body.*

All the heading that we have to this Act in the original copy, where the whole is thrown into one scene, is, "*Flourish. Enter Cæsar, Brutus, Cassius, Caska, Decius, Metellus, Trebonius, Cynna, Antony, Lepidus, Artemidorus, Publius, and* the *Soothsayer.*"—A *Flourish* is defined by **Johnson** "**a** kind of musical prelude." It is commonly, if **not always,** of trumpets. Webster has omitted this sense **of** the word. It is of continual occurrence in the stage directions of our old Plays; and Shakespeare has, **not** only in his *Richard the Third, iv.* 4,

"A flourish, trumpets!—strike alarum, **drums!**"

but in *Titus Andronicus, iv.* 2,

"Why do the emperor's **trumpets flourish thus?**"

283. **Doth** *desire you* **to** *o'er-read.*—*Over* (or *o'er*) in composition has four meanings:—1. Throughout (or over all), **which is** its effect here (answering to the *per* in the equivalent *peruse*); 2. Beyond, or in excess, as in *overleap, overpay;* 3. Across, as in one sense of *overlook;* 4. **Down** upon, as in another sense of the same verb.

283. **At** *your best leisure.*—Literally, **at the** leisure that **is** best **for** your convenience, that **best** suits you. The phrase, however, **had come to be** understood as implying **that the** leisure was **also to be as** early as could be made convenient.

283. *This his humble suit.*—*Suit* is from *sue* (which we also have in composition in *ensue, issue, pursue*); and *sue* is the French *suivre* (which, again, is from the Latin *sequor, secutus*). A *suit* of clothes is a set, one piece *following* or corresponding to another. *Suite* is the same word, whether used for a retinue, or for any other kind of succession (such as a *suite* of apartments).

285. *That touches us? Ourself shall be last served.*—This is the correction of Mr Collier's MS. annotator. The common reading is, "What touches us ourself shall be last served." To *serve*, or attend to, a *person* is a familiar form of expression; to speak of a *thing* as *served*, in the sense of attended to, would, it is apprehended, be unexampled. The "us ourself," however, would be unobjectionable. Whatever may be the motive or view which has led to the substitution of the plural for the singular personal pronoun in certain expressions, it is evident that the plurality of the pronoun could not conveniently be allowed to carry along with it a corresponding transformation of all the connected words. Although an English king might speak of himself as *We*, it would be felt that the absurdity was too great if he were to go on to say, "We the *Kings* of England." Hence such awkward combinations as "We ourself," or "Us ourself;" which, however, are only exemplifications of the same construction which we constantly employ in common life when in addressing an individual we say "You yourself." The same contradiction, indeed, is involved in the word *Yourself* standing alone. It may be observed, however, that the verb always follows the number of the pronoun which is its nominative, so that there is never any violation of the ordinary rule of grammatical concord. Upon the nature of the word *Self*, see Latham, *Eng. Lan.* 416. See also the note on 54, *Did lose his lustre*.

289. There is no such stage direction in the old editions as we now have at the end of this speech.

292. The stage direction attached to this speech is also modern.

295. *Look, how he makes to Cæsar.*—We should now say, he makes up to. And we also say to make *for*, with another meaning.—For the prosody of this verse, see note on 246.

296. *Casca, be sudden,* etc.—We should now rather say, Be quick. *Prevention* is hindrance by something happening before that which is hindered. *Vid.* 147.

296. *Cassius on Cæsar never shall turn back.*—The reading of all the old copies is "*or* Cæsar," and it is retained by most or all of the modern editors. It is interpreted by Ritson as meaning "Either Cæsar or I shall never return alive." But to *turn back* cannot mean to return alive, or to return in any way. The most it could mean would be to make a movement towards returning; which is so far from being the same thing with the accomplished return which this translation would have it to imply that it may almost be said to be the very opposite. Besides, even if to turn back could mean here to leave or get away from the Capitol alive, although Cassius, by plunging his dagger into his own heart, would indeed have prevented himself from so escaping, how was that act to bring with it any similar risk to Cæsar? I will slay myself, Cassius is supposed to say, whereby either I shall lose my life or Cæsar will his. The emendation of "*or* Cæsar" into "*on* Cæsar" was proposed and is strongly supported by Malone, although he did not venture to introduce it into his text. We have probably the opposite misprint of *on* for *or* in the speech of Paulina in the concluding scene of *The Winter's Tale*, where the old copies give us—

> "Then, all stand still:
> *On :* those that think it is unlawful business
> I am about, let them depart."

Although Mr Knight adheres to the *on* and the point.

297. *Cassius, be constant.—Vid.* 203.

297. *Popilius Lena speaks not of our purposes.*—Although this verse has twelve syllables, it is not for that an Alexandrine. Its rhythm is the same as if the last word had been merely the dissyllable *purpose*, or even a monosyllable, such as *act* or *deed*. It is completed by the strong syllable *pur-* in the tenth place, and the two unaccented syllables that follow have no prosodical effect. Of course, there is also an oratorical emphasis on *our*, although standing in one of those places which do not require an accented syllable, but which it is a mistake to suppose incapable of admitting such.

297. *Cæsar doth not change.*—In his manner of looking, or the expression of his countenance.

298. The stage direction attached to this speech is modern.

300. *He is addressed.*—To *dress* is the same word with to *direct*. Immediately from the French *dresser*, it is ultimately from the Latin *rectus* and *directus*, through the Italian *rizzare* and *dirizzare;* and its literal meaning, therefore, is, to make right or straight. Formerly, accordingly, anything was said to be *dressed* or *addressed* when it was in complete order for the purpose to which it was to be applied. Thus, in the *Second Part of King Henry the Fourth, iv.* 4, the King says, " Our navy is addressed, our power collected;" and in *A Midsummer Night's Dream, v.* 1, Philostrate, the Master of the Revels, makes his official announcement to Theseus thus;—" So please your Grace, the prologue is addressed." So *He is addressed* in the present passage means merely He is ready. The primary sense of the word is still retained in such phrases as To dress the ranks; and it is not far departed from in such as To dress cloth or leather, To dress a wound, To dress meat. The notion of decoration or embellishment which we commonly associate with dressing does not enter fully even into the expression To

dress the hair. In To *redress*, meaning **to set to rights again** that which has gone wrong, to make that which was crooked once more straight, we have the simple etymological or radical import of the **word** completely preserved. To redress is to re-rectify.

The following are some examples of the employment of the word *addressed* by writers of the latter part of the seventeenth century:—"When Middleton came to the King in Paris, he brought with him a little Scotish vicar, who was known to the King, one Mr Knox.... He said he was addressed from Scotland to the Lords in the Tower, who did not then know that Middleton had arrived in safety with the King;" etc.—*Clarendon, Hist., Book xiii.* "Thereupon they [the King's friends in England] sent Harry Seymour, who, being of his Majesty's bedchamber, and having his leave to attend his own affairs in England, they well knew would be believed by the King, and, being addressed only to the Marquis of Ormond and the Chancellor of the Exchequer, he might have opportunity to speak with the King privately and undiscovered;" etc.—*Id., Book xiv.* "Though the messengers who were sent were addressed only to the King himself and to the Chancellor of the Exchequer;" etc.—*Ibid.* "Two gentlemen of Kent came to Windsor the morning after the Prince [of Orange] came thither. They were addressed to me. And they told me;" etc.—*Burnet, Own Time*, I. 799.

301. *You are the first that rears your hand.*—In strict grammar, perhaps, it should be either "rears his" or "rear your;" but the business of an editor of Shakespeare is not to make for us in all cases perfect grammar, but to give us what his author in all probability wrote. A writer's grammatical irregularities are as much part of his style, and therefore of his mind and of himself, as any other characteristic.

302. Casca. *Are we all ready?* 303. Cæs. *What is*

now amiss, etc. There can, I think, be no doubt that Mr Collier's MS. annotator has here again given us the true reading, and a valuable restoration. What Casca could possibly mean by exclaiming " What is now amiss, That Cæsar and his Senate must redress ? " is nearly inconceivable. The question is plainly suitable to Cæsar only, to the person presiding; the proceedings could never have been so opened by any mere member of the Senate. And the absurdity of supposing it to have been spoken by Casca becomes still stronger when we have to consider it as a natural sequence of the " Are we all ready ? " which immediately precedes. Even if any one of the conspirators was likely to have made such a display, it was hardly Casca.

304. *Most puissant Cæsar.*—*Puissant,* and the substantive form *puissance,* are, I believe, always dissyllables in Milton; with Shakespeare they generally are so (as here), but not always. Thus in *King John, iii.* 1, the King says to the Bastard,

"Cousin, go draw our puissance together."

Walker, however, is mistaken in producing the line—

"Either past, or not arrived to pith and puissance"—

(from the Chorus before the Third Act of *King Henry the Fifth*) as necessarily to be read with the trisyllabic division of the word. It is not even probable that it ought to be so read,—barely possible. In Spenser too we have occasionally this pronunciation:—as in *F. Q. v.* 2, 7, "For that he is so puissant and strong;" and again in st. 17, " His puissance, ne bear himself upright."

305. *These crouchings.*—This is the correction (for the *couchings* of the old printed copies) of Mr Collier's MS. annotator. Surely it does not admit of a doubt.

305. *And turn pre-ordinance,* etc.—The reading of the old text here is " into the lane of children." Malone actually attempts an explanation of " the *lane* of children ;" he says it may mean " the narrow conceits of children,

which must change as their minds grow more enlarged"! The prostration of the human understanding before what it has got to hold as authority can hardly be conceived to go beyond this. Johnson conjectured that *lane* might be a misprint for *law;* and Mr Collier's MS. annotator, it appears, makes the same emendation. The new reading may still be thought not to be perfectly satisfactory; but at least it is not utter nonsense, like the other. In a passage which has evidently suffered some injury, we may perhaps be allowed to suspect that "*first* decree" should be "*fixed* decree." The word would be spelled *fixt*, as it is immediately afterwards in 310.

305. *Be not fond,* etc.—The sense in which *fond* is used here (that of foolish) appears to be the original one; so that when tenderness of affection was first called fondness it must have been regarded as a kind of folly. In like manner what was thought of doting upon anything, or any person, may be inferred from the import of the word *dotage.* In Chaucer a *fonne* is a fool; and the word *fondling* can scarcely be said to have yet lost that meaning (though it is omitted by Dr Webster).

305. *Such rebel blood, That will be thawed.*—*Vid.* 44.

305. *Low-crouched curt'sies.*—This is the correction of Mr Collier's MS. annotator: the Folios have "Low-crooked-curtsies" (with hyphens connecting all the three words). We say *to crouch low,* but not *to crook low. Curt'sies,* which we have here, is the same word which appears in the second line of the present speech as *courtesies.* It is akin to *court* and *courteous,* the immediate root being the French *cour;* which, again, appears to be the Latin *curia,*—or rather *curiata* (scil. *comitia?*), as is indicated by our English *court,* and the old form of the French word, which was the same, and also by the Italian *corte* and the Spanish *corte* and *cortes.* Mr Collier prints *curtesies.* It is *curtsies* in the Second Folio, as well as in the First.

305. *Know, Cæsar doth not wrong*, etc.—This is the reading of all the old printed copies, and Mr Collier expressly states that it is left untouched by his MS. corrector. We must take it as meaning, "Cæsar never does what is wrong, or unjust; nor will he be appeased (when he has determined to punish) without sufficient reason being shown." At the same time, it must be confessed both that these two propositions, or affirmations, do not hang very well together, and also that such meaning as they may have is not very clearly or effectively expressed by the words. "Nor without cause will he be satisfied" has an especially suspicious look. That "without cause" should mean without sufficient reason being shown why he should be satisfied or induced to relent is only an interpretation to which we are driven for want of a better. Now, all this being so, it is remarkable that there is good evidence that the passage did not originally stand as we now have it. Ben Jonson, in his *Discoveries*, speaking of Shakespeare, says, "Many times he fell into those things could not escape laughter; as when he said in the person of Cæsar, one speaking to him, 'Cæsar, thou dost me wrong,' he replied, 'Cæsar did never wrong but with just cause.'" And he ridicules the expression again in his *Staple of News*:—"Cry you mercy; you never did wrong but with just cause." We must believe that the words stood originally as Jonson has given them; and he had evidently heard of no alteration of them. Whoever may have attempted to mend them might perhaps have as well let them alone. After all, Cæsar's declaring that he never did wrong but with just cause would differ little from what Bassanio says in *The Merchant of Venice, iv.* 1 :—

> "I beseech you,
> Wrest once the law to your authority :
> To do a great right do a little wrong."

Shakespeare, however, may have retouched the passage himself on being told of Jonson's ridicule of it, though perhaps somewhat hastily and with less painstaking than Euripides when he mended or cut out, as he is said to have done in several instances, what had incurred the derisive criticism of Aristophanes.

306. *For the repealing*, etc.—To *repeal* (from the French *rappeler*) is literally to recall, though no longer used in that sense,—in which, however, it repeatedly occurs in Shakespeare. Thus in *Coriolanus, iv.* 1, after the banishment of Marcius, his friend Cominius says to him,

"If the time thrust forth
A cause for thy *repeal*, we shall not send," etc.

For the probable pronunciation of *banished* in this and in the preceding speech, see the note on 246.

307. *Desiring thee.*—We should now say in this sense "desiring of thee." To *desire*, from the Latin *desiderium* (through the French *désir*) is the same as to desiderate; but, like other similar terms, it has in different constructions, or has had in different stages of the language, various meanings according to the measure or degree of intensity in which that which it expresses is conceived to be presented. It may be found in every sense, from such wishing or longing as is the gentlest and quietest of all things (the *soft desire* of the common herd of our amatory versemongers) to that kind which gives utterance to itself in the most imperative style of command.

307. *An immediate freedom of repeal.*—A free unconditional recall. This application of the term *freedom* is a little peculiar. It is apparently imitated from the expression *freedom of a city*. As that is otherwise called the municipal *franchise*, so this is called *enfranchisement* in the next speech but one.

309. *As low as to thy foot.*—The Second Folio has "As *love*."

310. *I could be well moved.*—I could fitly or properly be moved.

310. *If I could pray to move, prayers would move me.*—

The meaning seems to be, "If I could employ prayers (as you can do) to move (others), then I should be moved by prayers (as you might be)." But it is somewhat dark. The commentators see no difficulty, or at least give us no help. "The oracles are dumb."

310. *But I am constant as the northern star.*—*Vid.* 203. Both in this line and in the two last lines of the present speech, the term *firm* would more nearly express the notion in our modern English.

310. *Resting quality.*—Quality or property of remaining at rest or immovable.

310. *But there's but one in all doth hold his place.*— That is, *its* place, as we should now say. *Vid.* 54.

310. *Apprehensive.*—Possessed of the power of apprehension, or intelligence. The word is now confined to another meaning.

310. *That unassailable*, etc.—*Holds on his rank* probably means continues to hold his place; and *unshaked of motion*, perhaps, unshaken by any motion, or solicitation, that may be addressed to him. Or, possibly, it may be, Holds on his course unshaken in his motion, or with perfectly steady movement.

312. *Wilt thou lift up Olympus?*—Wilt thou attempt an impossibility? Think you, with your clamour, to upset what is immovable as the everlasting seat of the Gods?

314. *Doth not Brutus bootless kneel?*—Has not Brutus been refused, and shall any other be listened to? It is surprising that Dr Johnson should have missed seeing this, and proposed to read "Do not, Brutus, bootless kneel." That, however (which Johnson does not appear to have known), is also the reading of the Second Folio, —except, indeed, that the point of interrogation is, notwithstanding, still preserved. Mr Collier in his regulated text adheres to the reading of the First Folio; but it does not appear that he has the sanction of any restoration of

that reading, or correction of that of the Second Folio, by his MS. annotator.

315.—The only stage direction after this speech in the original edition is, " *They stab Cæsar.*"

316. *Et tu, Brute.*—There is no ancient Latin authority, I believe, for this famous exclamation, although in Suetonius, I. 82, Cæsar is made to address Brutus Καὶ σὺ, τέκνον; (And thou too, my son?). It may have occurred as it stands here in the Latin play on the same subject which is recorded to have been acted at Oxford in 1582; and it is found in *The True Tragedy of Richard Duke of York*, first printed in 1595, on which the *Third Part of King Henry the Sixth* is founded, as also in a poem by S. Nicholson, entitled *Acolastus his Afterwit*, printed in 1600, in both of which nearly contemporary productions we have the same line:—"*Et tu, Brute?* Wilt thou stab Cæsar too?" It may just be noticed, as the historical fact, that the meeting of the Senate at which Cæsar was assassinated was held, not, as is here assumed, in the Capitol, but in the Curia in which the statue of Pompey stood, being, as Plutarch tells us, one of the edifices which Pompey had built, and had given, along with his famous Theatre, to the public. It adjoined the Theatre, which is spoken of (with the Portico surrounding it) in 130, 138, and 140. The mistake which we have here is found also in *Hamlet*, where (*iii.* 2) Hamlet questions Polonius about his histrionic performances when at the University: "I did enact Julius Cæsar," says Polonius; "I was killed i' the Capitol; Brutus killed me;" to which the Prince replies, "It was a brute part of him to kill so capital a calf there." So also, in *Antony and Cleopatra, ii.* 6:—

> "What
> Made the all-honoured, honest, Roman Brutus,
> With the armed rest, courtiers of beauteous freedom,
> To drench the Capitol?"

Even Beaumont and Fletcher, in their Tragedy entitled

The False One, in defending themselves from the imputation of having taken up the same subject which had been already brought on the stage in the present Play, say:—

> "Sure to tell
> Of Cæsar's amorous heats, and how he fell
> I' the Capitol, can never be the same
> To the judicious."

In the old copies the only stage direction at the end of this speech is the word "*Dies*."

319. *Ambition's debt is paid.*—Its debt to the country and to justice. Unless, as a friend suggests, the meaning may be—Ambition has now received its reward, its due.

325. *Nor to no Roman else.*—Where, as here, the sense cannot be mistaken, the reduplication of the negative is a very natural way of strengthening the expression. Steevens remarks that, according to Hickes, we have in the English of the times before the Conquest sometimes so many as four negatives employed in combination for this end.

327. *And let no man abide this deed.*—Let no man be held responsible for, or be required to stand any consequences that may follow upon any penalty that may have to be paid on account of, this deed. Another form of the verb to *abide* is to *aby*; as in *A Midsummer Night's Dream*, iii. 2:—

> "If thou dost intend
> Never so little shew of love to her,
> Thou shalt *aby* it;"

and in the same scene, a little before, "Lest to thy peril thou *aby* it dear;" and, a little after, "Thou shalt '*by* this dear." So in the Old Version of the *Psalms*, iii. 26, "Thou shalt dear *aby* this blow." It may be questioned whether *abide* in this sense has any connexion with the common word. To *aby* has been supposed by some to be the same with *buy*.—The original stage direction is *Enter Trebonius*.

328. *Where's Antony.*—In the original text, "Where is Antony."

329. *As it were doomsday.*—Assuming the proper meaning of *as* to be what was explained in the note on 44, *as it were* will mean literally no more than *that it were*, and there will be no express intimation of the clause being suppositive or conditional; that will be left to be merely inferred from the obvious requirements of the context, as many things in language continually are where no doubt can exist. The full expression would be "as *if* it were doomsday."—The *doom* of *doomsday* is no doubt the same word with *deem*, and means essentially only thought or judging, whether favourable or unfavourable. The Judges in the Isle of Man and in Jersey are called *Deemsters*, meaning, apparently, only pronouncers of judgment upon the cases brought before them. On the other hand, however, in Scotland formerly the *Dempster of Court* was the legal name for the common hangman. This might suggest a possible connexion between *deem* or *doom* and the Latin *damno* (or *demno*, as in *condemno*). But the name *Dempster* in Scotland also designated a species of judge. The Dempsters of Caraldstone in Forfarshire were so called as being hereditary judges to the great Abbey of Aberbrothock. Lord Hailes, under the year 1370, refers to an entry in the Chartulary recording that one of them had become bound to the Abbot and Abbey that he and his heirs should furnish a person to administer justice in their courts at an annual salary of twenty shillings sterling (*facient ipsis deserviri de officio judicis*, etc.).—*Annals*, II. 336 [edit. of 1819]. We continue to use *deem* indifferently; but another word originally of the same general signification, *censure*, has within the last two centuries lost its old sense, and has come to be restricted to that of pronouncing an unfavourable judgment. The other sense, however, is still retained in *census, recension,* and *censor*, with its derivative *censorship*

(as it is in the French forms for the two last-mentioned, *censeur* and *censure*).

331. *Why, he that cuts off*, etc.—The modern editors, generally, give this speech to *Cassius;* but it is assigned to *Casca* in all the old copies. We may suspect a misprint, —for not only is it more in the manner of Cassius, but it does not seem to be so suitable to the comparatively subordinate position of Casca at the present moment;—still, considerations of this kind are not decisive enough to warrant us in departing from the only text which claims to be of authority. No alteration is made by Mr Collier's MS. corrector. But it certainly would be nothing more than what we should expect that some confusion should have taken place in the printing of this Play between *Cassius* and *Casca*, as well as between *Lucilius* and *Lucius*.

332. *Stoop, then, and wash.*—So in *Coriolanus, i.* 10, we have—" *Wash* my fierce hand in his heart." In both passages *wash*, which is an Original English word (preserved also in the German *waschen*), is used in what is probably its primitive sense of immersing in or covering with liquid. Thus we say to *wash* with gold or silver. So in *Antony and Cleopatra, v.* 1, Octavius, on being told of the death of Antony, exclaims, " It is a tidings To *wash* the eyes of kings."

333. *In states unborn.*—The First Folio, and that only, has "In *state* unborn,"—palpably a typographical error, and as such now given up by everybody, but a reading which Malone, in his abject subservience to the earliest text, actually retained, or restored, interpreting it as meaning "in theatric pomp as yet undisplayed."

334. *That now on Pompey's basis lies along.*—At the base of Pompey's statue, as in 426.—In the copy of the First Folio before me it is " *lye* along ;" but I do not find such a variation anywhere noticed,—not even in Jennens's collation. *Lyes* is the word in the Second Folio.

335. *The men that gave their country liberty.*—This is

the reading of all the old copies, which Mr Knight has **restored, after** *their* had been turned into *our* by **the last century** editors (Malone included), not only unnecessarily and unwarrantably, **but also** without notice.

337. *With the* **most boldest.**—**In the** old version of the **Psalms we** are familiar with **the form** *the most Highest;* **and even** in the authorized translation of the Bible we have, **in** *Acts xxvi.* 5, "the **most** straitest **sect** of our religion." Nor **is** there anything intrinsically absurd in such a mode of expression. If we are not satisfied to consider it as merely an intensified superlative, we may say that *the most boldest* should mean those who are boldest among the boldest. So again in 426; "This was the most unkindest cut of all." **In** most cases, however, the double superlative **must be** regarded as intended merely to express **the extreme** degree more emphatically. Double comparatives **are** very common in Shakespeare.

339. *Say,* I *love Brutus.*—Mr Knight has, apparently by a typographical error, "I lov'd."

339. *May safely come to him, and be resolved.*—That is, have his perplexity or uncertainty removed. We might still say, have his doubts resolved. But we have lost the more terse form **of** expression, **by which** the doubt was formerly identified with **the doubter.** So again, in 426, Cæsar's blood is described by **Antony as**

"—rushing **out of** doors, **to** be resolved
If **Brutus so** unkindly knocked or no;"

and in 506 Brutus, referring to Cassius, asks of Lucilius, "How he received you, let me be resolved."—Mr **Collier's** MS. annotator appends the stage direction "*Kneeling*" to the first line of this speech, and "*Rising*" **to** the last.

340. *Tell him,* **so please** *him* **come** *unto this place.*—For the meaning of *so* here, **see the note on** "So with love I might entreat you," in 57. **There is** an ellipsis of the usual nominative (*it*) before the impersonal verb (*please*);

and the infinitive *come* also wants the customary prefix *to*. "So please him come" is equivalent to If it please (or may please) him to come.

342. *I know that we shall have him well to friend.*—So in *Cymbeline*, *i*. 5, Iachimo says, "Had I admittance and opportunity to friend." So Macbeth (*iii*. 3), "What I can redress, As I shall find the time to friend, I will." Even in Clarendon we have, "For the King had no port to friend by which he could bring ammunition to Oxford," etc.—*Hist., Book vii*. *To friend* is equivalent to *for friend*. So we say *To take to wife*. The German form of *to* (*zu*) is used in a somewhat similar manner: *Das wird mich zu eurem Freunde machen* (That will make me your friend). In the *Winter's Tale*, *v*. 1, We have "All greetings that a King at friend Can send his brother."

343. *Falls shrewdly to the purpose.*—The *purpose* is the intention; *to* the purpose is according to the intention, as *away from* the purpose, or *beside* the purpose, is without any such coincidence or conformity; and to *fall shrewdly to* the purpose may be explained as being to fall upon that which it is sought to hit with mischievous sharpness and felicity of aim. *Vid.* 186.

344. The original heading is "*Enter Antony.*"

345. *O mighty Cæsar! dost thou lie so low?*—Mr Collier states, in his *Notes and Emendations*, p. 400, that a stage direction of his MS. annotator requires Antony, on his entrance with this line, to kneel over the body, and to rise when he comes to "I know not, gentlemen, what you intend," etc.

345. *Who else is rank.*—Is of too luxuriant growth, too fast-spreading power in the commonwealth.

345. *As Cæsar's death's hour.*—This is the reading of all the old copies. Mr Collier prints "*death* hour."

345. *Nor no instrument.*—Here the double negative, while it occasions no ambiguity, is palpably much more forcible than either *and no* or *nor any* would have been.

345. *Of half that worth as.*—Vid. 44.

345. *I do beseech ye, if you bear me hard.*—See note on *Bear me hard* in 105.—The present line affords a remarkable illustration of how completely the old declension of the personal pronoun of the second person has become obliterated in our modern English. Milton too almost always has *ye* in the accusative. Thus (*Par. Lost, x.* 402):—"I call ye, and declare ye now, returned Successful beyond hope, to lead ye forth," etc. In the original form of the language *ye* (ge) is always nominative, and *you* (eów) accusative; being the very reverse of what we have here.

345. *Live a thousand years.*—Suppose I live; If I live; Should I live. But, although the suppression of the conditional conjunction is common and legitimate enough, that of the pronoun, or nominative to the verb, is hardly so defensible. The feeling probably was that the *I* in the next line might serve for both verbs.

345. *So apt to die.*—*Apt* is properly fit, or suited, generally, as here. So formerly they said *to apt* in the sense both of to adapt and of to agree. I apprehend, however, that such an expression as *apt to die* (for ready or prepared to die) would have been felt in any stage of the language to involve an unusual extension of the meaning of the word, sounding about as strange as *aptus ad moriendum* would do in Latin. We now, at all events, commonly understand the kind of suitableness or readiness implied in *apt* as being only that which consists in inclination, or addictedness, or mere liability. Indeed, we usually say *disposed* or *inclined* in cases in which *apt* was the customary word in the English of the last century; as in Smollett's *Count Fathom, Vol.* II. *ch.* 27, "I am apt to believe it is the voice of heaven." By the substantive *aptitude*, again, we mostly understand an active fitness. The word *apte* was wont to be not much used in French; some of the dictionaries do not notice it;

Richelet characterizes it as obsolete; adding, on the authority of Father Bouhours, that the noun *aptitude* is occasionally employed, although not considered to belong to the Court language. Like many other old-fashioned words, however, this has been revived by recent writers. Such expressions as "On est apte à juger," meaning "One has no difficulty in concluding," are common in modern books.

345. *As here, by Cæsar and by you, cut off.*—We may resolve the ellipsis by saying "as to be," or "as being cut off." And "*by* Cæsar" is, of course, beside Cæsar; "*by you*," through your act or instrumentality. A play of words, as it is called, was by no means held in Shakespeare's day to be appropriate only to sportive writing,— any more than was any other species of verbal artifice or ornament, such, for instance, as alliteration, or rhyme, or verse itself. Whatever may be the etymology of *by*, its primary meaning seems to be alongside of (the same, apparently, with that of the Greek παρά). It is only by inference that instrumentality is expressed either by it or by *with* (the radical notion involved in which appears to be that of joining or uniting). Vid. 620.

345. *The choice and master spirits of this age.*—*Choice* here may be understood either in the substantive sense as the *élite*, or, better perhaps, as an adjective in concord with *spirits*.

346. *O Antony! beg not your death of us.*—That is, If you prefer death, or if you are resolved upon death, let it not be of us that you ask it. The sequel of the speech seems decisive in regard to the *us* being the emphatic word.

346. *And this the bleeding business.*—Only a more vivid expression for the bloody business, the sanguinary act.

346. *Our hearts you see not, they are pitiful.*—Probably the primary sense of the Latin *pius* and *pietas* may have been nothing more than emotion, or affection, generally.

But the words had come to be confined to the expression of reverential affection towards a superior, such as the gods or a parent. From *pietas* the Italian language has received *pietà* (anciently *pietade*), which has the senses both of reverence and of compassion. The French have moulded the word into two forms, which (according to what frequently takes place in language) have been respectively appropriated to the two senses; and from their *piété* and *pitié* we have borrowed, and applied in the same manner, our *piety* and *pity*. To the former, moreover, we have assigned the adjective *pious*; to the latter, *piteous*. But *pity*, which meant at one time reverence, and afterwards compassion, has come in some of its uses to suffer still further degradation. By *pitiful* (or full of pity) Shakespeare, as we see here, means full of compassion; but the modern sense of *pitiful* is contemptible or despicable. "Pity," it has been said, or sung, "melts the soul to love;" but this would seem to show that it is also near akin to a very different passion. And, instead of turning to love, it would seem more likely that it should sometimes pass on from contempt to aversion and hatred. In many cases, too, when we say that we pity an individual, we mean that we despise or loathe him.

346. *As fire drives out fire, so pity pity.*—In this line the first *fire* is a dissyllable (like *hour* in 256), the second a monosyllable. The illustration we have here is a favourite one with Shakespeare. "Tut, man," says Benvolio to his friend Romeo (*Romeo and Juliet, i.* 2),

"—— one fire burns out another's burning,
One pain is lessened by another's anguish."

" One fire burns out one fire; one nail, one nail,"

exclaims Tullus Aufidius, in *Coriolanus* (*iv.* 7). But we have the thought most fully expressed in the soliloquy of Proteus in the Fourth Scene of the Second Act of *The Two Gentlemen of Verona:*—

> "Even as one heat another heat expels,
> Or as one nail by strength drives out another,
> So the remembrance of my former love
> Is by a newer object quite forgotten."

This is probably also the thought which we have in the heroic *Bastard's* exhortation to his uncle, in *King John*, v. 1:—

> "Be stirring as the time; be fire with fire;
> Threaten the threatener;" etc.

346. *For your part.*—We should not now use this phrase in the sense which it has here (in so far as regards you).

346. *Our arms, in strength of welcome.*—The reading in all the old printed copies is, "in strength of *malice*." Steevens interprets this, "strong in the deed of malice they have just performed," and Malone accepts the explanation as a very happy one. But who can believe that Brutus would ever have characterized the lofty patriotic passion by which he and his associates had been impelled and nerved to their great deed as *strength of malice?* It is simply impossible. The earlier editors, accordingly, seeing that the passage as it stood was nonsense, attempted to correct it conjecturally in various ways. Pope boldly printed "exempt from malice." Capel, more ingeniously, proposed "no strength of malice," connecting the words, not with those that follow, but with those that precede. But the mention of *malice* at all is manifestly in the highest degree unnatural. Nevertheless the word has stood in every edition down to that in one volume produced by Mr Collier in 1853; and there, for the first time, instead of "strength of *malice*," we have "strength of *welcome*." This turns the nonsense into excellent sense; and the two words are by no means so unlike as that, in a cramp hand or an injured or somewhat faded page, the one might not easily have been mistaken by the first printer or editor for the other. The "welcome" would probably

be written *welcōe*. Presuming the correction to have been made on documentary authority, it is one of the most valuable for which we are indebted to the old annotator. Even as a mere conjecture, it would be well entitled to notice and consideration.

346. *Of brothers' temper.*—Brothers, that is, to one another (not to you, Antony).

348. *Beside themselves.*—Other forms of the same figure are *Out of themselves, Out of their senses*. And in the same notion we say of a person whose mind is deranged that he is not himself.

348. *And then we will deliver you the cause.*—The history of the word *deliver* (properly to set free, to let go forth, and hence, as applied to what is expressed in words, to declare, to pronounce) presents some points worthy of notice. In Latin (besides *lĭber*, bark, or a book, and its derivative *delĭbrare*, to peel off, with which we have at present no concern), there are the adjective *lībĕr*, free (to which *lībĕri*, children, no doubt belongs), and the substantive *lĭbra*, signifying both a balance and the weight which we call a pound or twelve ounces. Whether *lībĕr* and *lĭbra* be connected may be doubted. The Greek form of *lĭbra*, λίτρα, and the probable identity of *lībĕr* with ἐλεύθερος are rather against the supposition that they are. At the same time, that which is *free*, whether understood as meaning that which is free to move in any direction, or that which hangs even and without being inclined more to one side than another, would be a natural enough description of a *balance*. And *libra* (a balance), it may be added, had anciently also the form of *libera*. At any rate, from *liber*, free, we have the verb *liberare*, to make free; and from *libra*, a balance, or weight, *librare*, to weigh.

So far all is regular and consistent. But then, when we come to the compound verb *deliberare*, we find that it takes its signification (and must therefore have taken its origin), not from *liberare* and *liber*, but from *librare* and *libra;* it means, not to free, but to weigh. And, such being the state of things in the Latin language, the French has from *deliberare* formed *délibérer*, having the same signification (to weigh); but it has also from *liber* formed another verb *délivrer*, with the sense of to free. From the French *délibérer* and *délivrer* we have, in like manner, in English, and with the same significations, *deliberate* and *deliver*. Thus the deviation begun in the Latin *deliberare* has been carried out and generalized, till the derivatives from *liber* have assumed the form that would have been more proper for those from *libra*, as the latter had previously usurped that belonging to the former.

It is from *deliver*, no doubt, that we have fabricated our modern abbreviation *clever*. The ancient forms for what we now call *clever* and *cleverly* were *deliver* and *deliverly*. Thus in Chaucer (*Prol. to C. T.* 84), the Knight's son, the young Squire, is described as "wonderly deliver, and grete of strengthe;" and in the Nuns' Priest's Tale of the Cock and the Fox (*C. T.* 15,422), we have—

"The Fox answered, In faith it shal be don:
And, as he spake the word, al sodenly
The Cok brake from his mouth *deliverly*,
And high upon a tree he flew anon."

Deliver, rapidly pronounced, became *dliver* or *dlever*, and that was inevitably converted into *clever* by the euphonic genius of the language, in which such a combination as *dl* cannot live.*

* According, indeed, to Dr Webster,—who, however, gives no hint of the above etymology,—*clever* would be actually only another way of writing *tlever*. One of his rules (the 23rd) for English pronunciation is as follows:—" The letters *cl*, answering to *kl*, are pronounced as if written *tl* : *clear*, *clean* are pronounced *tlear*, *tlean*. *Gl* are pronounced as *dl*: *glory* is pronounced *dlory*." I transcribe this from the edition of the "Dictionary of the English Language," in 2 vols. 4to, Lon. 1832, professing to be "reprinted by E. H. Barker, Esq., of Thetford, Norfolk, from a copy communicated by the author, and containing many

Somewhat curious, too, are the variations of import through which the word *clever* has passed, or among which it still wanders. Johnson, after giving its modern or common signification as " dexterous, skilful," and noticing that Pope has used it in the sense of "just, fit," and Arbuthnot in that of " well-shaped," concludes by describing it as "a low word applied to anything a man likes, without a settled meaning." Webster, omitting " well-shaped," gives the New England sense, " good-natured, amiable;" and then adds:—" In some of the United States, it is said, this word is applied to the intellect, denoting ingenious, knowing, discerning." This last, it need scarcely be observed, is in fact nearly the modern sense of the word in England. The American lexicographer erroneously supposes that its use in Great Britain is distinguished from its use in America by its being in the former country "applied to the body or its movements."

348. ***When I*** *struck him.*—In the original printed text it is "strooke him."

349. *Let each man render me his bloody hand.*—Give me back in return for mine. Here, according to the stage direction of Mr Collier's MS. annotator, Antony " takes one after another of the conspirators by the hand, and turns to the body, and bends over it, while he says, 'That I did love thee, Cæsar, O! 'tis true,'" etc.

---

manuscript corrections and additions." The American lexicographer's sense of hearing would appear to have been peculiarly constituted. Another thing that he tells us is, that, when he was in England, he paid particular attention to the practice of public speakers in regard to the sound of the vowel *u*, and was happy to find that very few of them made any distinction between the *u* in such words as *cube* or *duke* and the *u* in *rude* or *true*. I do not know whether he means to say that he found *cube* to be generally called *coob*, or *rude* to be pronounced as if it were written *ryude*. What is most surprising is that all this should have been reproduced by an English editor without either a word of dissent or so much as a note of admiration.

349. *Will I shake with you.*—It is not to be supposed that there was anything undignified in this phraseology in Shakespeare's age.

349. *Though last, not least.*—So in *King Lear*, i. 1, "Although the last, not least in our dear love;" as is noted by Malone, who adds that "the same expression occurs more than once in Plays exhibited before the time of Shakespeare." We have it also in the passage of Spenser's *Colin Clout's Come Home Again* in which Shakespeare has been supposed to be referred to:—

> "And there, though last, not least, is Ætion;
> A gentler shepherd may no where be found;
> Whose muse, full of high thought's invention,
> Doth like himself heroically sound."

This poem was published in 1595.

349. *You must conceit me.—Vid.* 142.

349. *Shall it not grieve thee dearer than thy death?*—Of this use of *dear* we have several other instances in Shakespeare. One of the most remarkable is in *Hamlet*, i. 2, where Hamlet exclaims—

> "Would I had met my *dearest* foe in heaven
> Ere I had seen that day!"

Horne Tooke (*Div. of Purley*, 612, etc.) makes a plausible case in favour of *dear* being derived from the ancient verb *derian*, to hurt, to annoy, and of its proper meaning being, therefore, injurious or hateful. His notion seems to be that from this *derian* we have *dearth*, meaning properly that sort of injury which is done by the weather, and that, a usual consequence of dearth being to make the produce of the earth high-priced, the adjective *dear* has thence taken its common meaning of precious. This is not all distinctly asserted; but what of it may not be explicitly set forth is supposed and implied. It is, however, against an explanation which has been generally accepted, that there is no appearance of connexion between *derian* and the contemporary word answering to *dear* in the sense of high-priced, precious, beloved, which is **deore**, *dúre*, or *dýre*, and is evidently from the same root, not with *derian*, but with **deóran**, or *dýran*, to hold dear, to love. There is no doubt about the existence of an old English **verb *dere*, meaning to** hurt, the unquestionable representative of the original *derian:* thus in Chaucer (*C. T.* 1824) Theseus says **to Palamon and** Arcite, in the Knight's Tale:—

"And ye shul bothe anon unto me swore
That never mo ye shul my contree *dere*,
Ne maken werre upon me night ne day,
But **ben** my frendes in alle that ye may."

But perhaps we may get most easily and naturally **at** the sense which *dear* sometimes assumes by supposing that **the notion** properly involved in it of love, having first become generalized into that of a strong affection of **any** kind, had thence passed on into that of such an emotion the very reverse of love. We seem to have it in the **intermediate sense in such instances as the following:—

" Some *dear* cause
Will in concealment wrap me up a while."—*Lear, iv.* 3.

"A precious ring; a ring that I must **use**
In *dear* employment."—*Romeo and Juliet, v.* 3.

And even when Hamlet speaks of his "*dearest* foe," or when Celia remarks to **Rosalind,** in *As You Like It, i.* 3, "**My father** hated his [Orlando's] father *dearly*," the **word need not be understood as** implying more than **strong or** passionate emotion.

349. *Here wast thou bayed.*—So afterwards, in 498, "We are at the stake, And bayed about with **many enemies."** It is not clear, however, in what **sense the verb** *to be bayed* **is** used in these passages. Does it mean to be embayed, **or enclosed?** or to be barked at? or to be **made to stand, as it is phrased, at bay?** The *bays* in these expressions appear to be all **different** words. According to Horne Tooke, *to bay,* meaning to enclose, undoubtedly

the same with a *bay* of the sea, is from the ancient *bygan*, to bend, and is essentially the same with both *bow* and *bough*. This is also, of course, the *bay* which we have in *bay-window.—Div. of Purley*, 464, 465. *To bay*, meaning to bark, again, Tooke conceives to be the same element which we have in the Greek βοάω (to call aloud, to roar), as well as in the Italian *abbaiare* and the French *aboyer*, and, understood as meaning to cry down, to vilify, to reproach, to express abhorrence, aversion, and defiance, to be the root of *bad* (quasi *bayed*), of *bane* (*bayen*), of the verb *to ban*, and of the French *bas* and its English derivative *base.—Id.* 357.—As for *at bay*, it is evidently the French *aux abois*, meaning in extremity, at the last gasp; and, whatever *abois* may be, it does not appear how it can have anything to do with *aboyer*, to bark. There are also to be accounted for *the bay*, a name for the laurel, and the colour called *bay*, applied to a horse, to salt, and to woollen thread. A division of a house or other building was formerly called a *bay*; as in *Measure for Measure*, ii. 1:—" If this law hold in Vienna ten years, I'll rent the fairest house in it after threepence a bay." For this, and also *Bay-window*, see Nares. In *Boucher* (or rather in the additions by his editors) will be found the further meanings of a boy, a stake, a berry, the act of baiting with dogs, round, to bend, and to obey. Spenser uses *to bay* for *to bathe*. In *The Taming of the Shrew, v.* 2, we have the unusual form *at a bay*:—" 'Tis thought your deer does hold you at a bay."

349. *Signed in thy spoil, and crimsoned in thy death.*—Instead of *death* the First Folio has *Lethee*, the others *Lethe;* and the passage is explained as meaning marked and distinguished by being arrayed in thy spoils (the power in the commonwealth which was thine), and made crimson by being as it were bathed in thy shed blood. But Steevens's note is entirely unsatisfactory: "*Lethe*," he says, "is used by many of the old translators

of novels for death;" and then he gives as an example the following sentence from the Second Part of Heywood's *Iron Age*, printed in 1632:—

"The proudest nation that great Asia nursed
Is now extinct in *lethe*."

Here *lethe* may plainly be taken in its proper and usual sense of forgetfulness, oblivion. No other example is produced either by the commentators or by Nares. Shakespeare, too, repeatedly uses *lethe*, and nowhere, unless it be in this passage, in any other than its proper sense. If, however, *lethe* and *lethum* (or *letum*),—which may, or may not, be connected,—were really sometimes confounded by the popular writers of the early part of the seventeenth century, they are kept in countenance by the commentators of the eighteenth. Steevens goes on to notice, as affording another proof that *lethe* sometimes signified death, the following line from *Cupid's Whirligig*, printed in 1616:—

"For vengeance' wings bring on thy *lethal* day;"

and he adds:—" Dr Farmer observes, that we meet with *lethal* for deadly in the Information for Mungo Campbell." It is not easy to understand this. Who ever doubted that *deadly* was the proper meaning of *lethalis* (from *lethum*)? But what has that to do with the signification of *lethe?* I do not know what it is that may have led Nares to imagine that, when *lethe* meant death, it was pronounced as a monosyllable. Seeing, however, that the notion of its ever having that signification appears to be a mere delusion, I have followed Mr Collier in supposing it to be here a misprint for *death*, which was the obvious conjecture of several of the editors of the last century, and is sanctioned by the authority of his MS. annotator.

349. *Strucken by many princes.*—It is *stroken* in the original edition.—In the preceding line, also, " the *heart*

of thee" is there misprinted "the *hart* of thee." But the two words are repeatedly thus confounded in the spelling in that edition.—Mr Collier strangely prefers making this exclamation, "How like a deer," etc., an interrogatory—as if Antony asked the dead body in how far, or to what precise degree, it resembled a deer, lying as it did stretched out before him.

351. *The enemies of Cæsar shall say this.*—Here again, as in "This shall mark Our purpose necessary" of 187, we have a use of *shall*, which now only remains with us, if at all, as an imitation of the archaic. *Vid.* 181. A singular consequence has arisen from the change that has taken place. By "*shall* say this" in the present passage Shakespeare meant no more than would now be expressed by "*will* say this;" yet to us the *shall* elevates the expression beyond its original import, giving it something, if not quite of a prophetic, yet of an impassioned, wrapt, and as it were vision-seeing character.

352. *But what compact.*—*Compact* has always, I believe, the accent upon the final syllable in Shakespeare, whether used as a substantive, as a verb, or as a participle.

352. *Will you be pricked in number of our friends?*—To *prick* is to note or mark off. The Sheriffs are still so nominated by a puncture or mark being made at the selected names in the list of qualified persons, and this is the *vox signata*, or established word, for the operation.

353. *Swayed from the point.*—Borne away, as by a wave, from the point which I had in view and for which I was making.

353. *Friends am I with you all.*—"This grammatical impropriety," Henley very well remarks, "is still so prevalent, as that the omission of the anomalous *s* would give some uncouthness to the sound of an otherwise familiar expression." We could not, indeed, say "*Friend* am I

R

with you all;" we should have to turn the expression in some other way. In *Troilus* and *Cressida*, iv. 4, however, we have "And I'll grow *friend* with danger." Nor does the pluralism of *friends* depend upon that of *you all*: "I am friends with you" is equally the phrase in addressing a single person. *I with you am* is felt to be equivalent to *I and you are*.

351. *Our reasons are so full of good regard.*—So full of what is entitled to favourable regard. Compare "many of the best respect" in 48.

354. *That, were you, Antony, the son of Cæsar.*—By all means to be thus pointed, so as to make *Antony* the vocative, the name addressed; not, as it sometimes ludicrously is, "were you Antony the son of Cæsar." *Son*, of course, is emphatic.

355. *Produce his body to the market-place.*—We now say "produce to" with a person only.

355. *Speak in the order of his funeral.*—*In the order* is in the course of the ceremonial.—Compare "That Antony speak in his funeral," in 357; and "Come I to speak in Cæsar's funeral," in 398.

357. The *Aside* here is not marked in the old copies.

358. *By your pardon.*—I will explain, by, or with, your pardon, leave, permission. "By your leave" is still occasionally used.

358. *Have all true rites.*—This is the reading of all the old copies. For *true* Pope substituted *due*, which is also the correction of Mr Collier's MS. annotator.

358. *It shall advantage more than do us wrong.*—This old verb, *to advantage*, is fast slipping out of our possession.—Here again we have, according to the old grammar, simple futurity indicated by *shall* with the third person. —*Vid.* 181.

359. *I know not what may fall.*—We now commonly say *to fall out*, rather than simply *to fall*, or *to befall*.

360. *You shall not in your funeral speech blame us.*—
The sense and the prosody concur in demanding an emphasis on *us*.

360. *And say you do't.*—We do not now in serious or elevated writing use this kind of contraction.

362. The original stage direction after this speech is, "*Exeunt. Manet Antony.*"

363. *O pardon me, thou bleeding piece of earth.*—So in all the early editions, and also in the greater number of those of the last century; but unaccountably altered into "thou piece of bleeding earth" in the Variorum edition of Malone and Boswell, the text of which was generally taken as the standard for subsequent reprints, till the true reading was restored by Mr Knight.

363. *That ever lived in the tide of times.*—This must mean, apparently, in the course or flow of times. *Tide* and *time*, however, properly mean the same thing. *Tide* is only another form of *Zeit*, the German word answering to our English *time*. *Time*, again, is the French *tems*, or *temps*, a corruption of the Latin *tempus* (which has also in one of its senses, the part of the head where time is indicated to the touch by the pulsations of the blood, been strangely corrupted, both in French and English, into *temple*,—distinguished, however, in the former tongue from *temple*, a church, by a difference of gender, and also otherwise written *tempe*).

363. *A curse shall light upon the loins of men.*—This is one of the most remarkable of the new readings for which we are indebted to Mr Collier's MS. annotator. The old printed text, "the limbs of men," was felt by every editor not enslaved to the First Folio to be in the highest degree suspicious. By most of them *the limbs of men* seems to have been understood to mean nothing more than the bodies or persons of men generally. Steevens, however, says ;—" Antony means that a future curse shall commence in distempers seizing on the *limbs*

of men, and be succeeded by commotion, cruelty, and desolation over Italy." A strangely precise style of prophecy! For *limbs* Warburton proposed to substitute *line*, Hanmer *kind*, and Johnson *lives*,—"unless," he adds, "we read these *lymmes* of men, that is, these bloodhounds of men." The *lymm*, *lym*, *lime*, *limer*, or *limehound* was used in hunting the wild boar. The *loins* of men means, of course, the generations of men. Even if proposed as nothing more, this would have been one of the most plausible of conjectures, and would probably have at once commanded general acceptance. Warburton hit upon nearly what seems to have been the meaning of Shakespeare with his *line* of men; but how much less Shakespearian the expression!

363. *Quartered with the hands of war.*—So afterwards, in 426, "Here is himself, marred, as you see, with traitors." *Vid.* 124. We should now rather regard the hands as the agents, and say "*by* the hands of war."

363. *With* Ate *by his side.*—This Homeric goddess had taken a strong hold of Shakespeare's imagination. In *Much Ado about Nothing*, ii. 1, Benedick, inveighing to Don Pedro against the Lady Beatrice, says, "You shall find her the infernal *Ate* in good apparel." In *King John*, iv. 1, John's mother, Queen Elinor, is described by Chatillon as "an *Ate* stirring him to blood and strife." And in *Love's Labour's Lost*, v. 2, Biron, at the representation of the Nine Worthies, calls out "More *Ates*, more *Ates*; stir them on! stir them on!" Where did Shakespeare get acquainted with this divinity, whose name does not occur, I believe, even in any Latin author?

363. *Cry Havoc!*—*Havoc* is the Original English *hafoc*, meaning waste, destruction; whence the *hawk*, so called as the bird of waste and ravage. Johnson states on the authority of a learned correspondent (known to be Sir William Blackstone), that, "in the military operations of old times, *havoc* was the word by which declaration was

made that no quarter should be given." Milton in one place makes a verb of this substantive:—"To waste and havoc yonder world" (*Par. Lost*, x. 617).

363. *Let slip the dogs of war.*—Notwithstanding the apparently considerable difference between *schlüpfen* and *schlafen*, by which they are severally represented in modern German, *slip* may possibly have been originally the same word with *sleep*. In the English of the time before the Conquest, although the common form is *slæpan* for *to sleep* and *slipan* for *to slip*, we find indications of *slepan* having been used for both. To sleep, or fall asleep, may have been regarded as a gliding, or softly moving, away.—To *let slip* a dog at a deer, etc., was, as Malone remarks, the technical phrase of Shakespeare's time. Hence the *leash*, out of which it was thus allowed to escape, was called the *slips*. The proper meaning, indeed, of *leash* (in French *lesse*, or *laisse*, from *laisser*) is that which lets go; and this is probably also the true meaning of the Spanish *lasso*; although, that which lets go, or from which we let go, being also necessarily that which has previously detained, *lesse*, *lasso*, *leash*, and also *lease*, have all, as well as *slip*, come to be regarded as involving rather the latter notion (of detention or tenure), that being really the principal or most important office which what is called a slip or leash seems to perform. It was perhaps in this way also that the verb *to let* acquired the sense (now nearly obsolete) of to hinder, as well as its more ordinary sense of to permit.

It is observed by Steele in *The Tatler*, No. 137, that by "the dogs of war" Shakespeare probably meant *fire*, *sword*, and *famine*, according to what is said in the Chorus to Act First of *King Henry the Fifth*:—

> "Then should the warlike Harry, like himself,
> Assume the port of Mars; and, at his heels,
> Leashed in like hounds, should Famine, Sword, and Fire
> Crouch for employment."

To this we might add what Talbot says, in the *First Part of King Henry the Sixth*, **iv.** 2, to the Captains of the French forces before Bordeaux:—

"You tempt the fury of my three attendants,
Lean Famine, quartering Steel, and climbing Fire."

In illustration of the passage from *Henry the Fifth* Steevens quotes what Holinshed makes that King to have said to the people of Roan (or Rouen):—"He declared that the Goddess of Battle, called Bellona, had three handmaidens ever of necessity attending upon her, as Blood, Fire, and Famine." And at that from *Henry the Sixth* Malone gives the following extract from Hall's Chronicle:—"The Goddess of War, called Bellona, . . . hath these three handmaids ever of necessity attending on her; Blood, Fire, and Famine; which three damosels be of that force and strength that every one of them alone is able and sufficient to torment and afflict a proud prince; and they all joined together are of puissance to destroy the most populous country and most richest region of the world."

It might, perhaps, be questioned whether the words, "And let slip the dogs of war" ought not to be considered as also part of the exclamation of Cæsar's spirit.

363. *That this foul deed*, etc.—So that.

363. *With carrion men.*—**Vid.** 177.—The stage direction in the original edition is "*Enter Octavio's Servant.*"

363. *You serve Octavius Cæsar.*—So called throughout both this Play and that of *Antony and Cleopatra*. He was properly now *Cæsar Octavianus*.

366. The stage direction, *Seeing the Body*, is modern.

367. *For mine eyes.*—This, which is clearly right, is the reading of the Second Folio. The First has "Passion I see is catching from mine eyes."

369. *Tell him what hath chanced.*—*Vid.* 69.

369. *No Rome of safety.*—*Vid.* 56.

369. *Till I have borne this corpse.*—*Corpse* (or *corse*) here is a modern conjectural substitution for the *course* of the First and Second Folios and the *coarse* of the Third and Fourth.

369. *The cruel issue of these bloody men.*—The result or end which they have brought about.

369. *According to the which.*—This archaism occurs occasionally in Shakespeare, as it does also in the common translation of the Scriptures:—" Every tree in the which is the fruit of a tree yielding seed" (*Gen. i.* 29).

369. *Lend me your hand.*—We should now rather say *a hand.*—The stage direction that follows is in the original edition, "*Exeunt. Enter Brutus and goes into the Pulpit, and Cassius with the Plebeians.*"

SCENE II.—*The same. The Forum.*

Enter BRUTUS *and* CASSIUS, *and a throng of* CITIZENS.

370. *Cit.* We will be satisfied; let us be satisfied.
371. *Bru.* Then follow me, and give me audience, friends.—
Cassius, go you into the other street,
And part the numbers.—
Those that will hear me speak, let 'em stay here;
Those that will follow Cassius, go with him;
And public reasons shall be rendered
Of Cæsar's death.
    1 *Cit.* I will hear Brutus speak.
373. 2 *Cit.* I will hear Cassius; and compare their reasons,
When severally we hear them rendered.
[*Exit* CASSIUS, *with some of the* CITIZENS.
BRUTUS *goes into the Rostrum.*
374. 3 *Cit.* The noble Brutus is ascended: Silence!
375. *Bru.* Be patient till the last.
Romans, countrymen, and lovers! hear me for my cause; and be silent, that you may hear: believe me for mine honour; and have respect to mine honour, that you may believe: censure me in your wisdom; and awake your senses, that you may the better judge. If there be any in this assembly, any dear friend of Cæsar's, to him I say, that Brutus' love to Cæsar was no less than his. If, then,

that friend demand, why Brutus rose against Cæsar, **this is my answer**;—Not that I loved Cæsar less, but that I loved Rome **more**. Had you rather Cæsar were living, and die all slaves, **than that** Cæsar were dead, to live all freemen? As Cæsar loved me, I **weep for him; as he was** fortunate, I rejoice at it; as he was valiant, I **honour him**: but, as he was ambitious, **I slew him**. There is tears, **for his** love; joy, for his fortune; honour, **for** his valour; and **death, for his** ambition. Who is here so base, that would be a bondman? If any, speak; for him have I offended. Who is here so rude, that would not be **a** Roman? If any, speak; for **him** have I offended. Who is here so vile, that will not love his **country**? If any, speak; for him have I offended. I pause for a reply.

376. *Cit.* None, Brutus, none. [*Several speaking at once*.
377. *Bru.* Then none have I offended. I have done no **more to** Cæsar than you shall do **to** Brutus. The question of his death is enrolled in the Capitol: his glory not extenuated, wherein he **was** worthy; nor his offences enforced, for which he suffered death.

Enter ANTONY *and others, with* CÆSAR'S **Body**.

Here comes his body, mourned **by** Mark Antony: **who**, though he had no hand in his death, shall receive the benefit **of his** dying, a place in the commonwealth; as which of you shall not? With this I depart; That, as I slew my best lover for the good of Rome, I have the same dagger for myself, when it shall please my country to need my death.

Cit. Live, **Brutus, live**! live!
1 *Cit.* Bring him with triumph home unto his house.
2 *Cit.* Give him a statue with his **ancestors**.
3 *Cit.* Let him be **Cæsar**.
382. 4 *Cit.* Cæsar's better parts
Shall now be crowned in Brutus.
1 *Cit.* We'll bring him **to his** house with shouts and clamours.
Bru. My countrymen,——
2 *Cit.* Peace; silence! Brutus speaks.
1 *Cit.* Peace, ho!
387. *Bru.* Good countrymen, let me depart alone,
And, for **my** sake, stay here with Antony:
Do grace to Cæsar's corpse, and grace his **speech**
Tending to Cæsar's glories; which Mark **Antony**,
By our permission, is allowed to make.
I do entreat you, not a man depart,
Save I alone, **till Antony have** spoke. [*Exit*.
1 *Cit.* Stay, ho! and let us hear Mark Antony.

  3 *Cit.* Let him go up into the public chair;
We'll hear him:—Noble Antony, go up.
390. *Ant.* For Brutus' sake, I am beholden to you.
  4 *Cit.* What does he say of Brutus?
  3 *Cit.* He says, for Brutus' sake,
He finds himself beholden to us all.
  4 *Cit.* 'Twere best he speak no harm of Brutus here.
  1 *Cit.* This Cæsar was a tyrant.
395. 3 *Cit.* Nay, that's certain:
We are blest that Rome is rid of him.
  2 *Cit.* Peace, let us hear what Antony can say.
  Ant. You gentle Romans,——
  Cit. Peace, ho! let us hear him.
399. *Ant.* Friends, Romans, countrymen, lend me your ears,
I come to bury Cæsar, not to praise him.
The evil that men do lives after them;
The good is oft interred with their bones:
So let it be with Cæsar. The noble Brutus
Hath told you, Cæsar was ambitious:
If it were so, it was a grievous fault;
And grievously hath Cæsar answered it.
Here, under leave of Brutus, and the rest
(For Brutus is an honourable man;
So are they all, all honourable men),
Come I to speak in Cæsar's funeral.
He was my friend, faithful and just to me:
But Brutus says, he was ambitious;
And Brutus is an honourable man.
He hath brought many captives home to Rome,
Whose ransoms did the general coffers fill:
Did this in Cæsar seem ambitious?
When that the poor have cried, Cæsar hath wept:
Ambition should be made of sterner stuff.
Yet Brutus says, he was ambitious;
And Brutus is an honourable man.
You all did see, that on the Lupercal
I thrice presented him a kingly crown,
Which he did thrice refuse. Was this ambition?
Yet Brutus says, he was ambitious;
And, sure, he is an honourable man.
I speak not to disprove what Brutus spoke,
But here I am to speak what I do know.
You all did love him once, not without cause;

What cause withholds you, then, to mourn for him?
O judgment, thou art fled to brutish beasts,
And men have **lost** their reason!—Bear with me;
My **heart** is in the coffin there with Cæsar,
And I must pause till it come back to me.
   1 *Cit.* Methinks, there is much reason in his sayings.
   2 *Cit.* If thou consider rightly of the matter,
Cæsar has had great wrong.
   3 *Cit.* Has he not, master?
I fear, there will a worse come in his place.

403. 4 *Cit.* Marked ye his words? He would not take the **crown**;
Therefore, 'tis certain he was not ambitious.

404. 1 *Cit.* If it be found so, some will dear abide it.
   2 *Cit.* Poor soul! his eyes are red as fire with weeping.
   3 *Cit.* There's not a nobler man in Rome than Antony.
   4 *Cit.* Now mark him, he begins again to speak.

408. *Ant.* **But** yesterday, the word of Cæsar might
Have stood against the world: now lies he there,
And none so poor to do him reverence.
Oh masters! if **I** were disposed to stir
Your hearts and minds to mutiny and rage,
I should do Brutus wrong, and Cassius wrong,
Who, **you all know,** are honourable men:
I will not **do them** wrong; I rather choose
To wrong the dead, to wrong myself, and you,
Than I will wrong such honourable men.
But here's a parchment, with the seal of Cæsar;
I found it in his closet; 'tis his will:
Let but the commons hear this **testament**
(Which, pardon me, **I do not mean to read**),
And they would go and kiss dead Cæsar's wounds,
And dip their napkins in his sacred blood;
Yea, beg a hair of him for memory,
And, dying, mention it within their wills,
Bequeathing it, as a rich legacy,
Unto their issue.
   4 *Cit.* We'll hear the will: Read it, Mark Antony.
   Cit. **The will,** the will: we will hear Cæsar's will.
   Ant. **Have** patience, gentle friends; I must not read it;
It is not meet you know how Cæsar loved **you.**
You are not wood, you are not stones, but men;
And, being men, hearing the will **of Cæsar,**
It will inflame you, it will make you mad.

'Tis good you know not that you are his heirs;
For if you should, O, what would come of it!
412. *4 Cit.* **Read the will**; we will hear it, Antony; you shall read us the will; Cæsar's will.
413. *Ant.* **Will you** be patient? Will you stay a while?
I have overshot myself, to tell you of it.
I fear, I wrong the honourable men,
Whose daggers have stabbed Cæsar: I do fear it.
   4 Cit. They were traitors: Honourable **men**!
   Cit. The will! the testament!
   2 Cit. **They** were villains, murderers: The will, read the will!
   Ant. **You will** compel me, then, to read the will?
Then make a ring about the corpse of Cæsar,
And let me show you him that made the will.
Shall I descend? And will you give me leave?
   Cit. Come down.
419. *2 Cit.* Descend.   [*He comes down from the pulpit.*
   3 Cit. You shall have leave.
   4 Cit. A ring; stand round.
422. *1 Cit.* Stand from the hearse, stand from the body.
   2 Cit. Room **for Antony;**—most noble Antony.
   Ant. Nay, press not so upon me; stand far off.
   Cit. Stand back! room! bear back!
426. *Ant.* If you have tears, prepare to shed them now.
You all do know this mantle: I remember
The first time ever Cæsar put it on;
'Twas on a summer's evening, in his tent,
That day he overcame the Nervii:—
Look! **in this** place, ran Cassius' dagger through:
See, **what a rent the** envious Casca made:
Through **this, the** well-beloved Brutus stabbed;
And, as he plucked his cursed steel away,
Mark how **the blood** of Cæsar followed it;
As rushing out **of doors, to be** resolved
If Brutus so unkindly **knocked, or no**;
For Brutus, as you **know, was Cæsar's angel**:
Judge, O you gods, how dearly Cæsar loved him!
This was the most unkindest **cut of all**:
For, when the noble Cæsar saw **him stab,**
Ingratitude, more strong **than traitors' arms,**
Quite vanquished him: then **burst his mighty heart;**
And, in his mantle muffling up his face,
Even at the base of Pompey's statue,

Which **all** the while ran blood, great Cæsar fell.
O, what **a** fall was there, my countrymen!
Then I, and you, and all of us fell **down**,
Whilst bloody treason flourished over us.
O, **now** you weep; and, I perceive, **you feel**
The **dint** of pity: these **are gracious drops**.
Kind souls, what, weep you, when you but behold
Our Cæsar's vesture wounded? Look you here,
Here is himself, marred, as you see, with traitors.

 1 *Cit.* O piteous spectacle!
 2 *Cit.* O noble Cæsar!
 3 *Cit.* O woeful day!
 4 *Cit.* O traitors, villains!
 1 *Cit.* O most bloody sight!
 2 *Cit.* We will be revenged; revenge; about,—seek,— burn,—fire,—kill,—slay!—let not a traitor live.

433. *Ant.* Stay, countrymen.
 1 *Cit.* Peace there:—Hear the noble Antony.
 2 *Cit.* We'll hear him, we'll follow him, we'll die with him.

436. *Ant.* Good friends, sweet friends, let me not stir you up
To such a sudden flood of mutiny.
They that have done this deed are honourable;
What private griefs they have, alas, I know not,
That made them do it; they are wise and honourable,
And will, no doubt, with reasons answer you.
I come not, friends, to steal away **your hearts**:
I am no orator, as Brutus is;
But, as you know me all, a plain blunt man,
That love my friend; and that they **know full** well
That gave me public leave to speak of him.
For I have neither wit, nor words, nor worth,
Action, nor utterance, nor the power of speech,
To stir men's blood: I only speak right on;
I tell you that which you yourselves do know;
Show you sweet Cæsar's wounds, poor, poor dumb **mouths**,
And bid them speak for me: But, were I Brutus,
And **Brutus** Antony, there were an Antony
Would ruffle up your spirits, and put a tongue
In **every** wound of Cæsar, that should move
The stones of Rome to rise and mutiny.

 Cit. We'll mutiny.
 1 *Cit.* We'll burn the house of Brutus.
 3 *Cit.* Away, then, come, **seek** the conspirators.

Ant. Yet hear me, countrymen; yet hear me speak.
Cit. Peace, **ho**! Hear Antony, most noble Antony.
Ant. Why, **friends,** you go to do you know not what:
Wherein hath Cæsar thus deserved your loves?
Alas, **you** know not:—I must tell you, then:—
You have forgot the will I told you of.
Cit. Most true;—the will;—let's stay, and hear the will.
444. *Ant.* Here is the will, and **under Cæsar's seal.**
To every Roman citizen he gives,
To every several man, seventy-five drachmas.
2 *Cit.* Most noble Cæsar!—we'll revenge his death.
3 *Cit.* **O royal Cæsar!**
Ant. Hear me with patience.
Cit. Peace, ho!
449. *Ant.* Moreover, he hath **left you all his walks,**
His private arbours, and **new-planted orchards,**
On this side Tiber; he **hath left them you,**
And to your heirs for ever; **common pleasures,**
To walk abroad, and **recreate yourselves.**
Here was a Cæsar: When comes **such another?**
450. 1 *Cit.* Never, never!—Come, **away, away!**
We'll burn **his** body in the holy place,
And with the brands fire the traitors' houses.
Take up the body.
2 *Cit.* Go, fetch fire.
3 *Cit.* Pluck **down benches.**
4 *Cit.* Pluck **down forms, windows,** anything.
[*Exeunt* CITIZENS, *with the body.*
454. *Ant.* **Now** let it work: Mischief, thou art afoot,
Take thou what course thou wilt!—How now, fellow?

Enter a SERVANT.

Serv. Sir, **Octavius is** already come to Rome.
Ant. Where **is he?**
Serv. He and Lepidus are at Cæsar's house.
458. *Ant.* And thither will I straight to visit him.
He comes upon a **wish.** Fortune is merry,
And in this mood **will give us** anything.
459. *Serv.* I heard them say, **Brutus** and Cassius
Are rid like madmen through the gates **of Rome.**
460. *Ant.* Belike they had some notice of the people,
How I had moved them. Bring me to Octavius. [*Exeunt.*

370. For *Cit.* here the original edition has *Ple.*; and afterwards for 1 *Cit.*, 2 *Cit.*, 3 *Cit.*, it has 1 *Ple.*, 2, 3; and for *Cit.* at 376, etc., it has *All.*

371. *And part the numbers.*—Divide the multitude.

371. *And public reasons shall be rendered.*—To render is to give back or in return for. Thus in 349, as we have seen, Antony asks Brutus and his confederates to *render* him their hands in return for his own. Here the act which had been done, the slaughter of Cæsar, is that in return or compensation for which, as it were, the reasons are to be given.—For the prosody of the present line see the note on "She dreamt to-night she saw my statue" in 246. It may be observed that in the First Folio, where the elision of the *e* in the verbal affix *-ed* is usually marked, the spelling is here *rendred;* but this may leave it still doubtful whether the word was intended to be represented as of two or of three syllables. It is the same in 373.

373. *Exit Cassius,* etc. *Brutus goes into the Rostrum.* —This stage direction is all modern. The Rostrum is the same that is called "the public chair" in 389, and "the pulpit" elsewhere: *Vid.* 318, 320, 355, 358, 360. *Rostrum* is not a word which Shakespeare anywhere uses. Nor, indeed, is it a legitimate formation. It ought to be *Rostra,* in the plural, as it always is in Latin. Nevertheless few persons in their senses will be inclined to go with Dr Webster for the immediate origin of *Rostrum,* in any of its English applications, to the Welsh *rhetgyr,* a snout, or *rhethern,* a pike.

374. *The noble Brutus is ascended.*—In this form of expression it is plain that we use the verb to *ascend* in quite a different sense from that which it has when we say "Brutus has ascended the pulpit." According to the one form, it is *Brutus* that *is ascended;* according to the other, it is *the pulpit* that *is ascended.* In point of fact, if to *ascend* be taken in its proper sense of to mount

or climb up, it is only the pulpit that can be ascended; in saying that Brutus is ascended we employ the verb as if its meaning were to lift, carry, or bear up. Clear, however, as is the violation of principle, the right of perpetrating it must be held to be one of the established liberties of the language. Even still we commonly say *is come, is become, is gone, is arrived, is fled, is escaped*, etc. In the freer condition of the language formerly such a mode of expression was carried a good deal farther. Thus, in the present Play, we have in 329 "[Antony is] fled to his house amazed;" in 399, "O judgment! thou art fled to brutish beasts;" in 459, "Brutus and Cassius Are rid like madmen through the gates of Rome;" in 510, "Hark, he is arrived;" in 624, "The deep of night is crept upon our talk;" in 704, "This morning are they fled away and gone;" in 722, "Time is come round;" and "My life is run his compass." This last instance carries the irregularity to its height; for here the verb *to run* is actually used at the same time in two senses; both in the sense in which we say "to run a ship on a rock," or "to run a nail into a door" (that is, to make move rapidly), and also in that in which we say "to run a race" (that is, to move rapidly through or over). In the first sense only can Cassius say that his life is run; in the second alone can he speak of it as running his—that is, its (*Vid.* 54)—compass. In the one case it is the thing moved that is run (the same as when we talk of running a thread through a cloth or a rope over a pulley, or of running a metal, or running off wine); in the other case, what is said to be run is the act or process through which the movement is made (the same as when we talk of running a risk, or running the gauntlet, or running a muck). This latter sense is not to be confounded with that which we have in "to run a mile;" there the verb is intransitive, and the noun expresses only the extent, or as it were manner, of the verbal action, and is no more governed by the verb than it is in the phrase "to live a year," or than the qualifying adverb is so governed in the phrase "to run fast." If Cassius had said that his life was run its compass halfway, we should have had a combination of all the three senses.

The following are examples of this form of construction from other plays:—

"Is our whole dissembly appeared?"
(*Dogberry, in Much Ado about Noth., iv.* 2);

"Prince John is this morning secretly stolen away."
Sexton, Ibid.);

"His lordship is walked forth into the orchard."
(*Porter, in Second Part of Henry IV., i.* 1);

"He said mine eyes were black, and my hair black,
And, now I am remembered, scorned at me."
(*Phebe, in As You Like It, iii.* 5);

"You being then, if you be remembered, cracking the stones."
(*Clown, in Meas. for Meas. ii.* 1);

"I telling you then, if you be remembered."—(*Ibid.*);

"But, if you be remembered,
I did not bid you mar it to the time."
(*Petrucio, in Tam. of Shrew, iv.* 3);

"If your majesty is remembered of it."
(*Fluellen, in Henry V., iv.* 7);

"Now, by my troth, if I had been remembered,
I could have given my uncle's grace a flout."
(*York, in Rich. III., ii.* 4);

"Be you remembered, Marcus, she's gone, she's fled."
(*Titus, in Titus Andronicus, iv.* 3).

375. *Romans, countrymen, and lovers.*—*Vid.* 260.

375. *Have respect to mine honour.*—That is, merely, look to (not look up to). We still employ such words as *respect* and *regard* in different senses according to circumstances. I look with regard, or with respect, upon this man, or upon that institution. With regard, or with respect, to another man or institution I have nothing to say but what is condemnatory, or nothing to say at all.

375. *Censure me.*—That is, merely, pass judgment upon me. *Vid.* 329.

375. *Any dear friend of Cæsar's, to him I say.*—It is "to *them* I say" in the second Folio.

375. *Not that I loved Cæsar less.*—Less than he (the "dear friend") loved Cæsar.

375. *But that I loved Rome more.*—More than he (the "dear friend of Cæsar") loved Rome.

375. *Had you rather.*—*Vid.* note on *Had as lief* in 54.

375. *To live all freemen.*—It is commonly printed "free men," in two words. But the writer cannot have intended that such prominence should be given to the term *men*, the notion conveyed by which is equally contained in *slaves;* for which, indeed, we might have had *bondmen*, with no difference of effect. If it ought to be "free men" here, it should be "Who is here so base that would be a bond man?" a few lines farther on. In the original edition it is "freemen."

375. *There is tears*, etc.—In many modern editions this is changed into "There *are*." But the tears, joy, etc., are regarded as making one thing. Instead of "There is," it might have been "This is," or "That is."

376. The stage direction is modern.

377. *The question of his death.*—The word *question* is here used in a somewhat peculiar sense. It seems to mean the statement of the reasons. In a note on the expression in *Hamlet, ii.* 2, "Little eyases, that cry out on the top of question," Steevens gives it as his opinion that *question* "in this place, as in many others, signifies *conversation, dialogue.*" And he quotes in corroboration Antonio's remark, in *The Merchant of Venice, iv.* 1, "I pray you, think you question with the Jew." But in that passage the meaning of the word is merely the ordinary one, you debate, argue, hold controversy, with. The following may perhaps be adduced as an instance of the use of the word in a somewhat larger sense, involving

s

little or nothing of the notion of a doubt or dispute:—
"Thou shalt accompany us to the place, where we will, not appearing what we are, have some question with the shepherd;" *Winter's Tale*, iv. 1.

377. *Nor his offences enforced.* — Dwelt upon and pressed, or more than simply stated. In the same sense in *Coriolanus*, ii. 3, the tribune Sicinius exhorts the populace touching Marcius:—"Enforce his pride, And his old hate unto you."

377. *As which of you shall not?*—We find *which* in our oldest English in the forms *hwile, hwyle,* and *hwelc*—forms which have been supposed to arise out of the combination of the relative *hwa* with *lic* (like), the annexation being designed to give greater generalization or indefiniteness of meaning to the pronoun. At all events, the word is used with reference to nouns of all genders, as is also its representative the *whilk*, or *quhilk*, of the old Scottish dialect, and as the English *which* too formerly was even when an ordinary relative (as we have it in the time-honoured formula "Our Father *which* art in heaven"), and still is both whenever it is interrogative and likewise when the antecedent to which it is relative is either suppressed or joined with it in the same concord and government. Thus, we say of persons as well as of things, "Which was it?". and "I do not know which of them it was," as Brutus, addressing his fellow-citizens, has here "*Which* of you;" and it is even allowable to say "Louis XVI., *which* king it was in whose reign—or, in the reign of *which* king it was—that the French Revolution broke out."—It is one of the many curiosities of Dr Webster's *English Dictionary* that he refuses to admit *which* to have anything to do with the ancient *hwile*, and suggests that it may be rather the same word with *quick!*

The stage direction in the original edition is, "*Enter Mark Antony, with Cæsar's* body."

377. *My best lover.*—Vid. 260.

382. *Shall now be crowned in Brutus.*—The *now* is not in the old texts, but was supplied by Pope, and has been retained by Malone and Boswell, as well as by Steevens. It may not be the true word, but that some word is wanting is certain. The dialogue here is evidently intended to be metrical, and "Shall be crowned in Brutus" is not a possible commencement of a verse. Mr Collier also in his regulated text retains the *now*, although it does not appear to have the sanction of his MS. annotator.

387. *Do grace to Cæsar's corpse.*—We have lost this idiom, though we still say "to do honour to."

390. *I am beholden to you.*—Both here and also in 392 the first three Folios have all *beholding*, which may possibly have been the way in which Shakespeare wrote the word (as it is that in which it was often written in his day), but may nevertheless be rectified on the same principle as other similar improprieties with which all modern editors have taken that liberty. Yet *beholding* is, I believe, always Bacon's word; as in his Tenth Essay:—"The stage is more beholding to love than the life of man." Even in Clarendon, reporting the words of Queen Henrietta to himself, we have:—"Her old confessor, Father Philips, . . . always told her, that, as she ought to continue firm and constant to her own religion, so she was to live well towards the Protestants who deserved well from her, and to whom she was *beholding*" (*Hist., Book xiii.*). The initial syllable of the word is of more interest than its termination.

The complete disappearance from the modern form of the English language of the verbal prefix *ge* is a remarkable fact, and one which has not attracted the notice which it deserves. This augment may be said to have been the favourite and most distinguishing peculiarity of the language in the period preceding the Norman Conquest. In the inflection of the verb it was not merely, as in modern German, the sign of the past participle passive, but might be prefixed to any other part; **and the words of all kinds which commenced with it, and in which** it was not inflexional, amounted **to** several thousands. Yet now **there is** no native English **word** having *ge* for **its** initial syllable **in** existence; **nor,** indeed, has there **been for** many centuries: there are **not** only **no** such **words** in Chaucer, **whose** age (the fourteenth century) **is** reckoned the commencement of the period **of what** is denominated Middle English; there are **none even** in Robert de Brunne, and very few, if any, in **Robert** of Gloucester, who belong to the thirteenth century, **or to** the age of what is commonly designated Early English. The inflexional *ge* is found **at a** comparatively **late date only in** the reduced or softened form of *y*, and **even so** scarcely after the middle of the sixteenth century (which **may be** taken **as** the date of the commencement of Modern English) except in a few antique words preserved **or** revived by Spenser. If **two** or three such words **as** *yclad* and *yclept* are to be found in Shakespeare, they **are** introduced with a view to a burlesque or grotesque effect, as they might be by a writer of the present day. They did not belong to the language of his age any more than they did to that of Thomson, who in **the** last century has sprinkled his *Castle of Indolence* with words of this description the better to keep up his imitation of Spenser. As for the "star-ypointing pyramid" attributed to Milton **(in** his lines **on** Shakespeare), **it** is in all probability **a** mistake **of** his modern editors: "ypoint*ed*" might **have** been credible, but "ypoint*ing*" scarcely is. **The true** reading probably is "starry-pointing." It has commonly been assumed that, with such rare and insignificant exceptions (if exceptions they are to be considered), the old prefix *ge* has entirely passed away or been ejected from the language in its present state,—that it has dropped off, like a decayed member, without anything being substi**tuted in its place. But** the fact is not so. It is certain, that, both in its inflexional and in its non-inflexional character, it still exists in a good many words in a disguised form,—in that namely of *be*. Many of our words beginning with *be* cannot be otherwise accounted for. Our modern *beloved*, for example, is undoubtedly the ancient *gelufed*. Another remarkable instance is that of the familiar word *belief* or *believe*. The Original English has no such verb as *belyfan*; its form for our *believe* is *gelyfan* (the same with the modern German *glauben*). Again, to *become* (at least in the sense of to suit) is the Original English *gecweman*: there is no *becweman*. *Become*, in this sense, it ought to be noticed, has apparently no connexion with *to come* (from *coman*, or *cuman*); we have its root *cweman* in the old English *to quem*, meaning to please, used by Chaucer. And the German also, like our modern English, has in this instance lost or rejected both the simple form and the *ge-* form, retaining, or substituting, only *bequem* and *bequemen*. Nor is there any *belang* or *belong*; our modern *belong* is from the ancient *gelang*. In like manner there is no such Original English verb as *besecan*; there is only *gesecan*, from which we have formed our *beseek* and *beseech*. So *tacn*, or *tacen*, is a token, from which is *getacnian*, to denote by a token or sign; there is no *betacnian*; yet we say to *betoken*. And there are probably other examples of the same thing among the words now in use having *be* for the commencing syllable (of which the common dictionaries give us about a couple of hundreds), although the generality of them are only modern fabrications constructed in imitation of one another, and upon no other principle than the assumption that the syllable in question may be prefixed to almost any verb whatever. Such are *bepraise, bepowder, bespatter, bethump*, and many more. Only between thirty and forty seem to be traceable to Original English verbs beginning with *be*.

The facts that have been mentioned sufficiently explain the word *beholden*. It has nothing to do with the modern *behold*, or the ancient *behealdan* (which, like its modern representative, signified to see or look on), but is another form, according to the corruption which we have seen to take place in so many other instances, of *gehealden*, the past participle passive of *healdan*, to hold; whence its meaning, here and always, of *held, bound, obliged*. It corresponds to the modern German *gehalten*, of the same signification, and is quite distinct from *behalten*, the past participle passive of the verb *behalten*, which signifies kept, preserved.

One word, which repeatedly occurs in Shakespeare, containing the prefix *ge*, has been generally misunderstood by his editors. What they all, I believe without exception, print *I wis*, or *I wiss*, as if it were a verb with its nominative, is undoubtedly one word, and that an adverb, signifying certainly, probably. It ought to be written *ywis*, or *ywiss*, corresponding as it does exactly to the modern German *gewiss*. It is true, indeed, that Sir Frederic Madden in the Glossary to his edition of *Syr Gawayne* (printed, for the Roxburgh Club, in 1839) expresses a doubt whether it were "not regarded as a pronoun and verb by the writers of the fifteenth century." But this supposition Dr Guest (*Phil. Proc. II.* 160) regards as wholly gratuitous. He believes there is not a single instance to be found in which *wiss*, or *wisse*, has been used in the sense of *to know*, "till our modern glossarists and editors chose to give it that signification." Johnson in his *Dictionary* enters *wis* as a verb, meaning to think, to imagine. Webster does the same. So also Nares in his *Glossary*. It is the only explanation which any of these authorities give of the form in question. "The preterite," adds Nares, "is *wist*. The present tense is seldom found but in the first person; the preterite was common in all the persons." In a note on the passage in *The Merchant of Venice*, ii. 9, " There be fools, alive, *I wis* [as they all print it], Silvered o'er," Steevens writes (*Variorum* edition, V. 71) :—" *I wis*, I know. *Wissen*, German. So in *King Henry the Sixth:* 'I wis your grandam had no worser match.' Again, in the Comedy of King Cambyses: 'Yea, I wis, shall you, and that with all speed.' Sydney, Ascham, and Waller use the word." The line here quoted from Shakespeare is not in *King Henry the Sixth*, but in *Richard the Third*, i. 3, and runs, " I wis [*Ywis*] your grandam had a worser match." So in the *Taming of the Shrew*, i. 1, " *Ywis*, it is not half way to her heart." Chaucer, though his adverb is commonly *ywis*, has at least in one instance simply *wis* :—

"Nay, nay, quod she, God help me so, as wis
This is to much, and it were Goddes wil."

C. T. 11,781.

The syllable *wis* is no doubt the same element that we have both in the German *wissen* and in our English *guess*.

395. *We are blest that Rome is rid of him.*—The Second Folio has "We are *glad*." But Mr Collier in his one volume restores *blest*, although it does not appear to be one of the corrections of his MS. annotator.

399. *Here, under leave of Brutus, and the rest.*—Compare " By your pardon" of 358.

399. *When that the poor have cried.*—The *that* in such cases as this is merely a summary or compendious expression of what follows, which was convenient, perhaps, in a ruder condition of the language, as more distinctly marking out the clause to be comprehended under the *when*. We still commonly use it with *now*, when it serves to discriminate the conjunction from the adverb, although not with other conjunctions which are never adverbs. Chaucer often introduces with a *that* even the clause that follows a relative pronoun; as (*C. T.* 982):—"The Minotaur

which *that* he slew in Crete;" or (*C. T.* 988) " With
Creon, which *that* was of Thebes king."

399. ***You all*** *did see, that on the Lupercal.—Vid.* 17.

399. *What cause withholds you, then, to mourn for him?*
We should now say, " Withholds you from mourning."
We could not use *withhold* followed by the infinitive.

403. *Has he not, masters?*— The **common** reading is
" Has he, masters ?" The prosody clearly demands the
insertion of some monosyllable; Capell accordingly inserted *my* before *masters;* but the word required **by** the
sense and the connexion evidently is *not*. The correction,
though conjectural, **is** therefore one which may be regarded **as** of nearly absolute necessity and certainty.—
Masters was the common term of address to a miscellaneous assembly formerly. So again in 408; where, however,
the word is *Maisters* in both the First and Second Folios,
although **not** usually so elsewhere.

404. ***Some*** *will dear abide* ***it.—Vid.*** 327.

408. *And none so poor to do him reverence.*—The
omission of one of two correlative words (such as the *as*
answering to the *so* here) is, when **no** ambiguity is thereby occasioned, allowable in almost all circumstances.—
The manner in which **the** clause is **hung on to** what precedes by the conjunction **is such as to preclude** the necessity of a new **copula or affirmative term.** It is as if it
were " **with none so poor,**" etc. And *and* is logically
(**whatever it may be etymologically**) equivalent to *with*.
So in **164, "Yes** every **man of them;** *and* no man here
But honours you."

408. *Let but* **the** *commons hear this testament.*—The
commonalty, the common people.

408. *And dip their napkins in* **his** *sacred blood.*—A
napkin (connected with *napery,* from **the** French *nappe,* a
cloth, which, again, appears to **be a** corruption of the
Latin *mappa,* of **the same** signification, the original **also**

of our *map*, and of the *mappe* of the French *mappemonde*, that is *mappa mundi*) is still the common name for a pocket handkerchief in Scotland. It is also that commonly employed by Shakespeare; See the Third Act of *Othello*, and the Fourth Act of *As you Like It*.—Compare 247.

412. *Read the will;* etc.—This and most of the subsequent exclamations of the populace need not be considered as verse.

413. *I have o'ershot myself, to tell you of it.*—That is, I have overshot myself (done more than I had intended) by telling you of it.

419. *He comes down,* etc.—This stage direction is not in the older copies.

422. *Stand from the hearse.*—The hearse was the frame or stand on which the body lay. It is the French *herse* or *herce*, meaning a portcullis or harrow; whence the English term seems to have been applied to whatever was constructed of bars or beams laid crosswise.

426. *That day he overcame the Nervii.*—These words certainly ought not to be made a direct statement, as they are by the punctuation of the *Variorum* and of most other modern editions, though not by that of Mr Collier's regulated text.

426. *As rushing out of doors, to be resolved.*— *Vid.* 339.

426. *This was the most unkindest cut of all.*— *Vid.* 337.

426. *For Brutus, as you know, was Cæsar's angel.*—I cannot think that the meaning can be, as Boswell suggests, his guardian angel. It is much more natural to understand it as being simply his best beloved, his darling.

426. *For when the noble Cæsar saw him stab.*—The *him* is here strongly emphatic, notwithstanding its occupation of one of the places assigned by the common rule to short or unaccented syllables. *Vid.* 436.

426. *Even at the base of Pompey's statue.*—*Vid.* 246. The measure, Malone remarks, will be defective (unless

we read *statua*) if *even* be a monosyllable, which he says it usually is in Shakespeare. He thinks that it would be all right with the prosody if *even* could be taken as a dissyllable!

426. *Which all the while ran blood.*—This is almost in the words of North's *Plutarch:*—"Against the very base whereon Pompey's statue stood, which ran all a gore of blood." *Gore* is an Original English word meaning anything muddy, possibly connected with the German *gähren*, to ferment, and other German words.

426. *Whilst bloody treason flourished over us.*—Surely this can mean nothing more than that treason triumphed,—put forth, as it were, its flowers,—shot up into vigorous efflorescence,—over us. Yet the only interpretation the *Variorum* commentators supply is that of Steevens, who says that *flourishes* means flourishes its sword, and quotes from *Romeo and Juliet*, *i.* 1, the line, "And flourishes his blade in spite of me,"—as if that would prove that *to flourish* used absolutely meant or could mean to flourish a sword.

426. *The dint of pity.*—*Dint* seems to be the same word with *dent*, or indentation, that is, the impression made as by a tooth. It is commonly *dent* in the old writers.

426. *These are gracious drops.*—Falling, the thought seems to be, like the bountiful and refreshing rain from heaven.

426. *Marred, as you see, with traitors.*—*Vid.* 363.

432. *We will be revenged*, etc.—This speech is printed in the First Folio as if it were verse, thus:—

> "We will be revenged: revenge;
> About,—seek,—burn,—fire,—kill,—slay!
> Let not a traitor live."

433. *Stay, countrymen.*—To this speech Mr Collier's MS. annotator appends the stage direction, "*They are rushing out.*"

436. *What private griefs they have.*—*Vid.* 129.—*Griefs* with Shakespeare involves the notion rather of to *aggrieve* than that expressed by to *grieve.* So again in 519: "Speak your griefs softly;" and "Enlarge your griefs."

436. *That gave me public leave to speak of him.*—The Second Folio has "That *give* me." Mr Collier restores *gave.*

436. *For I have neither* wit, etc.—This is the reading of the Second Folio. The First has *writ*, which Malone actually adopts and defends! Here is a most animated and admirable enumeration of the various powers, faculties, and arts by which a great orator is enabled "to stir men's blood," beginning, naturally, with that gift of imagination and invention which is at once the highest of them all and the fountain of most of the others; and this editor, rather than admit the probability of the misprint of a single letter in a volume swarming with undeniable typographical errata, would make Antony substitute the ridiculous remark that the first requisite for his purpose, and that in which he was chiefly deficient, was what he calls a *writ*, meaning a written speech! Is it possible that such a critic can have had the smallest feeling of anything in Shakespeare above the level of the merest prose? "Wit," he goes on to tell us, "in our author's time had not its present signification, but meant understanding." The fact is, that there are numerous passages in Shakespeare in which the word has exactly its present signification. "Sir Thurio," says Valentine to Silvia, in *The Two Gentlemen of Verona* (ii. 4), "borrows his wit from your ladyship's looks, and spends what he borrows, kindly, in your company." "Sir," replies Thurio, "if you spend word for word with me, I shall make your wit bankrupt." So in *Much Ado About Nothing*, i. 1, "There is a kind of merry war," says Leonato, speaking of his niece Beatrice, "betwixt Signior Benedick and her: they never meet but there is a skirmish of wit between them."

Or, to go no further, how would Malone, or **those** who think with him (if there be any), explain the conversation about Benedick's wit in the First Scene of the Fifth Act of the last-mentioned Play **without** taking the word as **there** used in the sense which **it now** ordinarily bears? In **the** passage before **us, to be** sure, **its** meaning is more comprehensive, corresponding nearly **to what it** still conveys in the expression "**the** wit of man."

We have the same natural conjunction **of terms** that we have here in *Measure for Measure, v.* **1, where** the Duke addresses the discomfited Angelo:—

"Hast thou or word, or wit, or impudence,
That yet can do thee office?"

436. *And bid them speak for me.*—The *them* here, emphatic and yet occupying a place in the verse in which it is commonly laid down **that** only a short or unaccented **syllable can** properly stand, is in precisely the same **predicament** with the *him* of "When the noble Cæsar saw *him* stab" of 426. *Vid.* 537.

444. *To every several man.*—*Several* is connected with the verb *sever*, which is from the Latin *separo*, through the French *sevrer* (though that language has also *séparer*, as we too have *separate*). "Every several man" is every man by himself or **in his individual** capacity. The phrase may be illustrated by **the legal** distinction between estates **in severalty** and in joint-tenancy or in common. So in **449** we have "common pleasures." "These properties of **arts or** policy, and dissimulation or closeness," says Bacon, in his 6th Essay, "are, indeed, habits and faculties several, **and to** be distinguished."

449. *He hath left them you.*—The emphasis is on *you*.

450. *And with the brands fire the traitors' houses.*—This is the reading of the First Folio: the Second has "**all** the traitors' houses," **which may** be right; for the prolongation of *fire* into a dissyllable, though it will give us the requisite number of syllables (which satisfies both

Malone and Steevens), will not make a very musical verse. Yet the harshness and dissonance produced by the irregular fall of the accent, in addition to the diæresis, in the case of the word *fire*, may be thought to add to the force and expressiveness of the line. Mr Collier omits the "all."

454. *Take thou what course thou wilt!—How now, fellow?*—It is impossible not to suspect that Shakespeare must have written " Take *now* what course thou wilt." The emphatic pronoun, or even a pronoun at all, is unaccountable here. The abruptness, or unexpectedness, of the appearance of the Servant is vividly expressed by the unusual construction of this verse, in which we have an example of the extreme licence, or deviation from the normal form, consisting in the reversal of the regular accentuation in the *last* foot. Thus we have in Milton, *Paradise Lost, x.* 840,

"Beyond all past example and future;"

and again, *xi.* 683,

"To whom thus Michael: These are the product."

At least, *future*, which is common in his verse, has everywhere else the accent on the first syllable. *Product* occurs nowhere else in Milton, and nowhere in Shakespeare.—The stage directions before and after this speech are in the original edition; — " *Exit Plebeians*," and " *Enter* Servant."

458. *He comes upon a wish.*—Coincidently with, as it were upon the back of, my wish for him. *Vid.* 589.

459. *I heard them say.*—In all the old copies it is " I heard *him* say;" which Jennens explains thus:—" *Him* evidently refers to Octavius, who, as he was coming into Rome, had seen Brutus and Cassius riding like madmen through the gates, and had related the same in the presence of the servant." The conjectural emendation of *them*, however, which appears to have been first proposed by Capell had been long generally received, and is con-

firmed by the authority of Mr Collier's manuscript annotator.

459. *Are rid like madmen.*—*Vid.* 374.

460. *Belike they had some notice of the people.*—This now obsolete word *belike* (probably) is commonly held to be a compound of *by* and *like.* But it may perhaps be rather the ancient *gelice* (in like manner), with a slight change of meaning. *Vid.* 390.—" Some notice of the people" is some notice respecting the people.

SCENE III.—*The same. A Street.*
Enter CINNA *the Poet.*

461. *Cin.* I dreamt to-night, that I did feast with Cæsar,
And things unlikely charge my fantasy:
I have no will to wander forth of doors,
Yet something leads me forth.

Enter CITIZENS.

  1. *Cit.* What is your name?
  2 *Cit.* Whither are you going?
  3 *Cit.* Where do you dwell?
  4 *Cit.* Are you a married man, or a bachelor?
  2 *Cit.* Answer every man directly.
  1 *Cit.* Ay, and briefly.
  4 *Cit.* Ay, and wisely.

469. 3 *Cit.* Ay, and truly, you were best.

470. *Cin.* What is my name? Whither am I going? Where do I dwell? Am I a married man, or a bachelor? Then to answer every man directly and briefly, wisely and truly. Wisely, I say, I am a bachelor.

471. *Cit.* That's as much as to say, they are fools that marry:—You'll bear me a bang for that, I fear. Proceed; directly.
  Cin. Directly, I am going to Cæsar's funeral.
  1 *Cit.* As a friend, or an enemy?
  Cin. As a friend.
  2 *Cit.* That matter is answered directly.
  4 *Cit.* For your dwelling,—briefly.
  Cin. Briefly, I dwell by the Capitol.
  3 *Cit.* Your name, Sir, truly.
  Cin. Truly, my name is Cinna.
  1 *Cit.* Tear him to pieces, he's a conspirator.

Cin. I am Cinna the poet, I am Cinna the poet.

4 *Cit.* Tear him for his bad verses, tear him for his bad verses.

483. *Cin.* I am not Cinna the conspirator.

484. 2 *Cit.* It is no matter, his name's Cinna; pluck but his name out of his heart, and turn him going.

3 *Cit.* Tear him, tear him. Come, brands, ho! fire-brands. To Brutus', to Cassius'; burn all. Some to Decius' house, and some to Casca's: some to Ligarius': away; go. [*Exeunt.*

461. *And things unlikely charge my fantasy.*—Instead of *unlikely* the old text has *unluckily*. *Unlikely*, which appears for the first time in Mr Collier's one volume edition, is the restoration of his MS. annotator. It at once, and in the most satisfactory manner, turns nonsense into sense.

461. *I have no will*, etc. — Very well illustrated by Steevens in a quotation from *The Merchant of Venice, ii.* 5, where Shylock says:—

"I have no mind of feasting forth to night:
But I will go."

The only stage direction here in the original edition is before this speech:—" *Enter Cinna the Poet, and after him the Plebeians.*"

469. *Ay, and truly, you were best.*—This is strictly equivalent to "You would be best," and might perhaps be more easily resolved than the more common idiom, "You had best." But all languages have phraseologies coming under the same head with this, which are not to be explained upon strictly logical principles. Witness the various applications of the Greek ἴχει, the French *il y a*, etc. In the following sentence from *As You Like It, i.* 1, we have both the idioms that have been referred to:— "I had as lief thou didst break his neck as his finger and thou wert best look to it."

470. *Wisely, I say, I am a bachelor.*—Cinna's meaning evidently is, Wisely I am a bachelor. But that is not

conveyed by the way in which the passage has hitherto been always pointed—" Wisely I say."

471. *You'll bear me a bang for that.*—You'll get a bang for that (from some one). The *me* goes for nothing. *Vid.* 89 and 205.

483. Cin. *I am not*, etc.—This speech was carelessly omitted in the generality of the modern texts, including that of the standard edition of Malone and Boswell, till restored by Mr Knight. It is given, however, in Jennens's collation (1774), and he does not note its omission by any preceding editor.

484. *Turn him going.*—Turn him off; let him go. The expression occurs also in *As You Like It, iii.* 1:—" Do this expediently, and turn him going." So in Sir Thomas Urquhart's translation of *Rabelais, B. i. ch.* 35; "Avoid hence, and get thee going."—This story of Cinna is told by Plutarch in his Life of Cæsar. He says, the people, falling upon him in their rage, slew him outright in the market-place.

The stage direction with which the Act terminates in the original edition is, " *Exeunt all the Plebeians.*"

ACT IV.

SCENE I.—*The same. A Room in* ANTONY'S *House.*

ANTONY, OCTAVIUS, *and* LEPIDUS, *seated at a Table.*

486. **Ant.** These many, then, shall die; their names are pricked.
 Oct. Your brother too must die. Consent you, Lepidus?
 Lep. I do consent.
 Oct. Prick him down, Antony.
490. **Lep. Upon** condition Publius shall not live,
 Who is **your sister's son,** Mark Antony.
491. **Ant. He shall not live; look, with a spot I** damn him.
 But, Lepidus, go you **to Cæsar's house;**
 Fetch the will hither, and we shall determine
 How to cut off some charge in legacies.

Lep. What, shall I find you here?
Oct. Or here, or at
The Capitol. [*Exit* LEPIDUS.

494. *Ant.* This is a slight unmeritable man,
Meet to be sent on errands: Is it fit,
The three-fold world divided, he should stand
One of the three to share it?
Oct. So you thought him;
And took his voice who should be pricked to die
In our black sentence and proscription.

496. *Ant.* Octavius, I have seen more days than you;
And though we lay these honours on this man,
To ease ourselves of divers slanderous loads,
He shall but bear them as the ass bears gold;
To groan and sweat under the business,
Either led or driven, as we point the way;
And, having brought our treasure where we will,
Then take we down his load, and turn him off,
Like to the empty ass, to shake his ears,
And graze on commons.
Oct. You may do your will;
But he's a tried and valiant soldier.

498. *Ant.* So is my horse, Octavius; and, for that,
I do appoint him store of provender.
It is a creature that I teach to fight,
To wind, to stop, to run directly on;
His corporal motion governed by my spirit.
And, in some taste, is Lepidus but so;
He must be taught, and trained, and bid go forth:
A barren-spirited fellow; one that feeds
On objects, arts, and imitations,
Which, out of use, and staled by other men,
Begin his fashion: Do not talk of him,
But as a property.
　　　　　　And now, Octavius,
Listen great things.—Brutus and Cassius
Are levying powers; we must straight make head:
Therefore let our alliance be combined,
Our best friends made, and our best means stretched out;
And let us presently go sit in counsel
How covert matters may be best disclosed,
And open perils surest answered.

499. *Oct.* Let us do so: for we are at the stake,

T

And **bayed** about with many enemies;
And some, that smile, have in their hearts, I fear,
Millions of mischiefs. [*Exeunt.*

The Same. A Room in Antony's House.—The original heading is only, " *Enter Antony, Octavius, and Lepidus.*" *The Same*, meaning at Rome, was supplied by Rowe. It is evident (especially from 492 and 493) that the scene is placed at Rome, although in point of fact the triumvirs held their meeting in a small island in the river Rhenus (now the *Reno*) near Bononia (*Bologna*), where, Plutarch says, they remained three days together.

486. *These many.*—An archaic form for so many, this number.

486. *Their names are pricked.*—*Vid.* 352.

490. *Who is your sister's son, Mark Antony.*—This is a mistake. The person meant is Lucius Cæsar, who was Mark Antony's uncle, the brother of his mother.

491. *Look, with a spot I damn him.*—Note him as condemned, by a mark or stigma (called pricking his name in 486, and pricking him down in 489, and pricking him in 495).

491. *Fetch the will hither, and we shall determine.*—This is the reading of all the old copies, and is properly retained by Mr Knight. In the Variorum edition we have (and without warning) *will* substituted for *shall;* and this alteration Mr Collier also adopts in his regulated text, although it does not appear to be one of the corrections of his manuscript annotator.

494. *This is a slight unmeritable man.*—So afterwards in 535, "Away, *slight* man!" said by Brutus, in momentary anger, to Cassius. *Vid.* 522. — *Unmeritable* should mean incapable of deserving.

494. *Meet to be sent on errands.*—*Errand* is an Original English word, *ærend* (perhaps from *ær*, or *ar*, before, whence also *ere* and *early*). It has no connexion with *errant*, wandering (from the Latin *erro*, whence also *err*, and *error*, and *erroneous*).

496. *To groan and sweat under the business.*—*Business* is commonly only a dissyllable with Shakespeare; and it may be no more here upon the principle explained in the note on "She dreamt to-night she saw my statue" in 246. There are a good many more instances of lines concluding with *business*, in which either it is a trisyllable (although commonly only a dissyllable in the middle of a line) or the verse must be regarded as a hemistich, or truncated verse, of nine syllables.

496. *Either led or driven*, etc.—The three last Folios, and also Rowe, have "*print* the way." The *we* of this line, and the *our* and the *we* of the next, are all emphatic. There is the common irregularity of a single short superfluous syllable (the *er* of *either*).

496. *And graze on commons.*—*In* is the reading of all the old copies. *On* is the correction of Mr Collier's MS. annotator.

498. *Store of provender.*—*Provender*, which Johnson explains to mean "dry food for brutes," and which also appears in the forms *provand* and *provant*, is immediately from the French *provende*, having the same signification; but the origin of the French word is not so clear. The Italian, indeed, has *provianda*, a feminine substantive in the singular; but this signifies victuals in general, or flesh-meat in particular, and is the same word with the French *viande* and the English *viands*, which are commonly traced to the Latin *vivere* (quasi *vivenda*), an etymology which receives some support from the existence of *vivanda* in the Italian as apparently only another form of *provianda*. Another derivation of the French *provende* brings it from *provenire* and *proventus*, in which case it would signify properly increase, growth, crop; and another would bring it from *provideo*, making it only a variation or corruption of *provision*. The parentage of the word, therefore, may be said to be contested between *vivo, venio,* and *video*. Possibly *vendo* might also put in

a claim. Webster has :—" It is said that *provend,* **pro-vender**, originally signified a vessel containing a **measure** of corn daily **given to a horse or** other beast." By whom this is stated, or in **what** language the words are said to have this **meaning, he does not inform us.** He also adduces the Norman *provender,* **a prebendary, and** *provendre,* **a prebend, and the Dutch** *prove,* **a prebend.** The Latin *præbenda* (from *præbeo*), the undoubted original of *prebend,* may have got confounded with *provende* in the obscurity enveloping **the origin** and proper meaning of the latter term.

498. *And, in some taste.*—It might seem at first **that this phrase,** as it may be said to be equivalent **in effect to our common "in some** sense," **so** is only another wording **of** the same conception or figure, what is called **a *sense* in the one form** being called a *taste* in the other. But, although taste is reckoned one of the senses, this would **certainly be** a wrong explanation. The expression "in some **sense" has** nothing **to do with the** powers of sensation or perception; *sense* here is signification, meaning, import. Neither does *taste* stand for the sense of taste in the other expression. The taste which is here referred to is a taste in contradistinction **to a** more **full** enjoyment or participation, a taste merely. **" In some taste"** is another way of saying, not **"in** some **sense," but "in** some measure, or degree."

498. *On objects, arts, and imitations,* etc.—This passage, as it stands in **the Folios,** with the sentence terminating at **"imitations," has much** perplexed the commentators, and, indeed, **may be** said to have proved quite inexplicable, **till a** comma was substituted for the full point by Mr Knight, which slight change makes everything plain and easy. Antony's assertion is, that Lepidus feeds, not **on** objects, arts, and imitations generally, but on such of them as are out of use and staled (or worn out : *Vid.* 50) **by** other people, which, notwithstanding, begin his fashion

(or with which his following the fashion begins). Theobald reduces the full point to a comma, as other editors do to a colon or a semicolon; but it is evident, nevertheless, from his note that he did not regard the relative clause as a qualification or limitation of what precedes it.

498. *Listen great things.*—*Listen* has now ceased to be used as an active verb.

498. *Our best friends made, and our best means stretched out.*—This is the reading of the Second Folio. It seems to me, I confess, to be sufficiently in Shakespeare's manner. The First Folio has " Our best Friends made, our meanes stretcht,"—which, at any rate, it is quite impossible to believe to be what he wrote.

498. *And let us presently go sit in counsel*, etc.—The more ordinary phraseology would be "Let us sit in consultation how," or "Let us consult how." The word in the First Folio is "Councell," and most, if not all, modern editions have "sit in council." But *Vid.* 263.

499. *And bayed about with many enemies.*—*Vid.* 349 (for *bayed*), and 363 (for *with*).

499. *Millions of mischiefs.*—This is the reading of all the old editions. Mr Knight has "mischief," no doubt by an error of the press. In the *Winter's Tale*, iv. 2, however, we have, in a speech of the Clown, " A million of beating may come to a great matter."

SCENE II.—*Before* BRUTUS's *Tent, in the Camp near Sardis.*

Drum.—*Enter* BRUTUS, LUCILIUS, TITINIUS, *and Soldiers:*
PINDARUS *meeting them:* LUCIUS *at a distance.*

Bru. Stand, ho!
Lucil. Give the word, **ho! and stand.**
502. *Bru.* What now, Lucilius? is Cassius near?
503. *Lucil.* He is at hand; and Pindarus is **come**
To do you salutation from his master.
[PINDARUS *gives a letter to* BRUTUS.
504. *Bru.* He greets me well.—Your master, Pindarus,

In his own change, or by ill officers,
Hath **given** me some worthy cause to wish
Things done undone : but, if he **be at hand,**
I shall be satisfied.
    Pin. I do not doubt
But that my noble master will **appear**
Such as he is, full of regard and **honour.**

506. *Bru.* He **is** not doubted.—
                    A word, Lucilius:
How he received you, let me be resolved.

507. *Lucil.* With courtesy, and with respect enough;
But not with such familiar instances,
Nor with such free and friendly conference,
As he hath used of old.

508. *Bru.* Thou hast described
A hot friend cooling : Ever note, Lucilius,
When love begins to sicken and decay,
It useth an enforced ceremony.
There are no tricks in plain and simple faith :
But hollow men, like horses hot at hand,
Make gallant show and promise of their **mettle ;**
But, when they should endure the bloody **spur,**
They fall their crests, and, like deceitful jades,
Sink in the trial. Comes his army on?

509. *Lucil.* They mean this night in Sardis to be quartered;
The greater part, the horse in general,
Are come with Cassius.   [*March within.*

510. *Bru.* Hark, he is **arrived :—**
March gently on **to** meet **him.**

              Enter CASSIUS *and Soldiers.*

    Cas. Stand, ho !
    Bru. Stand, ho ! Speak the word along.

513. *Within.* Stand.
514. *Within.* Stand.
515. *Within.* Stand.
    Cas. Most noble brother, you have done me wrong.
    Bru. Judge me, you gods ! Wrong I mine enemies?
And, if not so, how should I wrong a brother ?
    Cas. Brutus, this sober form of yours **hides** wrongs ;
And when you do **them**——

519. *Bru.* Cassius, be content :
Speak your griefs softly ;—I **do know you** well.—

Before the eyes of both our armies here,
Which should perceive nothing but love from us,
Let us not wrangle: Bid them move away;
Then in my tent, Cassius, enlarge your griefs,
And I will give you audience.
 Cas. Pindarus,
Bid our commanders lead their charges off
A little from this ground.
521. *Bru.* Lucius, do you the like; and let no man
Come to our tent, till we have done our conference.
Lucilius and Titinius, guard our door.   [*Exeunt*

 Scene II.—The original heading here is "*Drum. Enter Brutus, Lucillius, and the Army. Titinius and Pindarus meete them.*" The modern editors after the name of *Lucilius* introduce that of *Lucius.* See the note on 521.

 502. *What now, Lucilius? is Cassius near?*—Here the *ius* is dissyllabic in *Lucilius* and monosyllabic in *Cassius.*

 503. *To do you salutation.*—Another of the old applications of *do* which we have now lost. *Vid.* 147. The stage direction about the Letter is modern.

 504. *He greets me well.*—The meaning seems to be, He salutes me in a friendly manner. Yet this can hardly be regarded as a legitimate employment of *well.* For *greet* see 242.

 504. *In his own change,* etc.—The meaning seems to be, either through a change that has taken place in his own feelings and conduct, or through the misconduct of his officers.

 504. *Some worthy cause.*—Some reasonable or sufficient cause, some cause of worth, value, or power to justify the wish. Our modern *worth* is the ancient *weorth, wurth,* or *wyrth,* connected with which are *weorscipe,* worship, and *weorthian,* to hold in esteem or honour. But there may also perhaps be a connexion with *weorthan,* or *wurthan,* to become, or to be, the same word with the modern German *werden,* and still in a single fragment remaining in use among ourselves in the phrase *woe worth,* that is,

woe be. If this be so, either what we call *worth* is that which anything emphatically *is*, or, when we say **that a thing *is*, we are** only saying that it **is** *worth* in a broad or vague sense, according to a common manner of forming a term of general out of one of particular import. In the latter case *worth* may be connected with *vir*, and *virtus*, and *vireo*. *Vid.* 209.

506. *He is not* doubted.—*A word*, etc.—Brutus here, it will be observed, makes two speeches; first he addresses himself to Pindarus, then to Lucilius. Even **if the prosody** did not admonish us to the same effect, **it would, in** these circumstances, **be** better to print the passage as I have given it, with two hemistichs or broken lines.

506. *Let me be resolved.*—*Vid.* 339.

507. *But not with such familiar instances.*—The word still in use that most nearly expresses this obsolete sense of *instances* is, perhaps, *assiduities*. As *instance* should mean standing upon, so *assiduity* should mean sitting upon. *Assiduitas* is used by Cicero; *instantia*, I believe, is not found in the best age of the Latin tongue. The English word is employed by Shakespeare in other senses besides this that are now obsolete. "To comfort you the more," says the Earl **of Warwick to the** King, in **the** *Second Part of King Henry the Fourth, iii.* **1,**

"I have received
A certain *instance* that Glendower is dead;"—

that is, a certain assurance. Again, in *King **Richard** the Third*, "Tell him," says Lord Hastings in **reply to** the message from Lord Stanley, *iii.* 2,

"**Tell** him his fears are shallow, without *instance*;"—

that is, apparently, without **any fact to** support or justify them. Again, in *Hamlet*, ***iii.* 2, in** the Play acted before the King and Queen we have

> "The *instances* that second marriage move
> Are base respects of thrift, but none of love;"—

that is, the inducements, as we should now say, are base considerations of thrift, or pecuniary advantage. We now use *instance* in something like its proper sense only in the phrase "at the instance of," and even there the notion of pressure or urgency is nearly lost; the word is understood as meaning little, if anything, more than merely so much of application, request, or suggestion as the mere mention of what is wanted might carry with it. In another phrase in which it has come to be used, "in the first instance," it is not very obvious what its meaning really is, or how, at least, it has got the meaning which it appears to have. Do we, or can we, say "in the second, or third, instance?" By *instance* as commonly used, for a particular fact, we ought to understand a fact bearing upon the matter in hand; and this seems to be still always kept in mind in the familiar expression "for instance."

Shakespeare's use of the word may be further illustrated by the following passages:—" They will scarcely believe this without trial: offer them instances; which shall bear no less likelihood than to see me at her chamber window; hear me call Margaret, Hero; hear Margaret term me Claudio;" etc. (*Much Ado About Noth.*, ii. 2);—

> "Instance! O instance! strong as Pluto's gates;
> Cressid is mine, tied with the bonds of heaven:
> Instance! O instance! strong as heaven itself;
> The bonds of heaven are slipped, dissolved, and loosed;
> And with another knot, five-finger-tied,
> The fractions of her faith, orts of her love,
> The fragments, scraps, the bits and greasy reliques
> Of her o'ereaten faith, are bound to Diomed."
>   *Troil. and Cress.*, v. 2.

508. *Like horses hot at hand.*—That is, apparently,

when held by the hand, or led. Or rather, perhaps, when acted upon only by the rein. So in Harington's *Ariosto*, *vii*. 67, Melyssa says that she will try to make Rogero's griffith horse "gentle to the spur and hand." But has not "*at* hand" always meant, as it always does now, only near or hard by? That meaning will not do here. The commentators afford us no light or help. Perhaps Shakespeare wrote "*in* hand." The two expressions *in hand* and *at hand* are commonly distinguished in the Plays as they are in our present usage; and we also have *on hand* and *at the hands of* in the modern senses, as well as *to bear in hand* ("to keep in expectation, to amuse with false pretences"—*Nares*) and *at any hand* (that is, in any case), which are now obsolete. In *The Comedy of Errors*, *ii*. 1, *at hand*, used by his mistress Adriana in the common sense, furnishes matter for the word-catching wit of Dromio of Ephesus after he has been beaten, as he thinks, by his master:—"*Adr*. Say, is your tardy master now at hand? *Dro. E.* Nay, he's at two hands with me, and that my two ears can witness." In *King John*, *v*. 2, however, we have "like a lion fostered up at hand," that is, as we should now say, by hand. In another similar phrase, we may remark, *at* has now taken the place of the *in* or *into* of a former age. We now say To march *at* the head of, and also To place *at* the hend of, and we use *in the head* and *into the head* in quite other senses; but here is the way in which Clarendon expresses himself:—" They said . . . that there should be an army of thirty thousand men immediately transported into England with the Prince of Wales in the head of them" (*Hist., Book x.*); " The King was only expected to be nearer England, how disguised soever, that he might quickly put himself into the head of the army, that would be ready to receive him" (*Id., Book xiv.*); " These cashiered officers . . . found so much encouragement, that, at a time appointed, they put themselves into the heads of their regiments, and marched with them into the field" (*Id., Book xvi.*); "That Lord [Fairfax] had called together some of his old disbanded officers and soldiers, and many principal men of the country, and marched in the head of them into York" (*Ibid.*); "Upon that very day they [the Parliament] received a petition, which they had fomented, presented . . . by a man notorious in those times, . . . *Praise-God Barebone*, in the head of a crowd of sectaries" (*Ibid.*); "He [the Chancellor] informed him [Admiral Montague] of Sir George Booth's being possessed of Chester, and in the head of an army" (*Ibid.*).

508. *They fall their crests.*—This use of *fall*, as an active verb, is not common in Shakespeare; but it may be found in writers of considerably later date.

508. *Sink in the trial.*—One may suspect that it should be *shrink*.

509. Instead of the stage direction "*March within*" at the end of this speech, the original text has "*Low March within*" in the middle of 508. And instead of "*Enter Cassius and Soldiers*," it is there "*Enter Cassius and his powers.*"

513, 514, 515.—The *Within* prefixed to these three speeches is the insertion of the modern editors. In the First Folio the three repetitions of the "Stand" are on so many distinct lines, but all as if they formed part of the speech of Brutus. Mr Collier has at 515 the Stage Direction, "*One after the other, and fainter.*"

519. *Cassius, be content.*—That is, be continent; contain, or restrain, yourself.

519. *Speak your griefs softly.*—*Vid.* 129 and 436.

519. *Nothing but love from us.*—From each of us to the other.

519. *Enlarge your griefs.*—State them with all fulness of eloquent exposition; as we still say *Enlarge upon.*—*Vid.* 129 and 436. Clarendon uses the verb *to enlarge*

differently both from Shakespeare and from the modern language; **thus:**—"**As soon as his** lordship [the Earl of Manchester] had **finished his** oration, which was received with marvellous acclamations, Mr Pym enlarged himself, **in a speech** then printed, upon the **several** parts of the King's answer" (*Hist., Book vi.*).

521. *Lucius, do you the like;* etc.—The original text is—

"*Lucillius*, do you the like, and let no man
Come to our tent, till we have done our Conference.
Let *Lucius* and *Titinius* guard our doore."

To cure the prosody in the first line, Steevens **and** other modern editors strike out the *you*. It is strange that **no** one should have been struck with the absurdity of such an association as *Lucius* and *Titinius* for the guarding **of the door—an officer of rank and a** servant boy— the boy, **too,** being named first. The function of Lucius was to carry messages. As Cassius sends *his* servant Pindarus with a message to his division of the force, Brutus sends his servant Lucius with a similar message to his division. **Nothing** can be clearer than that *Lucilius* in the first line **is a** misprint for *Lucius*, and *Lucius* in the third a misprint for *Lucilius*. **Or** the error may have **been in** the copy; **and the insertion of** the *Let* was pro**bably an attempt of the printer,** or editor, **to** save the **prosody of** that **line, as** the omission of the *you* **is of** the modern **editors to save that** of the other. **The present** restoration sets everything to rights. At **the close** of the conference we have Brutus, in 580, again addressing himself **to** Lucilius and Titinius, who had evidently kept together all the **time it lasted.** Lucius (who in the original **text** is commonly **called the** *Boy*) **and** Titinius are nowhere mentioned together. **In the** heading of Scene III., indeed, the modern editors have again "*Lucius* and

Titinius at some distance;" but this is their own manufacture. All that we have in the old copies is, "*Manet Brutus and Cassius.*" See also 571.

SCENE III.—Within the Tent of BRUTUS. LUCILIUS *and* TITINIUS *at some distance from it.*

Enter BRUTUS *and* CASSIUS.

522. *Cas.* That you have wronged me doth appear in this:
You have condemned and noted Lucius Pella
For taking bribes here of the Sardians;
Wherein my letters, praying on his side,
Because I knew the man, were slighted off.
   Bru. You wronged yourself, to write in such a case.
524. *Cas.* In such a time as this, it is not meet
That every nice offence should bear his comment.
525. *Bru.* Let me tell you, Cassius, you yourself
Are much condemned to have an itching palm,
To sell and mart your offices for gold
To undeservers.
   Cas. I an itching palm?
You know, that you are Brutus that speaks this,
Or, by the gods, this speech were else your last.
527. *Bru.* The name of Cassius honours this corruption,
And chastisement doth therefore hide his head.
   Cas. Chastisement!
529. *Bru.* Remember March, the ides of March remember!
Did not great Julius bleed for justice sake?
What villain touched his body, that did stab,
And not for justice? What, shall one of us,
That struck the foremost man of all this world,
But for supporting robbers, shall we now
Contaminate our fingers with base bribes?
And sell the mighty space of our large honours
For so much trash as may be grasped thus?—
I had rather be a dog, and bay the moon,
Than such a Roman.
530. *Cas.* Brutus, bay not me;
I'll not endure it: you forget yourself,
To hedge me in: I am a soldier, I,
Older in practice, abler than yourself
To make conditions.

531. *Bru.* Go to; you are not, Cassius.
   Cas. I **am.**
   Bru. **I say, you** are not.
534. *Cas.* Urge me no more, **I** shall forget myself;
   Have mind upon your health, **tempt me no further.**
535. *Bru.* Away, slight man!
   Cas. Is't possible?
537. *Bru.* Hear me, for I will speak.
   Must I give way and room to your rash **choler?**
   Shall I be frighted, when a madman stares?
   Cas. O ye gods! ye gods! Must I endure all this?
539. *Bru.* All this? Ay, more: Fret till your proud heart break;
   Go, show your slaves how choleric you are,
   And make your bondmen tremble. Must I budge?
   Must I observe you? Must I stand and crouch
   Under your testy humour? By the gods,
   You shall digest the venom of your spleen,
   Though it do split you: for, from this day forth,
   I'll use you for my mirth, yea, for my laughter,
   When you are waspish.
   Cas. **Is it come** to this?
541. *Bru.* You say you are a better soldier:
   Let it appear so; make your vaunting true,
   And it shall please me well: For mine own part,
   I shall be glad to learn of abler men.
542. *Cas.* You wrong me every way, you wrong me, Brutus;
   I said an elder soldier, **not** a better:
   Did I say, better?
     Bru. If you did, I care **not.**
     Cas. When Cæsar lived he durst not thus have moved me.
     Bru. **Peace, peace; you durst** not so have tempted him.
     Cas. **I durst not?**
     Bru. No.
     Cas. What? durst not tempt him?
     Bru. For your life you durst not.
     Cas. Do not presume too much upon my love:
   I may do that I shall be sorry for.
551. *Bru.* You have **done** that you should be sorry for.
   There **is no terror, Cassius,** in your threats:
   For I am armed so strong in honesty,
   That they pass by me as the idle wind,
   Which I respect not. I did send to you
   For certain sums of gold, which you denied me;—

For I can raise no money by vile means:
By heaven, I had rather coin my heart,
And drop my blood for drachmas, than to wring
From the hard hands of peasants their vile trash
By any indirection. I did send
To you for gold to pay my legions,
Which you denied me: Was that done like Cassius?
Should I have answered Caius Cassius so?
When Marcus Brutus grows so covetous,
To lock such rascal counters from his friends,
Be ready, gods, with all your thunderbolts;
Dash him to pieces!
 Cas. I denied you not.
 Bru. You did.

554. *Cas.* I did not:—he was but a fool
That brought my answer back.—Brutus hath rived my heart:
A friend should bear his friend's infirmities,
But Brutus makes mine greater than they are.
 Bru. I do not, till you practise them on me.
 Cas. You love me not.
 Bru. I do not like your faults.
 Cas. A friendly eye could never see such faults.

559. *Bru.* A flatterer's would not, though they do appear
As huge as high Olympus.

560. *Cas.* Come, Antony, and young Octavius, come,
Revenge yourselves alone on Cassius!
For Cassius is aweary of the world:
Hated by one he loves; braved by his brother;
Checked like a bondman; all his faults observed,
Set in a note-book, learned and conned by rote,
To cast into my teeth. O, I could weep
My spirit from mine eyes!—There is my dagger,
And here my naked breast; within, a heart
Dearer than Plutus' mine, richer than gold:
If that thou beest a Roman, take it forth;
I, that denied thee gold, will give my heart:
Strike, as thou didst at Cæsar; for, I know,
When thou didst hate him worst, thou loved'st him better
Than ever thou loved'st Cassius.

561. *Bru.* Sheath your dagger:
Be angry when you will, it shall have scope;
Do what you will, dishonour shall be humour.
O Cassius, you are yoked with a lamb,

That carries anger as the flint bears fire;
Who, much enforced, shows a hasty spark,
And straight is cold again.

562. *Cas.* Hath Cassius lived
To be but mirth and laughter to his Brutus,
When grief, and blood ill-tempered, vexeth him?
   Bru. When I spoke that, I was ill-tempered too.
   Cas. Do you confess so much? Give me your hand.
   Bru. And my heart too.
   Cas. O Brutus!—
   Bru. What's the matter?

568. *Cas.* Have not you love enough to bear with me,
When that rash humour which my mother gave me
Makes me forgetful?

569. *Bru.* Yes, Cassius; and from henceforth,
When you are over-earnest with your Brutus,
He'll think your mother chides, and leave you so. [*Noise within.*

570. *Poet.* [*within*]. Let me go in to see the generals:
There is some grudge between 'em; 'tis not meet
They be alone.

571. *Lucil.* [*within*]. You shall not come to them.
   Poet. [*within*]. Nothing but death shall stay me.

Enter POET.

   Cas. How now? What's the matter?

574. *Poet.* For shame, you generals; What do you mean?
Love, and be friends, as two such men should be;
For I have seen more years, I'm sure, than ye.

575. *Cas.* Ha, ha; how vilely doth this Cynic rhyme!
   Bru. Get you hence, sirrah; saucy fellow, hence!
   Cas. Bear with him, Brutus; 'tis his fashion.

578. *Bru.* I'll know his humour when he knows his time:
What should the wars do with these jigging fools?
Companion, hence!
   Cas. Away, away, be gone!   [*Exit* POET.

Enter LUCILIUS *and* TITINIUS.

580. *Bru.* Lucilius and Titinius, bid the commanders
Prepare to lodge their companies to-night.

581. *Cas.* And come yourselves, and bring Messala with you,
Immediately to us.   [*Exeunt* LUCILIUS *and* TITINIUS.
   Bru. Lucius, a bowl of wine.
   Cas. I did not think you could have been so angry.
   Bru. O Cassius, I am sick of many griefs.

Cas. Of your philosophy you make no use,
If you give place to accidental evils.
   Bru. No man bears sorrow better :—Portia is dead.
   Cas. Ha! Portia?
   Bru. She is dead.
589. *Cas.* How 'scaped I killing, when I crossed you so?—
O insupportable and touching loss!—
Upon what sickness?
590. *Bru.* Impatient of my absence;
And grief, that young Octavius with Mark Antony
Have made themselves so strong;—for with her death
That tidings came;—with this she fell distract,
And, her attendants absent, swallowed fire.
   Cas. And died so?
   Bru. Even so.
593. *Cas.* O ye immortal gods!

Enter LUCIUS, *with wine and tapers.*

   Bru. Speak no more of her.—Give me a bowl of wine :—
In this I bury all unkindness, Cassius.   [*Drinks.*
   Cas. My heart is thirsty for that noble pledge :—
Fill, Lucius, till the wine o'erswell the cup;
I cannot drink too much of Brutus' love.   [*Drinks.*

Re-enter TITINIUS, *with* MESSALA.

596. *Bru.* Come in, Titinius :—Welcome, good Messala.—
Now sit we close about this taper here,
And call in question our necessities.
   Cas. Portia, art thou gone?
598. *Bru.* No more, I pray you.—
Messala, I have here received letters,
That young Octavius, and Mark Antony,
Come down upon us with a mighty power,
Bending their expedition toward Philippi.
599. *Mess.* Myself have letters of the self-same tenour.
   Bru. With what addition?
601. *Mess.* That by proscription, and bills of outlawry,
Octavius, Antony, and Lepidus
Have put to death an hundred senators.
   Bru. Therein our letters do not well agree:
Mine speak of seventy senators that died
By their proscriptions, Cicero being one.
   Cas. Cicero one?
604. *Mess.* Cicero is dead,

U

And by that order of proscription.—
Had you your letters from your wife, my lord?
Bru. No, Messala.
Mess. Nor nothing in your **letters writ of her?**
Bru. Nothing, Messala.
Mess. That, methinks, is strange.
Bru. **Why** ask you? hear **you** aught of **her in yours?**
Mess. **No, my lord.**
Bru. Now, as you are a Roman, tell me true.
Mess. Then like a Roman bear the truth I tell:
For certain she is dead, and by strange manner.

613. *Bru.* Why, farewell, Portia.—We must die, Messala:
With meditating that she must die once,
I have the patience to endure it now.
Mess. Even so great men great losses should endure.

615. *Cas.* I have as much of this in art as you,
But yet my nature could not bear it so.

616. *Bru.* Well, to our work alive. What do you think
Of marching to Philippi presently?
Cas. I do not think it good.
Bru. **Your** reason?

619. *Cas.* **This it is:**
'Tis better that the enemy seek us:
So shall he waste his means, weary his soldiers,
Doing himself offence; whilst we, lying still,
Are full of rest, defence, and nimbleness.

620. *Bru.* Good reasons must, of force, give place to better.
The people 'twixt Philippi and this ground
Do stand but in a forced **affection;**
For they have grudged us **contribution:**
The enemy, marching **along by them,**
By them shall make **a fuller number up,**
Come on refreshed, new-hearted, and encouraged;
From which advantage shall we cut him off
If at Philippi we do face him there,
These people at our back.
Cas. Hear me, good brother.

622. *Bru.* **Under** your pardon.—You must note **beside,**
That we have tried the utmost of our friends:
Our legions are brim-full, **our cause is ripe;**
The enemy increaseth every day;
We, at the height, are ready to decline.
There is a tide in the affairs of men,

Which, taken at the flood, leads on to fortune;
Omitted, all the voyage of their life
Is bound in shallows, and in miseries.
On such a full sea are we now afloat;
And we must take the current when it serves,
Or lose our ventures.

623. *Cas.* Then, with your will, go on;
We'll along ourselves, and meet them at Philippi.

624. *Bru.* The deep of night is crept upon our talk,
And nature must obey necessity;
Which we will **niggard** with a little **rest.**
There is no more to say?

625. *Cas.* No more. Good night;
Early to-morrow will we rise, and hence.

626. *Bru.* Lucius, my gown. [*Exit* LUCIUS.
Farewell, good Messala;—
Good night, Titinius :—Noble, noble Cassius,
Good night, and good repose.
Cas. O my dear brother,
This was an **ill** beginning of the night:
Never come such division 'tween our souls!
Let it not, Brutus.
Bru. Everything **is well.**
Cas. Good night, my lord.
Bru. Good night, good **brother.**
Tit. Mes. Good night, lord Brutus.
Bru. Farewell, **every** one.
[*Exeunt* CASSIUS, TITINIUS, *and* MESSALA.

Re-enter LUCIUS, *with the Gown.*

Give me the gown. Where is thy instrument?
Luc. Here, in the tent

634. *Bru.* **What,** thou speak'st drowsily?
Poor knave, **I blame** thee **not;** thou art o'erwatched.
Call Claudius, and some other of my men;
I'll have them sleep **on cushions in my tent.**

635. *Luc.* Varro and **Claudius!**

Enter VARRO *and* CLAUDIUS.

Var. Calls my lord?

637. *Bru.* I pray you, sirs, lie in my tent, **and sleep;**
It may be, I shall raise you by and by
On business to my brother Cassius.

Var. So please you, we will stand, and watch your pleasure.
639. *Bru.* I will not have it so: lie down, good sirs;
It may be I shall otherwise bethink me.
Look, Lucius, here's the book I sought for so;
I put it in the pocket of my gown.   [SERVANTS *lie down.*
    Luc. I was sure your lordship did not give it me.
641. *Bru.* Bear with me, good boy, I am much forgetful.
Canst thou hold up thy heavy eyes awhile,
And touch thy instrument a strain or two?
    Luc. Ay, my lord, an't please you.
    Bru. It does, my boy:
I trouble thee too much, but thou art willing.
    Luc. It is my duty, Sir.
645. *Bru.* I should not urge thy duty past thy might;
I know young bloods look for a time of rest.
    Luc. I have slept, my lord, already.
647. *Bru.* It was well done; and thou shalt sleep again;
I will not hold thee long: if I do live,
I will be good to thee.   [*Music and a song.*
This is a sleepy tune:—O murderous slumber
Lay'st thou thy leaden mace upon my boy,
That plays thee music?—Gentle knave, good night;
I will not do thee so much wrong to wake thee.
If thou dost nod, thou break'st thy instrument;
I'll take it from thee; and, good boy, good night.
Let me see, let me see;—Is not the leaf turned down,
Where I left reading? Here it is, I think.   [*He sits down.*

Enter the GHOST *of* CÆSAR.

How ill this taper burns!—Ha! who comes here?
I think, it is the weakness of mine eyes
That shapes this monstrous apparition.
It comes upon me:—Art thou anything?
Art thou some god, some angel, or some devil,
That mak'st my blood cold, and my hair to stare?
Speak to me what thou art.
648.   *Ghost.* Thy evil spirit, Brutus.
649.   *Bru.* Why com'st thou?
       Ghost. To tell thee, thou shalt see me at Philippi.
651.   *Bru.* Well; then I shall see thee again?
652.   *Ghost.* Ay, at Philippi.   [GHOST *vanishes*
653.   *Bru.* Why, I will see thee at Philippi then.—
Now I have taken heart, thou vanishest:

Ill spirit, I would hold more talk with thee.—
Boy! Lucius!—Varro! Claudius! Sirs, awake!—
Claudius!
Luc. The strings, my lord, are false.
Bru. He thinks, he still is at his instrument.—
Lucius, awake.
Luc. My lord!
Bru. Didst thou dream, Lucius, that thou so cried'st out?
Luc. My lord, I do not know that I did cry.
Bru. Yes, that thou didst Didst thou see anything?
Luc. Nothing, my lord.

661. *Bru.* Sleep again, Lucius.—Sirrah, Claudius!
Fellow thou! awake.
Var. My lord.
Clau. My lord.
Bru. Why did you so cry out, Sirs, in your sleep?
Var. Clau. Did we, my lord?
Bru. Ay: Saw you anything?
Var. No, my lord, I saw nothing.
Clau. Nor I, my lord.

669. *Bru.* Go, and commend me to my brother Cassius;
Bid him set on his powers betimes before,
And we will follow.
Var. Clau. It shall be done, my lord. [*Exeunt.*

522. *Wherein my letters . . . were slighted off.*—The printer of the First Folio, evidently misunderstanding the passage, gives us—

"Wherein my Letters, praying on his side,
Because I knew the man was slighted off."

The Second Folio has—

"Wherein my Letter, praying on his side,
Because I knew the man, was slighted off."

The received reading, therefore, though probably right, is only conjectural; unless we are to suppose, from its being adopted by Mr Collier, that it has the sanction of his manuscript annotator. Some of the modern editors print "slighted *of.*" At a date considerably later than Shakespeare we have still *slighted over* (for to treat or perform **carelessly**). **It is** used by Dryden in **the end of** the seventeenth century, **as it** had been by Bacon in **the** beginning. **The** connexion **of the various** modifications of the term *slight* is **sufficiently obvious.** They all involve **the notion of** quickly **and easily escaping or** being dispatched and got rid of. Perhaps not **only** *slight* and *sly*, **but even** *slide*, and *slink*, and *sleek* **ought to** be referred **to** the same **root.** In that **case the** modern **German** *schlau* (sly) may **be connected not** only with *schleichen* (to move softly), **but also with** *schlecht* (plain, simple, honest); **strange as** it **may be** thought that **the same** element should **denote** slyness or cunning in one **modification, and** simplicity or straightforwardness in another.

524. *That every nice offence*, etc.—*Nice* **is the ancient native** *nesc* **or** *hnesc*, tender, soft, gentle. In modern **English the word always** implies smallness or pettiness, **though not** always **in a** disparaging sense, but rather **most usually** in the **contrary.** So a *pet*, literally something **small, is the** common name for anything that is loved **and** cherished.—For "*his* comment" see 54.

525. *Let me tell you, Cassius*, etc. **Here** we have a line **with the first syllable wanting, which may be** regarded as **the converse of those wanting only the last syllable noticed in** the **note on** 246. **So,** lower down, **in** 541, **we have another speech** of Brutus commencing, with like abruptness, **with a line** which **wants the two** first syllables:—"You **say you are a** better **soldier."—For** the true nature **of the hemistich see the note on "** Made in her concave **shores" in 15.**

525. *Are* much condemned to have an itching palm.—*To condemn to* **is** now used only in the sense of sentencing to **the endurance of. In the** present passage the *to* **introduces the cause, not the** consequence, **of** the condemnation. **"You are condemned" is used as** a stronger expression for you are said, you are alleged, you are charged. —An *itching* palm **is** a covetous palm ; as we say an itch

for praise, an itch for scribbling, etc., or as in the translation of the Bible we read, in 2 *Tim. iv.* 3, of people "having *itching* ears" (being exactly after the original, κνηθόμενοι τὴν ἀκοήν).

525. *To sell and mart your offices.*—To make merchandise, or matter of bargain and sale, of your appointments and commissions. *Mart* is held to be a contraction of *market*, which is connected with the Latin *merx* and *mercor*, and so with *merchant, mercantile, commerce*, etc.

525. *To undeservers.*—We have lost both this substantive and the verb to *disserve* (to do an injury to), which Clarendon uses; though we still retain the adjective *undeserving*.

527. *And chastisement doth therefore.*—All the old copies have *doth*. Mr Collier, however, in his one volume edition substitutes *does*.

529, 530. *And bay the moon. . . . Brutus, bay not me.*—In the First Folio we have "*bay* the moon," and "*bait* not me;" in all the others, "*bait* the moon" and "*bait* not me." Theobald suggested "*bay* the moon" and "*bay* not me;" and it is a remarkable confirmation of this conjecture that it exactly accords with the reading given by Mr Collier's MS. annotator, who in 529 restores in the Second Folio the *bay* of the First, and in 530 corrects the *bait* of all the Folios into *bay*. To *bay* the moon is to bark at the moon; and *bay not me* would, of course, be equivalent to bark not, like an infuriated dog, at me. *Vid.* 349. To *bait*, again, from the French *battre*, might be understood to mean to attack with violence. So in *Macbeth, v.* 7, we have "to be *baited* with the rabble's curse." It is possible that there may have been some degree of confusion in the minds of our ancestors between *bait* and *bay*, and that both words, imperfectly conceived in their import and origin, were apt to call up a more or less distinct notion of encompassing or closing in. Perhaps something of this is what runs in Cassius's head when he subjoins, "You forget yourself, *To hedge me in*"—although Johnson interprets these words as meaning "to limit my authority by your direction or censure."—The present passage may be compared with one in *A Winter's Tale, ii.* 3 :—

> "Who late hath beat her husband,
> And now baits me."

A third Anglicized form of *battre*, in addition to *beat* and *bait*, is probably *bate*, explained by Nares as "a term in falconry; to flutter the wings as preparing for flight, particularly at the sight of prey." Thus Petrucio, in *The Taming of the Shrew, iv.* 1, speaking of his wife, after observing that his "falcon now is sharp, and passing empty" (that is, very empty, or hungry), goes on to say that he has another way to man his haggard (that is, apparently, to reduce his wild hawk under subjection to man),

> "That is, to watch her, as we watch those kites
> That bate, and beat, and will not be obedient."

Nares quotes the following passage from a letter of Bacon's as beautifully exemplifying the true meaning of the word:—"Wherein [*viz.* in matters of business] I would to God that I were hooded, that I saw less; or that I could perform more: for now I am like a hawk that *bates*, when I see occasion of service; but cannot fly, because I am tied to another's fist." The letter, which was first printed by Rawley in the First Part of the *Resuscitatio* (1657), is without date, and is merely entitled "A Letter to Queen Elizabeth, upon the sending of a New-year's Gift."

530. *I am a soldier, I.*—It is impossible to be quite certain whether the second *I* here be the pronoun or the adverb which we now write *Ay*. See the note on "I, as Æneas," in 54.

530. *To make conditions.*—To arrange the terms on which offices should be conferred.

531. *Go to.*—Johnson, in his Dictionary, explains this expression as equivalent to " Come, come, take the right course" (meaning, contemptuously or sarcastically). He adds, that, besides being thus used as " a scornful exhortation," it is also sometimes "a phrase of exhortation or encouragement ;" as in *Gen. xi.* 4, where the people, after the flood, are represented as saying, " Go to, let us build us a city and a tower," etc. But it must be understood to be used, again, in the scornful sense three verses lower down, where the Lord is made to say " Go to, let us go down, and there confound their language," etc.

534. *Have mind upon your health.*—*Mind*, is here remembrance, and *health* is welfare, or safety, generally ; senses which are both now obsolete.

535. *Away, slight man !*—*Vid.* 494 and 522.

537. *Hear me, for I will speak.*—The emphasis is not to be denied to the *will* here, although it stands in the place commonly stated to require an unaccented syllable. *Vid.* 426, 436, and 613.

539. *Must I observe you?*—Pay you observance, or reverential attention.

541. *You say you are a better soldier.*—*Vid.* 525.

541. *I shall be glad to learn of abler men.*—The old reading is " *noble* men ;" *abler* is the correction of Mr Collier's MS. annotator. Even if this were a mere conjecture, its claim to be accepted would be nearly irresistible. *Noble* here is altogether inappropriate. Cassius, as Mr Collier remarks, had said nothing about " noble men," whereas *abler* is the very expression that he had used (in 530) :—

>"I am a soldier, I,
> Older in practice, *abler* than yourself
> To make conditions."

542. *I said, an elder soldier.*—This is the reading of all the old copies. But Mr Collier prints *older*.

551. *You have done that you should be sorry for.*—The

emphasis, of course, is on *should*. The common meaning of *shall*, as used by Cassius, is turned, in Brutus's quick and unsparing replication, into the secondary meaning of *should* (ought to be). *Vid.* 181.

551. *Which I respect not.*—Which I heed not. Here *respect* has rather less force of meaning than it has now acquired; whereas *observe* in 539 has more than it now conveys. *Respect* in *Shakespeare* means commonly no more than what we now call *regard* or *view*. Thus, in *The Midsummer Night's Dream, i.* 1, Lysander says of his aunt, "She respects me as her only son;" and, in *ii.* 1, Helena says to Demetrius, "You, in my respect, are all the world." So, in *The Merchant of Venice, v.* 1, when Portia, on hearing the music from the lighted house as she approaches Belmont at night in company with Nerissa, says,—

"Nothing is good, I see, without respect;
Methinks it sounds much sweeter than by day,"—

she means merely that nothing is good without reference to circumstances, or that it is only when it is in accordance with the place and the time that any good thing can be really or fully enjoyed. As she immediately subjoins:—

"How many things by season seasoned are
To their right praise and true perfection!"

So afterwards Nerissa to Gratiano,—"You should have been *respective*, and have kept it" (the ring),—that is, you should have been mindful (of your promise or oath).

551. *And drop my blood.*—Expend my blood in drops.

551. *Than to wring.*—Although *had rather* (*Vid.* 54 and 57), being regarded as of the nature of an auxiliary verb, does not in modern English take a *to* with the verb that follows it (*Vid.* 1), it does so here in virtue of being equivalent in sense to *would* or *should prefer*.

551. *By any indirection.*—Indirectness, as we should now say.

551. *To lock such rascal counters.—As* to lock. *Vid.*
408. *Rascal* means despicable. It is an Original English word, properly signifying a lean worthless deer.

551. *Be ready, gods,* etc.—I cannot think that Mr Collier has improved this passage by removing the comma which we find in the old copies at the end of the first line, and so connecting the words " with all your thunderbolts," not with " Be ready," but with " Dash him to pieces."

551. *Dash him to pieces.*—This is probably to be understood as the infinitive (governed by the preceding verb *be ready*) with the customary *to* omitted. *Vid.* 1.

554. *Brutus hath rived my heart.*—*Vid.* 107.

559. *A flatterer's would not, though they do appear.*—This is the reading of all the old copies. Mr Collier's MS. annotator gives " *did* appear."

560. *Revenge yourselves alone on Cassius.* In this line and the next we have *Cassius* used first as a trisyllable and immediately after as a dissyllable.

560. *For Cassius is aweary of the world.*—Whatever may be its origin or proper meaning, many words were in the habit of occasionally taking *a* as a prefix in the earliest period of the language. Thence we have our modern English, *arise, arouse, abide, await, awake, aweary, etc.* Some of the words which are thus lengthened, however, do not appear to have existed in the Original English; while, on the other hand, many ancient forms of this kind are now lost. More or less of additional expressiveness seems usually to be given by this prefix, in the case at least of such words as can be said to have in them anything of an emotional character. Shakespeare has used the present word in another of his most pathetic lines,—Macbeth's "I 'gin to be aweary of the sun."—The *a* here seems to be the same element that we have in the "Tom's-*a*-*cold*" of *Lear, iii.* 4, and *iv.* 7, and also with the *an* that we have in the " When I was *an-hungered*" of the

New Testament, and Shakespeare's "They said they were *an-hungry*" (*Coriol. i.* 4).

560. **Conned by** *rote.*—The Original English *connan*, or *cunnan*, signifying to know, and also to be able,—its probable modification *cunnian*, to inquire,—and *cennan*, to beget or bring forth, appear to have all come to be confounded in the breaking up of the old form of the language, and then to have given rise to our modern *ken*, and *can*, and *con*, and *cunning*, with meanings not at all corresponding to those of the terms with which they severally stand in phonetic connexion. *Can* is now used only as an auxiliary verb with the sense of to be able, though formerly it was sometimes employed with the same sense as a common verb. "In evil," says Bacon, in his 11th *Essay* (Of Great Place), "the best condition is not to will; the second, not to can." *Ken* is still in use both as a verb and as a substantive. The verb Nares interprets as meaning to see, the substantive as meaning sight; and he adds, "These words, though not current in common usage, have been so preserved in poetic language that they cannot properly be called obsolete. Instances are numerous in writers of very modern date. . . . In Scotland these words are still in full currency." But the meaning of *to ken* in the Scottish dialect is not to see, but to know. And formerly it had also in English the one meaning as well as the other, as may be seen both in Spenser and in Shakespeare. The case is similar to that of the Greek εἴδω (οἶδα) and εἰδέω. *Cunning*, again, instead of being the wisdom resulting from investigation and experience, or the skill acquired by practice, as in the earlier states of the language, has now come to be understood as involving always at least something concealed and mysterious, if not something of absolute deceit or falsehood.

As for *con* its common meaning seems to be, not to

know, but to get by heart, that is, to acquire a knowledge of in the most complete manner possible. And *to con by rote* is to commit to memory by an operation of mind similar to the turning of a wheel (*rota*), or by frequent repetition. *Rote* is the same word with *routine*.

It is more difficult to explain the expression *to con thanks*, which is of frequent occurrence in our old writers and is several times used by Shakespeare. Nares explains it as meaning to study expressions of gratitude. But it really seems, in most instances at least, to signify no more than to give or return thanks. See a note on *Gammer Gurton's Needle* in Collier's edition of *Dodsley's Old Plays*, II. 30. *Con* in the present passage may perhaps mean to utter or repeat; such a sense might come not unnaturally out of the common use of the word in the sense of to get by heart. The case would be somewhat like that of the two senses assigned to the same word in the expressions "to *construct* a sentence" and "to *construe* a sentence." It is remarkable that in German also they say *Dank wissen* (literally to know thanks) for to give thanks.

Our common *know* is not from any of the Original English verbs above enumerated, but is the modernized form of *cnawan*, which may or may not be related to all or to some of them.

Corresponding to *cennan* and *connan*, it may finally be added, we have the modern German *kennen*, to know, and *können*, to be able or to know. But, whatever may be the case with the German *König* (a king), it is impossible to admit that our English *king*, the representative of the ancient *cyng, cyncg*, or *cyning*, can have anything to do with either *cennan* or *connan*. It is apparently of quite another family, that of which the head is *cyn*, nation, offspring, whence our present *kin*, and *kindred*, and *kind* (both the substantive and the adjective).

560. *Dearer than Plutus' mine.*—*Dear* must here be

understood, not in the derived sense of *beloved*, but in its literal sense of *precious* or *of value*. *Vid.* 349. It is "*Pluto's* mine" in all the Folios, and also in Rowe; nor does it appear that the mistake is corrected by Mr Collier's MS. annotator, although it is, of course, in Mr Collier's regulated text.

560. *If that thou beest a Roman.*—Our modern substantive verb, as it is called, is made up of fragments of several verbs, of which, at the least, *am*, *was*, and *be* are distinguishable, even if we hold *is*, as well as *are* and *art*, to belong to the same root with *am* (upon this point see Latham's *Eng. Lang.* 3rd edit. 346). In the original form of the language we have *eom* (sometimes *am*), *waes* (with *waere* and *waeron*, and *wesan*, and *gewesen*), *beo* (with *bíst* or *býst*, *beódh*, *beón*, etc.), *eart* (or *eardh*), *is* (or *ys*); and also *sý*, *seó*, *síg*, *synd*, and *syndon* (related to the Latin *sum*, *sunt*, *sim*, *sis*, etc.), of which forms there is no trace in our existing English. On the other hand, there is no representative in the written English of the times before the Conquest of our modern plural *are*. *Beest*, which we have here, is not to be confounded with the subjunctive *be*; it is *bíst*, *býst*, the 2nd pers. sing. pres. indic. of *beón*, to be. It is now obsolete, but is also used by Milton in a famous passage:—"If thou beest he; but oh how fallen! how changed," etc. *P. L. i.* 84.

561. *Dishonour shall be humour.*—*Vid.* 205.—Any indignity you offer shall be regarded as a mere caprice of the moment. *Humour* here probably means nearly the same thing as in Cassius's "that rash humour which my mother gave me" in 568. The word had scarcely acquired in Shakespeare's age the sense in which it is now commonly used as a name for a certain mental faculty or quality; though its companion *wit* had already, as we have seen, come to be so employed. *Vid.* 436. But what if the true reading should be "dishonour shall be *honour?*"

561. *O Cassius, you are yoked with a lamb.*—Pope prints,

on conjecture, "with a *man ;*" and "a *lamb,*" at any rate, can hardly be right.

562. *Blood ill-tempered.*—We have now lost the power of characterizing the blood as *ill-tempered* (except in imitation of the antique), although we might perhaps speak of it as *ill-attempered.* The epithet *ill-tempered,* now only applied to the sentient individual, and with reference rather to the actual habit of the mind or nature than to that of which it is supposed to be the result, was formerly employed, in accordance with its proper etymological import, to characterize anything the various component ingredients of which were not so mixed as duly to qualify each other.

568. *Have not you love enough to bear with me ?*—This is the reading of all the old copies, and is that adopted by Mr Knight. Both the *Variorum* text, which is generally followed, and also Mr Collier in his regulated text give us "Have you not."

569. *Yes, Cassius; and from henceforth.*—All the irregularity that we have in this line is the slight and common one of a superfluous short syllable (the *ius* of *Cassius*). Steevens, in his dislike to even this much of freedom of versification, and his precise grammatical spirit, would strike out the *from,* as redundant in respect both of the sense and of the measure.

569. *He'll think your mother chides.*—To *chide* is from the ancient *cid* or *cyd,* signifying strife or contention. It is now scarcely in use except as an active verb with the sense of to reprove with sharpness; but it was formerly used also absolutely or intransitively, as here, for to employ chiding or angry expressions. Shakespeare has both *to chide* and *to chide at.*

Instead of the stage direction "*Noise within,*" the original edition has "*Enter a Poet.*"

570. *Poet* [*within*].—The *within* is inserted here and before the next two speeches by the modern editors.—

The present incident (as well as the hint of the preceding great scene) is taken from **Plutarch's** life of Brutus. The intruder, however, is not a Poet in Plutarch, but one Marcus Favonius, who affected to be a follower of Cato, and to pass for a Cynic philosopher. And it will be observed that he is called a Cynic in the dialogue. There was probably no other authority than the Prompter's book for designating him a *Poet*.

571. *Lucil.* [*within*]. *You shall not come to them.*—In the *Variorum* and the other modern editions, **although** they commonly make no distinction between the **abbreviation** for *Lucilius* and that for *Lucius*, this speech must be understood to be assigned to Lucius, whose presence alone is noted by them in the heading of the scene. But in the old **text** the speaker is distinctly marked *Lucil*. **This is a** conclusive confirmation, if any were wanting, of **the restoration in 521.** How is it that the modern editors **have one and** all of them omitted to acknowledge the universal deviation here from the authority which they all profess to follow? Not even Jennens notices it.

574. *For I have seen more years, I'm sure, than ye.*—Plutarch makes Favonius exclaim, in the words of Nestor in the First Book of the Iliad:—

'Αλλὰ πίθεσθ'· ἄμφω δὲ νεωτέρω ἐστὸν ἐμεῖο·—

which North translates,

"My Lords, I pray you hearken both to me;
For I have seen more years than such ye three."

But this **last line can hardly** be correctly printed.—The Poet's quotation, it may be noted, is almost a repetition of what Antony has said to Octavius in 496.

575. *Ha, ha; how vilely doth this Cynic rhyme!*—The form of the **word in** all the Folios is *vildely*, or *vildly;* **and that is the form** which it generally, if not always, **has** in Shakespeare. The modern editors, however, have universally substituted the form now in use, as with *then*

(for *than*), *and* (for *an*), and other words similarly circumstanced.

578. *I'll know his humour when he knows his time.*—In this line we have what the rule as commonly laid down would make to be necessarily a short or unaccented syllable carrying a strong emphasis no fewer than four times:—*I'll—his—he—his.*

578. *With these jigging fools.*—"That is," Malone notes, "with these silly *poets*. A *jig* signified, in our author's time, a metrical composition, as well as a dance." Capell had proposed *jingling.*

578. *Companion, hence!*—The term *companion* was formerly used contemptuously, in the same way in which we still use its synonyme *fellow*. The notion originally involved in companionship, or accompaniment, would appear to have been rather that of inferiority than of equality. A companion (or *comes*) was an attendant. The *Comites* of the imperial court, whence our modern Counts or Earls, and other nobility, were certainly not regarded as being the equals of the Emperor, any more than a *Companion* to a lady is now looked upon as the equal of her mistress. We have our modern *fellow* from the ancient native *felaw; companion* (with *company*) immediately from the French *compagnon* and the Italian *compagno*, which have been variously deduced from *com-panis, com-paganus, com-bino* (Low Latin, from *binus*), *com-benno* (one of two or more riders in the same *benna*, or cart), etc. See *Menage, Dic. Etym. de la Langue Franç.* But, after all, Dr Webster may be right in what he says under the word *Company*:—"From *cum* and *pannus*, cloth, Teutonic *fahne*, or *vaan*, a flag. The word denotes a band or number of men under one flag or standard. What decides this question is, the Spanish mode of writing the word with *n* tilde, titled *n, compañia,* for this is the manner of writing *paño*, cloth; whereas *panis*, bread, is written *pan*. The orthography of the word in the other

x

languages is confirmatory of this opinion "—We have an instance of the use of *Companion* in the same sense in which we still commonly employ *fellow* even in so late a work as Smollett's *Roderick Random*, published in 1748:—"The young ladies [Roderick's cousins], who thought themselves too much concerned to contain themselves any longer, set up their throats all together against my protector [his uncle, Lieutenant Bowling]. 'Scurvy companion! Saucy tarpaulin! Rude impertinent fellow! Did he think to prescribe to grandpapa!'" *Vol.* I. *ch.* 3. In considering this meaning of the terms *companion* and *fellow* we may also remember the proverb which tells us that "Familiarity breeds Contempt."

Neither the entry nor the exit of Lucilius and Titinius is noticed in the old copies.

580. *Lucilius and Titinius, bid the commanders.*—The only irregularity in the prosody of this line is the common one of the one superfluous short syllable, the *ius* of *Titinius*.

581. *Immediately to us*, etc.—If this, as may be the case, is to form a complete line with the words of Brutus that follow, two of the six syllables must be regarded as superabundant. But there might perhaps be a question as to the accentuation of the *us*.

589. *Upon what sickness?*—That is, after or in consequence of what sickness. It is the same use of *upon* which we have in 458, and which is still familiar to us in such phrases as " upon this," "upon that," "upon his return," etc., though we no longer speak of a person dying *upon* a particular sickness or disease.

590. *Impatient of my absence;* etc.—This speech is throughout a striking exemplification of the tendency of strong emotion to break through the logical forms of grammar, and of how possible it is for language to be perfectly intelligible and highly expressive, sometimes, with the grammar in a more or less chaotic or uncertain

state. It does not matter much whether we take *grief* to be a nominative, or a second genitive governed by *impatient*. In principle, though not perhaps according to rule and established usage, "Octavius *with* Mark Antony" is as much entitled to a plural verb as "Octavius *and* Mark Antony." *Tidings*, which is a frequent word with Shakespeare, is commonly used by him as a plural noun; in this same Play we have afterwards "these tidings" in 729; but there are other instances besides the present in which it is treated as singular. It is remarkable that we should have exactly the same state of things in the case of the almost synonymous term *news* (the final *s* of which, however, has been sometimes attempted to be accounted for as a remnant of *-ess* or *-ness*, though its exact correspondence in form with the French *nouvelles*, of the same signification, would seem conclusively enough to indicate what it really is). At any rate *tiding* and *new* (as a substantive) are both alike unknown to the language.

590. *She fell distract.*—In Shakespeare's day the language possessed the three forms *distracted*, *distract*, and *distraught*; he uses them all. We have now only the first.

593. The original stage direction here is, "*Enter Boy with Wine and Tapers.*" The second "*Drinks*" at the end of 595 is modern; and the "*Re-enter Titinius*," etc., is "*Enter*," in the original.

596. *And call in question.*—Here we have probably rather a figurative expression of the poet than a common idiom of his time. Then as well as now, we may suppose, it was not things, but only persons, that were spoken of in ordinary language as *called in question*.

598. *Bending their expedition.*—Rather what we should now call their *march* (or *movement*)—though perhaps implying that they were pressing on—than their expedition (or enterprise).

599. *Myself have letters.*—We have now lost the right

of using such forms as either *myself* or *himself* as sufficient nominatives, though they still remain perfectly unobjectionable accusatives. We can say " He struck myself," and " I saw himself ;" but it must be " I myself struck him," and " He himself saw it." Here, as everywhere else, in the original text the *myself* is in two words, " My selfe." And *tenour* in all the Folios, and also in both Rowe's edition and Pope's, is *tenure*, a form of the word which we now reserve for another sense.

601. *That by proscription, and bills of outlawry.*—The word *outlawry* taking the accent on the first syllable, this line will be most naturally read by being regarded as characterised by the common peculiarity of a supernumerary short syllable—the *tion* or the *and*—to be disposed of, as usual, by the two being rapidly enunciated as one. It will in this way be exactly of the same prosody with another that we have presently :—" Struck Cæsar on the neck.—O you flatterers" (690). It might, indeed, be reduced to perfect regularity by the *tion* being distributed into a dissyllable—*ti-on*—, in which case the prosody would be completed at *out*, and the two following unaccented syllables would count for nothing (or be what is called hypercatalectic),—unless, indeed, any one should insist upon taking them for an additional foot, and so holding the verse to be an Alexandrine. But taste and probability alike protest against either of these ways of managing the matter. (See what is said in regard to the dissyllabication of the *tion* or *sion* by Shakespeare in the note on 246. *She dreamt to-night she saw my statue*). Nay, even the running together of the *tion* and the *and* is not necessary, nor the way that would be taken by a good reader; that is not how the line would be read, but only how it might be scanned : in reading it, the *and* would be rather combined with the *bills*, and a short pause would, in fact, be made after the *tion*, as the pointing and the sense require. So entirely unfounded is the notion

that a pause, of whatever length, occurring in the course of a verse can ever have anything of the prosodical effect of a word or syllable.

604. *Cicero is dead.*—In the original printed text these words are run into one line with "and by that order of proscription." The text of the *Variorum* edition presents the same arrangement, with the addition of *Ay* as a prefix to the whole. "For the insertion of the affirmative adverb, to complete the verse," says Steevens in a note, "I am answerable." According to Jennens, however, this addition was also made by Capell. In any case, it is plain that, if we receive the *Ay*, we must make two lines, the first ending with the word *dead*. But we are not entitled to exact or to expect a perfect observance of the punctilios of regular prosody in such brief expressions of strong emotion as the dialogue is here broken up into. What do the followers of Steevens profess to be able to make, in the way of prosody, of the very next utterance that we have from Brutus,—the "No, Messala" of 605? The best thing we can do is to regard Cassius's "Cicero one?" and Messala's responsive "Cicero is dead" either as hemistichs (the one the commencement, the other the conclusion, of a line), or, if that view be preferred, as having no distinct or precise prosodical character whatever. Every sense of harmony and propriety, however, revolts against running "Cicero is dead" into the same line with "And by that order," etc.

613. *With meditating that she must die once.*—For this use of *with* see 363.—*Once* has here the same meaning which it has in such common forms of expression as "Once, when I was in London," "Once upon a time," etc.—that is to say it means *once* without, as in other cases, restriction to that particular number. Steevens, correctly enough, interprets it as equivalent to "at some time or other;" and quotes in illustration, from *The Merry Wives of Windsor*, iii. 4, "I pray thee, *once* to-

night Give my **sweet** Nan this ring."—The prosody of the line is the same that has been noted in 426, 436, and 537.

615. *I have as much of this in art as you*, etc.—*In art* Malone interprets to mean "in theory." It rather signifies by acquired knowledge, or learning, as distinguished from natural disposition. The passage is one of the many in our old poets, more especially Shakespeare and Spenser, running upon the relation between nature and art.

616. ***Well, to our work*** *alive.*—This must mean, apparently, let us proceed to our living business, to that which concerns the living, not the dead. The commentators say nothing, though the expression is certainly one that needs explanation.

619. ***This*** *it is.*—" The overflow of the metre," Steevens observes, " and the disagreeable clash of *it is* with '*Tis* at the beginning of the next line, are almost proofs that our author only wrote, with a common ellipsis, *This*." He may very possibly be right. The expression "This it is" sounds awkward otherwise, as well as prosodically; and the superfluous, or rather encumbering, *it is* would be accounted for by supposing the commencement of the following line to have been first so written and then altered to '*Tis*.

620. ***Good reasons*** *must, of force.*—We scarcely now say *of force* (for of necessity, or necessarily); although *perforce* continues to be sometimes still employed in poetry. It may even be doubted if this be Milton's *meaning* in

" —our conqueror (whom I now
Of force believe almighty, since no less
Than such could have o'erpowered such **force** as ours)."—
P. L. i. 145.

620. ***The*** *enemy, marching along by them.*—This line, with the two weak syllables in the last places of two continuous feet (the second and third) might seem at first to be of the same kind with the one noted in 601.

But the important distinction is, that the first of the two weak syllables here, the *-y* of *enemy*, would in any circumstances be entitled to occupy the place it does in our heroic verse, in virtue of the principle that in English prosody every syllable of a polysyllabic word acquires the privilege or character of a strong syllable when it is as far removed from the accented syllable of the word as the nature of the verse requires. See *Prolegomena*, Sect. vi. The dissonance here, accordingly, is very slight in comparison with what we have in 601.—For " Along by them" see 200.

620. *By them shall make a fuller number up.*—For this use of *shall* see the note on *Cæsar should be a beast* in 238. —The "along by them" followed by the " by them" is an artifice of expression, which may be compared with the "by Cæsar and by you" of 345.

620. *Come on refreshed, new-hearted, and encouraged.* —" New-hearted" is the correction of Mr Collier's MS. annotator; the old reading is *new-added*, which is not English or sense, and the only meaning that can be forced out of which, besides, gives us merely a repetition of what has been already said in the preceding line, a repetition which is not only unnecessary but would be introduced in the most unnatural way and place possible, whereas *new-hearted* is the very sort of word that one would expect to find where it stands, in association with *refreshed* and *encouraged*.

620. *From which advantage shall we cut him off.*—Shakespeare most probably wrote 'we shall.'

622. *Under your pardon.*—*Vid.* 358.

622. *We, at the height*, etc.—Being at the height, are in consequence ready to decline—as the tide begins to recede as soon as it has attained the point of full flood.

622. *Omitted.*—The full resolution will be—which tide being omitted to be taken at the flood.

623. *Then, with your will*, etc.—In the original edition

"We'll along" is made part of the first line. Mr Collier prints, it does not appear on what, or whether on any, authority, " we will along," as had been done on conjecture by Rowe, Pope, and others. The " We'll along" gives us merely the very common slight irregularity of a single superabundant syllable.—" With your will" is equivalent to With your consent; "We'll along" to We will onward. But the passage is probably corrupt.

624. *The deep of night is crept.*—Vid. 374. This is the reading of all the old copies. But Mr Collier prints " has crept."

624. *Which we will niggard.*—*Niggard* is common both as a substantive and as an adjective; but this is probably the only passage in the language in which it is employed as a verb. Its obvious meaning is, as Johnson gives it in his Dictionary, "to stint, to supply sparingly."

624. *There is no more to say.*—There is no more for us to say. So, " I have work to do," "He has a house to let," etc. In Ireland it is thought more correct to announce a house as *to be let ;* but that would rather mean that it is going to be let.

625. *Early to-morrow will we rise, and hence.*—It might almost be said that the adverb *hence* is here turned into a verb; it is construed exactly as *rise* is:—" Will we rise," —" will we hence." So, both with *hence* and *home*, in the opening line of the Play:—

"Hence; home, you idle creatures."

626. *Lucius, my gown,* etc.—The best way of treating the commencement of this speech of Brutus is to regard the words addressed to Lucius as one hemistich and " Farewell, good Messala" as another. There are, in fact, two speeches. It is the same case that we have in 506.—In the old editions the stage directions are; after 625, " *Enter Lucius,*" and then, again, after 627, "*Enter*

Lucius with the gown." After 632 there is merely *"Exeunt."*

634. *Poor knave, I blame thee not; thou art o'er-watched.*—For *knave* see 647.—*O'er-watched,* or *over-watched,* is used in this sense, of worn out with watching, by other old writers as well as by Shakespeare, however irreconcilable such an application of it may be with the meaning of the verb *to watch.* We have it again in *Lear, ii.* 2:—

> "All weary and o'erwatched,
> Take vantage, heavy eyes, not to behold
> This shameful lodging."

634. *Some other of my men.*—By *some other* we should now mean some of a different sort. For some more we say *some others.* But, although *other* thus used as a substantive, with the plural of the ordinary form, is older than the time of Shakespeare, I do not recollect that he anywhere has *others.* Nor does it occur, I believe, even in Clarendon. On the other hand, it is frequent in Milton.

634. *I'll have them sleep.*—Such expressions as this, which are still familiar, show that *have* ought to be added to the verbs enumerated in the note on "You ought not walk," in 1, which may be followed by another verb without the prefix *to.*

635. *Varro and Claudius!*—In the old copies it is "*Varrus and Claudio,*" both in the speech and in the stage direction that follows.

637. *I pray you, Sirs.*—Common as the word *Sir* still is, we have nearly lost the form *Sirs.* It survives, however, in the Scottish dialect, with the pronunciation of *Sirce,* as the usual address to a number of persons, much as *Masters* was formerly in English, only that it is applied to women as well as to men.

639. *Servants lie down.*—This stage direction is modern.

641. *Canst thou* **hold** *up*, etc.—This and the next line are given in the Second Folio in the following blundering fashion, the result no doubt of an accidental displacement of the types:—

> "Canst thou hold up thy instrument a straine **or two.**
> And touch thy heavy eyes a-while."

The transposition is corrected by **Mr Collier's MS.** annotator.

645. *I know young bloods look.*—*Vid.* 56.

647. *It was well done.*—So in the old copies; but the Variorum edition has "It *is*," in which it has been followed by other modern editors,—though not by either **Mr** Knight or Mr Collier.

647. *Gentle knave, good night.*—*Knave*, from the ancient *cnafa*, or *cnapa*, having meant originally only a boy, and meaning now only a rogue, was in Shakespeare's time in current use with either signification. It was in its state of transition from the one to the other, and consequently of fluctuation between the two. The German *Knabe* still retains the original sense.

647. *I will not do thee so much wrong to wake thee.*—*Vid.* 408.

The stage direction "*He sits down*" is modern.

647. *It comes upon me.*—It advances upon me.

647. *Speak to me what thou art.*—We scarcely now use *speak* thus, for to announce or declare generally.

648, 649. *Thy evil spirit, Brutus*, etc.—It is absurd to attempt, as the modern editors do, to make a complete verse out of these two speeches. It cannot be supposed that Brutus laid his emphasis on *thou*. The regularities of prosody are of necessity neglected in such brief utterances, amounting in some cases to mere ejaculations or little more, as make up the greater part of the remainder of this scene.

651. *Well; then I shall see thee again?*—So the words

stand in the old copies. Nothing whatever is gained by printing the words in two lines, the first consisting only of the word *Well*, as is done by the generality of the modern editors.

652. *Ghost vanishes.*—This stage direction is not in the old editions.—Steevens has objected that the apparition could not be at once the *shade* of Cæsar and the *evil genius* of Brutus. Shakespeare's expression is the evil *spirit* of Brutus, by which apparently is meant nothing more than a supernatural visitant of evil omen. At any rate, the present apparition is afterwards, in 774, distinctly stated by Brutus himself to have been the ghost of the murdered Dictator:—

> "The ghost of Cæsar hath appeared to me
> Two several times by night: at Sardis, once;" etc.

So, also, in *Antony and Cleopatra*, ii. 6,—

> "Since Julius Cæsar,
> Who at Philippi the good Brutus ghosted."

Perhaps we might also refer to 744:—

> "O Julius Cæsar, thou art mighty yet
> Thy spirit walks abroad," etc.;

and to " Cæsar's spirit, ranging for revenge," in 363.

It may be well to append the two accounts of the incident given by Plutarch, as translated by North. In the life of Brutus the apparition is described merely as "a wonderful strange and monstruous shape of a body," and the narrative proceeds:—" Brutus boldly asked what he was, a god or a man, and what cause brought him thither. The spirit answered him, I am thy evil spirit, Brutus; and thou shalt see me by the city of Philippi. Brutus, being no otherwise afraid, replied again unto it, Well, then, I shall see thee again. The spirit presently vanished away; and Brutus called his men unto him, who told him that they heard no noise nor saw anything at all." In the life of **Cæsar the account is as** follows:—" Above all, the ghost that appeared unto Brutus showed plainly that the gods were offended **with** the murder **of** Cæsar. The vision was thus. **Brutus,** being ready **to** pass over his army from the city **of Abydos** to the **other** coast lying directly against it, slept every night (as **his** manner was) in his tent, and, being yet awake, thinking of his affairs, . . . he thought he heard a noise at his tent door, and, looking toward the light of the lamp that **waxed very dim, he saw a** horrible vision of a man, of **a** wonderful greatness **and** dreadful look, which **at** the **first** made **him** marvellously afraid. But when he saw that **it** did **him** no hurt, but stood at his bed-side and said nothing, at length he asked him what he was. The image answered him, **I am** thy ill angel, Brutus, and thou shalt see **me by the city of** Philippi. Then Brutus replied again, and said, **Well, I** shall see thee then. Therewithal the spirit presently vanished from him."

It is evident that Shakespeare **had both** passages in his recollection, though the **present** scene is chiefly founded **upon** the first. **Plutarch, however, it will be observed,** nowhere makes **the apparition to have been the ghost** of Cæsar.

653. *Why, I will see thee.*—This is an addition by Shakespeare to the dialogue **as** given by Plutarch in both lives. And even **Plutarch's** simple affirmative *I shall see thee* appears to be converted into an interrogation in **651.** It is remarkable that in our next English Plutarch, which passes as having been superintended by Dryden, **we have "I will see** thee" in both lives. The Greek is, in both passages, merely Ὄψομαι (I shall see thee).

653. *Boy! Lucius!—Varro! Claudius!*—Here **again,**

as in 635, all the Folios, in this and the next line, have *Varrus* and *Claudio*. So also in 661.

661. *Sleep again, Lucius,* etc.—It is hardly necessary to attempt to make verse of this. In the original text *Fellow* is made to stand as part of the first line.

669. *Go, and commend me to my brother Cassius.*—*Vid.* 279.

669. *Bid him set on his powers betimes before.*—The only sense which·the expression to *set on* now retains is to excite or instigate to make an attack. The other senses which it had in Shakespeare's day may be seen from 27 ("Set on; and leave no ceremony out"); from the passage before us, in which it means to lead forward or set out with; from 714 ("Let them set on at once"); from 746 ("Labeo and Flavius, set our battles on").—*Betimes* (meaning early) is commonly supposed to be a corruption of *by times*, that is, it is said, by the proper time. But this is far from satisfactory. Shakespeare has occasionally *betime*.

ACT V.

SCENE I.—*The Plains of Philippi.*

Enter OCTAVIUS, ANTONY, *and their Army.*

671. *Oct.* Now, Antony, our hopes are answered:
You said, the enemy would not come down,
But keep the hills and upper regions:
It proves not so; their battles are at hand;
They mean to warn us at Philippi here,
Answering before we do demand of them.

672. *Ant.* Tut, I am in their bosoms, and I know
Wherefore they do it: they could be content

To visit other places; and come down
With fearful bravery, thinking, by this face,
To fasten in our thoughts that they have courage;
But 'tis not so.

Enter a MESSENGER.

Mess. Prepare you, generals:
The enemy comes on in gallant show;
Their bloody **sign of battle is** hung **out**,
And something to be done immediately.

674. *Ant.* Octavius, lead your battle softly on,.
Upon the left hand of the even field.

675. *Oct.* Upon the right hand I; keep thou the left.

676. *Ant.* Why do you cross me in this exigent?
Oct. I do not cross **you**; but I will do so. [*March.*

Drum. Enter BRUTUS, CASSIUS, *and their Army;* LUCILIUS,
TITINIUS, MESSALA, *and others.*

678. *Bru.* They stand, and would have parley.
Cas. Stand fast, Titinius: We must out and talk.

680. *Oct.* Mark Antony, shall we give sign of battle?

681. *Ant.* No, Cæsar, we will answer on their charge.
Make forth; the generals would have some words.
Oct. Stir not until the signal.
Bru. Words before blows: Is it so, countrymen?
Oct. Not that we love words better, as you do.
Bru. Good words are better than bad strokes, Octavius.
Ant. In your bad strokes, Brutus, you give good words:
Witness the hole you made in Cæsar's heart,
Crying, *Long live!* **hail,** *Cæsar!*

687. *Cas.* Antony,
The posture of your **blows are** yet unknown;
But for your words, they rob the Hybla bees,
And leave them honeyless.
Ant. Not stingless too.
Bru. O, yes, and soundless too;
For you have stolen their buzzing, Antony,
And, very wisely, threat before you sting.

690. *Ant.* Villains, you did not so, when your **vile** daggers
Hacked **one another** in the sides **of** Cæsar:
You showed your **teeth like apes,** and fawned like hounds,
And bowed like bondmen, kissing Cæsar's feet;
Whilst damned Casca, like **a** cur, behind,
Struck Cæsar on the neck. O you flatterers!

691. *Cas.* Flatterers!—Now, Brutus, thank yourself:
This tongue had not offended so to-day,
If Cassius might have ruled.
692. *Oct.* Come, come, the cause: If arguing make us sweat,
The proof of it will turn to redder drops.
Look;
I draw a sword against conspirators;
When think you that the sword goes up again?—
Never, till Cæsar's three and thirty wounds
Be well avenged; or till another Cæsar
Have added slaughter to the sword of traitors.
693. *Bru.* Cæsar, thou canst not die by traitors' hands,
Unless thou bring'st them with thee.
   Oct. So I hope;
I was not born to die on Brutus' sword.
695. *Bru.* O, if thou wert the noblest of thy strain,
Young man, thou could'st not die more honourable.
   Cas. A peevish schoolboy, worthless of such honour,
Joined with a masker and a reveller.
   Ant. Old Cassius still!
698. *Oct.* Come, Antony; away.—
Defiance, traitors, hurl we in your teeth;
If you dare fight to-day, come to the field;
If not, when you have stomachs.
              [*Exeunt* OCTAVIUS, ANTONY, *and their Army.*
   Cas. Why now, blow, wind; swell, billow; and swim, bark!
The storm is up, and all is on the hazard.
700. *Bru.* Ho! Lucilius; hark, a word with you.
   Lucil. My lord.   [BRUTUS *and* LUCILIUS *converse apart.*
   Cas. Messala,—
   Mes. What says my general?
704. *Cas.* Messala,
This is my birth-day; as this very day
Was Cassius born. Give me thy hand, Messala:
Be thou my witness, that, against my will,
As Pompey was, am I compelled to set
Upon one battle all our liberties.
You know, that I held Epicurus strong,
And his opinion: now I change my mind,
And partly credit things that do presage.
Coming from Sardis, on our former ensign
Two mighty eagles fell, and there they perched,
Gorging and feeding from our soldiers' hands;

Who to Philippi here consorted us;
This morning are they fled away, and gone;
And in **their** steads, do ravens, crows, and kites
Fly o'er our heads, and downward look **on us**,
As **we were** sickly prey; their shadows **seem**
A **canopy** most fatal, under which
Our army lies, ready to give up the ghost.
   Mes. Believe not so.
706. *Cas.* I but believe it partly;
For I am fresh of spirit, and resolved
To meet all perils **very constantly**.
   Bru. Even so, **Lucilius**.
708. *Cas.* Now, **most noble** Brutus,
The gods to-day stand friendly; that **we may**,
Lovers in peace, lead on our days to age!
But, since the affairs of men rest still uncertain,
Let's reason with the worst that may befall.
If we do lose this battle, then is this
The very last time we shall speak together:
What are you then determined to do?
709. *Bru.* Even by the rule of that philosophy,
By which I did **blame** Cato for the death
Which he did give himself, I know not how,
But **I do find** it cowardly and vile,
For fear of what might fall, so to prevent
The term of life;—arming myself with patience,
To stay the providence of those high powers
That govern us below.
   Cas. Then, if we lose this battle,
You are contented to **be** led in **triumph**
Thorough the streets of Rome?
711. *Bru.* No, Cassius, no: think not, thou noble **Roman,**
That ever Brutus will go bound to Rome;
He bears **too great** a mind. But this same day
Must **end that work**, the ides of March begun;
And whether **we shall** meet again, I know not.
Therefore **our** everlasting farewell take:—
For ever, and for ever, farewell, Cassius!
If we do meet again, why we shall smile;
If not, why then **this** parting was **well made**.
   Cas. For ever, **and** for ever, farewell, Brutus
If we do meet again, we'll smile indeed;
If not, 'tis true, this parting **was** well made.

Bru. Why then, lead on.—O, that a man might know
The end of this day's business, ere it come!
But it sufficeth, that the day will end,
And then the end is known.—Come, ho! away!   [*Exeunt.*

The heading,—" *Scene I. The plains of Philippi,*"—
is modern, as usual.

671. *Their battles are at hand.*—*Battle* is common in
our old writers with the sense of a division of an army,
or what might now be called a battalion. So again in
674. When employed more precisely the word means
the central or main division.

671. *They mean to warn us.*—To *warn* was formerly
the common word for what we now call to summon.
Persons charged with offences, or against whom complaints were made, were *warned* to appear to make their
answers; members were *warned* to attend the meetings
of the companies or other associations to which they belonged; and in war either of the hostile parties, as here,
was said to be *warned* when in any way called upon or
appealed to by the other. Thus in *King John, ii.*
1, the citizens of Angiers, making their appearance in
answer to the French and English trumpets, exclaim,
" Who is it that hath *warned* us to the walls?" The
word, which is connected with *ware* and *wary*, is from the
Original English *warnian*. But the Anglo-Norman dialect of the French has also *garner* and *garnisher* with the
same meaning.

672. *With fearful bravery.*—Malone's notion is, that
"*fearful* is used here, as in many other places, in an
active sense,—*producing fear—intimidating.*" But the
utmost, surely, that Antony can be understood to admit
is that their show of bravery was *intended* to intimidate.
It seems more consonant to the context to take fearful
bravery for bravery in show or appearance, which yet is
full of real fear or apprehension. Steevens suggests that
the expression is probably to be interpreted by the fol-

y

lowing passage from the Second Book of Sidney's *Arcadia*:—"Her horse, fair and lusty; which she rid so as might show *a fearful boldness*, daring to do that which she knew that she knew not how to do." The meaning is only *so as showed* (not *so as should show*). In like manner a few pages before we have; "But his father had so deeply engraved the suspicion in his heart, that he thought his flight rather to proceed of a *fearful guiltiness*, than of an humble faithfulness."

672. *By this face.*— By this show or pretence of courage.

672. *To fasten in our thoughts that they have courage.*—We have now lost the power of construing to *fasten* in this way, as if it belonged to the same class of verbs with to *think*, to *believe*, to *suppose*, to *imagine*, to *say*, to *assert*, to *affirm*, to *declare*, to *swear*, to *convince*, to *inform*, to *remember*, to *forget*, etc., the distinction of which seems to be that they are all significant either of an operation performed by, or at least with the aid of, or of an effect produced upon, the mind.

674. *Octavius, lead your battle softly on.*—*Vid.* 671.

674. *Upon the left hand of the even field.*—Does this mean the smooth or level ground? Or is not "the even field" rather to be understood as meaning the even ranks, the army as it stands before any part of it has begun to advance, presenting one long unbroken line of front? I am not aware, however, of any other instance of such an application of the term *field*, unless it may be thought that we have one afterwards in the last line but one of the present Play :—"So, call the field to rest."

675. *Keep thou the left.*—Ritson remarks;—"The tenor of the conversation evidently requires us to read *you.*" He means, apparently, that *you* and *your* are the words used elsewhere throughout the conversation. But he forgets that the singular pronoun is peculiarly emphatic in this line, as being placed in contrast or opposi-

tion to the *I*. It is true, however, that *thou* and *you* were apt to be mistaken for one another in old handwriting from the similarity of the characters used for *th* and *y*, which is such that the printers have in many cases been led to represent the one by the other, giving us, for instance, *ye* for *the*, *yereof*, or *y'of*, for *thereof*, etc.*

676. *Why do you cross me in this exigent.*—This is Shakespeare's word for what we now call an exigence, or exigency. Both forms, however, were already in use in his day. *Exigent*, too, as Nares observes, appears to have then sometimes borne the sense of extremity or end, which is a very slight extension of its proper import of great or extreme pressure.

678. *Drum*, etc.—"*Lucilius, Titinius, Messala, and Others*" is a modern addition to the heading here.

680. *Shall we give sign of battle?*—We should now say "give *signal*."

681. *We will answer on their charge.*—We will wait till they begin to make their advance.

681. *Make forth.*—To *make*, a word which is still used

---

* This confusion in writing between the *th* and the *y* is, I have little doubt, what has given rise to such forms of expression as "The more one has, the more he would have," "The more haste, the less speed," etc. It is admitted that the *the* here cannot be the common definite article. *Vid.* Latham, *Eng. Lang.* 239, 264, 282. Neither in French nor in Italian is any article used in such cases. But it is the German that shows us what the word really is. "*Je* mehr einer hat, *je* mehr will er haben" is literally "*Ever* more one has, *ever* more he would have." And *je* represented according to the English system of spelling is *ye*. This is apparently what the pedantry of the book language, misled by the ignorance of transcribers, has perverted into our modern *the*. *Je* (or *ye*) is in fact the same word with our still not unfamiliar *aye*, always. Very probably it is also the same with *yea*, the adverb of affirmation. *Always*, or an equivalent term, would be in most cases a natural enough expression of affirmation or assent. In the word *every*, again, or *everye*, as it was anciently spelled, we have perhaps the opposite process of the conversion of *the* into *ye*; for the English "ever-*y* man" is, apparently, in form as well as in sense, the German "je-*der* mann."

with perhaps as much latitude and variety of application as any **other in** the language, **was, like** to *do*, employed formerly **in** a number of ways in **which** it has now ceased to serve **us**. Nares arranges its **obsolete** senses under seven heads, **no one** of which, **however, exactly** comprehends **the sense** it bears **in the present** expression. To *make forth* is **to** step forward. **In** preceding **editions I** had hastily assumed that Antony's " Make forth; the generals would have some words " was addressed to the **troops, in** which case *Make forth* would be a command **to them** to advance against the enemy. Yet Antony, it was observed, had just opposed **the** proposition of Octavius to **give** the signal of battle, and declared his determination **not** to move till the enemy should make their charge. **I have to** thank the writer **of** a communication dated from Victoria, in New South Wales, for calling my attention to what is probably, after all, the sense in which the passage is commonly understood, and at any rate approves itself to **be the** true sense as soon as it is suggested. What Antony says is addressed, not to the troops, but to Octavius; his meaning is, Let us go forward; the generals—Brutus and Cassius—would hold some parley with us.

687. *The posture of* **your** *blows are yet unknown.*—This **is the** reading of all **the** old copies. The grammatical irregularity is **still common.** "*Is* yet" is the correction of Mr Collier's MS. annotator. One would **be** inclined rather to suspect the word *posture*. It seems **a** strange word for what it is evidently intended to express.

690. *Whilst damned Casca.*—This is the reading of all the Folios. Mr Collier has *While*.

690. *Struck Cæsar on the neck.—O* **you** *flatterers!—* **The word in** the old text is *strook* (as in 348). There is the common prosodical irregularity **of a** superfluous short syllable. *Vid.* 601.

691. *Flatterers!—***Now, Brutus,** *thank yourself.*—The

prosodical imperfection of this line consists in the want of the first syllable. It is a hemistich consisting of four feet and a half.

692. *The proof of it.*—That is, the proof of our arguing. And by the *proof* must here be meant the arbitrement of the sword to which it is the prologue or prelude. It is by that that they are to prove what they have been arguing or asserting.

692. *Look ; I draw a sword*, etc.—It is perhaps as well to regard the *Look* as a hemistich (of half a foot) ; but in the original edition it is printed in the same line with what follows.

692. *Never, till Cæsar's three and thirty wounds.*—Theobald changed this to "three and *twenty*,"—"from the joint authorities," as he says, "of Appian, Plutarch, and Suetonius." And he may be right in believing that the error was not Shakespeare's. The "thirty," however, escapes the condemnation of Mr Collier's MS. annotator.

692. *Have added slaughter to the sword of traitors.*—This is not very satisfactory ; but it is better, upon the whole, than the amendment adopted by Mr Collier on the authority of his MS. annotator—" Have added slaughter to the *word* of traitor ;"—which would seem to be an admission on the part of Octavius (impossible in the circumstances) that Brutus and Cassius were as yet free from actual treasonable slaughter, and traitors only in word or name.

693. *Cæsar, thou canst not die by traitors' hands.*—In the standard Variorum edition, which is followed by many modern reprints, this line is strangely given as " Cæsar, thou canst not die by traitors." It is right in all Mr Knight's and Mr Collier's editions.

695. *O, if thou wert the noblest of thy strain.*—Strain, or *strene*, is stock or race. The word is used several times by Shakespeare in this sense, and not only by Chaucer and Spenser, but even by Dryden, Waller, and

Prior. The radical meaning seems to be anything stretched out or extended, hence a series either of progenitors, or of words or musical notes or sentiments.

695. *Thou could'st not die more honorable.*—This is not Shakespeare's usual form of expression, and we may be allowed to suspect that he actually wrote *honorably* (or *honourablie*).

698. The original stage direction is, "*Exit Octavius, Antony, and Army.*"

700. *Ho! Lucilius;* etc.—This is given as one verse in the original, and nothing is gained by printing the *Ho!* in another line by itself, as the modern editors do. The verse is complete except that it wants the first syllable,—a natural peculiarity of an abrupt commencement or rejoinder. So in 691.—In the original edition this speech is followed by the stage direction "*Lucillius and Messala stand forth;*" and there is no other after 701.

704. *As this very day.*—We are still familiar with this form of expression, at least in speaking. We may understand it to mean As is, or as falls, this very day; or rather, perhaps, as if, or as it were, this very day.

704. *On our former ensign.—Former* is altered to *forward*, it seems, by Mr Collier's MS. annotator; and the correction ought probably to be accepted. *Former* would hardly be the natural word unless it were intended to be implied that there were only two ensigns or standards.

704. *Who to Philippi here consorted us.*—Shakespeare's usual syntax is to *consort with;* but he has *consort* as an active verb in other passages as well as here.

704. *This morning are they fled away, and gone.*—*Vid.* 374.

704. *As we were sickly prey.*—As if we were.—*Vid.* 57.

706. *To meet all perils.*—So in the First Folio. The other Folios have *peril.*

708. *Lovers in peace.—Vid.* 260.

708. *But, since the affairs of men rest still uncertain.—* "*Rests* still *incertaine*" is the reading in the original edition.

708. *Let's reason with the worst that may befall.*—The abbreviation *let's* had not formerly the vulgar or slovenly air which is conceived to unfit it now for dignified composition. We have had it twice in Brutus's impressive address, 187. Shakespeare, however, does not frequently resort to it,—rather, one would say, avoids it.—*To befall* as a neuter or intransitive verb is nearly gone out both in prose and verse; as is also *to fall* in the same sense, as used by Brutus in the next speech.

709. *Even by the rule*, etc.—The pointing of this passage in the early editions is amusing:—

> "Even by the rule of that Philosophy,
> By which I did blame Cato, for the death
> Which he did give himselfe, I know not how:
> But I do find it," etc.

The construction plainly is, I know not how it is, but I do find it, by the rule of that philosophy, etc., cowardly and vile. The common pointing of the modern editors, which completely separates "I know not how," etc., from what precedes, leaves the "by the rule" without connexion or meaning. It is impossible to suppose that Brutus can mean "I am determined *to do by the rule* of that philsophy," etc.

709. *The term of life.*—That is, the termination, the end, of life. The common reading is "the *time* of life," which is simply nonsense; *term* is the emendation of Mr Collier's MS. annotator, and the same emendation had also been made conjecturally by Capell, though it failed to obtain the acquiescence of subsequent editors. For to *prevent* see 147 and 161. "To *prevent the term of life*," says Mr Collier (*Notes and Emendations*, 403), "means, as

Malone states, to anticipate the end of life; but **still he** strangely persevered in printing *time* for *term*." Did not Mr Collier himself do the same thing?

709. *To stay the providence of those high powers.*—To *stay* is here to await, not, as the **word** more commonly **means, to** hinder or delay.—" *Some* high powers " is the common reading; *those* is the correction of Mr Collier's **MS.** annotator, and might almost have been assumed on conjecture to be the true word.

711. *No, Cassius, no :* etc.—There has been some controversy about the reasoning of Brutus in this dialogue. Both Steevens and Malone conceive that there is an inconsistency between what he here says and his previous declaration of his determination not to follow the example of Cato. **But** how did Cato act? He slew himself that he might not witness and outlive the fall of Utica. This **was,** merely " for fear of what might fall," to anticipate the **end of life.** It did not follow that it would be wrong, in the **opinion** of Brutus, to commit suicide in order to escape **any** certain and otherwise inevitable calamity or degradation, such as being led in triumph through the streets of Rome by Octavius and Antony.

It is proper to remark, however, that Plutarch, upon whose narrative **the conversation is** founded, makes Brutus confess to **a change of** opinion. **Here** is the passage, in the Life **of** Brutus, as translated by **Sir** Thomas North :—" Then Cassius began to speak first, and said : The gods grant **us,** O Brutus, that this day **we may** win the field, and ever after to live all the rest **of** our life quietly, one with another. But, sith the gods have so **ordained it, that the** greatest and chiefest [things] amongst men are most uncertain, and that, if the battle **fall** out otherwise to-day than we wish or look for, we **shall** hardly meet again, what art thou then determined **to do?** to fly? or die? Brutus answered him: Being yet but a young **man,** and not over greatly experienced in the world, I trust [*trusted*] (I know not how) a certain rule of philosophy, by the which I did greatly blame and reprove Cato for killing of himself, as being no lawful nor godly act touching the gods, nor, concerning men, valiant; not to give place and yield to divine Providence, and not constantly and patiently to take whatsoever it pleaseth him to send us, but to draw back and fly. But, being now in the midst of the danger, I am of a contrary mind. For, if it be not the will of God that this battle fall out fortunate for us, I will look no more for hope, neither seek to make any new supply for war again, but will rid me of this miserable world, and content me with my fortune. For I gave up my life for my country in the Ides of March; for the which I shall live in another more glorious world."

This compared with the scene in the Play affords a most interesting and instructive illustration of the manner in which the great dramatist worked in such cases, appropriating, rejecting, adding, as suited his purpose, but refining or elevating everything, though sometimes by the slightest touch, and so transmuting all into the gold of poetry.

711. *Must end that work* **the ides of March begun.**— *Begun* is the word in the old editions. Mr Collier has *began*. The three last Folios all have "*that* Ides of March begun."

SCENE II.—*The same. The Field of Battle.*

Alarum.—Enter BRUTUS *and* MESSALA.

714. *Bru.* Ride, ride, Messala, ride, and give these bills
    Unto the legions on the other side: [*Loud Alarum.*
    Let them set on at once: for I perceive
    But cold demeanour in Octavius' wing,
    And sudden push gives them the overthrow.
    Ride, ride, Messala: let them all come down.   *Exeunt.*

714. *Give these bills.*—These billets, as we should now say.; but Shakespeare takes the word which he found in North's *Plutarch:*—"In the meantime Brutus, that led the right wing, sent little *bills* to the colonels and captains of private bands, in which he wrote the word of the battle."

As in all other cases throughout the Play, the notices of the locality of what are here called the Second and Third Scenes are modern additions to the old text, in which there is no division into scenes. The stage directions in regard to alarums, entries, etc., are all in the First Folio.

714. *But cold demeanour in Octavius' wing.*—The original text has "*Octavio's* wing." In 716, however, it is *Octavius*.

SCENE III.—*The same. Another part of the field.*

Alarums.—Enter CASSIUS *and* TITINIUS.

715. *Cas.* O, look, Titinius, look, the villains fly!
Myself have to mine own turned enemy:
This ensign here of mine was turning back;
I slew the coward, and did take it from him.

716. *Tit.* O Cassius, Brutus gave the word too early;
Who, having some advantage on Octavius,
Took it too eagerly; his soldiers fell to spoil,
Whilst we by Antony are all enclosed.

Enter PINDARUS.

717. *Pin.* Fly further off, my lord, fly further off;
Mark Antony is in your tents, my lord!
Fly therefore, noble Cassius, fly far off.
    Cas. This hill is far enough. Look, look, Titinius;
Are those my tents, where I perceive the fire?
    Tit. They are, my lord.

720. *Cas.* Titinius, if thou lov'st me,
Mount thou my horse, and hide thy spurs in him,
Till he have brought thee up to yonder troops
And here again; that I may rest assured,
Whether yond troops are friend or enemy.

Tit. I will be here again even with a thought. [*Exit.*
722. *Cas.* Go, Pindarus, get higher on that hill;
My sight was ever thick; regard Titinius,
And tell me what thou not'st about the field.—

[*Exit* PINDARUS.

This day I breathed first: time is come round,
And, where I did begin, there shall I end;
My life is run his compass.—Sirrah, what news?
   Pin. [*Above*]. O my lord!
   Cas. What news?
725. *Pin.* Titinius is enclosed round about
With horsemen, that make to him on the spur;—
Yet he spurs on.—Now they are almost on him.
Now, Titinius!—
Now some light :—O, he lights too :—
He's ta'en ;—and, hark! [*Shout.*
They shout for joy.
726. *Cas.* Come down; behold no more.
O, coward that I am, to live so long,
To see my best friend ta'en before my face

Enter PINDARUS.

Come hither, sirrah :
In Parthia did I take thee prisoner;
And then I swore thee, saving of thy life,
That, whatsoever I did bid thee do,
Thou should'st attempt it. Come now, keep thine oath!
Now be a freeman : and with this good sword,
That ran through Cæsar's bowels, search this bosom.
Stand not to answer: Here, take thou the hilts;
And when my face is covered, as 'tis now,
Guide thou the sword.—Cæsar, thou art revenged,
Even with the sword that killed thee. [*Dies.*
   Pin. So, I am free; yet would not so have been,
Durst I have done my will. O Cassius!
Far from this country Pindarus shall run,
Where never Roman shall take note of him. [*Exit.*

Re-enter TITINIUS, *with* MESSALA.

728. *Mes.* It is but change, Titinius; for Octavius
Is overthrown by noble Brutus' power,
As Cassius' legions are by Antony.
   Tit. These tidings will well comfort Cassius.

Mes. Where did you leave him?
Tit. All disconsolate,
With Pindarus his bondman, on **this hill**.
Mes. Is not that he, that lies upon the **ground**?
Tit. He lies not like the living. O **my heart**!
Mes. **Is** not that he?

735. *Tit.* **No**, this **was** he, Messala;
But Cassius is no more.—O setting sun!
As in thy red rays thou dost sink to night,
So in his red blood Cassius' day **is set**;
The sun of Rome is set! Our day is gone;
Clouds, dews, and dangers come; our deeds are done!
Mistrust of my success hath done this deed.

736. *Mes.* Mistrust of good success hath done this deed.
O hateful Error! Melancholy's child!
Why dost' thou show to the apt thoughts of men
The things that **are not**? O Error, soon conceived,
Thou never **com'st unto** a happy birth,
But kill'st the mother that engendered thee.
Tit. What, Pindarus! Where art thou, Pindarus?
Mes. **Seek** him, Titinius: whilst I go to meet
The noble Brutus, thrusting this report
Into his ears: I may say, thrusting it;
For piercing steel, and darts envenomed,
Shall be as welcome to the ears of Brutus
As tidings of this sight.

739. *Tit.* Hie you, Messala,
And I will seek for Pindarus **the while**.   [*Exit* MESSALA.
Why didst thou send me **forth**, brave Cassius?
Did I not meet thy friends? and did not they
Put on my brows this wreath of victory,
And bid me give it **thee**? Didst thou not hear their shouts?
Alas, **thou** hast misconstrued everything.
But hold thee, take this garland on thy brow;
Thy **Brutus** bid me give it thee, and I
Will do his bidding.—Brutus, come apace,
And see how I regarded Caius Cassius.—
By your leave, gods:—This is a Roman's part
Come, Cassius' sword, and find Titinius' heart.   [*Dies.*

Alarum.—*Re-enter* MESSALA, *with* BRUTUS, *young* CATO,
    STRATO, VOLUMNIUS, *and* LUCILIUS.

Bru. Where, where, Messala, doth his body lie?

sc. 3.] JULIUS CÆSAR. 333

741. *Mes.* Lo, yonder; and Titinius mourning it
   Bru. Titinius' face is upward.
   Cato. He is slain.
744. *Bru.* O Julius Cæsar, thou art mighty yet!
   Thy spirit walks abroad, and turns our swords
   In our own proper entrails.   [*Low alarums.*
745. *Cato.* Brave Titinius!
   Look, whe'r he have not crowned dead Cassius!
746. *Bru.* Are **yet two** Romans living such as these?—
   The last of all the Romans, fare thee well!
   It is impossible that ever Rome
   Should breed thy fellow.—Friends, I owe **moe tears**
   To this dead man, **than** you shall see me pay.—
   I shall find time, Cassius, I shall find time.—
   Come, therefore, and to Thassos send his body;
   His funerals shall not be **in our camp,**
   Lest **it discomfort** us.—Lucilius, **come;**—
   And come, young **Cato;** let us to the **field.**—
   Labeo, and Flavius, **set** our battles on:—
   'Tis three o'clock; and, Romans, yet e'er night
   We shall try fortune in a second fight.   [*Exeunt.*

715. *This ensign here of mine was turning back.*—Here the term *ensign* may almost be said **to be** used with the **double** meaning of both the standard and the standard-bearer.

716. *Took it too eagerly.*—Followed his advantage too eagerly.—**The** prosody of this **line,** with **its** two **superfluous** syllables, well expresses the hurry and impetuosity of the speaker.

717. *Fly farther off,* etc.—This is the reading of the old editions. Mr **Collier, as** usual, has *farther. Further* and *farther* correspond to *forth* and *far,* which, however, (*Vid.* 45) are only **diverse forms** of the same original word, *feor* or *forth.* Accordingly **here,** in the next line but one, we have "Cassius, fly *far* off."

720. *Whether yond troops.*—*Vid.* 65.

722. *Go, Pindarus, get higher on that hill.*—This is the **reading** of **the** First Folio; all the others **have** "get **hither."** The stage direction "*Exit Pindarus*" is modern.

722. *This day I breathed first.*—Compare this expression with what we have in 704:—" As this very day Was Cassius born."

722. *Time is come round.... My life is run his compass.*—Vid. 374.

722. *Sirrah, what news?*—The expressive effect of the break in the even flow of the rhythm produced by the superfluous syllable here, and the vividness with which it brings before us the sudden awakening of Cassius from his reverie, startled, we may suppose, by some sign of agitation on the part of Pindarus, will be felt if we will try how the line would read with " *Sir*, what news?"

725. *Titinius is enclosed round about*, etc.—The metrical arrangement here given is the same that we have in the First Folio. In many modern editions the following new disposition of the lines is substituted, the contrivance of Steevens or some one of the other editors of the latter part of the last century :—

> "Titinius is
> Enclosed round about with horsemen, that
> Make to him on the spur;—yet he spurs on.—
> Now they are almost on him : now, Titinius!
> Now some light :—O, he lights too :—he's ta'en ; and, hark!
> They shout for joy."

This alteration (made without notice) improves nothing, but seriously injures nearly every line over which it extends. And it also gives us a different prosodical manner from that which prevails throughout the present Play.

725. *With horsemen that make to him on the spur.*— One of the applications of the verb *to make* which we have now lost.—*Vid.* 681.

725. *Now, Titinius! Now some light : O, he lights too.* —It may be doubted whether the verb to *light* or *alight* have any connexion with either the substantive or the

adjective *light*. There evidently was, however, in that marvellous array in which the whole world of words was marshalled in the mind of Milton:—

> " So, besides
> Mine own that bide upon me, all from me
> Shall with a fierce reflux on me redound;
> On me, as on their natural centre, *light*
> Heavy."—*Par. Lost*, x. 741.

The prosodical irregularity of the present line is not greater than that of the " Now some light : O, he lights too :—he's ta'en ; and, hark !" of the other arrangement. In the original text, " He's ta'en " stands in a line by itself, as frequently happens in that edition with words that really belong to the preceding verse, and possibly, notwithstanding their detached position, were intended to be represented as belonging to it.

726. *Take thou the hilts.*—Formerly the *hilts* was rather more common than the *hilt*. Shakespeare uses both forms. *Hilt* is an Original English word, and is connected, apparently, with *healdan*, to hold.

726. *Even with the sword that killed thee.*—*Vid.* 363. —The stage directions, *Dies* and *Exit*, are modern; and for " *Re-enter Titinius, with Messala*" the old copies have " *Enter*," etc.

728. *It is but change.*—The battle is only a succession of alternations or vicissitudes.

735. *No, this was he, Messala.*—With the emphasis on *was*.

735. *As in thy red rays thou dost sink to night.*—The *to night* here seems to be generally understood as meaning this night. Both Mr Collier and Mr Knight print " to-night." But surely a far nobler sense is given to the words by taking *sink to night* to be an expression of the same kind with *sink to rest* or *sink to sleep*. The

colourless dulness of the coming night is contrasted with
the red glow in which the luminary is descending. "O
setting sun, Thou **dost** *sink*," meaning simply thou dost
set, is not much in Shakespeare's manner. Besides, we
hardly say, absolutely, that **the sun** *sinks*, whether we
mean that it is setting or only that it is descending. And
the emphasis given by the *to-night* to the mere expression
of the time seems uncalled-for and unnatural. There is
no trace of a hyphen in the old copies.

735, 736. *Mistrust of my success*, etc.—These **two**
lines may **show** us that the word *success* **was not** yet
when Shakespeare wrote quite fixed in the sense which
it now bears. It is plain that *success* simply was not
understood to imply all that was conveyed by the expression *good* *success*. By "mistrust of my success"
Titinius must be interpreted as meaning no more than
mistrust, doubt, or apprehension of what I had met with;
in conformity **with** what he afterwards **says in** apostrophizing Cassius, "Alas, thou hast misconstrued everything."—*Vid.* 229.

736. *O hateful Error! Melancholy's child!*—Error and
Melancholy are personages, and the words are proper
names, here.

736. *To the* **apt thoughts of** *men.*—*Vid.* **345.**

739. *Hie you, Messala.*—*Vid.* **139.**

739. *And I will seek for Pindarus the while.*—We
are still familiar enough **with** *the while*, for meanwhile,
or in the meantime, in **poetry,** in which so many **phrases
not of the day are** preserved; but **the expression no
longer** forms part of **what** can properly **be called our
living** English.

The stage direction, "*Exit Messala*," **is** modern.

739. *And bid me give it thee?* etc.—This is no **Alexandrine, but** only a common heroic verse with two **supernumerary** short syllables.

739. *But hold thee.*—Equivalent to our modern But. hold, or but stop.

739. *Brutus, come apace.*—*Apace* is literally at, or rather on, pace; that is, by the exertion of all your power of pacing. *Vid.* 65.

739. *By your leave, gods.*—*Vid.* 358. The stage direction that follows this speech in the original edition is;—"*Alarum. Enter Brutus, Messala, yong Cato, Strato, Volumnius, and Lucillius.*"

741. *Titinius mourning it.* An unusual construction of the verb *to mourn* in this sense. We speak commonly enough of mourning the death of a person, or any other thing that may have happened; we might even perhaps speak of mourning the person who is dead or the thing that is lost; but we only mourn *over* the dead body. So with *lament.* We lament the death or the loss, the man or the thing; but not the body out of which the spirit is gone.

744. *In our own proper entrails.*—That is, *into*, as we should now say. *Vid.* 122.

745. *Look whe'r he have not.*—That is, "*whether* he have not." *Vid.* 16. The word is here again printed "where" in the original edition.

746. *The last of all the Romans.*—This is the reading of all the Folios; and it is left untouched by Mr Collier's MS. corrector. "*Thou* last" is the conjectural emendation of Rowe.

749. *I owe moe tears.*—*Moe* (or *mo*) is the word as it stands in both the First and the Second Folio. *Vid.* 158.

746. *To Thassos send his body.*—*Thassos* is misprinted *Tharsus* in all the Folios, and the error escaped both Rowe and Pope. Nor does Mr Collier state that it is corrected by his MS. annotator. *Thassos* was first substituted by Theobald, who reasons thus :—" *Tharsus* was a town of Cilicia in Asia Minor; and is it probable that Brutus could think of sending Cassius's body thither out

of Thrace, where they were now encamped? *Thassos*, on the contrary, was a little isle lying close upon Thrace, and at but a small distance from Philippi, to which the body might very commodiously be transported. *Vid.* Plutarch, Appian, Dion Cassius, etc." It is sufficient to say that *Thassos* is the place mentioned by Plutarch (in his life of Brutus) as that to which the body was sent to be interred, and that the name, as Steevens has noted, is correctly given in North's translation, which Shakespeare had before him.

746. *His funerals.*—As we still say *nuptials*, so they formerly often said *funerals*. So *funérailles* in French and *funera* in Latin. On the other hand, Shakespeare's word is always *nuptial*. *Nuptials* occurs only in one passage of the very corrupt text of *Pericles:*—" We'll celebrate their nuptials " (*v.* 3), and in one other passage of *Othello* as it stands in the Quarto,—" It is the celebration of his nuptials (*ii.* 2)—where, however, all the other old copies have *nuptial*, as elsewhere.

746. *Labeo and Flavius*, etc.—In the First Folio, "*Labio* and *Flavio;*" in the others, "*Labio* and *Flavius*." For " set our battles on " see 669.

746. *'Tis three o'clock.*—In the original edition, " three a clocke." *Vid.* 85.

SCENE IV.—*Another part of the Field.*

Alarum.—*Enter, fighting,* Soldiers of both Armies; *then* BRUTUS, CATO, LUCILIUS, *and others.*

   Bru. Yet, countrymen, O, yet hold up your heads!
748. *Cato.* What bastard doth not? Who will go with me?
  I will proclaim my name about the field:—
  I am the son of Marcus Cato, ho!
  A foe to tyrants, and my country's friend.
  I am the son of Marcus Cato, ho!   [*Charges the enemy.*
   Bru. And I am Brutus, Marcus Brutus, I;

Brutus, my country's friend; know me for Brutus.
 [Exit, *charging the enemy.* CATO *is overpowered, and falls*
 Lucil. O young and noble Cato, art thou down?
 Why, now thou diest as bravely as Titinius;
 And may'st be honoured being Cato's son.
  1 *Sold.* Yield, or thou diest.
752. *Lucil.* Only I yield to die:
 There is so much, that thou wilt kill me straight;
 [*Offering money.*
 Kill Brutus, and be honoured in his death.
753. 1 *Sold.* We must not.—A noble prisoner!
  2 *Sold.* Room, ho! Tell Antony, Brutus is ta'en.
755. 1 *Sold.* I'll tell the news.—Here comes the general:—

Enter ANTONY.

Brutus is ta'en, Brutus is ta'en, my lord.
 Ant. Where is he?
 Lucil. Safe, Antony; Brutus is safe enough:
 I dare assure thee, that no enemy
 Shall ever take alive the noble Brutus:
 The gods defend him from so great a shame!
 When you do find him, or alive or dead,
 He will be found like Brutus, like himself.
758. *Ant.* This is not Brutus, friend; but, I assure you,
 A prize no less in worth: keep this man safe;
 Give him all kindness: I had rather have
 Such men my friends than enemies. Go on,
 And see whe'r Brutus be alive or dead:
 And bring us word unto Octavius' tent
 How everything is chanced. [*Exeunt.*

All that we have in the Folios for the heading of this Scene is, "*Alarum. Enter Brutus, Messala, Cato, Lucilius, and Flavius.*" And the only stage directions that we have throughout the Scene are "*Enter Soldiers, and fight,*" immediately before the speech of Brutus (747), and the "*Exeunt*" at the end.

748. *What bastard doth not?*—*Vid.* 177.

752. *There is so much, that thou wilt kill me straight.* The evident meaning of these words has

strangely **escaped** the acuteness **of** Warburton, **whose interpretation (1747) is**:—"So much resistance still **on foot,** that thou **wilt choose to** rid **me** out of the way, **that thou mayst go,** without the embarras of prisoners, to **the assistance of thy friends** who still want it." The true explanation is very well given **by** Heath **in** replying to **this** (in his *Revisal of Shakespeare's Text*, 1765):—"There **is so much money** for **thee, on** condition that **thou** wilt **kill me straight."**

753. *We must not.*—*A noble prisoner!*—The original edition places the entry of Antony immediately after **this** speech.

755. *I'll tell the news.*—This is the conjectural emendation **of** Theobald. All the Folios, and also both Rowe and Pope, have *thee* **for** *the*. Mr Collier adopts **the** emendation.

758. *And see whe'r Brutus be alive or dead.*—*Vid.* 16 **and 745.** It is "where" again in the original text.

758. *How everything is chanced.*—*Vid.* 69 and 374.

SCENE V.—*Another part of the Field.*

Enter BRUTUS, DARDANIUS, CLITUS, STRATO, *and* VOLUMNIUS.

Bru. Come, poor remains of friends, rest on this rock.
Cli. Statilius showed **the torch-light;** but, my lord,
He came not back; he is or ta'en, or slain.
761. *Bru.* Sit thee down, **Clitus**: Slaying is the word;
It is a deed in fashion. **Hark** thee, Clitus.— [*Whispering.*
Cli. What, I, my lord? **No,** not for all the world.
Bru. Peace, then; no words.
Cli. I'll rather kill myself.
Bru. Hark thee, Dardanius! [*Whispers him.*
Dar. Shall I do such a deed?
Cli. O, Dardanius!
Dar. O, **Clitus!**
Cli. What ill request did Brutus make to thee?
Dar. To kill him, Clitus. Look, he meditates.
771. *Cli.* **Now** is that noble vessel full of grief,
That it runs over even at his eyes.

Bru. Come hither, good Volumnius; list a word.
Vol. What says my lord?
774. *Bru.* Why, this, Volumnius:
The ghost of Cæsar hath appeared to me
Two several times by night: at Sardis, once;
And, this last night, here in Philippi fields.
I know my hour is come.
Vol. Not so, my lord.
776. *Bru.* Nay, I am sure it is, Volumnius.
Thou see'st the world, Volumnius, how it goes;
Our enemies have beat us to the pit: [*Low Alarums.*
It is more worthy to leap in ourselves
Then tarry till they push us. Good Volumnius,
Thou know'st, that we two went to school together;
Even for that our love of old, I pr'ythee,
Hold thou my sword hilts, whilst I run on it.
Vol. That's not an office for a friend, my lord. [*Alarum still.*
778. *Cli.* Fly, fly, my lord; there is no tarrying here.
779. *Bru.* Farewell to you;—and you;—and you, Volumnius.—
Strato, thou hast been all this while asleep;
Farewell to thee too, Strato.—Countrymen,
My heart doth joy, that yet, in all my life,
I found no man but he was true to me.
I shall have glory by this losing day,
More than Octavius, and Mark Antony,
By this vile conquest shall attain unto.
So, fare you well at once: for Brutus' tongue
Hath almost ended his life's history:
Night hangs upon mine eyes; my bones would rest,
That have but laboured to attain this hour.
                [*Alarum. Cry within;* Fly, fly, fly.
Cli. Fly, my lord, fly.
781. *Bru.* Hence; I will follow.
            [*Exeunt* CLITUS, DARDANIUS, *and* VOLUMNIUS.
I pr'ythee, Strato, stay thou by thy lord:
Thou art a fellow of a good respect;
Thy life hath had some smatch of honour in it:
Hold, then, my sword, and turn away thy face
While I do run upon it. Wilt thou, Strato?
Stra. Give me your hand first: Fare you well, my lord.
Bru. Farewell, good Strato.—Cæsar, now be still:
I killed not thee with half so good a will.
                [*He runs on his sword and dies*

Alarum.—Retreat. Enter OCTAVIUS, ANTONY, MESSALA,
LUCILIUS, *and their Army.*

Oct. What man is that?
Mes. My master's man.—Strato, where is thy master?
Stra. Free from the bondage you are in, Messala;
The conquerors can but make a fire of him;
For Brutus only overcame himself,
And no man else hath honour by his death.
    Lucil. So Brutus should be found.—I thank thee, Brutus,
That thou hast proved Lucilius' saying true.
788. *Oct.* All that served Brutus, I will entertain them.
Fellow, wilt thou bestow thy time with me?
789. *Stra.* Ay, if Messala will prefer me to you.
    Oct. Do so, good Messala.
791. *Mes.* How died my master, Strato?
    Stra. I held the sword, and he did run on it.
793. *Mes.* Octavius, then take him to follow thee,
That did the latest service to my master.
794. *Ant.* This was the noblest Roman of them all:
All the conspirators, save only he,
Did that they did in envy of great Cæsar;
He only, in a generous honest thought
Of common good to all, made one of them.
His life was gentle; and the elements
So mixed in him, that Nature might stand up,
And say to all the world, *This was a man!*
795. *Oct.* According to his virtue let us use him,
With all respect and rites of burial.
Within my tent his bones to-night shall lie,
Most like a soldier, ordered honourably.—
So, call the field to rest; and let's away,
To part the glories of this happy day.   [*Exeunt.*

The heading of *Scene V.*, with the locality, is, as usual, modern.

761. *Sit thee down.*—In this common phrase, apparently, the neuter verb to *sit* has taken the place of the active to *seat*. Or perhaps we ought rather to say that both in *Sit thee* and in *Hark thee*, which we have in the next line and again in 765, *thee* has usurped the function

of *thou*. We have a similar irregularity in *Fare* (that is, *go*) *thee well*.—The marginal "*Whispering*" at this speech is modern; and so is the "*Whispers him*" at 765.

771. *That it runs over.*— So that, as in 15.

774. *Here in Philippi fields.*—A common enough form of expression; as Chelsea Fields, Kensington Gardens. There is no need of an apostrophe to *Philippi*.

776. *Hold thou my sword hilts.*—*Vid.* 726.

778. *There is no tarrying here.*—So in *Macbeth*, v. 5, "There is nor flying hence, nor tarrying here." The expression is from North's *Plutarch :*—" Volumnius denied his request, and so did many others. And, amongst the rest, one of them said, *there was no tarrying for them there*, but that they must needs fly."

779. *Farewell to you;*—etc.—Mr Collier appends the stage direction, "*Shaking hands severally.*"

779. *Farewell to thee too, Strato.*—In all the Folios this stands;—"Farewell to thee, to Strato." The correction is one of the many made by Theobald which have been universally acquiesced in. It appears to have escaped Mr Collier's MS. annotator.

781. *Hence; I will follow.*—This is the reading of all the old copies. Pope added *thee*, in order to make a complete line of the two hemistichs.—The "*Exeunt Clitus*," etc., is modern.

781. *Thou art a fellow of a good respect.*—*Vid.* 48.

781. *Thy life hath had some smatch of honour in it.*—*Smatch* is only another form of *smack*, meaning taste. *Smack* is the word which Shakespeare commonly uses, both as noun and verb.

In the early editions, the stage direction after the last speech of Brutus (783) is, simply, "*Dies;*" and in the *Entry* that follows *Antony* is placed before *Octavius*, and "*their* Army" is "*the* Army."

788. *I will entertain them.*—Receive them into my service.

788. *Wilt thou bestow thy time with me?*—Here is another sense of *bestow*, in addition to that in 139, which is now lost. *Bestow thy **time with** me* means give up thy time to me.

789. *If Messala will **prefer** me to you.*—"To *prefer*," Reed observes, "seems to have been the established phrase for *recommending a servant*." And he quotes from *The Merchant of Venice, ii. 2*, what Bassanio says to Launcelot,—

"Shylock, thy master, spoke with me this day,
And hath preferred thee."

But to *prefer* **was** more than merely to recommend. It **was** rather to transfer, or **hand** over; as might be inferred even from what Octavius here rejoins, "Do **so**, good Messala." That it had **come** usually to imply **also** something of promotion **may be seen** from what Bassanio goes **on** to say:

—"if it be preferment
To leave a rich Jew's service, to become
The follower of so poor a gentleman."

The sense of the verb *to prefer* that we have in **Shakespeare** continued current down to a considerably later date. **Thus,** Clarendon **writes of** Lord Cottington:— "His mother was a Stafford, nearly allied to Sir Edward Stafford; ... by whom this gentleman was **brought** up, ... and by him recommended to Sir Robert Cecil ...; who preferred him to Sir Charles Cornwallis, when he went ambassador into Spain; where he remained for the **space** of eleven or twelve years in the condition of Secretary **or** Agent, without ever returning into England in all that time" (*Hist., Book xiii.*).

At an earlier date, again, we have Bacon, in the Dedication of **the** first edition **of** his *Essays* to his brother Anthony, thus writing:—Since **they** would not stay with their master, **but would** needs travail abroad, I have preferred them to you, that are next myself, dedicating them, such as they are, to our love," &c.

791. *How died my master, Strato?*—So the First Folio. The Second, by a misprint, omits *master*. The Third and Fourth have "*my lord*."

793. *Octavius, then take him,* etc.—That is, accept or receive him from me. It is not, I request you to allow him to enter your service; but I give him to you. *Vid.* 789.

794. *He only, in a generous honest thought Of common good,* etc.—We are indebted for this reading to Mr Collier's MS. annotator. It is surely a great improvement upon the old text—

"He only in a general honest thought,
And common good to all, made one of them."

To act "in a general honest thought" is perhaps intelligible, though barely so; but, besides the tautology which must be admitted on the common interpretation, what is to act in "a common good to all?"

794. *Made one of them.*—In this still familiar idiom *made* is equivalent to formed, constituted, and *one* must be considered as the accusative governed by it. *Fecit unum ex eis,* or *eorum* (by joining himself to them).

Here is the prose of Plutarch, as translated by North, out of which this poetry has been wrought:—"For it was said that Antonius spake it openly divers times, that he thought, that, of all them that had slain Cæsar, there was none but Brutus only that was moved to it as thinking the act commendable of itself; but that all the other conspirators did conspire his death for some private malice or envy that they otherwise did bear unto him."

794. *His life was gentle; and the elements,* etc.—This passage is remarkable from its resemblance to a passage in Drayton's poem of *The Barons' Wars*. Drayton's poem was originally published some years before the close

of the sixteenth century (according to Ritson, *Bibl. Poet.*, under the title of "*Mortemeriados*. . . . Printed by J. R. for Matthew Lownes, 1596," 4to); but there is, it seems, no trace of the passage in question in that edition. The first edition in which it is found is that of 1608, in which it stands thus:—

> "Such one he **was** (of him we boldly say)
> In whose rich soul all sovereign powers did suit,
> In whom **in peace** the elements all lay
> So mixt, as none could sovereignty impute;
> As all did govern, yet all did obey:
> His lively temper was so absolute,
> That 't seemed, when heaven **his** model first began,
> In him it showed perfection in a man."

In a subsequent edition published in 1619 it is re-modelled as follows:—

> "**He was a** man (then boldly dare to say)
> **In whose** rich soul the virtues well did suit;
> **In whom so** mixt the elements all lay
> That none to one could sovereignty impute;
> **As all did** govern, so did all obey:
> **He of a** temper was so absolute,
> As that it seemed, when nature him **began**,
> She meant to show all that might be in man."

Malone, who holds that Shakespeare's play of *Julius Cæsar* was probably produced about 1607, is inclined to think that Drayton **was the** copyist, even as his **verses** originally stood. "In the altered stanza," he adds, "he certainly was." Steevens, in the mistaken notion that Drayton's stanza **as found in** the edition of his *Barons' Wars* published in 1619 had appeared in the original poem, published, as he conceives, in 1598, had supposed that Shakespeare had in this instance deigned to imitate **or borrow** from his contemporary.

795. *To part the glories of this happy day.*—That is, to distribute to each man his **due** share in its glories.—The original stage direction is "*Exeunt omnes.*"

INDEX.

a-, an-, 560.
abide, 327.
aboard, 65.
aby, 327.
addressed, 300.
advantage, 358.
afeard, 244.
aim, 57.
alderliefest, 54.
alight, 725.
alive, 65.
all over, 175.
aloft, 65.
along by, 200.
an, 15.
and (an), 89, 575.
apace, 739.
apparent, 194.
approve, 147.
apt, 345.
aptitude, 345.
are, 129, 560.
arrive, 54.
art (s.), 615.
art (v.), 560.
as, 44, 57, 177, 329, 408, 704.
as well, 56.
ascended (is), 324.
aside, 65.
assembly, 246.
astir, 252.
at, 508.
Ate, 363.
attempered, 562.
augurer, 194.
aweary, etc., 560.
ay, 54, 530.
ay me!, 279.
aye, 675.

bad, 349.
bait, 529, 530.
ban, 349.
bane, 349.

base, 147, 349.
bastard, 177.
bate, 529, 530.
battle, 671.
bay, 349, 529, 530.
be, 560.
be (are), 67.
be-, 390, 460.
bear hard, 105.
become, 390.
been, 269.
beest, 560.
befall, 69, 708.
behaviours, 45.
beholden, 390.
believe, 390.
belike, 460.
belong, 390.
beloved, 390.
beseech, 390.
beshrew, 186.
beside, 348.
bestow, 139, 783.
betimes, 669.
betoken, 390.
bid, 1.
bills, 714.
bloods, 56.
bough, 349.
bow, 349.
break with, 182
bring, 106.
brook, 56.
business, 496.
bustle, 267.
busy, 267.
by, 124, 345.

can, 1, 560.
carrion, 177.
cast, 122.
cause, 1.
cautel, 177.
cautelous, 177.
censor, 329.

censorship, 329.
censure, 329, 375.
census, 329.
ceremonies, 16, 194
chance, 69.
charactery, 214.
charm, 209.
chew, 57.
chide, 569.
clean, 110.
clever, 348.
colour, 147
come home, 104.
comfort, 211.
command, 279.
commend, 279.
commerce, 525.
compact, 352.
companion, 578.
company, 578.
con, 560.
conceit, 142.
conclude, 249.
condemn to, 525.
condition, 205.
consort, 704.
constant, 263, 310
construct, 560.
construe, 560.
content, 519.
continence, 54.
contrite, 260.
contrive, 260.
council, 263, 498.
counsel, 263, 498.
countenance, 54.
court, 305.
courteous, 305.
courtesies, 305.
creature, 181.
cunning, 560.
curse, 186.
curst, 186.
curt'sies, 305.

damage, 147.
danger, 147.
dare, 1.
dear, 349, 560.
dearth, 349.
decent, 16.
deck, 16.
decorate, 16.
deem, 329.
degrees, 147.
deliberate, 348.
deliver, 348.
dent, 426.
desire, 307.
die, 16.
difference, 45.
dint, 426.
direct, 300.
disserve, 525.
distract, 590.
distraught, 590.
do, 1, 16, 147, **229,** 387, 503.
doom, 329.
dotage, 305.
dote, 305.
dress, 300.
drizzle, 233.
drown, 128.

early, 494.
earn, 259.
earnest, 259.
-ed, 16, 246.
either, 227.
element, 130.
emulation, 260.
endure, 1.
enforce, 377.
enlarge, 519.
ensign, 715.
entertain, 788.
envy, 187.
ere, 494.
errand, 494.
errant, 494.
erroneous, 494.
error, 494.
esteem, 57.
every, 675.
exigent, 676.
exorcise, 221.
expedition, 593.

factious, 129.

fall, 177, 359, 508, **708.**
fantasy, 194.
far, 45, 717.
fare thee, 761.
farther, 45, 717.
fasten, 672.
fault, 120, 143.
favour, 54, 130, **160.**
favoured, 54.
fear, 190, 244.
fearful, 672.
fellow, 578.
feverous, 130.
field, 674.
fire, 346.
firm, 107.
fleer, 129.
flourish, 283.
fond, 305.
fondling, 305.
forbid, 1.
force, 209.
force (of), **620.**
fore, 45.
foreign-built, 110.
forth, 45, 717.
fray, 267.
freedom, 307.
friend (to, at), 342.
friends (friend). 353.
from, 110, 194.
funerals, 746.
further, 45, 717.

garden, 143.
ge-, 390.
general, **147.**
genius, 155.
get me, 278.
get **thee** gone, **261.**
give sign, 680.
give way, 260.
given, 66.
glare, 109.
go along by, 200.
go to, 531.
gore, 426.
greet, 242.
griefs, 129, 436.
grievances, 129.
guess, 390

had best, 469.
had like, 57.
had rather, 57, **551.**

hail, 241.
hale, 241.
hand (at, in, on), 508.
handkerchief, 218.
hap, 69.
happen, 69.
happy, 69.
hark thee, **761.**
have, 634.
havoc, 363.
he, 54.
health, 534.
heap, 109.
hear, **1.**
hearse, 422.
heart's ease, **67.**
heir, 194.
help, 1.
hence, 625.
her, 54.
herd, 128.
herself, 56.
hie, 139.
hilts, 726, 776.
hind, 128.
hinder, 161.
himself, 56, 599.
his, 54.
hit (it), 54.
home, 625.
home-, 110.
hour, 256.
however, 103.
hug, 139.   [561.
humour, 105, 205, 240,
hurl, 233.
hurtle, 233.

I, 54.
I (me), **122.**
idle, 177.
-ile, 25.
improve, **186.**
in, 65, 122, 744.
incorporate, 134.
indirection, 551.
-ing, 1.
instance, 507
insuppressive, 177.
intend, 1.
is, 560.
it, 54.
-ite, 25.
i' the, 53.
itching, 525.

INDEX.

its, 54.
itself, 54, 56.
-ius, 61, 502, 560.

jealous, 50, 57.
jig, 578.
justle, 233.

keep, 211.
ken, 560.
kerchief, 218.
kin, 560.
kind, 560.
kindred. 560.
king, 560.
knave, 647.
know, 560.

lament, 741.
lease, 363.
leash, 363.
let, 1, 363.
let's, 708.
liable, 67, 249.
lief, 54.
light, 725.
like, 57, 85, 259.
likely, 57.
likes, 105.
listen, 498.
lover, 186, 260.

main, 194.
make, 1, 681, 725, 794.
make for, 295.
make to, 295.
manner, 45
mass, 408.
market, 525.
marry, 78.
mart, 525.
masters, 403, 637.
may, 1.
me, 89, 471.
mercantile, 25, 525.
merchant, 525.
merely, 45.
mettle, 102.
mind, 534.
mistook, 46.
moe, 158, 746.
mourn, 741.
must, 1.
my, 89, 205.
myself, 54, 56 599.

napery, 408.
napkin, 408.
neckerchief, 218.
news, 590.
nice, 524.
niggard, 624.
nor, 227.
not, 181.
nuptial, 746.

observe, 539.
occupation, 89.
o'clock, 65.
of, 50, 129.
on, 50, 65.
once, 613.
o' nights, 65.
only, 56.
ope, 89.
or, 227.
orchard, 143.
order, 355.
o' the, 53.
other, 78.
others, 634.
ought, 1.
ourself, 56.
out, 8.
over, 283.
overwatched, 634.
owe, 1.
owed, 1.
own, 1.

palter, 177.
paramour, 186.
pass, 15.
passion, 46.
path, 161.
patience, 46.
perforce, 620.
piety, 346.
pious, 346.
piteous, 346.
pitiful, 346.
pity, 346.
plucked, 160.
portent, 246.
power, 127.
prebend, 498.
prefer, 789.
prepare, 256.
present, 57.
pretend, 65.   [709.
prevent, 147, 161, 296,

prick, 352, 491.
proceed, 60.
proceeding, 249.
produce to, 355.
promised forth, 97.
proof, 147, 692.
proper, 12, 45.
provender, 498.
puissant, 304.

question, 377, 596.
quick, 267.
quite from, 194.

rascal, 551.
rathe, 54.
rather, 54.
recension, 329.
redress, 300.
regard, 375.
remorse, 147.
render, 219, 349, 371.
repeal, 306.
reprove, 186.
resolved, 339.
respect, 48, 375, 551.
retentive, 126.
rived, 107.
Rome, 56.
rostrum, 373.
rote, 560.
round, 147.
ruminate, 57.
rumour, 267.

scandal, 50.
scandalize, 50.
see, 1.
self, 54, 56.
sennet, 39.
sense, 498.
separate, 444.
set on, 225, 669.
sever, 444.
several, 444.
shake, 349.
shall, 1, 181, 238, 249, 351, 358, 491, 620.
she, 54.
shew, 186.
should, 56, 181, 238, 551.
shrew, 186.
shrewd, 186, 343.
shrewishness, 186

sign, 680.
sin, 16.
sing, 16.
-sion, 246.
sirs, 637.
sit thee, 761.
sleek, 522.
sleep, 363.
slide, 522.
slight, 494, 522.
slink, 522.
slip, 363.
slips, 363.
sly, 522.
smatch, 781.
so, 15, 44, 57, 147, **408**.
sooth, 268.
sore, 186.
sorrow, 186.
sorry, 186.
sort, 211.
sound, 128.
sour 186.
speak, 647.
stale, 50.
state, 50.
statue, 246.
stay, 709.
stirred, 252.
strain, 695.
strange-disposed, **110**.
strew, 186.
stricken, 46, 253.
struck, 46, 253.
strucken, 253, 349.
succeed, 229.
success, 229, 735, 736.
such, 57, 177.
sue, 283.
suit, 283.
suite, 283.
swagger, 107.
sway, 107, 353.
sweet, 267.
swing, 107.

swoon, 82, 83, 128.

tag-rag, 87.
taste, 498.
tempered, 562.
temple, 363.
tenure, 599.
terror, 190, 194.
th and y, 675.
than, 56, 575.
that, 15, 44, 57, **147**, 177, 399.
thatch, 16.
the more, etc., 675.
themselves, 56.
then (than), 56.
there's, 135.
these, 57.
these many, 486.
thews, 124.
thigh, 124.
think, 147, **189**.
this, 57.
this (time), 130.
this present, 57.
thou, **1**.
thunderstone, **120**.
thyself, 56.
tide, 363.
tidings, 590.
time, 363.
-tion, 246.
to, 1, 57, 551, 634.
toward, 53.
true man, 87.

unaccustomed, **194**.
undergo, 130.
undeservers, **525**.
unmeritable, **494**.
upon, 589.

viands, 498.
vile, 575.
villain, 186.

virtue, 209.
vouchsafe, 1.

ware, 671.
warn, 671.
wary, 671.
was, 560.
wash, 333.
wave, 107.
weak, 267.
weep, 16.
weigh, 107.
well, 504.
were, wert, best, 469.
when? 143.
whe'r, 16, **194, 745,** 758.
which, 369, **377**.
while (the), **739**.
whiles, 67.
whirl, 233.
whit, 181.
wicked, 267.
wight, 181.
will, 1, 181, 238, 249, 491.
wis, *v.* **ywis**.
wit, 436, 561.
with, 124, 315, 363, 613.
withhold, 399.
worship, 504.
worth, 504.
would, 218.
wrote, 46.

y-, 390.
ye, 345.
yea, 675.
yearn, 259.
yon, yond, yonder, 65.
you, 345.
yourself, 56.
ywis, 390.

THE END.

JOHN CHILDS AND SON, PRINTERS.

Educational Works.

THE ENGLISH OF SHAKESPEARE; ILLUSTRATED in a Philological Commentary on his Tragedy of 'Julius Cæsar.' By GEORGE LILLIE CRAIK, Professor of History and of English Literature in Queen's College, Belfast. Second Edition. Post 8vo

OUTLINES OF THE HISTORY OF THE ENGLISH LANGUAGE. For the use of the Junior Classes in Colleges, and the Higher Classes in Schools. By GEORGE L. CRAIK. Third Edition. Post 8vo.

PRACTICAL PERSPECTIVE. THE SUBSTANCE OF THE COURSE OF LECTURES ON LINEAR PERSPECTIVE, delivered at, and forming a part of the Course of Instruction in, the Training School, and in the Schools of Art in connection with the Department of Science and Art. By R. BURCHETT, Head Master of the Training and Normal School. Third Edition. Post 8vo, cloth, with Illustrations. 7s.

PRACTICAL GEOMETRY. THE COURSE OF CONSTRUCTION OF PLANE GEOMETRICAL FIGURES. By R. BURCHETT. With 137 Diagrams. Third Edition. Post 8vo, cloth. 5s.

DEFINITIONS OF GEOMETRY. 24mo, sewed. 5d.

THE CHARACTERISTICS OF STYLES. AN INTROduction to the Study of the History of Ornamental Art. By RALPH N. WORNUM. In royal 8vo, with very many Illustrations.

GRAMMAIRE FRANCAISE. By L. DIREY. Small 8vo, 3s.

ENGLISH GRAMMAR. By L. DIREY and A. FOGGO. Small 8vo, 3s.

DYCE'S ELEMENTARY OUTLINES OF ORNAMENT. 50 Selected Plates, small folio, sewed. Price 5s.

TEXT TO DYCE'S DRAWING-BOOK.—Fcap 8vo, 6d.

REDGRAVE'S MANUAL AND CATECHISM ON COLOUR. 24mo, sewed. Price 9d.

REDGRAVE ON THE NECESSITY OF PRINCIPLES IN TEACHING DESIGN. Fcap, sewed. Price 6d.

A SMALL DIAGRAM OF COLOUR. Small folio. Price 9d.

PRINCIPLES OF DECORATIVE ART. Folio, sewed. Price 1s.

LINDLEY'S SYMMETRY OF VEGETATION. 8vo, sewed. Price 1s.

DIRECTIONS FOR INTRODUCING ELEMENTARY DRAWING IN SCHOOLS AND AMONG WORKMEN. Published at the request of the Society of Arts. Small 4to, cloth. Price 4s. 6d.

ILLUSTRATIONS TO BE EMPLOYED IN THE PRACTICAL LESSONS ON BOTANY. Adapted to all classes. Prepared for the South Kensington Museum. By the Rev. PROFESSOR HENSLOW. With Illustrations. Post 8vo, Price 6d.

DRAWING FOR ELEMENTARY SCHOOLS; BEING A Manual of the Method of Teaching Drawing, specially adapted for the use of Masters of National and Parochial Schools. By ELLIS A. DAVIDSON, Head Master of the Chester School of Art. Post 8vo, cloth. 3s.

CHAPMAN AND HALL, 193, PICCADILLY.

www.ingramcontent.com/pod-product-compliance
Lightning Source LLC
Chambersburg PA
CBHW020225240426
43672CB00006B/415